Transforming Labor-Based Parties in Latin America
Argentine Peronism in Comparative Perspective

Why did some Latin American labor-based parties adapt successfully to the contemporary challenges of neoliberalism and working-class decline while others did not? Drawing on a detailed study of Argentine Peronism, as well as a broader comparative analysis, this book develops an organizational approach to party change. Levitsky's book breaks new ground in its focus on informal and weakly institutionalized party structures. It argues that loosely structured party organizations, such as those found in many populist labor-based parties, are often better equipped to adapt to rapid environmental change than are more bureaucratic labor-based parties. The argument is illustrated in the case of the Peronist party, a mass labor-based party with a highly fluid internal structure. The book shows how this weakly routinized structure allowed party reformers to undertake a set of far-reaching coalitional and programmatic changes that enabled Peronism to survive, and even thrive, in the neoliberal era.

Steven Levitsky is Assistant Professor of Government and Social Studies at Harvard University. He was a Visiting Fellow at the Kellogg Institute for International Studies in the fall of 1999. He has published articles on political parties and democracy in such journals as *Comparative Politics*, *World Politics*, *Studies in Comparative International Development*, *Party Politics*, *Journal of Democracy*, and the *Journal of Latin American Studies*.

Transforming Labor-Based Parties in Latin America

Argentine Peronism in Comparative Perspective

STEVEN LEVITSKY
Harvard University

PUBLISHED BY THE PRESS SYNDICATE OF THE UNIVERSITY OF CAMBRIDGE
The Pitt Building, Trumpington Street, Cambridge, United Kingdom

CAMBRIDGE UNIVERSITY PRESS
The Edinburgh Building, Cambridge CB2 2RU, UK
40 West 20th Street, New York, NY 10011-4211, USA
477 Williamstown Road, Port Melbourne, VIC 3207, Australia
Ruiz de Alarcón 13, 28014 Madrid, Spain
Dock House, The Waterfront, Cape Town 8001, South Africa

http: // www.cambridge.org

© Steven Levitsky 2003

This book is in copyright. Subject to statutory exception
and to the provisions of relevant collective licensing agreements,
no reproduction of any part may take place without
the written permission of Cambridge University Press.

First published 2003

Printed in the United States of America

Typeface Sabon 10/12 pt.   *System* LATEX 2_ε [TB]

A catalog record for this book is available from the British Library.

Library of Congress Cataloging in Publication Data
Levitsky, Steven.
Transforming labor-based parties in Latin America: Argentine Peronism in comparative perspective / Steven Levitsky.
    p.   cm.
Includes bibliographical references and index.
ISBN 0-521-81677-7 (hb.) – ISBN 0-521-01697-5 (pb.)
1. Movimiento Nacional Justicialista (Argentina)   2. Peronism – Argentina.
3. Political parties – Argentina.   4. Political parties – Latin America.   I. Title.
JL2098.M685 L48   2003
324.282′083–dc21   2002067726

ISBN 0 521 81677 7 hardback
ISBN 0 521 01697 5 paperback

To My Parents,
Carol Levitsky and David Levitsky

And to Liz

Contents

Figure and Tables		*page* viii
Acknowledgments		xi
1	Labor-Based Party Adaptation in the Neoliberal Era: Rethinking the Role of Party Organization	1
2	Origins and Evolution of a Mass Populist Party	35
3	An "Organized Disorganization": The Peronist Party Structure in the 1990s	58
4	Populism in Crisis: Environmental Change and Party Failure, 1983–1985	91
5	From Labor Politics to Machine Politics: The Transformation of the Peronist Party–Union Linkage	107
6	Menemism and Neoliberalism: Programmatic Adaptation in the 1990s	144
7	A View from Below: Party Activists and the Transformation of Base-Level Peronism	186
8	The Paradox of Menemism: Party Adaptation and Regime Stability in the 1990s	217
9	Crisis, Party Adaptation, and Democracy: Argentina in Comparative Perspective	231
References		251
Index		271

Figure and Tables

FIGURE

1.1 A Typology of Parties Based on the Dimensions of Routinization and Mass Organization — *page* 23

TABLES

3.1	The PJ's Membership-to-Voter Ratio in Comparative Perspective	61
3.2	Social Linkages of Surveyed Base Units in the Federal Capital and Greater Buenos Aires	64
3.3	The Organizational Form of Surveyed Base Units	69
4.1	Changes in the Sectoral Composition of the Argentine Labor Movement	97
5.1	Presidential and Legislative Electoral Results, 1983–9	120
5.2	The Erosion of Union Representation in the PJ National Council, 1983–95	134
5.3	PJ Trade Unionists Elected to the Chamber of Deputies in the Five Largest Industrialized Districts, 1983–2001	134
5.4	The Erosion of Peronist Union Representation in the Chamber of Deputies, 1983–2001	135
5.5	Local Union Participation in the PJ in the 1990s	138
5.6	National Union Participation in the PJ in the 1990s	139
5.7	National Party and Union Leaders' Views of the Menem Economic Program	142
5.8	Local Party and Union Leaders' Views of the Menem Economic Program	142
6.1	National Party Leaders' Views of the Menem Economic Program	151

6.2	Local Party Leaders' Views of the Menem Economic Program	152
6.3	Party Members' Views of the Menem Economic Program (1992)	153
6.4	Party Members' Views of the Menem Economic Program, by Income Level (1996)	154
6.5	Argentine Electoral Results, 1991–9	182
7.1	Social Welfare Activities of Surveyed Base Units	188
7.2	Activists' Views of the Menem Economic Program	192
7.3	Activists' Views of Government Policies toward Business, Unions, and Workers	192
7.4	Peronist *Punteros* and Activists, by Year of Entry into Party Politics	193
7.5	Activists' Views of the Menem Program, by Year of Entry into the Party	194
7.6	Patronage Distribution in PJ Base Units	195
7.7	Activist Responses to the Question: "What Level of Party Activity Is Most Important to You"?	201
7.8	Comparing Neoliberal and Opposition Activists' Views of What Level of Party Activity Is Most Important	201
7.9	Comparing Three Types of Base Units	206
7.10	The Increasing Role of Selective Material Benefits in Fostering PJ Activist Participation	209
7.11	The Volatility of the Peronist Vote in the Federal Capital, 1989–99	213
9.1	Electoral Performance of Six Latin American Labor-Based Parties in the 1980s and 1990s	244

Acknowledgments

As I write these pages, Argentina is in the midst of one of the most profound political-economic crises in its history. Millions of Argentines have reached a level of poverty and desperation that few had thought imaginable. In early 2002, in the aftermath of the massive riots that buried Fernando De la Rua's presidency two years before the end of his mandate, Peronism again found itself in power during a period of crisis and change. This book will argue that the Peronist party's combination of organizational strength and flexibility has enabled it to adapt and survive through many difficult times. Peronism's capacity to manage the contemporary crisis remains unclear. In the meantime, many of the Argentines who gave so generously to me while I was living in their country are now living in despair. I desperately wish it were otherwise.

In researching and writing this book, I have incurred many debts of gratitude. My research benefited from the guidance of many advisors, both formal and informal. I am deeply grateful to David Collier and Ruth Berins Collier, my advisors at the University of California at Berkeley. Ruth, who shares my concern for the fate of working-class parties, was a primary source of intellectual inspiration for this project. David's patient, rigorous, and enthusiastic teaching had an enormous impact on my intellectual development. He made me into a professional scholar. Peter Evans offered tough criticism and sage advice throughout the research and writing process. Christopher Ansell helped me make sense of the data I brought back from the field. His conceptual and theoretical insights can be found throughout the book.

The research for this project would not have been possible without the generous financial support of the National Science Foundation; the Tinker Foundation; the Center for Latin American Studies at the University of California, Berkeley; the Fulbright-Hays Doctoral Dissertation Research Abroad (DDRA) program; and the Social Science Research Council. The Helen Kellogg Institute for International Studies at the University of Notre Dame provided both financial assistance and a warm and intellectually stimulating environment in which to write.

Excerpts from Chapter 1 of this book first appeared in Steven Levitsky, "Peronism and Institutionalization: The Case, the Concept, and the Case for Unpacking the Concept," *Party Politics* 4, no. 1: 77–92; copyright 1998 by Sage Publications, Inc., reprinted with permission of Sage Publications, Inc. Excerpts from Chapter 2, Chapter 3, Chapter 6, and Chapter 7 appeared in "An 'Organized Disorganization': Informal Organization and the Persistence of Local Party Structures in Argentine Peronism," *Journal of Latin American Studies* 33, no. 1 (February): 29–66; copyright 2001 by Cambridge University Press; reprinted with permission. Excerpts from Chapter 1, Chapter 5, Chapter 6, and Chapter 9 appeared in Steven Levitsky, "Organization and Labor-Based Party Adaptation: The Transformation of Argentine Peronism in Comparative Perspective," *World Politics* 54, no. 1 (October 2001): 27–56, copyright 2001 by Johns Hopkins University Press; reprinted with permission.

I am deeply indebted to a large number of friends and colleagues in the United States and Argentina. I learned an immense amount from my graduate student colleagues at Berkeley, particularly Zackary Elkins, Kenneth Greene, Natalia Ferretti, Sarah Kelsey, Marcus Kurtz, James Mahoney, Matt Marostica, Carol Medlin, Michael Sinatra, Aaron Schnieder, and Richard Snyder. Sebastian Etchemendy was a consistent source of friendship, challenging criticism, and lively conversation about Argentine politics. Among the larger community of scholars, Manuel Alcántara, Katrina Burgess, Michael Coppedge, Javier Corrales, Robert Fishman, Edward Gibson, Frances Hagopian, Mark Healey, Terry Karl, Scott Mainwaring, Gerardo Munck, María Victoria Murillo, Guillermo O'Donnell, Susan Stokes, and J. Samuel Valenzuela provided invaluable comments and criticism. James McGuire, whose study of Peronism had an enormous influence on my own work, has generously provided his knowledge and insights since my early days in graduate school. Finally, Jorge Domínguez and Kenneth Roberts read and commented on the entire manuscript, and both were invaluable sources of advice.

In Argentina, I benefited enormously from my affiliation with the Centro de Estudios del Estado y Sociedad (CEDES). I am indebted to Roberto Frenkel, Juan José Llovet, and the entire third floor of economists for their friendship and enthusiastic support for my research. Sofres Ibope, Hugo Haime y Asociados, and the Instituto de Estudios sobre el Estado y Participación (IDEP) generously provided me with survey and other data. Mariano Cabello, Roberto García, Santiago Diehl, and, later on, Alicia Llosa offered invaluable research assistance. Finally, the night shift at the Argentine Library of Congress made my archival research both feasible and bearable.

A large number of Argentine scholars, journalists, and politicians assisted my research. Juan Manuel Abal Medina (h), Gerardo Adrogúe, Ernesto Calvo, Rosendo Fraga, Carlos Gervasoni, Marcela Gonzalez, Ines Gonzales Bombal, Ricardo Gutierrez, Elisabeth Jelin, Artemio López, Andres

Malamud, Hector Mazzei, Ana María Mustapic, Marcos Novaro, Vicente Palermo, Hector Palomino, Diego Schurman, Ernesto Seman, Santiago Senen Gonzalez, Catalina Smulovitz, Mariano Tomassi, and Juan Carlos Torre all took time to listen to and debate my ideas, and to share their own. I am particularly grateful to Pablo Gonzalez, Moira Mackinnon, and Cecilia Senen Gonzalez, whose friendship I hold dear. Peronist leaders José Alberto Cuneo Verges, Roberto García, Fernando Maurette, Miguel Angel Toma, and particularly Rodolfo Díaz repeatedly took time out of their busy schedules to teach me about their party.

Three individuals profoundly influenced my understanding of Peronism. Javier Auyero, whose research in Greater Buenos Aires coincided with my own, was a source of inspiration, friendship, support, and hours of fascinating discussion. Mario Wainfeld, the best analyst of Peronist politics I have ever met, was like a father to me in Argentina. His ideas, which I tried desperately to absorb over a long series of coffees and dinners, permeate this entire book. Finally, I owe an enormous debt to my friend Pierre Ostiguy. The impact of Pierre's teaching, which began with a series of all-night conversations in Buenos Aires nearly a decade ago and continues to this day, is difficult to overstate.

My greatest debt, however, is to the hundreds of Peronist activists who opened their homes and base units to me. I cannot thank them all, but I am particularly indebted to the following individuals: in the Federal Capital: Salvador Corraro, Julio Cosentino, Ernesto Duhalde, Amilcar and Ignacio Fidanza, Isidoro, María Lenz, Reinaldo Mendoza, Ricardo Morato, Mate Ocampo, Kelly Olmos, Cesar and Daniel Torres, and particularly Carlos Racedo and Raúl Roa; in La Matanza: Angel Bustamante, Abraham "Toto" Delgado, Hector Drewes, Fernando Espinoza, Mate, Raúl Matteau, Miguel Pretto, and Federico Russo; and in Quilmes: Miguel Angel Cuello, Buby Federico, Angel García, Dora García, Quique Gonzales, Reymundo Gonzalez, Hugo Guerreño, Marcelo Mayo, Claudio Oliveras, José Rivela, José Luis Salussi, and Mario Scalisi. I am especially grateful to Elba Quiroga for her kindness and friendship.

One Peronist deserves singular recognition: Claudio Britos. A *puntero* from La Matanza, Claudio took me under his wing and brought me inside Peronism, teaching me the language and the rules of the game. He taught me how Peronism "really works." He showed me the best and worst of Peronism. He also protected me. My base-level research simply could not have been done without him. My debt to him is enormous. Claudio, you will never read this, but thank you.

My final debts are personal: to Lucan Way, a true friend, intellectual companion, and collaborator, and most of all, to Liz Mineo, my wife, best friend, and toughest critic. Busy with her own work, Liz didn't help me much in the research or writing of this book. But she helped me see beyond it, and the book is immeasurably better for it.

CHAPTER 1

Labor-Based Party Adaptation in the Neoliberal Era: Rethinking the Role of Party Organization

The new world economic order has not been kind to labor-based political parties. Changing trade and production patterns, increased capital mobility, and the collapse of the Soviet bloc dramatically reshaped national policy parameters in the 1980s and 1990s. Traditional left-wing programs were discredited, and policies based on Keynesian and "import-substituting" models were increasingly dismissed as populist and inflationary. At the same time, long-term changes in class structure eroded the coalitional foundations of labor-based parties. The decline of mass production and expansion of the tertiary and informal sectors weakened industrial labor organizations, limiting their capacity to deliver the votes, resources, and social peace that had been the foundation of the traditional party-union "exchange." These changes created an incentive for labor-based parties to rethink their programs, redefine their relationship with unions, and target new electoral constituencies. Such change is not easy. Because adaptive strategies generally run counter to parties' traditional programs and the perceived interests of many of their constituents, party leaders often prove unwilling or unable to carry out such strategies. Yet if they do not adapt, labor-based parties face the prospect of electoral decline and political marginalization. Party adaptation may have important implications for democracy. In Latin America, the failure of established labor-based parties to respond effectively to the economic crises of the 1980s and 1990s at times resulted in party system decomposition and the breakdown, or near breakdown, of democratic regimes.

By virtually any measure, the Argentine (Peronist) Justicialist Party (PJ) is a case of successful labor-based adaptation. Closely aligned with the powerful General Labor Confederation (CGT), Peronism had opposed liberal economic policies since its birth in the 1940s. Yet beginning in the mid-1980s, the PJ underwent a dual transformation. First, it redefined its relationship with organized labor, dismantling traditional mechanisms of union participation and replacing its union-based mass linkages with patronage-based

1

territorial organizations. By the early 1990s, the PJ had transformed itself from a labor-based party in which unions were at times the dominant partner into an increasingly clientelistic party in which unions played a relatively minor role. Second, the PJ adapted its socioeconomic program. After taking office in 1989, the PJ government of President Carlos Menem dismantled the statist, inward-oriented economic model established under Juan Perón in the 1940s and implemented a set of neoliberal policies that sharply contradicted the party's traditional program. These changes were carried out with striking political success. The Menem government faced little opposition among party leaders and cadres, and the party retained the bulk of its traditional working- and lower-class base. The PJ won four straight national elections after 1989, including Menem's landslide reelection in 1995. Peronism's adaptation and survival contributed in an important way to democratic governance during the 1990s. The PJ's linkages to working- and lower-class society helped the Menem government carry out radical economic reforms within a democratic context, and party's electoral success helped to stabilize the party system, which allowed for relatively smooth executive-legislative relations and limited the prospects for antisystem outsider candidates.

Although labor-based parties in a variety of countries adopted market-oriented programs in the 1980s and 1990s, the PJ case stands out in several respects. First, the reforms carried out by the Menem government were more radical than those of most comparable cases. According to one crossnational study of economic liberalization, the Argentine reforms were the second most far-reaching in the world in the 1990–5 period, and they were faster and more far-reaching than those of Margaret Thatcher in England, Augusto Pinochet in Chile, and Solidarity in Poland (Gwartney et al. 1996).[1] Second, unlike similar cases in Chile, France, and Spain, where socialist parties downplayed their shift to the center and continued to present themselves as the least conservative option in the party system, the Menem-led PJ leap-frogged its main rivals and positioned itself as Argentina's principal pro-market party in the 1990s. Finally, the PJ stands out in terms of its electoral success. Whereas many historically labor-based parties in Latin America – including the Institutional Revolutionary Party (PRI) in Mexico, the American Popular Revolutionary Alliance (APRA) in Peru, and Democratic Action (AD) in Venezuela – experienced steep electoral decline during the 1990s,[2] the PJ's electoral base remained remarkably stable.[3] Hence, although the PJ's

---

[1] Also Inter-American Development Bank (1997).
[2] The PRI electoral base eroded by nearly a third during the 1990s, and AD and APRA saw their electoral support decline by more than 50 percent.
[3] The PJ averaged 44.0 percent of the presidential vote during the 1990s, compared to 43.7 percent during the 1980s. The Chilean Socialist Party and the Bolivian Revolutionary Nationalist Movement also maintained stable electoral bases in the 1990s.

transformation entailed abandoning key aspects of its traditional program and loosening ties to core constituencies such as organized labor, these changes may have contributed in an important way to the party's survival in the neoliberal era.

Drawing on an analysis of the Peronist case, this book seeks to explain the capacity of labor-based parties to adapt to the opportunities and constraints posed by a changing socioeconomic environment. Building on recent research on parties in the advanced industrial countries (Koelble 1991, 1992; Kitschelt 1994a), it adopts an organizational approach to party change, treating parties' internal structures as intervening variables that mediate their responses to environmental change. Yet it also refines this literature by highlighting the importance of informal and noninstitutionalized party structures. The dominant literature on party organization, which is based almost entirely on studies of advanced industrialized countries, tends to take institutionalized party structures for granted. Yet in Latin America and elsewhere, many parties – including some very important ones – are characterized by informally structured and internally fluid organizations. As this book demonstrates, variation on the dimension of institutionalization may have important implications for party behavior. A central argument of the book is that lower levels of institutionalization – though often a source of inefficiency, disorder, and ineffective representation – tend to enhance parties' flexibility during periods of crisis. Thus, loosely structured party organizations, such as those characteristic of many populist parties, are often better equipped to adapt and survive in a context of economic crisis or change than are well-institutionalized party structures such as those characteristic of many social democratic and communist parties.

The Argentine case illustrates this argument. The PJ's rapid adaptation was made possible by a party structure that is mass-based but weakly institutionalized. Although the PJ maintains a powerful mass organization with deep roots in working- and lower-class society, it differs from more prototypical working-class parties in that its internal structure is fluid. Due in large part to its populist origins, the PJ lacks a central bureaucracy, effective party organs, and routinized internal rules and procedures. Though often a source of inefficiency and disorder, such internal fluidity provides the party with a substantial degree of strategic flexibility. This flexibility contributed in at least three ways to the PJ's adaptation and survival in the neoliberal era. First, the weakly institutionalized nature of the Peronist party–union linkage permitted the rapid dismantling of traditional mechanisms of labor participation when union influence began to hinder the party's electoral performance. Second, the absence of stable career paths and secure tenure patterns facilitated the removal of old-guard leaders and permitted the entry and rise of new blood into the party leadership. Third, the absence of stable norms of accountability or routinized decision rules provided President Menem with substantial room to maneuver in designing and implementing a radical economic reform program.

The book thus seeks to bridge the predominantly European literature on party organization with Latin American cases. Notwithstanding the long tradition of research on party organizations in Europe and the United States,[4] Latin American party organizations have received remarkably little scholarly attention.[5] As a result, we know very little about how even some of the region's largest and most successful parties function internally. Theoretically informed analyses of Latin American party organizations will help to broaden the scope of a literature that has traditionally been based on studies of a few advanced industrialized countries. Although research on European and North American party organizations has generated important knowledge and insights, the fact that it captures only a narrow slice of the empirical universe of party organizations limits the generalizability of the concepts and theories that emerge from this literature.

This introductory chapter is structured as follows. First, it outlines the programmatic and coalitional challenges facing contemporary labor-based parties and examines the implications of party adaptation (or nonadaptation) for regime stability in Latin America. It then presents a basic framework for analyzing party change, making the case for an approach that focuses on party organization. It shows how the PJ case may help us refine contemporary theories about the relationship between party organization and adaptation. The chapter then presents the central theoretical argument of the study: that lower levels of institutionalization may, under certain conditions, facilitate party adaptation and survival. It concludes with an overview of how this argument is applied to the Peronist case.

A NEW CRITICAL JUNCTURE: THE DUAL CHALLENGE FACING LATIN AMERICAN LABOR-BASED PARTIES

Labor-based parties are parties whose core constituency is *organized labor*.[6] Such parties depend to a significant extent on trade union support (in the form of financial and organizational resources, the delivery of votes, and social peace when the party is in office) for their political success, and as a result, unions exercise an important degree of influence over the party leadership in

---

[4] On European party organizations, see Michels (1911), Duverger (1954), Panebianco (1988), Kitschelt (1989a, 1994a), Koelble (1991), and Katz and Mair (1992, 1994). On U.S. party organizations, see Ostrogorski (1902), Key (1949), Eldersveld (1964), Mayhew (1986), Shefter (1994), and Aldrich (1995).

[5] Exceptions include recent work by Coppedge (1994), Mainwaring and Scully (1995), and Mainwaring (1999), as well as the comparative study of Latin American party organizations currently being undertaken by Manuel Alcántara and his colleagues at the University of Salamanca.

[6] The term "core constituency" is taken from Gibson (1996: 12–13).

terms of strategy, the party program, and candidate selection.[7] While labor-based parties vary ideologically (from communism to social democracy to different forms of populism), they have historically shared an aversion to liberal economic policies. Committed to some type of state-directed redistributionism, usually in the form of demand enhancement policies, labor-based parties of all types have historically played a leading role in efforts to oppose, regulate, or mitigate the negative effects of market capitalism.

The contemporary era of social and economic change, which has been characterized as a new "critical juncture" (Collier and Collier 1991: 772–4; Collier 1992: 2–7), poses a fundamental challenge to labor-based parties. Postwar party-labor alliances were sustained by the constellation of production patterns, international political and economic conditions, and macroeconomic and social policies associated with the Keynesian or import substituting industrialization (ISI) era. During this period, a steady global economic expansion provided governing labor-based parties with the resources and policy-making autonomy to carry out expansionary policies based on wage growth and redistributive social welfare programs. At the same time, mass production patterns created conditions under which relatively homogeneous working classes could be organized, and in which organized labor could deliver both social peace and working-class votes to their party allies (Pizzorno 1978; Howell and Daley 1992).

The decline of the Keynesian-ISI model posed a twofold challenge for labor-based parties: a *programmatic* challenge and a *coalitional* challenge. In the programmatic realm, the breakdown of the Bretton Woods system, the increased volume and competitiveness of international trade, and the economic shocks of the 1970s eroded the foundations of the postwar economic order (Piore and Sabel 1984). As lower growth rates generated fiscal crises and inflationary pressure, national economic models came under increasing strain. In Latin America, these developments were exacerbated by the debt crisis, which imposed severe fiscal constraints on governments and substantially reduced their leverage vis-á-vis international financial institutions. In the 1980s, the International Monetary Fund (IMF) and other financial institutions began to condition debt refinancing on the implementation of orthodox stabilization and adjustment programs. These changes dramatically reshaped policy parameters, reducing the feasibility of traditional pro-labor policies (Roberts 1997a). When in power, labor-based parties found their policy-making autonomy limited by an increasingly uncertain, competitive, and globalized economy. In Western Europe, the limits of

---

[7] This definition includes parties in which trade unions hold a dominant position within the party (labor parties) and parties in which labor holds a privileged, yet still subordinate, position (such as many European social democratic parties and Latin American populist parties). It does not include parties that depend on working- or lower-class votes but in which trade unions do not play significant role.

policy-making autonomy were seen in the failure of the French Socialist government's expansionary policies in the early 1980s and the difficulties faced by the Swedish social democratic government as it pursued a "third road" in the early 1990s. In Latin America, the comparative weakness of national economies and the constraints imposed by debt obligations reduced government autonomy even further. The costs of breaking with orthodox policies were clearly seen in the case of Peru, where the APRA government's heterodox program resulted in a cutoff of international finance and a deep hyperinflationary crisis in the late 1980s (Pastor and Wise 1992).

In the coalitional realm, evolving class structures have eroded the social bases of party-labor alliances, making close social and organizational linkages between parties and unions more difficult to sustain. The globalization of production, the decline of mass production forms, and the growth of tertiary, informal, and self-employed sectors have weakened industrial unions and centralized labor confederations. As workforces have become less concentrated in large factories and more heterogeneous in their skills, work experiences, and interests, organized labor's capacity to represent them has eroded. Membership in industrial unions has declined in most countries, and even where it has not, the capacity of unions to mobilize or negotiate on behalf of their bases has been reduced. As a result, labor organizations have less to offer parties in terms of the traditional party-union "exchange": They can deliver fewer votes, they are less necessary to ensure social peace, and they have fewer resources to invest in the political arena (Howell and Daley 1992).

Changing class structures have also eroded labor-based parties' electoral bases. The decline of industrial unionism and blue-collar workforces, together with increased levels of wealth and education and the influence of mass media technologies, has led to a weakening of class identities and an increase in electoral volatility (Dalton, Flanagan, and Beck 1984; Franklin, Mackie, and Valen 1992). In the advanced industrial countries, these changes have been associated with the emergence of an increasingly white-collar, "postmaterialist" electorate (Inglehart 1977; Dalton, Flanagan, and Beck 1984). In Latin America, postindustrialism has simultaneously taken two forms. While one segment of the workforce has followed the advanced industrial path toward white collarization, another segment has been pushed into the self-employed and informally employed sectors (Castells and Portes 1989; Tokman 1992). Geographically fragmented, heterogeneous in their forms of work, and generally unorganized, urban informal and self-employed workers tend to differ markedly from blue-collar workers in their interests and political identities (Castells and Portes 1989: 31–2).

To maintain their political viability, contemporary labor-based parties have had to make a twofold adjustment. First, when they are in government, they are under pressure to abandon key elements of their traditional socioeconomic programs in favor of more market-oriented policies. Although left-of-center governments – particularly in the advanced industrialized countries – still possess an important degree of macroeconomic policy-making autonomy (Garrett and Lange 1991; Garrett 1998), it is reasonable to suggest that all labor-based parties that seek to govern face pressure to shift toward the programmatic center. Second, to avoid tying themselves to an increasingly narrow social base, labor-based parties must rearticulate their old linkages to the working and lower classes (Howell and Daley 1992; Koelble 1992). In most cases, this has entailed reducing the influence of organized labor and broadening the party's appeal in an effort to capture a larger share of the white-collar and/or informal sector vote.[8]

Yet the existence of new environmental opportunities and constraints is no guarantee that party leaders will have either the will or capacity to respond to them. Indeed, labor-based parties have responded to the neoliberal challenge in a variety of ways and with varying degrees of success (Koelble 1992; Kitschelt 1994a; Burgess and Levitsky 2003). On the one hand, we find clear cases of failure. Some parties, such as the French and Chilean Communist parties, did not adapt and became increasingly marginal players in the political arena. Others, such as the Peruvian APRA, turned leftward initially and suffered steep electoral declines and long periods out of power. In other cases, such as AD in Venezuela, leaders attempted radical programmatic reforms but failed due to opposition both from within the party and from the electorate. Other labor-based parties adapted and fared well in the 1980s and 1990s. For example, the Spanish Socialist Workers Party (PSOE) and the Australian Labor Party, as well as the Argentine PJ, shifted toward market-oriented policies and were able to maintain themselves in power for substantial periods of time. Between these successful and failed cases lies a range of parties, such as the Austrian Socialist Party and the Mexican PRI, which adapted slowly and experienced at least a moderate electoral decline.

PARTY ADAPTATION AND DEMOCRACY IN LATIN AMERICA

The question of whether and how labor-based parties adapt to changes in the socioeconomic environment has important implications not only for the parties themselves, but also for party systems and in some cases political regimes. When major parties fail, party systems may fragment or decompose, and young democratic regimes may become vulnerable. The relationship between party adaptation and regime stability can be clearly seen in contemporary Latin America. As in Western Europe, labor-mobilizing parties were central actors in many postwar Latin American party systems, including those in

---

[8] This phenomenon has, of course, been observed in Western Europe since the 1960s (Kirchheimer 1966).

Argentina, Chile, Mexico, Peru, and Venezuela (Collier and Collier 1991). Yet whereas European labor-based parties tended to survive and eventually correct failed strategies in the 1980s and 1990s (Koelble 1992: 52),[9] often leaving party systems virtually intact, in Latin America, failed party strategies tended to have deeper long-term consequences. In large part, this was due to the depth of the 1980s' socioeconomic crisis, during which failed policies often resulted in massive economic contractions and/or hyperinflation. Not surprisingly, these crises often had devastating effects on governing parties' electoral performance. Electoral failures were exacerbated by the fact that Latin American parties tend to be less deeply rooted in society than their advanced industrial counterparts (Mainwaring 1999: 28–35). As a result, the electoral declines suffered by parties such as AD in Venezuela, the Peruvian APRA, and the Chilean Communist Party in the 1990s were far more precipitous than those experienced by the British Labour Party or the German Social Democrats in the 1980s. In theory, party failure may be expected to lead to a partisan realignment in which old parties are replaced by newer, more representative parties. However, in contemporary Latin America, labor-based party failure has more often resulted in party system *decomposition* (Roberts 1997b). Due to the predominance of media-based, candidate-centered politics and the increasing volatility of electorates, most of the new parties that have emerged in the wake of established party failure have been loosely structured, personalistic, and often short-lived organizations. As a result, emerging party systems are often fragmented, fluid, and highly unstable.

Party system decomposition may have important implications for democratic stability in Latin America. Parties remain central actors in contemporary democracies. Notwithstanding the generalized trend toward weaker party organizations and media-based, candidate-centered politics (Katz 1990; Katz and Mair 1995; Perelli 1995), parties continue to be the most effective available means of structuring electoral choices and organizing the legislative process. Although neighborhood associations, nongovernmental organizations, identity-based social movements, and other nonparty organizations have emerged as important political actors,[10] such organizations cannot effectively substitute for parties as mechanisms for coordinating citizens' political activities, aggregating their interests at the macro- or national-level, or providing them with regular access to the state (Hagopian 1998: 123–6; Roberts 1998a: 70–3). Where parties are weak, politics tends to be characterized by extreme electoral volatility, executive-legislative conflict, policy ineffectiveness, and the rise of "outsider" or antisystem candidates (Mainwaring and Scully 1995; Mainwaring 1999; Levitsky and Cameron 2003). These

---

[9] The British Labour Party in the 1990s is perhaps the clearest example of such a recovery.
[10] See Escobar and Alvarez (1992), Oxhorn 1995, Chalmers et al. (1997), Alvarez, Dagnino, and Escobar (1998), and Keck and Sikkink (1998).

phenomena tend to undermine the quality, and often the stability, of young democratic regimes.

Indeed, evidence from Latin America suggests that labor-based party adaptation and survival may have been critical to regime stability in the 1990s, particularly in countries with "labor-mobilizing" party systems (Roberts 1997b). Where powerful labor-based parties collapsed during the neoliberal era, as in Peru and Venezuela, party systems decomposed and democratic regimes either broke down or were brought to the brink of collapse.[11] In Peru, the collapse of APRA in the wake of Alan García's failed heterodox policies contributed to a process of party system disintegration that made possible both the election of outsider Alberto Fujimori and the 1992 *autogolpe* in which Fujimori assumed dictatorial powers. In Venezuela, the failure of AD president Carlos Andres Pérez's neoliberal experiment fueled an intensifying political and socioeconomic crisis that resulted in the collapse of the established party system, two coup attempts, and the eventual election of populist military rebel Hugo Chávez. By contrast, in countries where labor-based parties adapted successfully to the challenges of the neoliberal era, such as Argentina and Chile, both party systems and regimes remained relatively stable.

EXPLAINING PARTY ADAPTATION: AN ORGANIZATIONAL APPROACH

These divergent outcomes highlight the importance of understanding why some labor-based parties adapted successfully to the neoliberal challenge while others did not. Party adaptation can be understood as a set of changes in *strategy* and/or *structure*, undertaken in response to (or anticipation of) changed environmental conditions, that contribute to a party's capacity to meet its "primary goal" (Harmel and Janda 1994: 265). Although labor-based parties pursue a variety of goals, winning elections is clearly a predominant one.

For a party to adapt successfully, it must accomplish three things. First, its leaders must choose an appropriate strategy. Party leaders may fail to respond to environmental change or they may respond too slowly. Alternatively, they may choose ineffective strategies. Second, reformers must sell the strategy to (or impose it upon) the rest of the party. Both programmatic and organizational change may be expected to meet resistance from old-guard leaders, trade unionists, and activists with a stake in the party's traditional project. Third, the party must sell the new strategy to the electorate. No adaptive strategy can succeed unless it wins votes. Successful adaptation thus requires not only that parties undertake strategic change, but also that they

---

[11] For a comparative analysis of these party systems transformations, see Roberts (1997b, 2002).

win enough votes to maintain (if not improve) their electoral performance vis-á-vis the precrisis period.[12]

The causes of party change may be analyzed at different levels. The "ultimate" causes of party change lie in the external environment (Katz and Mair 1992: 9; also Harmel and Janda 1982; Panebianco 1988). Although party strategies are shaped by many aspects of the environment (Harmel and Janda 1982), the most important of these is probably the electoral environment. Because winning public office is a primary goal of most major parties, their strategies tend to be heavily influenced by the structure and preferences of the electorate (Downs 1957; Schlesinger 1984: 383–4). Parties that do not adapt to changes in the electorate are likely to suffer defeat and/or decline. Because such defeats generally result in a loss of resources for parties and party leaders, they can be expected to serve as a stimulus for party change. Party strategy is also shaped by the structure of electoral competition. For example, whereas two-party systems create incentives for parties to converge on the center in pursuit of the median voter (Downs 1957), in a multiparty context, parties may be induced to adjust their strategies in response to competition on their own flank (Kitschelt 1994a: 128–30; Harmel and Svasand 1997).

Parties must also respond to changes in the economic environment. In all countries, but particularly in lower- and middle-income countries, economic constraints often limit the degree to which governing parties can pursue vote-maximizing strategies. Indeed, economic crisis may induce programmatic choices that have little to do with the immediate preferences of the electorate. In Latin America, for example, the economic crisis of the 1980s led many governing parties to adopt policies that ran directly counter to the programs on which they campaigned (Stokes 2001). The dramatic policy reversals carried out by governments in Argentina, Bolivia, Peru, and Venezuela were responses to deep economic crises, rather than vote- or office-maximizing strategies. Although these policy switches had important electoral consequences, in some cases benefiting populist parties that successfully stabilized the economy (Gervasoni 1997; Stokes 2001), the link between programmatic choice and electoral preferences in these cases was far from clear. In most of these countries, policy choices were made in a context of high uncertainty and an ill-informed and often skeptical electorate.

Although environmental factors explain why contemporary labor-based parties have incentives to adapt, they cannot explain whether and how parties *actually respond* to these incentives. Analyses that focus primarily on the electoral or economic context have difficulty explaining diverging

---

[12] Although strategic change and electoral performance do not necessarily go hand in hand, in Latin America in the 1980s and 1990s, the heavy costs associated with failed adaptation meant that in practice, the two frequently did vary together.

outcomes across cases facing similar environments.[13] Such approaches offer little insight into why some parties pursue optimal electoral strategies while others do not.

An alternative approach to party adaptation looks for its causes within parties, and particularly within party leaderships. Some scholars have highlighted the role of party leaders in determining whether parties adapt or fail. For example, Richard Rose and Thomas Mackie argue that the "voluntary choices of party leaders" are of "first importance" in explaining party adaptation (1988: 557). Similarly, Frank Wilson describes party leaders as "the key intervening variable" that determines whether parties "respond to...factors that make transformation possible or desirable" (1994: 264). Perhaps due to the region's history of personalistic leaderships and presidential dominance, such leader-centered approaches have been especially prevalent in studies of Latin American parties.[14]

Other analysts argue that party adaptation is facilitated by leadership *change*, or the recomposition of what Angelo Panebianco calls the party's "dominant coalition" (1988: 242–4; also Harmel and Janda 1994). Scholars have linked environmental crisis and leadership change through what Harmel and Janda (1994) call an "integrated approach" to party change. According to this framework, poor performance resulting from environmental change "acts as a catalyzer" for party change by weakening oldguard leaderships and increasing the likelihood that they will be replaced by reform-oriented leaders (Panebianco 1988: 242–4; also Harmel and Janda 1994: 266–8).

Although leadership and leadership change are often critical to explaining party adaptation, they cannot be understood apart from the organizational context in which they occur. Party structures mediate leaders' responses to external challenges, encouraging some strategies and discouraging others. For example, whereas some party organizations grant leaders substantial room for maneuver in searching for and implementing adaptive strategies, others limit leadership autonomy through strict rules of accountability. Similarly, whereas some party structures facilitate leadership renovation, others are characterized by entrenched oligarchies and slow, incremental leadership change.

This book adopts an organizational approach to party change. In the tradition of Roberto Michels, Maurice Duverger, and Panebianco, it treats

---

[13] Thus, Przeworski and Sprague's conclusion that the erosion of industrial working classes would result in the decline of electoral socialism (1986: 183–5) proved overly pessimistic, as studies have found no relationship between working-class decline and labor-based party performance in the advanced industrialized countries (Kitschelt 1994a; Merkel 1995).

[14] See, for example, Graham (1990) on APRA's failures under García in the 1980s, Corrales (2000, 2002) on the diverging fates of AD and the PJ in the 1990s, and Córdoba (1994) on the PRI's adaptation under Carlos Salinas. For a critique of these leadership-centered explanations, see Burgess and Levitsky (2003).

parties as complex systems whose strategies are shaped by their organizational structures and internal dynamics. In this sense, it departs from approaches that treat parties as rational unitary actors, such as those that follow in the tradition of Anthony Downs (1957). Downsian models of party behavior assume that parties will either pursue vote (or office) maximizing strategies or be eliminated via electoral competition (Downs 1957: 25, 123; Schlesinger 1984: 384). They therefore pay little attention to intraparty factors. Yet there are clear analytical costs to assuming away party organization. Parties – particularly mass parties – are composed of multiple actors with diverse and often competing goals. Party organizations shape both the strategies that these actors pursue and their capacity to execute those strategies. Thus, even when party leaders can determine optimal strategies, intraparty dynamics often limit their capacity to pursue them. Indeed, recent studies of European and Latin American parties have found that organizational dynamics frequently produce strategies that are suboptimal from the standpoint of the party as a whole. For example, Koelble (1991, 1992) and Kitschelt (1994a, 1994b) have shown that the internal coalitions and organizational structures of European social democratic parties often hindered their responses to economic and electoral change in the 1980s. In Latin America, Coppedge (1994: 54–63) and Mainwaring (1999: 170–1) have found that factional dynamics (in Venezuela's AD) and patronage politics (in Brazilian clientelistic parties) often result in the selection of suboptimal presidential candidates, and Roberts (1998a: 47–8) has shown that the Chilean Communist Party's highly structured organization limited its capacity to modify its strategies in the face of political and economic liberalization.

Thus, parties' pursuit of optimal strategies is best treated as an outcome to be explained rather than as an assumption. It therefore seems reasonable to analyze party change in terms of a two-level or "nested" game (Tsebelis 1990; Koelble 1992), in which party leaders are located at the intersection of environmental and intraorganizational dynamics. An organizational approach to party change thus assumes that although leaders who seek to increase their political power (or that of their parties) must respond to changes in the external environment, their choices of strategies, as well as their capacity to carry out those strategies, are mediated by their parties' organizational structures and the "power games" within them. Such an approach, which has been employed in several recent studies of party behavior in the advanced industrialized countries,[15] avoids both the excessive structuralism of some environment-centered approaches and the excessive voluntarism of many leadership-centered approaches.

---

[15] Studies that examine how party organization affects parties' coalitional bargaining strategies include Strom (1990a, 1990b) and Maor (1995, 1998). Studies that examine how parties' organizational structures mediate their responses to changing electoral environments include Koelble (1991, 1992) and Kitschelt (1994a).

Party Organization, Adaptive Capacity, and the Question of Institutionalization

Recent research on party organization in the advanced industrialized countries (Panebianco 1988; Koelble 1991, 1992; Kitschelt 1994a) has generated important insights into how parties' organizational structures affect parties' adaptive capacities. These studies point to several organizational features that help parties adapt and survive during periods of environmental crisis. The first is strategic flexibility, or the capacity to modify party strategy in response to external challenges. Two factors are said to enhance strategic flexibility. The first factor is leadership autonomy. To be able to respond quickly and decisively to external challenges, party leaders require a certain amount of room to maneuver within the organization. Thus, to the extent that its leaders' strategic initiatives are restricted or slowed down by rules, procedures, and routines that ensure accountability to lower-level authorities, a party's adaptive capacity will be limited (Strom 1990b: 577; Kitschelt 1994a: 212–13). Strategic flexibility is also enhanced by leadership renovation. Where old-guard leaders remain entrenched in the party hierarchy, limiting the entry and rise of new members, it is less likely that the party will undertake rapid or far-reaching change. Thus, parties that facilitate the entry of fresh blood into their hierarchies are said to be more open to change than those with entrenched bureaucracies, strict career paths, and internal recruitment filters (Kitschelt 1994a: 212; Roberts 1998a: 47).

Another set of factors that facilitates adaptation and survival regards parties' rootedness in society. In its extreme form, societal rootedness is associated with mass party structures and organizational encapsulation (Sartori 1968: 122; Wellhofer 1979a, 1979b). By "incorporating within the political party as many of the everyday life activities of the membership as possible" through the sponsorship of unions, youth and women's branches, sports clubs, cooperatives, and other organizations, mass parties created distinct party subcultures or "communities of fate" (Wellhofer 1979b: 171). Such encapsulation raises the threshold at which voters decide to abandon their party, creating, in effect, "electorates of belonging" (Panebianco 1988: 267). According to Panebianco, an electorate of belonging is

> that portion of the party electorate integrated into the party's subculture. This type of voter is virtually a "born" supporter.... His loyalty and identification with the party are so strong that he votes for the party independently of the party's strategy (1988: 278, footnote 38).

Although the organizational encapsulation characteristic of some turn-of-the-century European parties no longer exists anywhere in the world, many parties continue to possess extensive base-level organizations, large activist bases, and relatively stable core electorates. Even in this weakened form, such societal rootedness provides an electoral cushion that enables parties to make strategic changes – or mistakes – without suffering substantial short-term losses.

The literature on party organization and change suggests a trade-off between societal rootedness and strategic flexibility. This trade-off centers on the question of mass organization. On the one hand, mass organizations tend to be associated with electoral stability. Although mass linkages weakened over the course of the twentieth century (Katz 1990; Katz and Mair 1995), the persistence of party subcultures and identities – together with the human, organizational, and patronage resources provided by mass party structures – continues to yield long-term electoral benefits (Wolinetz 1990: 310–12; Ware 1992: 73–5). On the other hand, mass organization is widely associated with bureaucratization, which is said to limit strategic flexibility. Over time, the mass party organizations created during earlier periods of electoral mobilization tended to bureaucratize (Michels 1911). Although Michels viewed bureaucratization as strengthening the hand of party elites vis-á-vis rank-and-file members, bureaucratic mass party structures have also been associated with entrenched decision rules and elaborate procedures to ensure leadership accountability (Strom 1990b: 577–9). In addition, bureaucratic hierarchies generally maintain strict recruitment filters and stable career paths, which limit leadership renovation (Kitschelt 1994b: 17–21). For this reason, mass parties are said to "lack the flexibility to adapt easily to new challenges" (Deschouwer 1994: 83).[16]

The flexibility-stability trade-off can be seen in Panebianco's (1988) distinction between mass bureaucratic and electoral-professional parties. Mass bureaucratic parties – which are characterized by extensive territorial organizations, powerful central bureaucracies, large memberships and activist bases, and stable "electorates of belonging" (1988: 264) – are said to be stable but comparatively inflexible (Kitschelt 1994a: 216). By contrast, electoral-professional parties, which lack mass memberships and entrenched bureaucracies and tend to be characterized by more media-based, candidate-centered appeals, tend to be more flexible but less electorally stable than mass bureaucratic parties (Panebianco 1988: 264–7).

Yet the flexibility-stability trade-off may not be as steep as the literature suggests. As the Peronist case clearly demonstrates, mass organizations may exist without strong central bureaucracies, stable career paths, or institutionalized mechanisms of leadership accountability. Although the PJ is unquestionably a mass party, its mass organization is informal rather than bureaucratic, and the rules and procedures that govern the internal life of the party are fluid, contested, widely manipulated, and often ignored. Such informal and weakly institutionalized party structures are relatively common in Latin America. Indeed, they are characteristic of most populist and clientelistic

---

[16] Also Michels (1911/1962: 189), Sjoblom (1983: 393–5), and Kitschelt (1994a: 216).

parties. Nevertheless, these dimensions have received relatively little attention in the dominant literature on party organization and change.[17]

The failure to take informal and weakly institutionalized party structures into account reflects a pronounced advanced country bias in the literature on party organization. Much of the leading scholarship on party organization and change takes for granted that parties' internal structures, as well as the behavior patterns within them, are institutionalized.[18] Intraparty rules and procedures are assumed to be stable, well-defined, and widely known and accepted by members, and party organizations are assumed to correspond more or less to the formal structures outlined in their statutes. Hence, mass organizations are often treated as invariably bureaucratic.[19] Although such assumptions may be appropriate for studies of many European parties, they have significant conceptual and theoretical costs when applied to Latin America. Not only do parties vary considerably on the dimension of institutionalization, but this variation has important implications for parties' capacity to adapt to environmental change.

Unpacking the Concept of Institutionalization

Although several scholars have suggested that institutionalization has an important effect on parties' capacity to adapt (Huntingon 1968: 13–17; Kesselman 1970; Panebianco 1988: 261; Appleton and Ward 1997; Levitsky 1998b), they differ substantially over what that effect is. In large part, this is due to the fact that although the term *institutionalization* is widely used in studies of political parties, it is attached to a variety of different meanings and analytic approaches.[20] As a result, one finds surprisingly little scholarly agreement about what institutionalization is or what its affects are.

A variety of meanings of *institutionalization* can be found in the literature on political organizations. Definitions of *institution* range from a relatively narrow focus on formal rules (Ostrom 1986; Tsebelis 1990) to broad conceptions that include beliefs, myths, knowledge, and other aspects of culture (March and Olsen 1989; Powell and DiMaggio 1991). It is possible to identify at least three distinct organizational phenomena that have been associated with institutionalization in recent research on political parties. The first of these is electoral or organizational stability, which is often measured

---

[17] Mainwaring (1999: 21–5) similarly argues that the leading theoretical work on party systems pays insufficient attention to weakly institutionalized party systems.
[18] Panebianco (1988) is an exception in this regard.
[19] See Wellhofer (1972: 156); Panebianco (1988: 264); Strom (1990b); and Kitschelt (1994a: 212–13); also Michels (1911/1962: 187).
[20] For discussions of the concept of party or party system institutionalization, see Welfling (1973); Janda (1980: 19–28); Panebianco (1988: 49–68); Dix (1992); Mainwaring and Scully (1995: 4–6), Schedler (1995); McGuire (1997: 7–11); Levitsky (1998a); and Mainwaring (1999: 25–39).

in terms of a party's age, the continuity of its name or organization, or its electoral volatility (Janda 1980: 19–27; Mainwaring and Scully 1995: 6–7; Appleton and Ward 1997: 356). However, to avoid problems of tautology, in which stability is simultaneously treated as an indicator and an outcome of institutionalization,[21] this phenomenon may be better understood as a *product* of institutionalization than as a defining feature of it.

A second phenomenon that is associated with party institutionalization, and which underlies the definitions put forth by scholars such as Selznick (1957) and Huntington (1968), is what McGuire (1997: 8) calls "value infusion." These definitions treat institutionalization as a process by which an organization becomes "infused with value beyond the technical requirements of the task at hand" (Selznick 1957: 17). According to this conceptualization, institutionalization occurs when actors' goals shift from the pursuit of particular objectives *through* an organization to the goal of perpetuating the organization per se. Thus, an institutionalized organization is "valued for its own sake" and "develops a life of its own quite apart from the specific functions it may perform at any given time" (Huntington 1968: 15).

A third phenomenon that is commonly associated with institutionalization is the routinization of the rules and procedures *within* organizations (Krasner 1988; North 1990a; Knight 1992). Scholars who focus on this dimension view institutions as "regularized patterns of interaction that are known, practiced, and regularly accepted," as well as the "rules and norms formally or informally embodied in those patterns" (O'Donnell 1994: 57–9). According to Douglass North (1990a: 4), institutions are "perfectly analogous to the rules of the game in a competitive team sport," in that they structure behavior through a combination of "rules and informal codes." When rules, norms, and procedures are institutionalized, stable sets of expectations form around them. Actors' behavior becomes regularized and predictable, thereby "providing a structure to everyday life" (North 1990a: 3).

Scholars often treat two or more of these phenomena as dimensions of a single concept (Janda 1980: 19; Panebianco 1988: 53, 58–60; McGuire 1997: 7–12; Mainwaring 1999: 26–7). In some cases, the dimensions are treated as distinct but are said to vary together.[22] In other cases, they are simply conflated.[23] Although multidimensional concepts are often useful, such

---

[21] For discussions of the problems of tautology associated with some definitions of *institutionalization*, see Tilly (1973: 431), Sigelman (1979: 215), and Levitsky (1998a: 85).

[22] For example, see McGuire (1997: 7–8).

[23] For example, Panebianco defines *institutionalization* as value infusion, writing that a party is institutionalized when it "becomes valuable in and of itself, and its goals become inseparable and indistinguishable from it" (1988: 53). However, his indicators of institutionalization include bureaucratization, the regularization of finance, the homogenization of organizational subunits, and an increasing "correspondence between a party's statutory norms" and its "actual power structure," all of which are more closely related to routinization than to value infusion (1988: 58–60).

aggregation also has potential analytic costs. Organizations may score very differently on the various dimensions. For example, an organization may be infused with value without being internally routinized. These ambiguities are clearly seen in the case of Peronism. According to the value infusion definition, the PJ is well institutionalized, for its members exhibit a commitment to the party that transcends its original goals. Peronists have remained committed to the movement and its organizations through periods of severe adversity – such as the party's proscription beginning in 1955, Perón's death in 1974, and the brutal repression of the 1976–83 dictatorship – and despite important changes in the organization's goals and strategies, such as the Menem government's neoliberal turn. According to the routinization definition, however, the PJ is weakly institutionalized. As this book demonstrates, the rules of the game that govern the internal life of the party have never been stable or taken for granted. Rather, they are routinely circumvented, ignored, or modified in line with the short-term strategies of party leaders. Not surprisingly, then, scholars differ considerably in their assessment of the PJ's level of institutionalization. Whereas some scholars characterize the PJ as "highly institutionalized" (Jones 1997: 272), others view it as "weakly institutionalized" (McGuire 1997: 1).

Such conceptual ambiguity poses a serious problem for causal analysis. Diverging understandings of the meaning of institutionalization, or a failure to distinguish among different aspects of institutionalization, may limit our capacity to develop and assess arguments about its causes and consequences. This problem is made manifest in the scholarship on institutionalization and organizational adaptation. Different definitions of *institutionalization* are associated with opposing arguments about the causal relation between institutionalization and party adaptation. For example, the value infusion conception views institutionalization as *facilitating* adaptation (Huntington 1968), in that members of a valued organization will seek to preserve it even after its goals change or are met. When individuals have a stake in an organization's persistence, then the goal of maintaining the organization per se will override particular organizational goals, and members will be likely to accept changes in those goals in order to ensure the organization's survival.[24] By contrast, the routinization conception views institutionalization as *reducing* the adaptive capacity of organizations. Institutionalization in this second sense is understood to constrain actors. Routinization reduces the options considered by actors and raises the social, psychic, or material costs of departing from established patterns (March and Olsen 1984: 740). Consequently, sudden or far-reaching change in the context of routinized rules and procedures tends

---

[24] Thus, Huntington argues that institutionalized nationalist parties in postcolonial states (such as the Indian Congress Party) were able to shift their goals and functions during the postindependence period (1968: 17), whereas noninstitutionalized parties presumably could not.

to be widely resisted within organizations (Zucker 1977: 729), and organizational change tends to take place "slowly and laboriously" (Panebianco 1988: 58).

In light of these ambiguities, it may be useful to disaggregate institutionalization into clearly specified components.[25] This book focuses on the dimension of internal routinization, which may be defined as a state in which the rules and procedures within an organization are widely known, accepted, and complied with. Highly routinized rules are internalized and even "taken for granted" by actors (Jepperson 1991: 147). Routinization may be formal or informal. *Formal* rules are officially sanctioned and generally written down. Where there is a tight fit between these rules and actual behavior patterns, we may speak of *formal routinization*. Where behavior follows widely known and accepted patterns, but these patterns either deviate from or are unrelated to formal rules, we may speak of *informal routinization*. Finally, *weak* or *nonroutinization* is a state in which (formal or informal) rules and procedures are fluid, contested, and routinely circumvented or ignored.

Routinization and Party Adaptation

A central claim of this book is that routinization limits the capacity of organizations to respond quickly to environmental challenges, and that *weakly routinized* organizations may be better equipped to adapt to rapid environmental change than highly routinized organizations. In normal times, of course, routinization is associated with organizational efficiency. Established routines and taken-for-granted rules, procedures, and roles are critical to the everyday functioning of complex organizations (Nelson and Winter 1982: 74–110; March and Olsen 1989: 24). As North writes, routinization "allow[s] people to go about the everyday process of making exchanges without having to think out exactly the terms of an exchange at each point and in each instance" (1990a: 83). By contrast, low routinization is generally associated with organizational inefficiency. In the absence of clearly defined and widely accepted rules of the game, organizational actors must invest substantial amounts of time and energy into resolving internal conflicts or procedural disputes, coordinating activities, and monitoring the actions of others.

Yet routinization may also handicap organizations in a context of crisis or rapid environmental change, for it limits the speed and flexibility with which actors are able to devise and implement adaptive strategies.[26] These limitations may be understood in both cognitive (or norm-based) and rational

---

[25] Thus, the PJ could be scored as moderately high on the dimension of value infusion in the 1990s, but relatively low on the dimension of routinization.

[26] Thompson (1967: 150) makes a similar observation, which he calls the "paradox of administration."

actor (or calculus-based) terms. From a cognitive perspective, routinized decision-making processes narrow the range of alternatives considered by leaders (Nelson and Winter 1982: 74–83). When rules, procedures, and roles are routinized, stable sets of expectations form around them. They become "taken for granted" (Jepperson 1991: 147), as actors come to view them as "part of the 'objective situation'" (Zucker 1983: 5). Consequently, actors often comply with routinized rules and procedures without evaluating the immediate costs and benefits of such compliance (Zucker 1977: 728; Dimaggio and Powell 1991: 11). Indeed, studies have shown that organizational actors frequently stick to routines even in the midst of crises (Nelson and Winter 1982: 122; March and Olsen 1989: 33). From a rational actor perspective, routinized structures become entrenched because actors invest in skills, learn strategies, and create organizations that are appropriate to the existing rules of the game (North 1990b: 364–5). These investments give actors a stake in the preservation of existing arrangements, as well as a greater capacity to defend them, which raises the transaction costs of carrying out organizational change.

Routinized organizations thus tend to be "sticky," in that they do not change as quickly as underlying preferences and power distributions. This leaves such organizations vulnerable to external shocks, for it limits the speed with – and often the extent to – which they can adapt. Decision makers in a highly routinized organization will – at least initially – tend to consider a narrower range of strategic alternatives, none of which may be appropriate in a context of crisis or rapid environmental change. Moreover, even when leaders do come up with viable adaptive strategies, established routines and decision rules may limit their capacity to implement them. These limitations may be critical. In a context of environmental crisis, the failure to respond quickly may have devastating consequences for organizations (Nelson and Winter 1982: 126; Krasner 1988: 82). By contrast, weakly routinized organizations may be better equipped to respond to environmental shocks. Because more is "up for grabs" in the short run, actors have greater room to maneuver as they search for and carry out adaptive strategies, and because rules and procedures are not buttressed by vested interests or taken-for-grantedness, actors have less difficulty modifying them when it serves their short-term goals. Thus, nonroutinized organizations tend to be less sticky, as lags between institutional outcomes and underlying distributions of power and preferences can be closed with relative ease.

With respect to political parties, routinization may be said to affect strategic flexibility along three dimensions: (1) leadership renovation, or the ease with which old-guard leaders may be removed and reformers may rise up through the ranks of the party hierarchy; (2) leadership autonomy, or the room for maneuver available to party leaders; and (3) structural pliability, or the ease with which the party's organizational structure can be modified in response to environmental challenges.

Leadership Entrenchment versus Leadership Fluidity

As noted previously, strategic flexibility is enhanced by leadership renovation. Where party hierarchies are routinized, often in the form of bureaucracies, leadership renovation tends to be slow. In such organizations, old-guard leaders often become entrenched in the party hierarchy, and internal recruitment filters and established career paths ward off reformist movements (Kitschelt 1994b: 17–21). Because party leaderships exercise substantial control over the bureaucratic advancement process, aspiring leaders find that the only way to rise through the party ranks is to allow themselves to be "co-opted by the center" (Panebianco 1988: 61; also Michels 1911/1962: 174–6). Thus, those who succeed in the organization do so because they have played by the rules and have proven their loyalty to the party leadership (Wellhofer 1972: 171–5). Consequently, bureaucratic organizations are often dominated by what Downs (1967: 96–7) calls "conservers," or middle-level officials who "seek to maximize their security and convenience" and therefore "tend to be biased against any change in the status quo."[27] In such contexts, reformers tend to be "drowned in a sea of conventional party stalwarts" (Kitschelt 1994b: 10). Bureaucratized party hierarchies thus frequently take the form of oligarchies, in which leadership turnover occurs "gradually and slowly" and "never through a sudden, massive, and extended injection of new blood" (Schonfeld 1981: 231).

In parties that lack bureaucratized hierarchies, movement into, up, and out of the party leadership is generally more fluid. Old-guard leaders and cadres may be more easily removed from the party hierarchy, and reformers may rise up quickly through the leadership ranks. In the absence of strict recruitment filters and bureaucratic career paths, parties tend to be more permeable to exogenous influences (Kitschelt 1994a: 214; Roberts 1998a: 47). New activists find it relatively easy to enter the party and rise up through the ranks. Although such openness often brings higher levels of dissidence and factionalism, it also promotes internal debate and the circulation of ideas, which facilitates programmatic adaptation and change (Roberts 1998a: 47).

Strategic Constraint versus Strategic Autonomy

Strategic flexibility is also enhanced by leadership autonomy. To the extent that party leaders are constrained from within, their ability to search for and implement adaptive strategies will be limited (Panebianco 1988: 15; Kitschelt 1994a: 213–16). Although routinization may be accompanied by a centralization of authority, as in the case of Leninist parties (Kitschelt 1994a: 214), more frequently it tends to "drastically limit internal actors' margins of maneuverability" (Panebianco 1988: 58). In a highly routinized setting, established routines limit the array of options considered by party

---

[27] Also see Michels (1911/1962: 189).

leaders, which may delay the search for appropriate responses to environmental shocks. For example, in his study of the Norwegian Labour Party, Olsen (1983) found that the party leadership operated within established routines even in the midst of a deep cabinet crisis and in the face of a possible electoral defeat. Moreover, most routinized parties possess complex rules of internal accountability, such as the division of leadership into competing powers and requirements that leadership decisions be approved by lower-level bodies (Strom 1990b: 577–8; Kitschelt 1994a: 223–5).

Routinization may also limit innovation from below (Kitschelt 1994a: 212; Roberts 1998a: 46). To the extent that party subunits are vertically integrated into a central bureaucracy, their room to maneuver vis-á-vis higher-level bodies will be limited. Bureaucratic procedures ensure that decisions made by the party leadership are carried out by lower-level branches, thereby limiting the degree to which those branches may innovate or experiment with alternative strategies.

By contrast, weakly routinized party structures tend to yield greater strategic autonomy, both to party leaderships and to lower-level subunits. The absence of established bureaucratic routines allows party leaders to consider a wider range of strategic options, and the absence of established mechanisms of accountability gives leaders greater autonomy to carry out strategies (Harmel and Svasand 1993: 68). Moreover, lower-level bodies have more freedom to experiment with new strategies, and in the absence of bureaucratized career paths, innovations from below will be less likely to be suppressed by middle-level bureaucrats or "conservers."

Structural Rigidity versus Structural Pliability

Finally, routinized party organizations themselves tend to be resistant to change. Routinized party structures, particularly those of mass party organizations, tend to be path-dependent or subject to "increasing returns" (Panebianco 1988: xii–xiv).[28] In such a context, actors throughout the party are likely to have internalized existing organizational arrangements and developed strategies and skills appropriate to those arrangements. Power holders at all levels of the organization are thus likely to have learned how to win internal power games by the existing rules. These actors can be expected to oppose changes in those rules. Even when a substantial number of party members develop an interest in changing the structure of the organization, the coordination problems – or transaction costs – involved in carrying out such changes are often exceedingly high. Efforts to change structures that are buttressed by vested interests and taken-for-grantedness tend to generate internal resistance. The costs of overcoming that resistance, together with the costs entailed by a disruption of established routines and the enforcement of new ones, often outweigh the expected benefit of the change.

---

[28] On path-dependence and increasing returns in politics, see Pierson (2000).

As a result, structural change in routinized mass parties tends to be a slow, arduous process. Such changes often fail to keep pace with changes in the external environment. In weakly routinized parties, by contrast, key aspects of the party structure tend to be less entrenched or taken for granted, which facilitates their modification or removal.

In sum, the absence of bureaucratic hierarchies, stable routines, and norms of accountability may be expected to facilitate party adaptation in a context of environmental crisis or change. Although there is no guarantee that weakly routinized parties will adopt appropriate strategies in response to external crises, their loosely structured organizations create a greater *opportunity* for adaptation than exists in highly routinized parties.

Mass Populist Parties: Combining Rootedness and Flexibility

To the extent that mass parties are weakly routinized, then, they may avoid the flexibility-stability trade-off discussed in the previous section. In other words, parties that combine societal rootedness with low levels of bureaucratization may possess a distinct advantage in terms of adaptive capacity. Many Latin American mass populist parties[29] – including the PJ, Bolivian MNR, Mexican PRI, and Peruvian APRA[30] – fall (to varying degrees) into this category. Mass populist parties are mass-based in that they possess extensive national organizations, large membership and activist bases, and strong linkages to working- and lower-class society. In many cases, these linkages include strong ties to the labor movement. It is in this sense that mass populist parties may be distinguished from other Latin American parties that have been identified as populist, such as the parties created by Arnulfo Arias in Panama, Manuel Odría in Peru, Gustavo Rojas Pinilla in Colombia, and José María Velasco Ibarra in Ecuador.

Despite their mass organizations and ties to organized labor, Latin American mass populist parties have historically differed from most European working-class parties – such as social democratic and communist parties – in four ways.[31] First, their support bases were more heterogeneous, as they included elements of the unorganized urban and rural poor, the middle sectors, and, in some cases, the peasantry. Second, their ideologies were generally amorphous or eclectic, rather than Marxist or social democratic. Third, they were characterized by a strong element of mobilization from above,

---

[29] On Latin American populism, see Di Tella (1965b), Drake (1978), Conniff (1982, 1999), Collier and Collier (1991), Roberts (1995), and Weyland (2001).

[30] Arguably, the Chilean Socialist Party (PSCh) also falls into this category. Although the PSCh transformed itself into a class-based Marxist party in the 1950s, its origins were populist and it never developed a highly structured and disciplined organization (Drake 1978; Roberts 1998a: 48).

[31] This definition draws heavily on Di Tella (1965b), Collier and Collier (1991: 788), and Roberts (1995: 88–9).

Mass Linkages	Low Routinization	High Routinization
Strong	Mass Populist Party	Mass Bureaucratic Party
Weak	Personalistic Electoral Party	Electoral-Professional Party

FIGURE 1.1. A Typology of Parties Based on the Dimensions of Routinization and Mass Organizaion

often from actors within the state.[32] Finally, populist parties were characterized by personalistic – and in some cases charismatic – leaderships.[33]

Due to their top-down origins and personalistic leaderships, mass populist parties developed organizational structures that differed considerably from those of most European working-class parties. Many European communist and social democratic parties emerged as highly structured, disciplined, and collectively led organizations. Over time, these parties evolved into highly routinized, bureaucratic organizations with stable, oligarchic leaderships. In contrast, most populist parties did not develop stable bureaucratic structures, as personalistic leadership tended to inhibit the routinization of internal rules, hierarchies, and organizational patterns. As a result, many of them fell apart soon after losing power. When they survived, however, mass populist parties often evolved into strikingly flexible organizations. Although most of these parties maintain extensive base-level organizations and strong loyalties among the subaltern sectors of society, key legacies of populism – including fluid internal structures, nonbureaucratic hierarchies, and relatively autonomous leaderships – provide them with a high degree of strategic flexibility.

Figure 1.1 adds the dimension of routinization to Panebianco's (1988: 262–7) ideal-typical distinction between mass bureaucratic and electoral-professional parties. Mass-based parties are distinguished from electoral parties by the existence of extensive base-level organizations. On the right side

---

[32] APRA, which was born in opposition and never gained substantial access to the state during its formative period, is a partial exception.
[33] The PRI is an exception in this regard.

of the figure are the routinized parties that predominate in the literature. In the upper-right corner, one finds routinized mass parties, which correspond to Panebianco's mass bureaucratic parties. Many Northern European social democratic parties fall into this category. Such parties tend to be electorally stable but comparatively inflexible. In the lower-right corner, one finds routinized nonmass parties, which correspond to Panebianco's electoral-professional parties. These parties are more flexible, but less electorally stable, than mass bureaucratic parties. On the left side of Figure 1.1 are weakly routinized parties. In the lower-left corner, one finds nonroutinized parties without mass organizations, such as the personalistic vehicles that predominated in Peru and Russia in the 1990s. Such parties are highly flexible but often ephemeral. Finally, the upper-left corner corresponds to nonbureaucratic mass parties, such as mass populist parties. These parties are characterized by a distinctive combination of stability and flexibility, for although they are mass-based, they lack many of the bureaucratic constraints that are common to routinized mass parties. Hence, such parties may be particularly well equipped to adapt to contemporary processes of socioeconomic change.

THE CASE OF PERONISM: THE ADAPTATION AND SURVIVAL
OF A LABOR-BASED POPULIST PARTY

This book examines the relationship between low routinization and party adaptation through a study of the PJ's response to the challenges of neoliberalism and working-class decline. At the outset of the neoliberal era, the PJ was a mass – and labor-based – populist party. It was a mass party in that it possessed a powerful local infrastructure, a large activist base, and stable loyalties among the vast majority of working- and lower-class voters. It was labor-based in that its core constituency was organized labor. Yet the PJ differed from many other established working-class parties in that its mass organization was informal and weakly routinized. Unlike most European labor-based parties, for example, Peronism had populist origins. Created from above by a highly personalistic leader, the party never developed a disciplined, hierarchical organization. Perón constantly thwarted efforts to establish a stable set of internal rules of the game, both during his initial presidency and during his long exile after 1955. Even after Perón's death, Peronists failed to reach a consensus on new rules of the game for organizing the party or distributing authority. As a result, the PJ organization that emerged from the 1983 democratic transition was weakly routinized and thoroughly nonbureaucratic. The party hierarchy lacked recruitment filters, stable career paths, and secure tenure patterns. In addition, intraparty rules and procedures surrounding questions such as leadership and candidate selection and executive decision making were fluid, contested, and widely manipulated. Even core features of the PJ's organizational structure, such as its executive bodies and party–union linkages, were weakly routinized.

Although the PJ's internal fluidity frequently resulted in inefficiency and disorder, it also provided the party with a degree of flexibility that is uncharacteristic of most working-class parties. In the wake of the 1983 democratic transition, trade unions dominated the PJ to a degree that far exceeded most European and Latin American labor-based parties. Yet because it lacked the "stickiness" associated with a routinized party–union linkage and a bureaucratic internal structure, the PJ was more open to change than most of its European and Latin American counterparts. Thus, whereas most social democratic and communist parties adapted slowly and incrementally to changes in the socioeconomic environment, the PJ was able to change more quickly in line with these changing political and economic conditions.

This book shows how the PJ's weak routinization enabled reform-oriented leaders to undertake rapid and far-reaching changes in the party's *structure* and *strategy* in the late 1980s and early 1990s. Changes in organizational structure permitted the PJ to adapt coalitionally by substantially reducing trade union influence in the party. While unions historically had enjoyed great influence within Peronism, their position in the party was never routinized. Though largely accepted in the 1960s and 1970s, Peronism's traditional mechanisms of union participation were neither formalized in the party's statutes nor widely taken for granted. Thus, Peronist labor's "political arm," the "62 Organizations" (or "62"), lacked statutes, offices, and clear rules of operation, and Peronism's traditional mechanism for placing unionists on its leadership bodies and candidate lists, the *tercio* (or one-third) system, was neither broadly accepted nor rigorously enforced. Due to this lack of routinization, when politicians' dependence on union resources declined in the mid-1980s, the "62" and the *tercio* were easily dismantled. Without any institutional channels for participation in the 1990s, union influence quickly eroded. As politicians replaced union resources with state resources, the urban PJ was transformed from a union-based party into a patronage-based party in which unions played a relatively marginal role. This process of deunionization was faster and more far-reaching than in most other labor-based parties in Latin America and Europe.

Low routinization also facilitated changes in party strategy, which permitted the rapid adoption of a market-oriented program in the 1990s. Although President Menem's bold strategies and skilled leadership were critical to the success of his programmatic turn, such strategies would not have been possible were it not for a party structure that granted him substantial room for maneuver. Few national PJ leaders, and even fewer local and provincial party leaders, shared President Menem's reform agenda in 1989. Nevertheless, Menem encountered little intraparty resistance as he brought neoliberal economists, business leaders, and right-wing politicians into his government, struck an alliance with the conservative Democratic Center Union, and carried out a set of radical liberalizing reforms. This strategic autonomy was largely a product of the PJ's organizational structure. In the absence of a strong central bureaucracy with stable career paths and secure tenure patters, officials at all levels of the party hierarchy have an incentive to remain on good terms with office-holding party leaders. Rather than entrenched "oligarchs" or bureaucratic "conservers," old-guard leaders become "bandwagoners," defecting to winning factions in the hope of maintaining their positions. Intraparty bandwagoning was critical to the success of the Menem program, as much of the left-of-center Renovation faction that controlled the party in 1989 defected to Menem after he took office. Menem's strategic autonomy was further enhanced by the absence of regularized mechanisms of consultation. The PJ's formal leadership bodies, the National Congress and National Council, played virtually no role in shaping party strategy. The government's programmatic shift was never debated or voted on in the party congress, and the National Council found itself either ignored by, or serving as a rubber stamp for, the Peronist-controlled executive branch. Finally, Menem's strategic autonomy was enhanced by the absence of effective horizontal links among secondary party leaders, which undermined their capacity to act collectively. Placed in a hub-and-spokes relationship with the national leadership, secondary leaders found themselves vulnerable to strategies of cooptation and repeatedly failed in their efforts to build coalitions to check the power of the national leadership.

The Peronist adaptation was critical to its survival as a major political force in the 1990s. By replacing its union-based structures with patronage-based territorial organizations, the PJ created mass linkages that were more compatible with both deindustrialization and neoliberalism. And by enabling the Menem government to stabilize the economy, the PJ's programmatic adaptation helped it avoid the heavy political costs paid by governing populist and labor-based parties – such as AD in Venezuela and APRA in Peru – that failed to resolve their countries' economic crises.

The PJ's capacity to adapt and survive in the neoliberal period also contributed to democratic stability in Argentina. Given the Menem government's apparent lack of interest in strengthening representative institutions, this outcome may appear somewhat paradoxical. Indeed, the Menem government's concentration (and at times abuse) of power led scholars to characterize it as a textbook case of "delegative democracy" during the 1990s (O'Donnell 1994; Diamond 1999: 34–5). Moreover, the PJ's programmatic about-face may have had important costs in terms of the quality of democratic representation, as policy switches erode voters' ability to make informed electoral choices and may undermine their confidence in the electoral process (Stokes 2001). Yet the PJ's adaptation and survival in the 1990s also contributed to democratic stability in at least three ways. First, the PJ's links to organized labor and working- and lower-class voters limited popular sector mobilization against neoliberal reforms, which permitted the Menem government to combine radical reform and democracy in a way that was virtually unparalleled in the region. Second, the PJ's survival as a major political force helped to stabilize the party system at a time when political identities were in flux and outsider and even antisystem candidates were on the rise. Not only did the PJ's continued hold on the working- and lower-class electorate limit the prospects for political outsiders, but it also provided the Menem government with the support it needed to push its reform program through the legislature. Finally, by reconciling with the economic elite – without breaking its ties to labor – the PJ put an end to the stalemated party system dynamic that had been viewed as a major source of Argentina's postwar regime instability.

Peronism as a Labor-Based Party

This book treats the PJ as a labor-based party,[34] arguing that it faced coalitional and programmatic challenges in the 1980s and 1990s that were in many ways similar to those faced by social democratic, labor, and communist parties in the advanced industrialized countries. Such a characterization is by no means an uncontroversial one. Peronism has long been characterized by its heterogeneity, ideological eclecticism, and malleability (De Ipola 1987; Buchrucker 1988, 1998). Its electoral coalition was always more heterogeneous than those of most European working-class parties. In urban areas, Peronism originally drew from both the established industrial working class and an expanding pool of poor migrants from the interior (Germani 1965, 1973; Smith 1972; Kenworthy 1975), while in the less developed provinces of the interior, it was supported by a heterogeneous mix of rural workers and lower-to-middle-income townspeople (Smith 1972; Llorente 1980; Mora y Araujo 1980).[35] Peronism has been even more heterogeneous in the ideological realm, spanning from the leftist Montonero guerrillas to ultranationalist paramilitary groups such as *Comando de Organización*. Perón himself was notoriously eclectic in both his rhetoric and his alliances, and Peronist policy making was always characterized by a high degree of pragmatism. Although they are best known for their redistributive, pro-labor policies, Peronist governments implemented relatively orthodox stabilization programs in 1952 and 1975. This heterogeneity and ideological eclecticism has made Peronism very difficult to label in left–right terms,[36] and as a result, many scholars have simply characterized the movement as "pragmatic" (De Ipola 1987; Pinto 1995: 84).

Notwithstanding this internal heterogeneity, however, Peronism maintained a trade unionist and working-class core. Organized labor remained

---

[34] Such a characterization is in line with work such as Di Tella (1965b, 1998), Torre (1983, 1990), Collier and Collier (1991), and McGuire (1997).

[35] Since the 1950s, Peronism's strongest electoral support has come from this latter "peripheral coalition" (Gibson 1997; also Llorente 1980; Mora y Araujo 1980).

[36] For a compelling analysis of why Peronism cannot be understood in traditional left–right terms, see Ostiguy (1998).

Peronism's core constituency throughout the movement's turbulent history. Edward Gibson defines a party's core constituencies as

those sectors of society that are most important to its political agenda and resources. Their importance lies not necessarily in the number of votes they represent, but in their influence on the party's agenda and capacities for political action. A party's core constituencies shape its identity; they are necessary to its existence (1996: 7).

Although the Peronist–trade union alliance was never formalized as it was in many European social democratic and communist parties, labor's weight in the Peronist coalition historically rivaled – and at times exceeded – that of many of its European counterparts. Trade unions played a fundamental role in Perón's initial rise to power in the 1940s and were critical to the movement's survival during the 1955–73 proscription period. After Perón's death in 1974, union leaders gained a near-hegemonic position in the party leadership. Throughout these periods, the unions constituted Peronism's primary linkage to the urban working and lower classes. When Perón was in power, the unions delivered votes, mobilized supporters, served as channels for the distribution of social welfare benefits, and, critically, provided social peace. When Peronism was out of power, the unions' vast human, financial, and organizational resources were essential to the movement's very survival.

With respect to its electoral coalition, although the PJ was never a pure working-class party, it was Argentina's "party of the poor" (Mora y Araujo 1995: 52). In every election in which the PJ participated between 1946 and 1999, it won the vast majority of working- and lower-class votes and was virtually hegemonic among the poor (Mora y Araujo 1980, 1995: 52–3; Ostiguy 1998: 346–51). In urban industrialized areas, this base had a strong working-class component. Survey and electoral data from the 1946–55 period (Smith 1972; Llorente 1980; Germani 1980: 258–61; Schoultz 1983: 30–1), the 1960s (Kirkpatrick 1971; Schoultz 1983), and the 1973 election (Mora y Araujo and Smith 1980; Cantón 1986; Miguens 1988) all find a strong positive correlation between industrial working-class status and the Peronist vote.[37]

Finally, although the Peronist program was nowhere near as ideologically coherent as European social democracy, it did maintain certain core components. For example, despite their substantial internal differences, virtually all Peronists shared an aversion to free-market capitalism and a commitment to organized labor and a state-led development model. Specifically, the core Peronist program included: (1) a state-led industrialization strategy that centered around the state's promotion, protection, and, in some cases, ownership of key industries; (2) Keynesian or demand-enhancement policies aimed at expanding the domestic market; and (3) a staunch commitment to

---

[37] Thus, urban Peronism could be described as "essentially a working class–based movement" (Mora y Araujo 1980: 431–2).

bread-and-butter unionism, which included a defense of union wage demands, job protection, basic worker benefits, moderately redistributive social welfare policies, and the corporatist legal and organizational framework established during the first Perón government.

Rethinking the Peronist Party Structure: The Role of Informal Organization

This book also departs from most work on Peronism in that it centers on the PJ as an organization. Although substantial research has been carried out on Peronism's social bases,[38] the leadership of Juan and Eva Perón,[39] the policies of particular Peronist governments,[40] and Peronist unions,[41] guerrilla movements,[42] ideology,[43] and identity,[44] the Peronist party organization has rarely been the object of scholarly investigation.[45] As a result, we know remarkably little about how the PJ functions internally. This lack of scholarly attention reflects the widely held view that the Peronist party is weak or inoperative and therefore is unworthy of serious attention.[46] Scholars have dismissed the original Peronist party as a "cadaver" (Luna 1984: 60) and "little more than an appendage of state bodies" (Cavarozzi 1988: 4). Similarly, the contemporary PJ has been described as a "mere name plate" (Cerruti 1993: 338) and an "electoral committee" run by a small circle of "operators" in Buenos Aires (Novaro 1995: 60). Indeed, Peronists themselves commonly claim that their party "doesn't exist."

However, a second look at the PJ organization reveals a strikingly different picture. In many ways, the PJ is among the best-organized parties in Latin America. It maintains a mass membership, a large activist base, and an extensive base-level infrastructure with deep roots in working- and lower-class society. This base-level infrastructure was critical to Peronism's survival through eighteen years of proscription, periods of harsh repression, and the death of its founder, as well as to its extraordinary record of electoral success.

---

[38] See Di Tella (1965a); Germani (1965, 1973); Murmis and Portantiero (1970); Kirkpatrick (1971); Mora y Araujo and Llorente (1980); Schoultz (1983); Gibson (1997); and Ostiguy (1998).

[39] Kirkpatrick (1971); Navarro (1981); Page (1983); and Madsen and Snow (1991).

[40] De Riz (1981); Di Tella (1983); Waisman (1987); Plotkin (1993); Gerchunoff and Torre (1996); and Palermo and Novaro (1996).

[41] See Torre (1983, 1988a, 1988b, 1990, 1998); James (1988); Godio (1991a, 1991b); Ranis (1995); McGuire (1997); and Murillo (2001).

[42] Gillespie (1987); Bonasso (1997).

[43] Buchrucker (1987, 1988).

[44] Martucelli and Svampa (1997) and Ostiguy (1998).

[45] Exceptions include Ciria (1972, 1983), Palermo (1986a), Mackinnon (1995, 1998), and Mustapic (1996).

[46] For example, historian Félix Luna has written that "no one will be able to write the history of the Peronist party between 1946 and 1955 because it never existed" (1984: 60).

A major reason why the PJ organization has been consistently understated and even ignored by scholars is that it is almost entirely informal. The anthropologists Luther P. Gerlach and Virginia H. Hine once observed that scholars tend to assume that organizations are hierarchical and have a "well-defined chain of command" (1970: 33). Thus, "in the minds of many, the only alternative to a bureaucracy or a leader-centered organization is no organization at all" (1970: 34). Such has arguably been the case in studies of Peronism. The PJ's formal or bureaucratic structure *is* largely inoperative. A visit to the party's national offices reveals a strikingly underdeveloped bureaucracy. Beyond custodial personnel, the headquarters are generally empty. The party's top executive body, the National Council, lacks a professional staff, possesses little data on provincial party branches, and has virtually no record of its own membership or activities prior to 1990. Provincial and local party headquarters are even less active. The few existing analyses of the PJ focus primarily on this formal structure (Ciria 1972, 1983; Jackisch 1990; Mustapic 1996). This may explain the conventional view that the PJ is weak, and that party leaders maintain a personalistic and largely unmediated relationship with the Peronist rank and file (Novaro 1994: 76–89; Palermo and Novaro 1996: 370–6).

Yet attention to the weakness of the PJ bureaucracy tends to obscure the powerful informal organization that surrounds it. The Peronist organization consists of a vast collection of informal, neighborhood-based networks that operate out of a range of different entities, including local clubs, cooperatives, soup kitchens, and often activists' homes. These entities are self-organized and -operated. They do not appear in party statutes, are rarely registered with local party authorities, and maintain near-total autonomy from the party bureaucracy. Nevertheless, they routinely participate in party activity, playing a critical mediating role between the party leadership and its base. They recruit new members, distribute patronage, channel local demands, and – most important – deliver votes in internal and general elections. Studies of the PJ that focus on the party's formal structure miss this organizational infrastructure, and as a result, they miss the vast bulk of Peronist party activity.

To understand how the PJ and many other Latin American parties function, then, it is essential to go beyond party statutes and formal bureaucratic structures and to examine informal patterns of organization.[47] In many Latin American parties, informal structures constitute the "meat" of the party organization. Indeed, it is only when one examines these structures that the bulk of the party organization becomes visible.

Understanding how the PJ functions in practice is critical to the utility of both its behavior and the behavior of its members. In analyzing how

---

[47] These arguments are developed in Levitsky (2001a, 2001b). On the importance of informal institutions in Latin America more generally, see O'Donnell (1996).

Peronism's informal structure shapes the choices of party leaders and activists, this book helps to shed new light on Peronist behavior patterns that have previously been explained in vague, often cultural, terms. For example, whereas President Menem's personalistic leadership is often understood as a continuation of Peronism's "populist" or "verticalist" tradition (Nun 1995; Ostiguy 1998), this study highlights the organizational factors – such as a segmented structure and the absence of horizontal links – that contribute to or reinforce such leadership patterns. Similarly, whereas the PJ's programmatic flexibility has been attributed to a tradition of ideological "pragmatism" (De Ipola 1987; Pinto 1995: 84), this study suggests that such flexibility is rooted in (or at least enhanced by) weakly routinized organizational structures. Finally, whereas observers often attribute Peronist "bandwagoning" behavior – such as that which occurred after Menem defeated Antonio Cafiero in the 1988 presidential primary – to an opportunistic or "power-seeking" party culture, this study explains such behavior as a response to insecure tenure patterns in the party hierarchy.

Overview of the Research

This book is based primarily on research carried out in Argentina by the author in 1994 and 1996–7. Research on the national party organization included interviews with eighty-seven national PJ legislators, thirty-nine members of the PJ National Council (some of whom were also legislators), and a variety of former party, union, and guerrilla leaders. It also included informal interviews with dozens of Congressional staff members who are party activists in their home provinces. Research on the party-union linkage included interviews with the leaders of thirty-nine national unions and the leaders of thirty-six local unions in the Federal Capital and Greater Buenos Aires, as well as with four former CGT general secretaries and the general secretaries of the dissident Argentine Workers Movement (MTA) and Argentine Workers Congress (CTA).

The analysis of the PJ's base-level organization draws on research in three urban districts: the Federal Capital, which is a relatively wealthy and predominantly middle-class district, and La Matanza and Quilmes, which are located in the industrial suburbs of Greater Buenos Aires and have larger working- and lower-class populations.[48] This research included interviews

---

[48] La Matanza and Quilmes were selected because they are relatively representative of Greater Buenos Aires Peronism. The two districts lie near the median on several demographic and socioeconomic dimensions, and they each possess characteristics of the zone's first and second "belts." The first belt is a more established, industrialized zone with larger middle- and working-class populations, while the second belt is poorer, less developed, and populated by a larger number of internal migrants. Many of these migrants live in shantytowns or slums. Though strong in both belts, the PJ is particularly dominant in the second belt.

with 75 municipal-level PJ leaders and 112 neighborhood leaders (*punteros*) from these districts. It also included two surveys: (1) a survey of 112 local party branches (base units, or UBs),[49] based on visits to the UBs and in-depth interviews with the activists who ran them; and (2) a survey of 611 party activists, based on a thirty-nine-point questionnaire distributed to activists in each of the surveyed UBs. UBs were selected so as to be as representative as possible of the socioeconomic, geographic, and internal factional make-up of each municipality.

Although the Federal Capital, La Matanza, and Quilmes are not representative of the country as a whole, most of the organizational patterns observed in these municipalities were confirmed through interviews with party leaders and activists both from other municipalities in Greater Buenos Aires[50] and from several other provinces.[51] Hence, there is reason to think that the findings of this study are generalizable. Nevertheless, it is important to note that the book's primary focus is on urban Peronism. As noted previously, Peronism has historically been based on a dual electoral coalition of industrial workers (organized by unions) in urban areas and a mix of lower- and middle-classes (organized into traditional patron-client networks) in poorer, nonindustrial provinces. Although scholars are correct to point out the weight of "peripheral Peronism" in the PJ electoral coalition (Gibson 1997; Gibson and Calvo 2000), and although it is true that the power of provincial Peronism increased in the 1980s and 1990s, the importance of urban Peronism should not be understated. The five large industrialized districts of Buenos Aires, Cordoba, the Federal Capital, Mendoza, and Santa Fe accounted for two-thirds of the PJ vote and three-quarters of the overall electorate in 1997, and these provinces remain essential to the creation of any kind of dominant coalition in the PJ.

The Plan of the Study

The book is organized as follows. Chapters 2 and 3 examine the origins, evolution, and contemporary structure of the Peronist party organization. Chapter 2 locates the roots of the PJ's weakly routinized structure both in its populist origins in the 1940s and in the movement's decentralized and even anarchic response to its proscription in the post-1955 period. Chapter 3 describes the PJ's contemporary party structure, which the chapter characterizes as mass-based, but informal and weakly routinized. It then develops

---

[49] Of these, fifty-four were in the Federal Capital, thirty-one were in La Matanza, and twenty-seven were in Quilmes.
[50] These include Avellaneda, Beratazegui, Hurlingham, Ituzaingo, José C. Paz, Lanus, and Tres de Febrero.
[51] These include Chaco, Córdoba, Mendoza, Salta, Santa Cruz, Santa Fe, Santiago del Estero, and Tucumán.

an argument about how this fluid internal structure may facilitate adaptive change.

Chapter 4 examines the electoral and economic challenges facing PJ leaders in the 1980s. It argues that the de facto labor party that emerged from military rule was a poor fit with an environment characterized by a shrinking industrial working class and the crisis of the ISI state. It then makes the case that the PJ's surprising electoral defeat in 1983 was largely a product of its initial failure to adapt to this new environment.

Chapters 5 and 6 examine the PJ's coalitional and programmatic adaptation in the 1980s and 1990s. Chapter 5 focuses on Peronism's coalitional adaptation, tracing its transformation from a labor-dominated party into a mass patronage-based party. This transformation occurred on two levels. At the base level, as local politicians gained access to public office beginning in 1983, they built patronage organizations that replaced the unions as the PJ's primary linkage to the mass base. At the elite level, party reformers contested and eventually dismantled the PJ's informal and weakly routinized mechanisms of union participation, leaving unions without any role in the party leadership. As a result, union influence declined precipitously. Chapter 6 analyzes the PJ's programmatic adaptation under Menem. After showing that a substantial number of local and national Peronist leaders had serious doubts about the neoliberal reforms, the chapter shows how the PJ's weakly routinized structure facilitated their implementation. First, the absence of tenure security or stable career paths provoked a large-scale "bandwagoning" process in 1989 in which members of the center-left Renovation faction defected to Menemism. Second, the weakness of the PJ's formal leadership bodies and the absence of norms of internal accountability left Menem with substantial room to maneuver in designing and carrying out his adaptive strategies.

Chapter 7 moves to the base level, asking why PJ activists – many of whom disagreed with the neoliberal program – remained in the party in the 1990s. It argues that although continued participation can be attributed in part to activists' increased access to state resources, it was also a product of the PJ's highly decentralized structure. Peronist activists were able to pursue local-level strategies that had little to do with the PJ's national profile, thereby avoiding a stark choice between neoliberalism and leaving the party. Yet if base-level Peronism remained largely "un-Menemized" during the 1990s, it was transformed in other ways. The consolidation of machine politics began to erode the PJ's long-established social, cultural, and organizational linkages to working- and lower-class society, which may have important electoral consequences in the future.

Chapter 8 examines the implications of the Peronist adaptation for Argentine democracy. Notwithstanding the Menem government's concentration and abuse of power, Argentine democracy strengthened over the course of the 1990s. This outcome was in large part a product of the transformation and political success of Peronism. The PJ government's capacity to deliver both labor acquiescence and the bulk of the working- and lower-class vote on behalf of neoliberal reforms was critical to their implementation in a democratic context. Moreover, the PJ's adaptation and survival helped to stabilize the party system during a period of profound political and economic crisis, thereby limiting the space available to the kind of antisystem populist leaders who undermined liberal democratic institutions in Peru and Venezuela.

The conclusion places the PJ case in comparative and theoretical perspective. It examines the fate of five other Latin American labor-based parties in the 1990s, arguing that nonpopulist – and hence better routinized – parties, such as the Venezuelan AD and the Chilean Communist Party, adapted more slowly and less successfully to the neoliberal challenge. Finally, the chapter offers some final thoughts about the implications of the Peronist transformation, both for future research on parties and party change and for the future of working-class representation in Argentina.

CHAPTER 2

Origins and Evolution of a Mass Populist Party

> *Those who get stuck in one system and become excessively stable lose perfectibility. Perfectibility comes with evolution.... One cannot go changing organizations every day, but one also cannot constantly stay with the same organization. One has to make it evolve in line with the times and the situation.*
>
> – Juan Perón[1]

Party organizations, particularly those of mass parties, are both shaped and constrained by the past. Large-scale organizations rarely re-create themselves from scratch, even when it may be more efficient for them to do so. Wholesale organizational change entails substantial costs, both in terms of overcoming vested interests and established routines and in terms of coordinating, overseeing, and enforcing new sets of rules, procedures, roles, and routines. Because these costs are frequently higher than the benefits associated with the new, more efficient structure, change within mass party organizations tends to be slow, arduous, and incremental. For this reason, party development has been characterized as a path-dependent process, in the sense that contemporary organizations tend to reflect the choices and political conflicts of earlier periods (Panebianco 1988). According to Panebianco, a party's

organizational characteristics depend more upon its history, i.e. on how the organization originated and how it consolidated, than upon any other factor. The characteristics of a party's origin are in fact capable of exerting a weight on its organizational structure even decades later. Every organization bears the mark of its formation, of the crucial political-administrative decisions made by its founders, the decision which "molded" the organization (1988: 50).

---

[1] Perón (1951/1971: 28).

Thus, Panebianco claims that "few aspects of an organization's functioning...appear comprehensible if not traced to its formative phase" (1988: xiv).

This chapter sets up the book's central argument by examining the roots of the PJ's mass-based, but weakly routinized, party organization. It argues that the PJ's fluid internal structure can indeed be traced to its formative phase. Peronism's origins were populist. Although the movement mobilized a massive working- and lower-class base and forged strong ties to organized labor, it differed from most European working-class parties in that it was created from above by a highly personalistic leader. Consequently, in contrast to the highly structured, disciplined, and collectively led working-class parties that emerged in many European countries (Duverger 1954/1963), the early Peronist Party was charismatic.[2] According to Panebianco, charismatic parties are characterized by

> an absence of "rules," internal "career patterns," and a clear division of labor. The direct loyalties and the personal and arbitrary delegation of authority by the organization's leader are the only criteria for the organization's functioning. The charismatic organization thus substitutes total uncertainty and instability for the stability of the expectations that guide bureaucratic and traditional organizations.... [T]he division of labor is constantly redefined at the leader's discretion, career uncertainties are considerable, no accepted procedures exist, and improvisation is the only real organizational "rule" (1988: 144–6).

Because such extreme personalism inhibits the development of bureaucratic hierarchies and stable internal rules of the game, charismatic parties tend to be highly unstable (Panebianco 1988: 161–2). Indeed, many of them dissolve after the departure of their founding leaders (Panebianco 1988: 162).

Yet parties' organizational structures are also shaped by historical developments that occur after their formative phases. This is particularly true of parties with highly discontinuous organizational trajectories, such as the PJ. The Peronist organization was transformed in fundamental ways by Perón's overthrow and its subsequent eighteen-year proscription. During this period, Peronism fell into a semi-anarchic state in which subunits operated with substantial autonomy, both of each other and of the national leadership. No authority structure gained control over these subunits, and no institutional settlement was reached around a binding set of internal rules of the game. Key elements of this decentralized "movement" structure persisted into the contemporary period.[3] Hence, the contemporary PJ organization

---

[2] James McGuire (1997: 14–18) makes a similar argument.
[3] The Peronist case thus did not conform to Panebianco's (1988: 162) hypothesis that postcharismatic parties will either disappear or institutionalize as centralized organizations after the departure of their founding leader.

must be understood as a product of both Peronism's populist origins *and* its post-1955 transformation.

This chapter traces Peronism's organizational development through three periods. The first section examines the movement's populist origins (1943–55). During this initial period, Juan Perón organized – and repeatedly reorganized – the Peronist Party from above, which created a highly personalistic, fluid, and state-dependent structure. The second section examines the post-1955 proscription period, during which the Peronist Party collapsed and Peronism was transformed into a loosely structured "movement" organization. During this period, Peronists repeatedly failed to converge around basic rules of the game for governing themselves, and as a result, a plethora of different rules, organizations, and authority structures coexisted and competed with each other. The third section examines the PJ's post-1983 process of "partyization." During this period, Peronist subgroups were integrated into party activity and the PJ underwent an important internal democratization process. However, party reformers were unable to establish a stable bureaucratic structure or impose a binding set of rules and procedures on the party, and Peronist subunits remained largely autonomous from the party bureaucracy.

The chapter thus highlights two fundamental continuities in Peronism through the 1945–89 period. First, the movement was always labor-based. Although the Peronist-labor alliance was less institutionalized than those of most European labor-based parties, unions nevertheless played a central (and at times dominant) role in the movement, and the Peronist electoral base was always concentrated in the working and lower classes. Second, the Peronist organization was persistently underroutinized. Throughout the 1945–89 period, Peronists repeatedly failed to reach an institutional settlement around a single organizational structure or set of internal rules of the game. Consequently, the movement never developed an effective bureaucratic structure, a stable leadership hierarchy, or a binding set of intraparty rules and procedures to govern key areas such as leadership and candidate selection, the relationship between higher- and lower-level authorities, or trade union participation.

POPULIST ORIGINS: THE BIRTH OF A CHARISMATIC LABOR-BASED PARTY (1943–55)

The origins of the Peronist party were both labor-based and populist. Peronism's emergence was closely linked to the rise of the industrial working class (Torre 1988b, 1990; Collier and Collier 1991).[4] In the 1930s and

---

[4] The nature of the original Peronist coalition has been widely debated. See, for example, Germani (1965, 1973); Di Tella (1965a); Murmis and Portantiero (1970); Smith (1972); Kenworthy (1975); Mora y Araujo and Llorente (1980); Torre (1988a, 1988b, 1990); De Ipola (1989); and Madsen and Snow (1991).

1940s, industrialization and large-scale internal migration lay the foundation for the rapid growth of the Argentine working class. Labor scarcity, European immigration, and the concentration of production in large factories and a few industrial centers created favorable conditions for unionization and the crystallization of strong class identities (Palomino 1987: 77). Although industrial workers never constituted as large a share of the electorate as they did in Western Europe, the Argentine proletariat was the largest, best organized, and most cohesive in Latin America (Collier and Collier 1991: 91–7; McGuire 1997: 263–9). At its peak, the labor movement encompassed more than 50 percent of the salaried work force – the highest rate in Latin America, and one that compared favorably to most Western European countries (Godio, Palomino, and Wachendorfer 1988: 79; McGuire 1997: 268). This sector formed the nucleus of the Peronist coalition.

Yet if Peronism was rooted in the industrial working class, it differed from most European working-class parties in that its origins were unambiguously populist. Colonel Juan Domingo Perón originally came to power as part of the United Officers Group (GOU), which played a leading role in the military coup that toppled President Ramón Castillo in June 1943. Beginning in late 1943, Perón used his position as labor secretary to build a base of support among the urban working and lower classes. He achieved this support through the extension of a variety of union and worker benefits (Torre 1990; Collier and Collier 1991: 337–8), as well as an unprecedented social and cultural appeal to the lower sectors of society (Ostiguy 1998). Although Perón probably did not intend to rely heavily on working-class support, the events of 1945 and 1946 pushed Peronism in a decidedly mass-based direction. Perón's removal and jailing by fellow officers in October 1945 provoked a massive working-class mobilization that forced his release and the calling of elections for February 1946 (Torre 1990: 107–40). Perón won the election with overwhelming working- and lower-class support (Schoultz 1983: 30–1).

The October 17 mobilization and the February 1946 elections created an opening for the formation of a strong labor-based party in Argentina. Within a week of Perón's release, union leaders founded the Labor Party (PL) as a means of channeling working-class support for Perón. The union leaders who founded the PL – including party president Luis Gay of the telephone workers union and vice president Cipriano Reyes of the meat packers union – envisioned it as a European-style labor-based party, in which unions would collectively affiliate their members, operate local branches, and enjoy a hegemonic position in the leadership (Pont 1984: 37–47; Torre 1990: 148–55). Indeed, the PL's internal structure was explicitly modeled on the British Labour Party (Torre 1990: 153).

The *laborista* project quickly collapsed, however. Despite the fact that the PL delivered the bulk of Perón's votes in the 1946 election (Little 1988: 286; Torre 1990: 194–5), the new president dissolved the PL, together with pro-Perón parties such as the UCR Renovating Juntas and the conservative

Independent Centers, soon after taking office. In their place, Perón created the Single Party of the National Revolution (PURN), which later became the Peronist Party (PP). Although many union leaders opposed this move, their capacity to challenge it was limited by Perón's mass appeal and their own political inexperience (Beveraggi Allende 1954: 41; Pont 1984: 48–53; Torre 1990: 232–7).

The PP was a thoroughly populist party. Organizationally, it differed from the PL (and most European labor-based parties) in four important ways. First, it was created from above, by actors within the state. Designed to "retain rather than achieve power" (Little 1973: 659), the PP was largely run from within the government. Local branches were financed by the state,[5] and much of the party's organizational activity was directed from the public affairs ministry (Ciria 1983: 201). As a result, the PP never developed an autonomous organization.

Second, the PP was highly personalistic. The PP's 1954 statutes declared Perón to be the party's "Supreme Leader," granting him the authority to "modify or declare null and void the decisions of party authorities," and to "inspect, intervene, and replace" party leaderships (Ciria 1972: 6–7). The statutes even forbade party branches from displaying any photographs other than those of Perón and his wife Eva (Ciria 1983: 169). The PP's leadership bodies were thoroughly subordinated to Perón. Provincial branches were "permanently intervened" by the party leadership (Ciria 1983: 151),[6] and local candidates were often hand-picked by national leaders (Little 1973: 652; Pont 1984: 59).[7] Moreover, party leaders with independent support bases were routinely purged and replaced by "ultra-loyalists" who depended exclusively on Perón (Zorrilla 1983b; Mackinnon 1995: 238–41). Because Peronists' political careers hinged primarily on their ties to Perón, no stable career paths or bureaucratic hierarchy emerged. Indeed, turnover in the party hierarchy was strikingly high. For example, when the party was reorganized in January 1947, turnover in the top leadership bodies was 100 percent (Mackinnon 1995: 241).

Third, the Peronist Party structure was extremely fluid. In classic charismatic fashion, Perón repeatedly reorganized his movement from above, thereby preventing the emergence of a stable organization or internal rules of the game. As noted previously, the PL was dissolved just three months after the 1946 election. Its successor, the PURN, also lasted less than a year.

---

[5] This point was confirmed in the author's interviews with a several Peronist activists from the 1950s.

[6] According to Tcach, such interventions were "part of the normal, 'typical' functioning of the Peronist Party" (1990: 12).

[7] According to Tcach (1991: 161), the national leadership chose all but one of the Córdoba party's legislative candidates in 1948. One local PP leader complained that "the candidacies proclaimed in Córdoba came from Buenos Aires in a sealed envelope" (Little 1973: 652).

When the PURN was reorganized and renamed the PP, its National Executive Junta was replaced by a Superior Council with an entirely new leadership (Mackinnon 1995: 241). The Peronist party structure remained in a "fluid state" through the end of the decade (Mackinnon 1998: 27). According to Little, the Superior Council routinely gave "detailed instructions for the performance of Party activities that... were rarely carried out" (1973: 659). In 1951, Perón again reorganized the party structure, creating a parallel hierarchy based on a national "strategic command" and provincial "tactical commands." Although these bodies were supposed to consist of representatives of the PP leadership, the Women's Peronist Party and the CGT (Ciria 1983: 11), in practice, Juan and Eva Perón served as the strategic command, and the tactical commands were run by the governors and national "intervening" delegates (Chumbita 1989: 95; Tcach 1991: 202). Perón began to describe this new structure as a "movement," of which the party was only a part. The structure was formalized in the 1954 party statutes, which changed the PP's name to the Peronist Movement and divided it into political, women's, and labor branches (Ciria 1983: 182–4). In practice, however, no effective branch-based structure had emerged at the time Perón was overthrown in 1955.

Finally, the PP lacked a stable party-union linkage. Unlike the Labor Party, which collectively affiliated union members with the party and guaranteed union leaders a privileged position in the leadership, the PP's statutes included no formal mechanism of labor participation (Partido Peronista 1948). The "movement" structure that emerged in the early 1950s recognized labor as one of Peronism's three branches, and the CGT quickly took on the role of Peronism's labor branch. According to the movementist tradition that emerged out of this period, the labor branch held the right to a third – or *tercio* – of Peronist candidacies and leadership positions. However, the *tercio* system was neither formalized in party statutes nor rigorously practiced at the time of Perón's overthrow.[8]

The weakly routinized nature of the early Peronist Party should not be taken to mean that it lacked a mass organization. Indeed, thousands of PP and Women's Peronist Party branches were established throughout the country in the late 1940s.[9] These local organizations served as hubs for the distribution of material benefits and provided a space for political, social, and cultural interaction for hundreds of thousands of working-class Argentines (Bianchi and Sanchís 1988: 80–6; Tcach 1991: 204–5). Nevertheless, the PP's populist roots left it without an autonomous bureaucratic structure. As

---

[8] According to one former Consejo Superior member, the *tercio* "was not a written norm, but rather something that was verbally agreed upon" (Pont 1984: 59).

[9] Approximately fifty-two hundred base units are said to have been in operation in 1954 (Ciria 1983: 161), and the Women's Peronist Party is said to have established three thousand base units and recruited half a million members alone in the late 1940s and early 1950s (Fraser and Navarro 1985: 107–9; Bianchi and Sanchís 1988: 90–1).

a result, at the time of Perón's overthrow, the Peronist Party lacked a stable hierarchy and even minimally routinized rules and procedures to structure internal authority relations, leadership and candidate selection, or trade union participation.

Peronism emerged from the 1943–55 period as the dominant political representative of the working and lower classes. Despite the repeated efforts of post-1955 governments to eradicate Peronism from the labor movement, Argentine unions remained overwhelmingly Peronist through the end of the century. Peronism also retained the support of the vast majority of working- and lower-class Argentines. Survey and electoral data suggest that in every election in which Peronism participated after 1955, it won a majority of working-class votes and was virtually hegemonic among the poor (Kirkpatrick 1971; Mora y Araujo and Llorente 1980; Schoultz 1983; Cantón 1986; Ostiguy 1998). This hegemony over the working- and lower-class vote established Peronism as Argentina's dominant electoral force, with a stable core of supporters that scholars have estimated at roughly 30–5 percent of the electorate.[10] Yet Peronism's embeddedness in working- and lower-class society was not accompanied by the consolidation of a stable party organization. As the following sections demonstrate, the post-1955 Peronist organization fell into a fluid semi-anarchic state – an arrangement that would persist for more than three decades.

FROM CHARISMATIC PARTY TO MOVEMENT ORGANIZATION: PERONISM IN OPPOSITION, 1955–83

On September 16, 1955, sectors of the armed forces commanded by General Eduardo Lonardi launched a rebellion that would result, four days later, in the overthrow and exile of President Perón. PP offices were closed and Peronist parties banned from electoral competition, and the CGT and many of its member unions were intervened and purged. Peronism would be proscribed from politics – and Perón himself kept in exile – for the next eighteen years. Proscribed and intermittently repressed, Peronism moved underground. The movement survived within the trade unions, which remained legal and, despite the best efforts of the military regime, overwhelmingly Peronist. Peronists also operated out of thousands of clandestine neighborhood-based networks, or "working groups," many of which met secretly under the guise of barbeques or birthday parties.[11] These clandestine networks organized study groups, midnight graffiti-painting brigades, masses for Evita, the circulation of Perón's messages, and literature

---

[10] This figure corresponds to estimates made by Di Tella (1968: 65), Kirkpatrick (1971: 90); O'Donnell (1973: 172), and Ostiguy (1998: 346). Although Peronists liked to claim a "natural majority," it is more accurate to say that the party maintained a stable plurality.

[11] On the initial postcoup Resistance period, see James (1988).

distribution at dance halls and soccer games. These activities were critical to the movement's post-1955 survival.

Yet Peronism's organizational response to repression differed strikingly from that of many other European and Latin American working-class parties. Whereas parties such as the German Social Democrats, the French and Chilean Communists, and the Venezuelan AD survived periods of repression by "internalizing" their organizational subunits and creating highly disciplined structures based on a "formal hierarchy of branches, committees, and organizations" (Tarrow 1994: 136–40, 148; also Duverger 1954/1963: 49), Peronism fell into a state of virtual anarchy. With Perón in exile, Peronism's centralized structure broke down. The Peronist Party, which had been held together by charisma and state power rather than an autonomous organization, disintegrated, and the old-guard PP leadership quickly passed into oblivion (McGuire 1997: 78). The movement's resurgence after 1955 occurred in a bottom-up, decentralized manner. Initial acts of Peronist resistance were "spontaneous, atomized initiatives," carried out in the "absence of a coherent, national leadership" (James 1988: 52). Organization took the form of self-constituted "commandos" based on preexisting factory or neighborhood networks (James 1988: 78). Linkages among the commandos were "tenuous at best," and the bodies created to coordinate their activities, such as Center of Resistance Operations and the Peronist Grouping of Insurrectionary Resistance, were ineffective (James 1988: 78, 143–4). Although the movement stabilized somewhat after 1956, its organization remained little more than a "loose federation of different groups loyal to Perón" (James 1988: 184).

Rather than being a disciplined, centralized organization, then, post-1955 Peronism took the form of what Gerlach and Hine (1970) call a "movement organization." Movement organizations differ from bureaucratic organizations in that they lack an overarching authority structure with the capacity to coordinate subunits or "make decisions binding on all of the participants in the movement" (Gerlach and Hine 1970: 36–7). Rather, subunits organize themselves autonomously, and as a result, each subunit "tends to develop a... 'style' of its own," and "has different ideas about how to achieve the more general objectives of the movement" (1970: 42). To use Duverger's terms, movement organizations lack horizontal links, which facilitate communication and coordination among subunits, and vertical links, which facilitate centralization and internal discipline (1954/1963: 47–53).

Between 1955 and 1983, Peronism closely approximated a movement organization. Unlike socialist party branches and communist party cells (Duverger 1954/1963: 23–36), Peronist "working groups" were not integrated into a central hierarchy and in fact maintained little contact with higher-level authorities. Higher-order Peronist organizations took a variety of forms. In urban areas, Peronism's primary organizational base was the trade unions, which provided protection, jobs, money, office space, printing presses, and other resources. Other activists joined nonparty cadre organizations such as the paramilitary *Comando de Organizacion* (C de O), the ultranationalist Iron Guard, the more technocratic Technological Commands, the leftist Montonero guerrillas, and their Peronist Youth (JP) allies.[12] These organizations, which pursued goals ranging from socialist revolution (the Montoneros) to the violent defeat of the left (C de O), operated with near-total autonomy from the national leadership and remained at the margins of party activity even during periods of electoral opening. In the interior, many activists joined neo-Peronist parties, or Peronist-led parties that used other names in order to circumvent the ban on the Peronist (after 1958, Justicialista) Party.[13] These included aspiring national organizations such as the Popular Union, Social Justice, and Three Banners, as well as strictly provincial parties such as Neuquén Popular Movement, the Federal Democratic Movement (Salta), and Provincial Action (Tucumán). Neo-Peronist parties competed against each other – and at times against representatives of the "official" PJ – for Peronist votes. No overarching structure encompassed these various subgroups or coordinated their activities. Instead, each union, cadre organization, and neo-Peronist party maintained an organizational life of its own. Moreover, the movement's boundaries were fluid and ill-defined: anyone could call herself a Peronist, create an organization, and become part of the movement.

In the absence of an overarching authority structure, Peronism became a highly decentralized organization. Peronist subgroups did not require official recognition to constitute themselves, and they routinely developed and carried out strategies without approval from above. No single leadership body had the capacity to discipline or control them. Although Perón remained the movement's undisputed leader, he could not (and did not attempt to) control its day-to-day activities. Moreover, Perón's delegates in Argentina, including the hand-picked leadership bodies that he occasionally placed at the top of the Peronist hierarchy, were unable to discipline or impose binding decisions effectively upon Peronist subgroups. For example, the Superior and Coordinating Council, which Perón created in 1958, found that its orders were routinely ignored by Peronist unions and neo-Peronist parties (Quevedo 1991: 56–8; Arias and García Heras 1993). Similarly, the Tactical Command, which Perón created in the early 1970s, exercised only marginal influence over the cadre organizations that dominated the movement during that period (Bonasso 1997).[14] Even Perón's direct orders were sometimes ignored. In 1963, for example, nearly a dozen neo-Peronist parties disobeyed Perón's

---

[12] Smaller left-wing cadre organizations included Base Peronism, the Peronist Armed Forces (FAP), the Revolutionary Armed Forces (FAR), and Descamisados (Shirtless Ones).
[13] On neo-Peronist parties, see Arias and García Heras (1993) and Arias (1998).
[14] Thus, the Technological Commands publicly declared themselves to be "autonomous of the Tactical Command" (Bonasso 1997: 210).

instructions to boycott the legislative and gubernatorial elections (Arias and García Heras 1993: 108–9). Although Peronists who disobeyed Perón's orders were sometimes "expelled" from the movement, in practice, such expulsions were often ignored and were almost never permanent.[15] Thus, when Perón expelled the Montoneros in 1974 for insubordination, Montonero leader Dardo Cabo declared, "No one has the right to throw us out. No one can fire us!"[16]

This semi-anarchic structure was reinforced by two factors. First, Perón himself clearly benefited from – and indeed promoted – such an arrangement (James 1988: 185–6; McGuire 1997: 80–164). In addition to filling Perón's personal proclivity for "governing in chaos" (Bonasso 1997: 55), an organizational "big tent" helped the exiled leader maintain control over a highly heterogeneous movement. Tolerance for a diversity of organizations, ideologies, and tactics reduced the risk of permanent schism (as occurred in Venezuela's AD) and allowed Perón to weaken internal rivals by playing them against one another. Second, a semi-anarchic structure was consistent with Peronism's "movementist" ideology. Peronists considered themselves a broad movement of which the party was only a part. After 1955, the boundaries and hierarchies of the movement lacked definition, and over time, movementism came to be associated with subgroup autonomy. If one could be outside the party but inside the movement, and if no clear boundaries or hierarchy existed within the movement, then virtually any kind of organizational activity was legitimate.

The Peronist organization also remained weakly routinized in the post-1955 period. No single group or actor – including Perón – was able to impose a binding set of internal rules of the game. Although Perón's charismatic authority was challenged by important union and provincial-based routinizing projects, the exiled leader remained powerful enough to block the consolidation of any alternative project. Consequently, no single structure or set of internal rules of the game prevailed, and a diversity of rules, organizations, and authority structures therefore coexisted and competed with each other. The failure to reach an institutional settlement could be seen during two periods of electoral opening: the 1957–66 semidemocratic period, during which Peronism was banned but neo-Peronist activity was at times tolerated, and the 1973–6 democratic period, during which Peronism briefly returned to power.

---

[15] An example is Catamarca boss Vicente Saadi, who was expelled from the movement twice. Saadi had been removed as governor and jailed by Perón in the late 1940s, but he regained control over Catamarca Peronism after the 1955 coup and later reconciled with Perón. In 1958, Saadi was again expelled after his neo-Peronist Populist Party disobeyed Perón's order to support Arturo Frondizi in the presidential election. Nevertheless, Saadi retained control of Catamarca Peronism, and in 1961, he was reinstated in the party.

[16] Quoted in De Riz (1981: 153–4).

The 1957–66 period gave rise to unprecedented efforts to routinize Peronism by transforming it into a stable electoral organization. The post-1957 political opening created a strong incentive for Peronist leaders to seek ways to reintegrate themselves into the electoral arena (Arias and García Heras 1993; Arias 1998). In the interior, neo-Peronist projects were launched by provincial bosses such as Deolindo Bittel (Chaco), Ricardo Durand (Salta), Vicente Saadi (Catamarca), and Elías and Felipe Sapag (Neuquén), who maintained independent support bases and could therefore expect to win local elections even in Perón's absence. Military leaders often tolerated these efforts, in the apparent hope that neo-Peronist parties would fragment the Peronist vote and weaken Perón's control over the movement (McGuire 1997: 84). Thus, although most provincial Peronist *caudillos* heeded Perón's calls to boycott the 1957 Constituent Assembly election and support Intransigent Radical Civic Union presidential candidate Arturo Frondizi in 1958, by the early 1960s, many of them had created neo-Peronist parties with the aim of participating in future legislative and gubernatorial elections (Arias and García Heras 1993: 102–9). Declaring that Peronists were not a "flock of sheep" and that the movement could not be run "by remote control" (Arias 1998: 62), neo-Peronist leaders such as Elías Sapag made it clear that they would participate in elections even if it meant disobeying Perón (Quevedo 1991: 56–8; Arias and García Heras 1993: 103).

In the industrialized provinces, pressure for routinization emerged from within the labor movement.[17] Due to their legal status and control over vital financial, organizational, and human resources, unions became the dominant force in urban Peronism after 1955 (James 1988: 156; McGuire 1997: 89–90). Under the leadership of metal workers union (UOM) boss Augusto Vandor, a group of Peronist unions attempted to translate this vast organizational strength into electoral power (McGuire 1997: 93–145). Lacking a vehicle through which to channel their demands in their political arena, Vandor and his allies in the 62 Organizations launched a labor-based party-building project. In 1962, the "62" aligned with the neo-Peronist Popular Union (UP) with the aim of participating in that year's legislative and gubernatorial elections. Due to their control over critical resources, the unions quickly established a hegemonic position in the UP,[18] converting it into a de facto labor party (James 1988: 154; McGuire 1997: 89–90).[19] The UP's

---

[17] These dynamics are analyzed in detail by McGuire (1997). Much of the following section draws on this work.

[18] According to former UOM leader Osbaldo Pérez, "Vandor had all the politicians in his bag.... All the politicians would come knocking on the doors of the unions, because they knew that if they didn't reach an agreement with us, they couldn't get elected" (author's interview, October 29, 1996).

[19] According to McGuire, the "62" "took control of the candidate-selection process" in 1962, claiming half of the UP candidacies in the largest districts (1997: 89–90). In Buenos Aires, trade unionists received six of every eleven legislative candidacies, while in the capital the

victories in Buenos Aires and other major provinces, which led the military to annul the elections, placed the *Vandoristas* in an unprecedented position to "challenge Perón for the right to act as broker for the Peronist votes" (McGuire 1997: 93).

Perón fiercely resisted these routinizing projects, and his efforts to reassert charismatic authority generated a series of conflicts that prevented the consolidation of any stable internal rules of the game. In late 1963, the exiled leader responded to the growing strength of neo-Peronist parties by reorganizing the national PJ leadership and creating a four-member Reorganizing Junta made up of ultraloyalists (James 1988: 177; McGuire 1997: 113). This effort failed, however, as Vandor used his influence in the labor movement to force a restructuring of the junta, which was quickly transformed into a seven-member body with a pro-Vandor majority (McGuire 1997: 113). The new junta announced plans to reorganize the PJ "from the bottom up" (McGuire 1997: 113), which, according to one neo-Peronist leader, would result in the creation of a "democratic and solidly structured party."[20] In June 1964, a pro-Vandor list won intraparty elections and gained control of the party leadership (McGuire 1997: 113–14),[21] thereby laying the foundation for a national neo-Peronist party.[22] The following year, the *Vandorista* leadership unified the various neo-Peronist factions into a single legislative bloc and created a labor-dominated Board of Analysis to prepare the party for the 1967 elections (James 1988: 179; McGuire 1997: 123–6). In October 1965, a Vandor-dominated party congress called for the "immediate institutionalization of the Peronist movement... from the bottom up" – a process that was clearly aimed at limiting Perón's authority (McGuire 1997: 125).

Perón ultimately derailed these party-building efforts. Using both his wife Isabel (who traveled to Argentina in late 1965 to mobilize opposition to Vandor) and Vandor's rivals within the labor movement, Perón skillfully reconstructed a loyalist coalition (McGuire 1997: 124–41). In April 1966, Perón won a decisive victory over Vandor when the two backed opposing candidates in the Mendoza gubernatorial election.[23] The election effectively destroyed the neo-Peronist project. As a result, when the June 1966 military

---

unions gained the first five spots on the UP legislative list (James 1988: 154; McGuire 1997: 90).

[20] Oscar Albrieu, interviewed in *Primera Plana*, May 5, 1964, p. 5 (cited in McGuire 1997: 121).

[21] Although Perón was named party president, the active leadership was placed in the hands of "62" ally Alberto Iturbe (McGuire 1997: 114).

[22] According to the weekly *Primera Plana*, Vandor "did what had seemed impossible: he created a true labor party" (cited in McGuire (1993: 195)). *Primera Plana* observed that "not a shred of political decision-making power would remain in [Peron's] hands if the party were controlled by leaders chosen... in the internal election" (cited in McGuire (1997: 125)).

[23] Vandor backed neo-Peronist leader Alberto Serú García, while Perón backed Ernesto Corvalán Nanclares. Although the conservative Emilio Jofré won the election, Corvalán

coup did away with electoral politics, Peronism remained without any effective rules of the game for governing itself.

Peronism also failed to reach an institutional settlement during the 1972–6 political opening. The PJ's legalization in January 1972 and the calling of elections for March 1973 created an imperative to establish a single national party structure for the first time since 1955. Although this was formally achieved in the June 1972 party congress, in practice, few Peronists took party activity seriously during this period. Many of the most important players within the movement – including cadre organizations such as the JP/Montoneros, Iron Guard, and C de O – advanced explicitly antiparty or movementist agendas. The JP and Montoneros, whose ascendance within the movement was actively encouraged by Perón, openly disparaged electoral politics, and many JP/Montonero cadres never even joined the PJ (Palermo 1986a: 82–3; Bonasso 1997: 341; Perdía 1997: 126–7). Consequently, the National Council, which was formally the party's highest authority, hardly functioned, and PJ General Secretary Horacio Farmache found himself virtually powerless. Real authority rested largely in the hands of Perón (who held no formal party post), Perón's appointed delegate in Argentina, Hector Cámpora, and the (also appointed) general secretary of the movement, Juan Manuel Abal Medina. Indeed, most Peronists viewed "movement" leadership bodies such as the Tactical Command and the Superior Council, which were essentially fictitious entities created by Perón to legitimize de facto authority relations that he had set up (and which lacked statutes, offices, regular meetings, clearly defined hierarchies, or rules of leadership selection and rotation), as higher authorities than the National Council (Bonasso 1997: 238–9).

The PJ's institutional fluidity was clearly seen in the 1972–3 leadership and candidate selection process. In the days prior to the June 1972 congress, party and union leaders could not agree on how to select the National Council or even how many members it would have (Bonasso 1997: 238–43). Cámpora devised a modified version of the old movementist system of political, women's, and labor branches, incorporating the JP as the "youth branch" and creating a sixteen-member National Council whose seats would be evenly distributed among the branches (Bonasso 1997: 240). The system never functioned in practice, however. Because the "political" and "women's" branches did not actually exist, their representatives were chosen behind closed doors by Perón's top delegates (Zorrilla 1983a: 68–9; Bonasso 1997: 340–1). Moreover, because the party congress ignored the "62"'s request to name the union representatives, the unions boycotted the body entirely (Zorrilla 1983a: 68–70; Bonasso 1997: 238–43). The candidate selection process was also chaotic. Although Perón's right to impose

---

outpolled Serú García by nearly two to one. For a detailed account of the Mendoza conflict, see McGuire (1997: 141–4).

Cámpora as the party's presidential candidate was not seriously contested, the leadership's efforts to impose gubernatorial candidates on local branches generated institutional crises in most major provinces. In several of these provinces, including Chubut, Formosa, Neuquén, Salta, Santa Fe, Santiago del Estero, and Tucumán, Peronism suffered schisms and thus fielded more than one candidate (Bonasso 1997: 352).[24]

Although the PJ briefly took a more centralized form following Perón's return to the presidency in late 1973,[25] after Peron's death in July 1974, the party fell into a state of virtual anarchy. Without Perón's charismatic leadership to bind together the movement's disparate parts, and without any effective rules of the game for structuring authority or resolving internal conflicts, Peronism became an arena for praetorian struggles among leftist guerrillas, ultranationalist paramilitary groups, and unions. During the initial months of Isabel Perón's government, a shadowy group of advisors and cabinet members, led by Social Welfare Minister José Lopez Rega, sought to create a personalistic regime around Perón's widow (Wainfeld 1983). This project eventually led to a confrontation with the unions, which, under the leadership of UOM boss Lorenzo Miguel, toppled López Rega with a massive two-day general strike in July 1975 (Torre 1983: 135–6).

The fall of López Rega ushered in a period of unprecedented union hegemony in the party. However, this power was entirely de facto. Labor leaders used their vast organizational and mobilizational muscle to fill the vacuum left by Perón, but they made little effort to establish stable rules of the game for union participation (McGuire 1997: 166–9). Indeed, the only Peronist group that advanced a routinizing agenda during this period, the "antiverticalist" faction led by Senate President Italo Luder, PJ Vice President Angel Robledo, and Buenos Aires Governor Victorio Calabró, was easily pushed aside by the "62" (McGuire 1997: 167–8). In the end, labor's triumph was a Pyrrhic one. Argentina descended into political and economic chaos, and on March 24, 1976, the PJ government was toppled by a military coup.

In sum, Peronism never developed a coherent organizational structure between 1955 and 1983. There was not one Peronist party but many, and most Peronist organizations operated outside of all of them. Moreover, the movement failed to develop stable rules of the game to select its leaders, structure internal authority relations, or govern trade union participation. Indeed,

---

[24] For example, after the Buenos Aires branch nominated a gubernatorial ticket of Manuel de Anchonera and UOM leader Luis Guerrero, Abal Medina intervened the provincial party and imposed leftist Oscar Bidegain instead (Bonasso 1997: 342–5). In Neuquén, Salta, and Santiago del Estero, efforts by the national leadership to bypass traditional *caudillos* provoked party schisms, as old-guard leaders abandoned the PJ and competed against it.

[25] PJ candidate Cámpora won the March 1973 election but resigned four months later, calling new elections in which Perón would be allowed to run. In September 1973, Perón was elected president with 62 percent of the vote.

despite the fact that unions played a central – and at times hegemonic – role in urban Peronism, the party-union linkage remained fluid and ill-defined.

THE TRANSITION TO ELECTORAL POLITICS: "PARTYIZATION" WITHOUT ROUTINIZATION

Peronism again fell into a state of anarchy during the 1976–83 military regime. In urban areas, Peronists flocked to the unions for protection, with many taking jobs as advisors, lawyers, or accountants. A smaller number remained active in cadre organizations. Although the Montoneros were decimated by repression, right-wing cadre organizations such as C de O and the Iron Guard, protected by allies in the military, remained largely intact. Finally, thousands of activists worked out of clandestine neighborhood-based networks.[26] Despite the fact that party offices were closed down, many Peronists remained active in neighborhood-based "working groups," front organizations such as study centers,[27] or nongovernmental organizations such as cooperatives, soup kitchens, neighborhood clubs, and church groups. Although little data exist on clandestine Peronist organization during the dictatorship, the number of activists who engaged in at least low-level participation appears to have been significant. Of the 112 PJ base units surveyed for this study, 28.6 percent operated clandestinely during the *Proceso*, and 58 percent were led by an activist who had participated in a Peronist organization during that period. As a result of this persistent organization, when the military regime collapsed in 1982, Peronism reemerged in an impressive manner. Base units mushroomed up, seemingly out of nowhere, and proliferated throughout the country. By mid-1983, the PJ had signed up more than 3 million members, which was more than all other parties combined.[28]

Peronism underwent an unprecedented process of "partyization"[29] in the 1980s. Whereas leading Peronist subgroups had previously operated outside the PJ and pursued nonelectoral goals, the emergence of a stable democratic regime after 1983 induced most of these organizations to integrate themselves into party activity. Thus, unlike in the 1970s, Peronist cadre organizations participated actively in party politics in 1983. For example, Iron Guard

---

[26] Although most subunits were highly localized, others were linked into larger *agrupaciones*. In the capital, for example, a group of ex–Peronist Youth (JP) and Iron Guard cadres created a clandestine network called the Force, which inserted activists into local clubs, cooperatives, soup kitchens, church, groups, and unions. Through this coordinated "community work," the Force was able to survive the worst years of repression, and when the dictatorship ended, it resurfaced as the Peronist Unity Front (FUP).

[27] In Formosa, a group of ex–Iron Guard cadres operated base units disguised as "Scalabini Ortiz Institutes," while in Rio Negro, a major faction worked through "Institutes of Rio Negro Studies."

[28] *Clarin*, April 23, 1983, p. 6, and July 21, 1983, p. 4.

[29] Palermo (1994: 317) also uses this term.

created scores of base units in the Federal Capital, Buenos Aires, and Santa Fe, and it elected six of its members to Congress. C de O underwent a similar change. Although it continued to describe itself as "movementist," C de O routinely participated in elections in its home district of La Matanza and even elected leader Alberto Brito Lima to Congress. Many JP/Montonero cadres entered party politics via the Intransigence and Mobilization (IM) faction, which competed in internal elections throughout the country. Though led by Catamarca boss Vicente Saadi, IM was based on Montonero networks and financed by the Montoneros.[30]

Trade unions also invested heavily in party activity. At the national level, the "62" and "25" union factions served as key allies of the Orthodox and Renovation factions, respectively, backing candidates in internal elections throughout the country. At the provincial level, unions such as the UOM, oil workers, and auto workers became powerful intraparty actors in the industrialized districts. The vast majority of Peronist unions participated in local and provincial politics. Of the thirty-nine national unions surveyed for this study, thirty-five participated in PJ politics in the 1980s, and thirty-one of them placed members on PJ legislative lists or in provincial or national party leaderships during that period.[31]

Only a handful of Peronist subgroups continued to operate outside the party in the 1980s. These organizations, which included the union-based *Ubaldinismo*[32] and small cadre networks such as Revolutionary Peronism (ex-Montoneros) and Liberators of America (ex-Iron Guard), focused primarily on social movement activities such as anti-IMF protests and rallies in support of CGT general strikes. Somewhat paradoxically, these last vestiges of movementism were absorbed into party activity by Carlos Menem's 1988 campaign for the PJ presidential nomination. Menem's movementist appeal attracted ex-cadre organizations such as C de O, the Liberators of America, and Revolutionary Peronism, as each of them viewed Menemism as a means

---

[30] Author's interviews with ex-IM members Nilda Garré (November 24, 1997) and Oscar Nievas (November 19, 1996), and with ex-Montonero leader Roberto Perdía (June 3, 1997).

[31] This evidence runs counter to McGuire's (1992) claim that two of the four largest Peronist union factions, the *Ubaldinistas* and the "15," did not participate in PJ activity in the 1980s. Although these factions did not work closely with the party, individual unions within them did so, particularly at the local level. For example, *Ubaldinista* unions such as the public administration workers, construction workers, and textile workers and "15" unions such as the oil workers, retail workers, and auto workers all placed members in local or national party leadership bodies in the 1980s.

[32] A loosely organized social movement that supported CGT General Secretary Saúl Ubaldini, *Ubaldinismo* mobilized both unions and nonunion activists behind labor protests and on behalf of issues such as opposition to debt payments. Ubaldini, a self-described "movementist" who "never belonged to the party," shunned party activity in the 1980s, repeatedly turning down offers to join the PJ leadership or run for public office (author's interview, October 2, 1997).

of blocking the PJ's transformation into a "European-style party."[33] Yet by reorienting them toward electoral politics, Menem's campaign brought each of these groups into the party. Thus, although Peronists continued to refer to themselves as a movement in the 1990s, in practice, all major Peronist subgroups devoted themselves primarily to party activity.

"Partyization" was not accompanied by routinization or bureaucratization, however. Peronism reemerged from the dictatorship in a bottom-up, semi-anarchic manner. Local party organizations were constructed at the margins of the PJ bureaucracy, as activists opened their own branches, or base units, without the approval (or even knowledge) of the party hierarchy. In other words, the party bureaucracy did not create, finance, or directly operate its own branches. In fact, it had no say over who could create them, how many were created, or where they were located.

The PJ organization that emerged in 1983 thus retained key features of its post-1955 movement structure. Cadre organizations, union-based factions, and informal territorial networks maintained their own distinct structures, sponsored their own base units, and pursued their own strategies. No overarching structure linked these subgroups together or imposed an organizational order onto them. The national party organization was thus little more than a loose collection of disparate subunits; a handful of weak territorial factions[34] coexisted with the union-based "62," rump cadre organizations such as the JP, C de O, Iron Guard, and the Montonero-based IM, "ultraverticalist" cliques of the old Isabelista guard, and the independent fiefdoms of provincial *caudillos* such as Mario Franco (Rio Negro), Herminio Iglesias (Buenos Aires), Carlos Juarez (Santiago del Estero), and Carlos Menem (La Rioja). These diverse subgroups were not integrated vertically into a national hierarchy, and no party organ could effectively discipline or control them.

The PJ also remained weakly routinized. At the outset of the 1983 transition, three distinct institutional projects coexisted within the party. A few Peronists, including former antiverticalists such as Angel Robledo, called for the creation of a stable territorial organization and the direct election of leaders and candidates. In their view, Peronism's survival in the new democratic era required a "transition from Perón's charismatic leadership to a rational leadership."[35] Yet other Peronists, including the bulk of the union leadership, preferred the traditional "movement" structure, in which Peronism's political, women's, and labor branches each received receive a quota (or *tercio*) of leadership posts and candidacies.[36] Finally, a handful of "ultraverticalist"

---

[33] According to Liberators leader Javier Mouriño, "Menem based his campaign on all those sectors outside the party, but inside the movement" (author's interview, July 1, 1997).
[34] These included Peronist Convegence; the Movement of Unity, Solidarity, and Organization; the Coordination of Justicialista Action; and the Movement of Doctrinal Reaffirmation.
[35] Peronist intellectual Julio Bárbaro, quoted in *Clarín*, November 9, 1983, p. 7.
[36] *Clarín*, April 24, 1983, p. 8; June 15, 1983, p. 14.

Isabel Perón loyalists refused to recognize the authority of the PJ leadership on the grounds that only Isabel or her appointees could legitimately lead the party. Although Isabel remained in Spain and showed no interest in returning to politics, few Peronists were willing to challenge her authority. Indeed, many party leaders, believing that Isabel might exercise veto power over party decisions, repeatedly sent telegrams to Madrid to gauge her opinion.[37]

The lack of consensus around the rules of the game for organizing and governing the party persisted throughout the 1983 electoral process, and as a result, it was often unclear who the PJ's "real" authorities were and how they were being selected. The party's formal statutes, which called for a conventional territorial structure, were not widely known, accepted, or adhered to (Palermo 1986a: 88–91). Neither the National Council nor acting party president Deolindo Bittel possessed substantial authority. Real power lay in the hands of labor bosses such as Lorenzo Miguel and Diego Ibañez (oil workers union), who, despite holding no formal party posts, dominated both the March 1983 party congress and the candidate selection process that followed it. Although the PJ held internal elections to choose delegates to a September 1983 party congress, which would then choose a new National Council and the presidential ticket, in reality, this electoral process was largely circumvented. "62" leaders, who continued to insist on the traditional branch system, pressured party leaders to negotiate "unity" lists that would make elections unnecessary.[38] Indeed, the presidential ticket of Italo Luder and Bittel emerged out of back-room negotiations at the margins of the primary process and was widely viewed as having been imposed by the "62" (Cordeu et al. 1985: 29). According to one PJ leader, the "62" let it be known that Luder was to be the candidate several weeks before the primaries even began.[39] At the same time, ultraverticalists rejected the internal elections altogether, declaring that "with Isabel at the helm, campaigns for the nomination are unnecessary."[40] When the September 1983 party congress nominated Luder as the PJ's presidential nominee, the ultraverticalists abandoned the congress, vowing to obtain a "veto" from Isabel and calling on Isabel to name a "Superior Council" to replace the National Council.[41] Several other losing candidates, including Carlos Menem, traveled (or sent representatives) to Madrid after the congress in an effort to modify the outcome.[42]

---

[37] For example, in July, "62" leader Lorenzo Miguel sent Isabel a telegram "on behalf of all three branches," asking her to clarify her position on the PJ's reorganization and presidential nomination (*Clarín*, July 21, 1983, p. 4).
[38] *Clarín*, May 12, 1983, p. 12; June 5, 1983, p. 13.
[39] Author's interview with José Octavio Bordón, November 26, 1997.
[40] *Clarín*, July 18, 1983, p. 4.
[41] *Clarín*, September 6, 1983, p. 3; October 12, 1983, p. 7, and Cordeu et al. (1985: 39).
[42] *Clarín*, September 11, 1983, p. 6; September 12, 1983, p. 2–3; September 13, 1983, p. 7; September 15, 1983, p. 10.

Origins and Evolution of a Mass Populist Party

The PJ's defeat in the 1983 presidential election plunged the party into another round of institutional crisis. Although the defeat generated widespread opposition to the Orthodox leadership, the party lacked routinized mechanisms for removing it. In a strategy that recalled Peronism's movementist period, anti-Orthodox factions circumvented formal party channels and created new leadership structures at the margins of the formal authorities. The result was dual and competing authority structures, which eroded the authority of the already weak National Council.

The National Council was challenged by two parallel authority structures in 1984. One was the Federal Council, which was created by provincial bosses such as Carlos Juarez and Carlos Menem. Although PJ statutes described the Federal Council as an advisory body, the governors sought to substitute it for the National Council as the PJ's top executive authority until the party was reorganized.[43] A few months later, Isabel Perón returned to Argentina and created a second parallel authority structure: a "Superior Command" that claimed to be "above all other party organs" and to possess the authority to "determine the national and international policy positions of the movement."[44] The new body was composed almost entirely of former members of the *Isabelista* government and close friends of Isabel. Few of its members had ties to the PJ leadership, and most were no longer active in politics.[45] Yet because few Peronists questioned Isabel's authority,[46] and because the Superior Command controlled access to Isabel, the body quickly emerged as a parallel leadership structure with the authority to speak on behalf of the party.[47] Even the National Council was forced to petition the body for an audience with Isabel.[48] For much of 1984, the Superior Command and National Council operated as parallel authorities, meeting separately with government officials and developing separate party programs.[49] The National Council was badly weakened by these challenges. The body met irregularly and was often unable to gain a quorum, and when circumstances compelled the PJ to take a public position, the Council was forced to invite the Federal Council, the Superior Command, and the

---

[43] *Clarín*, November 8, 1983, p. 6; November 14, 1983, p. 5; November 15, 1983, p. 11; December 1, 1983, p. 10.
[44] *Clarín*, May 25, 1984, p. 8; August 10, 1984, p. 10.
[45] *Clarín*, May 25, 1984, p. 8; June 8, 1984, p. 6.
[46] For example, "62" leaders accepted the creation of the Superior Command as "the right of Mrs. Perón," declaring that the PJ would "obey, in a disciplined way, whatever Mrs. Perón says" (*Clarín*, June 6, 1984, pp. 8–9; May 14, 1984, p. 4).
[47] *Clarín*, May 6, 1984, p. 16; Mar 7, 1984, p. 5; May 22, 1984, p. 4; May 24, 1984, p. 14.
[48] *Clarín*, December 7, 1983, p. 8; December 9, 1983, p. 10; December 12, 1983, p. 35.
[49] For example, while the Superior Command adopted a conciliatory posture toward the government, the National Council adopted a hard-line oppositionist stance (*Clarín*, May 22, 1984, pp. 2–4; June 20, 1984, p. 8). The legislative process was stalled for several weeks while the government waited "for it to become clear who is in charge in Peronism" (*Clarín*, January 29, 1984, pp. 10–11; February 14, 1984, p. 15).

"62" to its meetings in order to make a binding decision on behalf of the party.

Although the Superior Council faded into oblivion in the latter months of 1984, the party's institutional crisis persisted. In late 1984, the Orthodox-led National Council was challenged by a new routinizing movement called the Renovation, which sought direct elections for all party posts and candidacies. Led by Antonio Cafiero, Carlos Grosso, and Carlos Menem, the Renovators initially sought to remove the *Ortodoxos* at the December 1984 party congress at the Odeon Theater. However, when their reform efforts were blocked through fraud and intimidation, the Renovators opted for an extra-institutional solution. In February 1985, they organized a parallel congress in Rio Hondo, which elected a new leadership and approved a system of direct elections.[50] The PJ remained divided into competing Peronist parties until July 1985, when a pact between the Orthodox leadership and a group of provincial bosses produced a unity congress in which Catamarca *caudillo* Vicente Saadi was elected party president.

Formal unification did not solve the party's institutional crisis, however. The July congress failed to generate a consensus around new rules of the game for selecting party authorities. Because the congress did not establish a system of direct internal elections, many Renovators refused to recognize the legitimacy of the new Orthodox-dominated National Council. Declaring that they were "not worried about formal party names or statutes," hard-line Renovators asserted their open "disobedience" of the Saadi leadership.[51] One group of Renovators relaunched the Federal Council, seeking to transform it into a provisional party leadership,[52] while others pushed for a complete break with the PJ and the creation of a "Renovation Party."[53] Ultimately, however, Renovation leaders decided to simply "act as if the [Saadi leadership] did not exist,"[54] and establish themselves as a parallel leadership.[55] Thus, the Renovation elected its own national leadership, organized its own legislative bloc, and publicly distanced itself from the positions adopted by the National Council.[56]

The failure to reach an institutional settlement left the PJ in a state of near anarchy between 1985 and 1987. The Saadi-led National Council never gained effective control over the party, as many provincial branches – particularly those led by Renovators – refused to recognize its authority or comply

---

[50] *Clarín*, February 3, 1985, pp. 2–3; February 4, 1985, pp. 2–3.
[51] *Clarín*, July 12, 1985, p. 7.
[52] *Clarín*, November 26, 1985, p. 11; November 28, 1985, p. 13; December 3, 1985, p. 13.
[53] This position was adopted by the "25" union faction and much of the Peronist left, including the journal *Unidos*.
[54] *Clarín*, April 15, 1987, p. 14.
[55] *Clarín*, October 4, 1986, p. 11.
[56] *Clarín*, July 9, 1986, p. 12; July 10, 1986, p. 14; July 12, 1986, p. 6.

Origins and Evolution of a Mass Populist Party   55

with its directives.⁵⁷ In Mendoza, for example, when the National Council sent delegate Mario Gurlioli to oversee the operations of the provincial branch, the local Renovators who ran the party simply ignored him.⁵⁸ In Córdoba and Neuquén, National Council interventions (or threatened interventions) of provincial branches fractured the party, as dominant Renovation factions abandoned the official PJ and competed against it. Orthodox-controlled branches suffered schisms as well. In Buenos Aires, Herminio Iglesias' effort to fend off a reformist challenge by twice canceling internal elections led to a massive Renovation defection in 1985, and in Corrientes, long-time *caudillo* Julio Romero's repeated cancellation of elections and expulsion of internal opponents resulted in the emergence of parallel Peronist parties in both the 1985 and 1987 elections.

By early 1987, the authority of the Saadi-led National Council had eroded to such an extent that the Renovation became the PJ's de facto leadership. Although they held no positions in the party leadership, the Renovators publicly represented the PJ on all issues of national importance in 1987.⁵⁹ They also ran the PJ's 1987 electoral campaign, creating a parallel "electoral command" that developed the party's program and electoral strategy.⁶⁰ After the election, which the PJ won, the Renovators launched a party reorganization process at the margins of the National Council. In a series of informal summits in the Hotel Bauen, the Renovators drew up a new leadership slate and called a party congress for November 28.⁶¹ The National Council refused to recognize the congress or step down before its mandate expired,⁶² but the Renovators gathered an overwhelming majority of delegates and forced the National Council to resign.⁶³ The new leadership was not formally elected but rather "proclaimed" into existence in a governors' conference in early 1988.⁶⁴ The Renovation takeover brought a thorough housecleaning of the

---

57 For example, many provincial branches refused to comply with Saadi's instructions to align with the Developmentalist Integration Movement (MID) in the 1985 elections, even after he threatened to intervene or take over noncompliant branches (*Clarín*, September 6, 1985, p. 8; September 8, 1985, p. 11; September 9, 1985, pp. 2–3; September 10, 1985, pp. 2–3).
58 *Los Andes*, September 21, 1986, p. 12; September 29, 1986, p. 5; *Clarín*, October 6, 1986, p. 10.
59 For example, it was the Renovators who led the opposition to both the government's *Obedencia Debida* legislation and its new austerity program in mid-1987 (*Clarín*, June 3, 1987, p. 5; July 21, 1987, pp. 2–3).
60 *Clarín*, April 12, 1987, p. 14; June 23, 1987, p. 12; June 24, 1987, pp. 8–9; July 8, 1987, p. 14; July 9, 1987, p. 9.
61 *Clarín*, September 14, 1997, p. 5; September 16, 1987, p. 9; October 10, 1987, p. 5; October 11, 1987, p. 5.
62 *La Prensa*, October 29, 1987, p. 5; November 12, 1987, p. 4; November 25, 1987, p. 6; November 26, 1987, p. 11.
63 Outgoing PJ Vice President Julio Romero described the move as a "true coup d'état" (*La Prensa*, November 29, 1987, p. 4; November 30, 1987, p. 1).
64 *Clarín*, January 11, 1988, p. 3.

PJ hierarchy. Only one member of the National Council Executive Board – Santa Fe Governor Victor Reviglio – retained his post.

In sum, the PJ underwent five leadership changes between 1983 and 1987. None of these changes took place by means of widely accepted rules and procedures, and none of the leaderships elected during this period survived its four-year mandate. Moreover, the authority of the National Council was repeatedly challenged, both by parallel leadership bodies and by rebellious provincial branches.

The 1987–9 Renovation process, which is discussed in detail in Chapter 5, put an end to the institutional chaos of the 1983–7 period. The November 1987 party congress established a territorial structure in which leaders and candidates would be selected through direct primaries. The new system was broadly accepted within the party, putting a definitive end to alternative charismatic or corporatist projects. Moreover, under the leadership of new party president Antonio Cafiero, the Renovators paid unprecedented attention to the PJ's formal structure. Party organs such as the National Council met more frequently, the party bureaucracy began to keep internal records, and a greater effort was made to adhere to party statutes. The consolidation of the electoral-territorial structure put in place after 1987 was made manifest by the fact that it survived the passing of the Renovation itself. Despite the fact that the Renovators lost control of the party after Carlos Menem defeated Cafiero in the 1988 presidential primaries,[65] the formal structure that emerged from the 1987 congress remained intact.

Yet the degree of routinization that occurred under the Renovation should not be overstated. Although Renovation leaders clearly sought to establish a stable intraparty regime based on the model of European mass parties (Abos 1984: 60; Palermo 1986a, 1986b), in practice, the PJ organization never resembled the bureaucratic party structure outlined in the new statutes. Indeed, in many respects, the Renovators did little to change the way the PJ functioned. As the next chapter shows, the post-Renovation PJ continued to lack an effective central bureaucracy with the capacity to discipline or control lower-level organizations. It also lacked a bureaucratic hierarchy with stable career paths or secure tenure patterns. Indeed, the Renovators reinforced the PJ's leadership fluidity by carrying out a thorough housecleaning of the party hierarchy, removing old-guard leaders before their mandates expired. The Renovation process also failed to establish the National Council as the undisputed arena for party decision making or to infuse it with an authority that was autonomous of those who controlled key power resources. The conflicts of the 1984–7 period, during which the Renovators repeatedly operated at the margins of the party's formal leadership bodies, left the PJ's authority structures virtually as weak as ever. Moreover, the Renovators fell short of

---

[65] Menem gained de facto control of the party after winning the 1988 primary. He did not assume formal control of the party until 1990.

Origins and Evolution of a Mass Populist Party

establishing stable internal rules of the game in a variety of areas. Many of the rules and procedures governing the internal life of the party did not become widely known, accepted, or taken for granted, but rather remained fluid and contested. Finally, no clear party-union linkage emerged from the Renovation period. Indeed, as Chapter 5 shows, the Renovators contested and eventually dismantled traditional mechanisms of union participation, leaving the unions without any institutional links to the party.

The PJ thus entered the 1990s as a mass-based, but weakly routinized, party. Although most Peronist subgroups were integrated into party activity after 1983, and although the Renovation of the late 1980s established a stable territorial structure and introduced important democratizing reforms, the PJ nevertheless retained a fluid leadership hierarchy, weak leadership bodies, and ill-defined rules of the game for structuring union participation.[66] Peronism's contemporary structure is the focus of Chapter 3.

---

[66] This point raises questions about claims that Carlos Menem's personalistic leadership had a "deinstitutionalizing" effect on the PJ in the 1990s (Manzetti 1993: 109; Aboy Carlés 1996: 29; McGuire 1997: 241–6). Many of the phenomena that are generally associated with low institutionalization – including a fluid leadership hierarchy, weak formal authority structures, and the absence of binding internal rules of the game – had long been present in Peronism and did not change substantially under the Renovation. Menemism should therefore be viewed as perpetuating the PJ's underroutinization rather than causing it.

CHAPTER 3

An "Organized Disorganization": The Peronist Party Structure in the 1990s

The contemporary PJ retains important features from its populist and movementist past. Although it possesses a powerful mass organization with deep roots in working- and lower-class society, that organization lacks a central authority structure, an effective bureaucracy, and widely accepted and binding rules of the game. This internal fluidity has led scholars to conclude that the PJ's organizational structure is inoperative or even nonexistent, and that party leaders maintain personalistic and largely unmediated relationships with the Peronist rank and file (Novaro 1994: 76–89; Palermo and Novaro 1996: 370–6; Weyland 1999).

This chapter presents a somewhat different view. It characterizes the PJ as an informal mass party. It is a mass party in that it maintains both a large membership and activist base and an extensive base-level organization with deep roots in working- and lower-class society. Yet the PJ differs from prototypical mass working-class parties (such as European social democratic and communist parties) in that it is *informally organized* and *weakly routinized*.[1] It is informal in that most Peronist subunits are self-organized and -operated networks – run out of unions, clubs, nongovernmental organizations, and even activists' homes – that do not appear in the party's statutes or records, and which remain unconnected to (and autonomous of) the party bureaucracy. It is weakly routinized in that its internal rules and procedures are not widely known, accepted, and complied with, but rather are fluid, contested, and widely circumvented or ignored. This combination of societal rootedness and internal fluidity, the chapter argues, underlies the PJ's striking adaptive capacity.

The chapter is divided into two sections. The first section describes how the contemporary PJ is organized and functions internally. It argues

---

[1] McGuire (1997: 10–11) makes a similar point when he distinguishes between the PJ's electoral and organizational strength and its weak institutionalization.

that the Peronist party structure exhibits key features of its post-1955 movement organization. Peronist subunits continue to organize themselves autonomously of the party bureaucracy, and the party lacks an overarching authority structure with the capacity to coordinate and discipline subunits. It also shows that the PJ remains weakly routinized in three critical respects. First, its formal leadership bodies lack independent authority and are often not taken seriously by either party leaders or lower-level Peronist organizations. Second, the party's leadership hierarchy remains fluid, as it lacks bureaucratic filters, stable career paths, or tenure security. Third, the rules of the game regarding trade union participation remain informal, contested, and unstable. The second part of the chapter examines the implications of the PJ's informal and weakly routinized structure. It argues that although this fluid structure is inefficient and at times chaotic, and although it seriously limits the PJ's capacity to effectively represent and channel the demands of constituencies such as organized labor, it also provides Peronism with a striking degree of strategic flexibility. This flexibility, in turn, gives the PJ a capacity to adapt to environmental change or external crises that is rare among established labor-based parties.

AN INFORMAL MASS PARTY

The PJ is formally structured along the lines established by the Renovation in the late 1980s. This means that on paper, the PJ organization is not altogether different from that of many European mass bureaucratic parties. The post-Renovation party statutes call for a territorial structure based on a bureaucratic chain of command running from the National Council to provincial and municipal branches down to neighborhood base units (UBs). The formal hierarchy consists of four levels: (1) the national leadership, which includes the party congress and the National Council; (2) provincial-level branches, which are governed by provincial party councils; (3) municipal-level branches, which are governed by municipal councils; and (4) neighborhood-level base units. The highest body of authority is the party congress, which has the power to determine the party program, modify the party statutes, and intervene provincial party leaderships (Partido Justicialista 1991: articles 20-1). Day-to-day leadership of the party is in the hands of the National Council. The National Council is composed of 110 members: twenty-four district-level presidents, seventeen union representatives, ten women's representatives, ten youth representatives, and forty-nine at-large members. With the exception of the district presidents (who are automatic members), all National Council members, including the party president, are elected directly by the membership (Partido Justicialista 1991: article 24). The National Council is governed by a thirty-two member Executive Board, which is elected from within the council.[2]

In practice, however, the PJ organization differs considerably from that which is outlined in the party statutes. In the words of one Peronist mayor, the party remains an "organized disorganization."[3] Although it is mass-based, in that it possesses an extensive base-level organization with deep roots in working- and lower-class society, the PJ's organizational structure is informal and internally fluid. Peronist subunits continue to operate at the margins of the party bureaucracy, and many – perhaps most – do not appear in party records. At the same time, the rules of the game governing key areas of party life – including leadership and candidate selection, the authority of leadership bodies, and trade union participation – are fluid, contested, and frequently circumvented or manipulated by party leaders.

A Mass Organization

The PJ remained a predominantly mass party through the 1990s. Although no current parties encapsulate their members to the same degree that some turn-of-the-century European mass parties did, the PJ maintains what is by contemporary standards an extensive and deeply rooted mass organization. This can be seen in three senses.[4] First, the PJ maintains an extensive mass membership. Party membership fluctuated between 3.0 million and 4.1 million in the 1980s,[5] and it stood at 3.85 million in December 1993 (Jones 1997: 274). This figure constituted a striking 18 percent of the overall electorate. Indeed, as Table 3.1 shows, the PJ's membership-to-voter ratio of 54.2 in 1993 exceeded those of most postwar European social democratic parties (Bartolini and Mair 1990: 234).[6] Although it is important to note that party membership entails a lower level of commitment in Argentina than it does in most European mass parties (for example, PJ members do not pay regular dues), the Peronist figure is nevertheless strikingly high.

---

[2] In the 1990s, day-to-day leadership was formally delegated to a Mini-Board (*Mesa Chica*) consisting of the president, vice presidents, and secretaries.
[3] Author's interview with Hurlingham Mayor Juan José Alvarez, July 18, 1997.
[4] Scholars have employed a variety of indicators of party organization, the most common of which are membership (Duverger 1954/1963; Bartolini and Mair 1990) and number of organizational subunits (Wellhofer 1979a). Ignazi (1996: 551) suggests a more elaborate set of indicators, including number of party members and activists, number and strength of ancillary organizations, amount of autonomously collected resources, number of controlled sources of information, and number of "quasi-autonomous non-governmental organizations."
[5] *Clarín*, April 23, 1983, p. 6; July 21, 1983, p. 4; July 9, 1988, p. 2.
[6] Scholars commonly use membership-to-voter ratio as an indicator of organizational density (Duverger 1954/1963; Pelinka 1983; Bartolini and Mair 1990; Kitschelt 1994a). The PJ figure is based on the 7,103,155 votes it received in the 1993 legislative elections (Fraga 1995: 34).

TABLE 3.1. *The PJ's Membership-to-Voter Ratio in Comparative Perspective*

Political party	Membership/voter ratio (percentage)
Venezuelan Democratic Action (1988)	58
Argentine Justicialista Party (1993)	54
Swedish Social Democratic Party (1966–85)	38
Austrian Social Democratic Party (1966–85)	32
Chilean Communist Party (1969)	29
Italian Communist Party (1963)	21
Norwegian Labour Party (1966–85)	15
Danish Social Democratic Party (1966–85)	11
British Labour Party (1966–85)	6
German Social Democratic Party (1966–85)	6
Spanish Socialist Workers Party (1983)	3

Sources: Argentina: Jones (1997: 274) and Fraga (1995: 34); Chile: Furci (1984: 107, 122); Italy: Morlino (1996: 13); Spain: Pelinka (1983: 41); Venezuela: Coppedge (1994: 29); all others: Bartolini and Mair (1990: 234).

Second, the PJ maintains a dense organizational infrastructure, particularly in working- and lower-class neighborhoods. Although the party's failure to keep records of its base units makes it difficult to measure the density of its organization, evidence from La Matanza, Quilmes, and the provincial capital of San Miguel de Tucumán suggests that the PJ's base-level infrastructure remains both extensive and densely organized. In La Matanza, estimates of the number of base units ranged from five hundred to one thousand in the late 1990s, but the figure of seven hundred offered by local party president Juan Carlos Piris appears roughly accurate.[7] Using this figure, we can estimate that there was approximately one base unit per 1,750 residents in the late 1990s, and that there were 1.8 base units per square kilometer.[8] In Quilmes, 126 UBs were officially registered with the party in 1996, but estimates of the actual number of UBs ranged from two hundred to five hundred.[9] A conservative estimate of three hundred yields a total of approximately one UB per eighteen hundred residents and 3.28 UBs per square kilometer. The PJ's organizational density is roughly similar in the provincial capital of San Miguel, Tucumán, where the PJ had an estimated 250 UBs in 1997, or approximately one UB per 2,400 residents.[10]

---

[7] Author's interview, December 12, 1997.
[8] The population of La Matanza in 1996 was an estimated 1.2 million, and its area is 392.2 square kilometers (*Informe de Coyuntura*, published by the Centro de Estudios Bonaerense, November–December 1996, p. 98).
[9] Based on interviews with party president Jose Rivela (May 22, 1997) and party administrator Elba Quiroga (November 26, 1996), as well as with a variety of local leaders and activists.
[10] Estimate based on interviews with local PJ leaders and activists.

Third, the PJ remains deeply embedded in working- and lower-class society through linkages to a variety of (formal and informal) organizations. At the most basic level, local PJ organizations maintain extensive links to informal social networks in working- and lower-class neighborhoods. In lower-class zones, most of the "natural leaders" or "problem solvers" (Auyero 2000) of the neighborhood are Peronist.[11] Although many of these local brokers are not full-time party activists, almost all of them maintain ties – through friends, neighbors, or relatives – to informal party networks. These ties are periodically activated both from below and from above: Neighborhood "problem-solvers" use them to gain access to government resources, while local *punteros* use them to recruit people for elections or other mobilizations. There is a dark underside to this social embeddedness. Because urban slums are frequently centers of illicit activity such as drug trafficking, prostitution, and gambling, Peronist networks are inevitably linked to these forms of organization as well.[12]

Local party organizations also maintain linkages to a variety of social organizations. Historically, the most important of these have been unions. The vast majority of Argentine unions are run by Peronists, and although labor influence in the PJ has declined considerably since the mid-1980s (see Chapter 5), most unions remained active in local Peronist politics through the late 1990s. Indeed, of the thirty-six local unions surveyed for this study, thirty-three participated in party activity in 1997. Some of these unions contributed money or activists to political factions. Others directly sponsored or operated base units.

PJ organizations are also linked to urban social movements such as squatters' movements and shantytown organizations. In the Federal Capital, the vast majority of shantytown organizations were run by Peronists in the 1990s, and citywide organizations of shantytown dwellers, such as the Shantytown Movement and the Social Front, maintained close ties to the PJ. In San Francisco de Solano, Quilmes, leaders of a twenty thousand-member squatters' movement that had carried out a series of land invasions in the early 1980s formed a political organization, Social Justice, which joined the PJ in 1983 (Fara 1989: 184–5). In La Matanza, which contains more than one hundred squatter settlements and shantytowns, five of thirty-one UBs surveyed for this study were linked to squatter settlements,[13] and the coordinator of the Roundtable of Squatter Settlements, which claimed to represent

---

[11] For an insightful account of Peronist "problem-solving networks," see Auyero (2000).
[12] For journalistic accounts of these linkages, see Lopez Echague (1996) and Otero (1997).
[13] For example, the Perón and Evita base unit, led by Graciela Diaz, works closely with a neighboring eight hundred–family squatter settlement (named "The Graciela Settlement"), PJ activist Cacho Inés is president of the seven hundred–family "24 de Febrero" squatter settlement in Laferrere, and the "August 22" faction has close ties to the "January 22" squatter settlement in Ciudad Evita.

sixty shantytown organizations, was elected to the local PJ leadership in 1995.[14] At least two La Matanza factions, "August 22" and "Immortal Evita," also built alliances with organizations of garbage collectors in the 1990s.

Base-level PJ organizations are also linked to a variety of nongovernmental organizations, including *sociedades de fomento* (neighborhood development associations), school and health center cooperatives,[15] women's associations, and soup kitchens. In Quilmes, the Federation of *Sociedades de Fomento*, which claimed to represent 90 of the municipality's 150 *sociedades*, placed its president in the local PJ leadership in 1995.[16] In the Federal Capital, shantytown organizers estimated that between 70 and 80 percent of the city's 150 soup kitchens are run by Peronists.[17] Similar estimates have been made for the Greater Buenos Aires districts of Hurlingham, Lanus, and Quilmes.[18] A smaller number of UBs maintain ties to church organizations. For example, members of the "United or Dominated" UB in the capital entered the PJ via a progressive Catholic youth organization in the early 1980s, and the base unit continued to work with the local parish in a variety of charity activities through the 1990s.

Peronist organizations also maintain extensive ties to local clubs. Of particular importance are soccer clubs, especially those in the second or "B" division. Soccer clubs are a central part of social and cultural life in working- and lower-class zones, and links to these clubs provide the PJ with access to important human and organizational resources. Local Peronist leaders often use soccer fan clubs to mobilize youths for rallies, to paint graffiti, and, not infrequently, to intimidate opponents. The fan clubs thus serve as an important channel for recruiting activists into the party. Scores of party-club linkages exist in the Federal Capital and Greater Buenos Aires. For example, union leader Luis Barrionuevo's control over the Chacarita soccer club helped him establish a powerful political base in Greater Buenos Aires. In La Matanza, where the three largest clubs – Almirante Brown, Huracan, and Laferrere – were run by Peronists throughout most of the 1990s,[19] the

---

[14] Author's interview with Raul Tuncho, president of the roundtable of squatter settlements in La Matanza, August 30, 1997.

[15] These are voluntary organizations created to support particular schools or health clinics.

[16] Author's interviews with Cornelio Melgares, president of the Quilmes Federation of Neighborhood Associations (April 2, 1997), and José Luis Saluzzi, Quilmes director of non-governmental organizations (September 4, 1997). Based on interviews by the author in 1997.

[17] Based on interviews by the author in 1997.

[18] The Hurlingham figure is based on the author's interview with Hurlingham Mayor Juan José Alvarez, July 18, 1997. The Lanus figure is based on research carried out by Javier Auyero (personal communication). The figure for Quilmes is based on the author's interview with José Luis Saluzzi, Quilmes director of non-governmental organizations, September 4, 1997.

[19] Former PJ school board president and mayoral candidate Aníbal Stela, who led the Work and Production faction, served as president of Huracan, while former Public Works Secretary

TABLE 3.2. *Social Linkages of Surveyed Base Units in the Federal Capital and Greater Buenos Aires*

Social linkages	Number	Percentage of sample (n = 104)
Base units with ties to at least one social organization	59	56.7
Base units with ties to at least two social organizations	38	36.5
School cooperative	23	22.1
Sociedad de fomento	21	20.2
Neighborhood club	21	20.2
Self-help organization	21	20.2
Union	15	14.4
Church organization	9	8.7
Squatter organization	7	6.7

Note: Sample size is 104 because no information was available for 8 of the 112 base units surveyed for this study.

local party used the Laferrere soccer fan club for mobilizations and graffiti painting. In the Federal Capital, former city council member Raúl Padró used the Defenders of Belgrano fan club as an organizational base, while the UOM's ties to the Nueva Chicago club strengthened its political presence in Mataderos and other southern neighborhoods. Party–club linkages are also common in the interior provinces. In Tucumán, for example, the two largest soccer clubs were controlled by Peronists in the late 1990s, and one of them – Club Atlético – was led by Senator (and later, Governor) Julio Miranda. Similarly, in San Juan, the San Martin Club helped launch the political careers of legislator Juan José Chica Rodriguez and Governor Jorge Escobar in the early 1990s.

Overall, of the base units surveyed for this study, 57 percent showed evidence of a linkage to one or more civic organizations, and 37 percent were linked to two or more such entities. These data are summarized in Table 3.2. Of the base units surveyed, 22.1 percent had ties to a school or child care cooperative, 20.2 percent had ties to a local club, 20.2 percent had ties to a *sociedad de fomento*, 20.2 percent had ties to a soup kitchen or other self-help organization, 14.4 percent had ties to a union, 8.7 percent had ties to a church organization, and 6.7 percent had ties to a squatter organization.

This infrastructure of base units, unions, nongovernmental organizations, and informal social networks enables the PJ to maintain a stable political

Hugo Fernandez, who led the Immortal Evita faction, was president of Almirante Brown. Local PJ activists described Almirante Brown and Huracan as "100 percent Peronist."

presence in working- and lower-class class areas.[20] These zones are characterized by the persistence of a strong Peronist subculture – a common body of language, traditions, symbols, beliefs, organizational practices, and historical interpretations that unites Peronists of different ages, regions, social backgrounds, and ideologies – and identity. Though somewhat weakened by generational change, this identity and subculture provides the PJ with a sizeable "electorate of belonging" (Panebianco 1988). As Pierre Ostiguy (1998) has argued, for many lower-class voters, the Peronist identity extends beyond party politics to the social and cultural realms. For this segment of the electorate, Peronism is less a party choice than an encompassing identity. One does not just *vote* Peronist; one *is* Peronist (Ostiguy 1998: 394–482). Such voters provide the PJ with a relatively stable floor of support. Although the size of this core electorate is difficult to measure, surveys carried out by Hugo Haime and Associates in the mid-1990s found that between 25 and 30 percent of voters – and as many as 40 percent of lower-income voters – identified themselves as Justicialist.[21]

An Informal Organization

The PJ's mass linkages remain informal and decentralized rather than bureaucratic. The formal party structure is largely ignored, and power, resources, information, and even political careers pass through informal, self-organized subunits with only weak and intermittent links both to each other and to the party bureaucracy.[22] This section describes the PJ's informal organization at the local, provincial, and national levels. It shows how the party organization remains informal, in that power and resources pass through self-organized subgroups that operate at the margins of the party bureaucracy; segmented, in that subunits are not linked horizontally; and decentralized, in that subunits are not linked vertically into a central bureaucracy.

---

[20] Although no comprehensive studies exist of PJ electoral performance in lower-class areas, local studies reveal a striking degree of Peronist electoral hegemony. In her survey of residents in a squatter settlement in Quilmes, for example, Judy Lawton found that 76 percent of residents who were party members were Peronist (1994: 14). The survey found that 90.2 percent of respondents voted Peronist in 1989 and 76.4 percent voted for the PJ in 1991 (1994: 15). In La Matanza, the PJ vote hovered around 70 percent vote in lower-class zones such as Gonzales Catan, Laferrere, and Rafael Castillo in the early 1990s (Ostiguy 1998: 549).

[21] Surveys carried out in Greater Buenos Aires by Hugo Haime and Associates in October 1993 and April 1994, and a national survey carried out by Hugo Haime and Associates in April 1995. Data provided to the author by Hugo Haime and Associates.

[22] As one local leader put it, "Peronism is a giant informal network. Some work in the base units, others in their homes, and others in the *sociedades de fomento*. But they are all part of the network. This network is always there, sometimes latent, but always ready to be activated" (author's interview with José Montenegro, August 26, 1997).

Neighborhood-Level Organization: Base Units

According to PJ statutes, base units (UBs) constitute "the primary organ of the party" (Partido Justicialista 1991: article 12). They are the neighborhood branches out of which activists operate. Formally, UBs must have at least fifty members and must be governed by a Base Unit Council that is elected every two years by the membership.[23] In practice, however, they tend to be run by either a small group of activists or a single *puntero* (neighborhood broker) and her inner circle of friends and family.[24] Only 4.8 percent of the UBs surveyed for this study held regular elections with leadership turnover, while 22.1 percent held nominal elections in which the same leader always won and 73.1 percent held no regular elections at all.

Formally, UBs are part of the party bureaucracy. According to party statutes, UBs register with, and fall under the direct authority of, local party councils. The local party council determines the jurisdiction of each UB, and in some districts it has the authority to intervene in UBs that do not properly carry out their functions.[25] In reality, however, UBs are autonomous from the party bureaucracy. They are not created by the party, and their offices are not party property. Rather, they are created, privately, by the activists themselves. Anyone can open a UB at any time and in any place. Frequently, *punteros* establish UBs in their own homes and thus literally become their "owners." As one local leader put it:

We don't have to ask, "may we open up a Peronist community center?" No. In Peronism you have the freedom to create what you want. No one tells you what to do.[26]

Of the surveyed UBs, 67.6 percent were created "from below" by activists or *punteros*, 11.7 percent were created as outgrowths of existing UBs, 12.6 percent were created "from above" by local factions (or *agrupaciones*), and 8.0 percent were created by unions. Not a single UB was created by the party bureaucracy.

Not only do local party bureaucracies lack control over how many UBs exist or where they are located, but they often do not even have a record of the UBs under their jurisdiction. In Quilmes, party officials estimated in 1997 that they had a record of about a third of the existing UBs.[27] In La Matanza,

---

[23] Partido Justicialista (1991: articles 14 and 16) and Partido Justicialista de la Provincia de Buenos Aires 1988: articles 20, 22, and 23).

[24] Of the base units surveyed in this study, only 7.2 percent exhibited the degree of role specialization stipulated by the party charter. By contrast, 54 percent were run by a single *puntero*, and 39 percent were run by a small core of activists.

[25] Partido Justicialista (1991: article 13); Partido Justicialista de la Provincia de Buenos Aires (1988: article 28).

[26] Author's interview with José Montenegro, August 26, 1997.

[27] Author's interviews with PJ-Quilmes administrator Elba Quiroga, November 26, 1996, and party president José Rivela, May 22, 1997.

party administrators claimed to possess no records at all of existing UBs. Although party leaders have occasionally attempted to bring UBs under the control of the party bureaucracy, these efforts have repeatedly failed. In Quilmes in the mid-1980s, for example, party president Roberto Morguen enacted a policy whereby only officially recognized base units would be permitted to operate in each neighborhood. Yet because the party had no means of enforcing the policy, it was widely ignored.[28] Similarly, in the Federal Capital, Menemist factions proposed a reform in 1997 to limit party offices to one officially recognized branch per ward. It, too, was viewed as impossible to enforce. As one local leader put it:

Who would finance and run these offices? And how are they going to close down the other base units, if the base units are owned by the *punteros*? Are they going to throw the *punteros* out of their homes?[29]

Virtually all UBs carry out a set of core activities that include signing up members, competing in internal elections, and campaigning in general elections. Between elections, most UBs play a brokerage role between their neighborhoods and local factions, or *agrupaciones* (see the next subsection). On the one hand, most of them seek to maximize their support in the neighborhood, a task that often involves, but is not limited to, the distribution of material resources. On the other hand, most *punteros* seek to expand their access to state and party resources. *Punteros'* primary currency of exchange is their control over votes in internal elections. Particularly in lower-income zones, most citizens do not vote in internal elections on their own. They must be coaxed, bribed, and quite often physically transported to the polls. This task is performed by the *punteros*. *Punteros* seek to maximize the number of votes they can credibly claim to control. They use personal ties, persuasion, and material favors to build up a clientele, which allows them to act as gatekeepers to the neighborhood's votes. They then bring these votes to the table in negotiations with local politicians, who offer jobs and other state resources in exchange for their support.

Notwithstanding these common activities, UBs take diverse forms. While some take the form stipulated by the party statutes, others take the form of informal "working groups," which operate out of activists' homes, without a sign outside or any kind of formal recognition from the party. Legitimated by Perón's proscription era motto that "every house is a base unit," working groups are formed by activists without the numbers or resources to maintain an office, or by *punteros* who prefer informality because it gives them more

---

[28] Author's interviews with Roberto Morguen (May 13, 1997) and José Luis Saluzzi (September 4, 1997).

[29] Author's interview with Raul Roa, member of the PJ Metropolitan Council, November 10, 1997.

"room to maneuver."[30] Other UBs operate out of civic associations such as cooperatives, community centers, or soup kitchens. Although these working groups and civic associations do not "exist" as UBs on paper, in that they are not registered with (or recognized by) the party, they operate in exactly the same way as base units: They sign up members, compete in internal elections, and campaign in general elections. According to Liliana Monteverde, who runs the "Companions" UB in the capital,

> We put on different hats. One day we are a base unit; the next day a child care center, and the next day a civic association. But we always have the same Peronist ideology.[31]

In some areas, a majority of UBs operate out of civic associations. In San Miguel de Tucuman, for example, most UBs function as "neighborhood centers," while in the province of Santa Cruz, many UBs are organized into "community centers." Finally, some UBs are actually neighborhood annexes of local party factions. Neighborhood annexes differ from other UBs in that they are created (and often staffed) from the outside, rather than by neighborhood activists. Like working groups and civic associations, however, they are not sanctioned by, or subject to the authority of, local party authorities.

Local PJ organizations thus consist of a heterogeneous mix of UBs, working groups, civic organizations, and nonprofit organizations. For example, in the Lugano neighborhood in the Federal Capital, the infrastructure of one leading faction included a child care center, a soup kitchen, a "mother's center," a community center, and several working groups, while in Quilmes, the Loyalty faction included a church group, a mother's association, a children's rights group, and several community centers. In La Matanza, the Universal Evita faction had nineteen working groups and no base units in 1997 because, according to leader Adalberto Dal Lago, "they cost less and are easier to manage."[32] Table 3.3 shows the distribution of organizational forms taken by the UBs surveyed for this study. Less than half (42.9 percent) took the form stipulated by the party charter; 22.3 percent were informal working groups; 21.4 percent operated out of civic associations; and 11.6 percent were neighborhood annexes sponsored by local factions. A small number (1.8 percent) operated out of unions.

---

[30] Miguel Pinnaccio, who runs a working group in La Matanza, claims he does not work out of an office because "to have an office you have to depend on someone, which means that you have to answer to someone. This way, I'm free" (author's interview, April 5, 1997).

[31] Author's interview, June 30, 1997. Similarly, an activist whose "Heirs of Perón and Evita" base unit was transformed into a soup kitchen said, "We had to take down the Peronist sign to get funding as a nonprofit, but everyone knows it is still a base unit" (author's interview, March 24, 1997).

[32] Author's interview, May 23, 1997.

TABLE 3.3. *The Organizational Form of Surveyed Base Units*

Organizational form	Number	Percentage
Formal base unit	48	42.9
Informal working group	25	22.3
Civic association/nonprofit	24	21.4
Annex of *agrupación*	13	11.6
Union	2	1.8
TOTAL	112	100.0

Municipal-Level Organization

UBs are linked to the party through informal organizations called *agrupaciones*. *Agrupaciones* are clusters of UBs that compete for power in the party at the local level. They may be led by government officials, city council members, provincial or national legislators, unions, or outside political entrepreneurs seeking to build a base. They range in size from four or five UBs to more than one hundred, although most contain between ten and thirty. Two or three dozen *agrupaciones* may exist in each municipality, but usually only a handful are politically influential.[33] *Agrupaciones* vary considerably in terms of their organizational structures. Some are loosely organized and short-lived, emerging prior to internal elections and then disappearing after the election. Others are highly organized, stable, and enduring.[34]

Agrupaciones build alliances with *punteros* throughout the municipality. In exchange for their support, *punteros* seek direct financing for their UBs, material resources to distribute to their constituents, and government jobs. Because those in the best position to offer such resources are public office holders, most *agrupaciones* are held together by state patronage. Public officials use money from kickbacks, resources from the state agencies they run, and low-level government jobs to finance their *agrupaciones*. Food and medicine from social welfare ministries are routinely diverted to UBs, and *punteros* are widely employed as staff in government and legislative offices.[35] Others – known as *noquis*[36] – receive fictitious contracts that enable them to earn full-time salaries while they work in the UBs. Of the UBs surveyed

---

[33] In 1997, at least eighteen *agrupaciones* existed in Quilmes and least twenty-three existed in the Federal Capital. In La Matanza, the local party has a list of fifty-eight *agrupaciones*, although the author could confirm the existence of only thirty-five.

[34] For example, the Peronist Unity Front in the Federal Capital and Peronist Loyalty in La Matanza were created in the 1970s and endured into the late 1990s.

[35] According to Carnota and Talpone, the PJ controlled more than one thousand patronage jobs in the Federal Capital city council alone in the early 1990s (1995: 54).

[36] It is traditional in Argentina to eat *noquis* on the 29th of every month. Those who have contracts but don't actually work are called *noquis* because they are said to only go into work at the end of the month – *noqui* day – to pick up their paychecks.

for this study, 93 percent belonged to an *agrupación*, and most of the others were in transition from one *agrupación* to another.

Agrupaciones are thoroughly informal organizations. They are not mentioned in the party statutes, and local party offices generally keep no record of them. Because they organize and finance themselves, *agrupaciones* enjoy substantial autonomy from the party bureaucracy. They do not have to conform to either the dictates of party statutes or the decisions of local party authorities. This organizational autonomy is legitimated by Peronism's movementist tradition. Because the movement is understood to be broader than the party, and because the movement lacks any kind of (formal or informal) structure or hierarchy, Peronists often view their *agrupaciones* as lying outside the party, but inside the movement.[37] As a result of these ill-defined boundaries, *agrupaciones* may float in and out of the PJ with relative ease. In the 1980s and 1990s, scores of *agrupaciones* left the PJ for an election or two – either running on their own or in alliance with another party – without leaving the "movement."[38] In the Federal Capital, for example, Peronist Victory (VP) left the party in 1996 to back the mayoral candidacy of Gustavo Beliz of the New Leadership party. Over the next two years, VP maintained "one foot in and one foot out of the party," calling itself a "Peronist *agrupación* outside the structure of the PJ."[39] In 1997, it aligned with the Action for the Republic party, but in 1998, it returned to the PJ to join Eduardo Duhalde's presidential campaign.[40] Similarly, in many *agrupaciones* in Greater Buenos Aires defected to the ultranationalist Movement for Dignity and Independence (MODIN) in the early 1990s, only to return after MODIN's collapse a few years later.

Despite their informal nature, *agrupaciones* function as the *de facto* Peronist party organization. It is the *agrupaciones*, not the party bureaucracy, that link the PJ to its activist base. The vast bulk of party

---

[37] Thus, despite the fact that it participates in internal elections and campaigns for the PJ in general elections, *Comando de Organización* in La Matanza considers itself "part of the movement, but not part of the party," and therefore in no way subject to the discipline of the local party (author's interview with *Comando de Organización* leader Alberto Brito Lima, April 8, 1997).

[38] A well-known case of such a temporary defection was the Renovation Front in Buenos Aires, which abandoned the Orthodox-led PJ in 1985 after party boss Herminio Iglesias canceled internal elections. The Renovation Front competed against, and defeated, the Iglesias-led PJ in that year's midterm elections, after which it returned to the PJ and quickly took over the party leadership.

[39] Author's interviews with VP leaders Jorge Arguello (May 19, 1997) and Victor Pandolfi (June 5, 1997).

[40] *Agrupaciones* may also float into the PJ from the outside. For example, when a group of leaders and activists from the right-wing Center Democratic Union (UCeDe) joined the PJ's Federal Capital branch in the early 1990s, UCeDe city council member Francisco Siracusano created the People's Conservative Movement, which established six base units and began competing in intraparty elections.

resources – particularly patronage and other unregulated forms of finance – pass through the *agrupaciones*,[41] and as a result, the agrupaciones "have much more money than the party itself."[42] And crucially, it is the *agrupaciones* that finance – and to some extent, coordinate – the party's base units. Of the UBs surveyed for this study, 85.6 percent received most or all of their resources from an *agrupación*, while 14.4 percent were either self-financed or were financed through private sector donations. Not a single base unit was financed by the party bureaucracy. The *agrupaciones'* organizational infrastructures thus tend to dwarf those of the party bureaucracy. According to former Federal Capital party treasurer Raúl Roa,

> The party bureaucracy just maintains the headquarters, which is nothing more than one office and the ten employees that run and clean the place. The rest of the organization is financed and coordinated by the leaders of the various *agrupaciones*. The party's real infrastructure, meaning the base units, is in the hands of the *agrupaciones*.[43]

Agrupaciones also carry out the bulk of the party's mobilizational work. *Punteros* mobilize their supporters for activities sponsored by the *agrupación*, carry out instructions that are channeled through the *agrupación*, and distribute material goods and literature supplied by the *agrupación*. *Punteros* get the bulk of their information from assemblies run by their *agrupación*, and to the extent that UBs are able to channel demands upward through the party, they do so via the *agrupación*. By contrast, UBs rarely participate in events sponsored by the local party leadership. In La Matanza, for example, local Peronists described the party council as a group that "just meets to play cards,"[44] and one council member claimed to have never been sworn in and to never have attended a meeting of the body.[45]

Agrupaciones also have a greater capacity to impose discipline on local leaders than does the party bureaucracy. For example, despite the fact that the Federal Capital party charter stipulates that elected officials must contribute 10 percent of their salaries to the local party,[46] only three of six congressional deputies did so in 1997.[47] By contrast, *every one* of the elected officials belonging to the Liberators of America and Peronist Unity Front

---

[41] Although public finance is channeled through the party bureaucracies, this amounts to a relatively small percentage of party finance. Most private donations – and, crucially, *all patronage resources* – are channeled through the *agrupaciones*.

[42] Author's interview with former Federal Capital party treasurer Raúl Roa, May 12, 1997. Similarly, former Quilmes party president José Rivela claimed that the local party "has no money. All the money is in the *agrupaciones*" (author's interview, May 22, 1997).

[43] Author's interview, May 12, 1997.

[44] Author's interview with Claudio Britos, an alternate member of the PJ-La Matanza party council, November 15, 1997.

[45] Author's interview with Tuncho, August 30, 1997.

[46] Partido Justicialista Metropolitana (1986: article 80).

[47] Author's interview with Roa, May 12, 1997.

regularly contributed 10 percent of their salaries to their *agrupaciones*.[48] A similar situation exists in Quilmes, where "fewer than half" of elected officials meet their obligation to contribute 5 percent of their salaries to the party.[49] Similarly, while *agrupaciones* can generally ensure that all of their base units attend their assemblies, local parties have no means of compelling base units to attend party-sponsored meetings. For example, in the late 1990s, Quilmes party president José Rivela's "mandatory" base unit assemblies were attended only by the UBs that belonged to his *agrupación* and those of his allies. According to Rivela, Peronists

> ignore the party.... They respond to the *agrupaciones* because that is where the money comes from.... The *agrupaciones* can provide them with something – some financing to pay the rent, food or blankets to give away. The party can't offer anything at all, so no one pays any attention to it.[50]

Even political careers are channeled through *agrupaciones*. Because leadership recruitment and candidate selection is done almost entirely by the *agrupaciones*, emerging politicians invest in *agrupaciones* rather than build careers in the party bureaucracy. *Punteros* work their way up through *agrupaciones* by building up territorial bases and exchanging votes for candidacies or government posts. Once in office, they use patronage jobs to sponsor other base units and build their own *agrupaciones*.

Provincial-Level Party Organization

At the provincial level, *agrupaciones* aggregate into competing *líneas internas*, or provincial factions. Provincial factions are generally created and run by public officials, such as governors, national or provincial cabinet members, or legislators. In Buenos Aires, for example, two factions dominated the provincial party in the mid-1990s: the Federal League, which was run by Chamber of Deputies President Alberto Pierri and provincial Public Works Minister Hugo Toledo; and the Buenos Aires Peronist League (LIPEBO), led by provincial Chamber of Deputies President Osvaldo Mercuri. Similarly, in Tucumán in the mid-1990s, the dominant True Peronism and Peronism of Hope factions were led by Senators Olijela Rivas and Julio Miranda, respectively.

---

[48] Author's interviews with Roa of FUP and Victor Columbano of Liberators of America, May 12, 1997.
[49] Author's interview with PJ-Quilmes party president Rivela, May 22, 1997.
[50] Author's interview with PJ-Quilmes party president Rivela, May 22, 1997. The weakness of local party structures vis-á-vis the *agrupaciones* is clearly seen in La Matanza. Throughout the 1990s, the de facto headquarters of the PJ's La Matanza branch was the office of the Militancy and Renovation (MyRP) *agrupación*, which was led by local boss (and Chamber of Deputies President) Alberto Pierri. Known as the Big House (*La Casona*), the MyRP headquarters was far better financed, better staffed, and more frequently visited than the party headquarters itself. Party membership data were located in a MyRP computer center, and information on the party's base units was reportedly located Pierri's offices in the Chamber of Deputies.

The primary currency of exchange between provincial factions and *agrupaciones* is patronage: *Agrupaciones* exchange votes for positions in provincial governments or on national or provincial legislative lists. Like *agrupaciones*, provincial factions vary in their organizational structures. Some are loosely organized factions that emerge for internal elections and then disappear. Others, such as the Peronist Renovation Movement in Santa Cruz, the Orange List in Mendoza, and Peronist Convergence in La Pampa, were relatively well-organized and stable throughout much of the 1980s and 1990s. Although a few provincial factions are collectively led and maintain coherent programmatic profiles, most are personalistic, with many taking on the name of their leader.[51]

Power, resources, and careers pass through the provincial factions, rather than party bureaucracies, and as a result, provincial party bureaucracies tend to be weak. For example, the Buenos Aires party branch, which represents more than a million party members, was open for only three half days every week in 1997, and it possessed virtually no paid staff. The provincial council rarely met, and when it did, it often had to call acting party president Alberto Pierri to have the office unlocked.[52] By contrast, the party's two dominant factions, the Federal League and LIPEBO, maintained powerful organizations and kept detailed records of local-level party activity. It was the provincial factions, and not the party, that organized and financed the party's campaigns, mobilized Peronists for rallies, and disciplined local organizations. In Tucumán, when the dominant factions temporarily stopped funding the party in 1997, the provincial headquarters were left without phone service, a functioning bathroom, or funds for the upcoming electoral campaign.[53] Hence, without control over the provincial factions, control of the bureaucracy means very little. Indeed, when the party's formal leadership is not aligned with the dominant factions, it becomes virtually powerless.[54]

---

[51] Examples in the 1990s included *Jaurismo* (after Governor Carlos Juarez) in Santiago del Estero, *Romerismo* (after Governor Juan Carlos Romero) in Salta, and *Saadismo* (after Vicente and Ramon Saadi) in Catamarca.

[52] Author's interview with Oscar Guida, a member of the PJ-Buenos Aires provincial council, November 22, 1996.

[53] Author's interview with PJ-Tucumán party president Amado Juri, December 8, 1997. Likewise, in San Juan in 1995, the provincial party was left without money to pay its gas and phone bills, as all party resources were concentrated in the dominant Front of Hope faction (*Clarín*, December 5, 1995, p. 22).

[54] This was clearly seen in the case of the 1990 referendum in Buenos Aires on a set of reforms to the provincial constitution that would have permitted Governor Antonio Cafiero to run for reelection. When the measure was handily defeated, with many Peronists voting against it, the outcome was taken as a major surprise given that Cafiero controlled the entire party "apparatus." Yet two of the party's three major factions, the Federal League and Menem Leadership, did not work in favor of the measure and, in many places, quietly worked against it. By August 1990, when the referendum was held, the well-financed Federal League had grown substantially in the province, leaving Cafiero with a minority of the "real" party.

Provincial branches vary considerably with respect to their power configurations and organizational structures. Where the party controls the governorship, provincial branches frequently consolidate into centralized machinelike organizations. In peripheral provinces such as Catamarca, Chaco, Corrientes, La Rioja, and Santiago del Estero, these organizations were led in the 1980s by traditional *caudillos*, many of whom served as governor in the 1946–55 period and/or the 1973–6 period. These party leaderships tended to be traditional, in that they were based as much on personal and familial ties as on patronage.[55] Party structures tended to be highly personalistic;[56] candidate lists were often drawn up by the party boss himself, and top candidacies and party posts were often given to close friends and relatives. As traditional leaderships eroded in the 1990s, organizations became more machinelike. In provinces such as Buenos Aires, La Pampa, San Luis, and Santa Cruz, governors used patronage to coopt all significant internal factions into a broad governing coalition. Lacking the resources to compete with the governor, secondary leaders generally chose to join the dominant coalition rather than confront it and risk political marginalization. Consequently, internal competition was reduced and power became concentrated in the hands of the party boss. When such machines consolidate, competitive intraparty elections are rare. Leadership and candidate selection tends to take place through "unity lists," which are drawn up by the party boss and a small circle of leaders. Elections are either canceled altogether or are rubber-stamp affairs in which dominant lists face only nominal opposition.

Where the PJ is out of power, it is more difficult for a single leader to consolidate machinelike control over the party. Rather, factions led by mayors, provincial or national legislators, or members of the national government

---

[55] In Catamarca, long-time party boss Vicente Saadi turned the provincial PJ into a virtual Saadi clan in the 1980s, with his son Ramon serving as governor, Vicente as senator, and several other Saadis or in-laws serving as mayors, provincial legislators, or cabinet members. After Vicente Saadi's death in 1988, the party leadership was passed on to Ramon. Another Saadi son, Luis, was elected to Congress, and his daughter Alicia was elected senator. In Corrientes, long-time boss Julio Romero was accused by internal rivals of "running the PJ as if it were a plantation" (*Clarín*, August 2, 1986, p. 10). In the late 1980s, Romero passed the party leadership on to his son Humberto, although the latter was unable to maintain control over the party. In Santiago del Estero, long-time PJ leader Carlos Juarez maintained a highly personalistic relationship with the party base. During the 1976–83 dictatorship, in which he was exiled, Juarez is said to have sent annual Christmas and birthday cards to each of his followers. In the 1990s, Juarez twice placed his wife at the top of the party's legislative list.

[56] In Tucumán, one local leader claims, "If the party congress decided that so and so was to be the candidate, and Governor Riera decided it was to be someone else, they would have to call another congress to select the candidate that Riera wanted" (author's interview with José Antonio Cuneo Verges, September 25, 1997). In Santiago del Estero, Juarez was said even to hold veto power over city council lists.

compete for power in the party. Politics remains patronage-based, but rather than consolidating into a single centralized machine, the party remains pluralistic and competitive. To use Wolfinger's (1972: 174–5) term, these are cases of "machine politics" without the consolidation of a single machine. In some cases, such as Córdoba, Chubut, Neuquén, and Rio Negro during the 1990s, the provincial party is organized into relatively stable systems of competing factions. In other districts, the PJ has decomposed into a state of near-anarchy, in which dozens of weak factions and localized *agrupaciones* compete to establish themselves, but no strong factions emerge. Examples include Chaco and the Federal Capital in the late 1990s.

The National Organization: The Absence of Horizontal and Vertical Links

The PJ lacks a national-level structure. The party's formal bodies of authority are weak and largely inoperative. The National Council is, in effect, an empty shell. Its offices are often empty, and it lacks resources, full-time professional staff, and even basic data on the activities of lower-level branches. In fact, the National Council possesses virtually no record of its own activities and leadership rosters before 1990. Indeed, when the private Juan D. Perón Institute called the national headquarters to invite National Council members to its public inauguration in 1997, the party's secretarial staff was unable to come up with the phone numbers or addresses of the body's membership. According to former acting party president Roberto García, when he took office in 1990, the PJ headquarters were located in a "small office that did not even have a sign outside."[57] García claimed that he was "the only bureaucrat in the party" during his three years as president,[58] and that no other party leaders visited the party office regularly. Given the bureaucracy's lack of resources, PJ politicians find they can best advance their careers through positions in the government, rather than the party. Many bypass the party entirely, never holding a position in local party or provincial party councils. According to García,

> the party is not valued or seen as worth anything. If you say you want to be the president of the party, everyone will tell you, "why don't you go for a seat in congress, which is worth more?"[59]

The national PJ organization lacks strong horizontal and vertical links. Because no stable mechanism links provincial bosses horizontally, national-level factions tend to be weak and ephemeral. Only one stable national faction – the Renovation – emerged during the 1983–99 period, and it

---

[57] Author's interview with Roberto García, June 23, 1997. As García put it, "It's hard to imagine. We were the biggest party on the continent and we didn't even have a sign outside."
[58] Author's interview with Roberto García, June 23, 1997.
[59] Author's interview, June 23, 1997.

disintegrated soon after its defeat in the 1988 primaries.[60] Due to the absence of horizontal and vertical links, when the PJ is out of national office, it becomes fragmented and decentralized. In such a context, the National Council exerts little authority over internal factions or provincial branches.[61] By contrast, when the PJ controls the national executive, it generally takes a more centralized form. In such cases, the lines of authority pass through the national executive, rather than the party bureaucracy. Lacking the resources or independent authority to compete with office-holding party leaders, the formal party hierarchy "ceases to function."[62] As a result, "the government runs the party."[63]

In sum, the contemporary PJ organization is both informal and decentralized. Its formal bureaucratic structure is largely inoperative and exercises little control over lower-level party organizations. In this sense, the PJ structure shares important characteristics with the Brazilian clientelistic parties described by Mainwaring (1999: 153–65) and the U.S. party machines described by scholars such as Key (1949), Eldersveld (1964), and Mayhew (1986). It differs markedly from more centralized and bureaucratic parties such as Venezuela's AD and the French and Chilean communist parties, in which the central bureaucracy tightly controls local party organizations.

The Weak Routinization of Internal Rules and Procedures

The rules of the game governing how the PJ is organized and functions remained weakly routinized in the 1990s. For example, the correspondence between the PJ's formal rules and the actual behavior of party leaders remains low. Party statutes are said to be in a "state of permanent infraction."[64]

---

[60] The Orthodox faction was, in reality, little more than a loose grouping of labor and party leaders who controlled the national party organization. It never functioned as a coherent faction. Although Menemism emerged as a national-level faction in the 1987–8 period, it only functioned as a campaign alliance and disappeared after the 1988 internal election.

[61] The weakness of the party bureaucracy could be seen in party president Antonio Cafiero's inability to take advantage of it in his 1988 bid for the presidential nomination. It is often argued that Menem defeated Cafiero despite Cafiero's control over the party "apparatus." This is only partially true. Although Cafiero controlled the party's formal bureaucracy, Menem was supported by the vast bulk of the labor movement and important *agrupaciones* and factions throughout the country, particularly in Buenos Aires, Catamarca, Corrientes, La Rioja, Mendoza, Santa Cruz, Santa Fe, and Tucuman.

[62] Author's interview with Senator Omar Vaquir, September 24, 1997.

[63] Author's interview with Hurlingham Mayor Juan José Alvarez, July 18, 1997.

[64] Author's interview with Roa, treasurer of the PJ's Federal Capital branch, May 12, 1997. According to national deputy Angel Abasto, "not only is it the case that activists do not know the rules in the party charter, but leaders don't know them either" (author's interview, September 18, 1997).

According to one party leader, party rules are

constantly infringed.... If you break the law, there is a judge to punish you. If you break the party statutes, there is no one to sanction you. There is no tribunal to punish you.[65]

Rather than taking the party statutes for granted, party leaders view them instrumentally. As one lower-level party leader put it, "we use the party statutes when they are useful. When they are not useful, we don't use them."[66]

Not only are the rules outlined in the party statutes often ignored, but they are also highly fluid. According to Ricardo Morato, the legal representative of the PJ's Federal Capital branch, the PJ "governs itself by constantly modifying the party statutes, or by making exceptions."[67] Party leaders with the power to change existing rules and procedures in pursuit of their goals routinely do so. Thus, party rules are "modified according to the needs of the leadership."[68] Rather than a taken-for-granted set of rules to govern intraparty behavior, then, the party statutes are little more than "a product of the momentary balance of power at any given time."[69] As former party general secretary José Luis Manzano put it,

The party statutes are the written agreement of how power is organized at a particular time. They are an instrument for one faction to impose itself on another. They are not the rules by which the factions play.[70]

The relative absence of routinization can be seen in three areas of party activity: (1) the authority of party leadership bodies; (2) career paths and leadership change; and (3) the party–union linkage.

Party Leadership Bodies: The Absence of Taken-for-Granted Authority

According to the party statutes, the National Congress and National Council are the PJ's maximum authorities and are responsible for resolving intraparty conflicts, developing the party program, and directing the party's electoral campaigns.[71] However, party leaders are quick to point out that such authority exists "only in theory."[72] The National Council has never achieved

---

[65] Author's interview with Roa, treasurer of the PJ Federal Capital branch, May 12, 1997. Similarly, Congressional Deputy Eduardo Rollano claims that the party statutes are "openly violated all of the time" (author's interview, June 24, 1997).
[66] Author's interview with Daniel Checker, advisor to Senator José Figueroa, September 9, 1997.
[67] Author's interview, September 26, 1997.
[68] Author's interview with Congressional Deputy José Lopez, September 15, 1997.
[69] Author's interview with Congressional Deputy Lorenzo Dominguez, September 25, 1997.
[70] Author's interview, December 5, 1997.
[71] Partido Justicialista (1991: articles 19–25).
[72] Author's interview with former interior minister and National Council member Gustavo Béliz, July 21, 1997.

taken-for-granted status as the party's ultimate decision-making arena. One local PJ leader, comparing the PJ to Argentina's other major political party, the Radical Civic Union (UCR), put it the following way:

> In the UCR they can't do anything if they don't talk about it in the party council. We don't pay attention to the party council. This is because we are a movement, not a party.[73]

Crucially, the National Council is not endowed with authority that is autonomous from office-holding party leaders. As a result, the body is frequently ignored, particularly when the PJ controls the executive branch.[74] According to another party leader, "People don't go to debate in the National Council meetings because they know it isn't going to go anywhere."[75]

Little consensus exists among Peronists as to the role of the party's leadership bodies. Whereas some party leaders argue that the National Council should "function independently of the government,"[76] playing a "role of control and criticism"[77] and "generating and diffusing its own policies,"[78] others insist that the party bureaucracy should "only function during elections. After that, things should be run by the president."[79] Of thirty-one National Council members surveyed for this study, only three (9.7 percent) claimed that the National Council "functions as the party charter says it should." By contrast, twenty-four National Council members (77.4 percent) said the body "does not function as the party charter says it should." Four others (12.9 percent) said the National Council does not function according to the party charter but suggested that such nonfunctioning was in accordance with Peronist tradition.

The lack of autonomous authority of the PJ's leadership bodies is made manifest by the repeated creation of ad hoc parallel bodies to perform functions formally reserved for the National Council or the party congress. In 1983, the bulk of party decision making, including candidate selection and the development of campaign strategies, took place in informal "summits" – organized and run by the "62 Organizations" – at the margins of the National Council. In 1987, the Renovation faction created a parallel "Electoral Command" – at the margins of the Orthodox-led National Council – to lead the party in that year's midterm elections. And after Menem's defeat

---

[73] Author's interview with Mario Scalisi, undersecretary of culture in Quilmes, May 8, 1997.
[74] According to Congressional Deputy Jorge Yoma, "for other parties, the party structure is a dogma, a corset. In the UCR, collective debate becomes problematic, due to the structure with all of the committees and the like. In the case of Peronism, we only open the doors of the party bodies when there are elections" (author's interview, September 25, 1997).
[75] Author's interview with Roa, treasurer of the PJ-Federal Capital branch May 12, 1997.
[76] Author's interview with National Deputy Ernesto Kaehler, November 19, 1997.
[77] Author's interview with National Deputy Pascual Rampi, November 18, 1997.
[78] Author's interview with National Deputy Juan Valcarcel, December 2, 1997.
[79] Author's interview with National Deputy Mario Cámara, November 20, 1997.

of party president Antonio Cafiero in the 1988 presidential primaries, the running of the party passed into the hands of an ad hoc body called the "Commission of Ten," which led the party into the 1989 presidential campaign.

The weakness of the PJ's formal leadership bodies again suggests a parallel to Brazil's leading clientelistic parties (Mainwaring 1999: 153–5). It clearly distinguishes the PJ from most European labor-based parties, as well as Latin American labor-based parties such as AD, the Brazilian Workers Party (PT), and even the Mexican PRI.[80] It also distinguishes the PJ from the UCR, in which the National Convention and other formal party authorities carry substantial weight.

The Party Hierarchy: Career Paths and Leadership Selection

The rules of the game surrounding issues such as career advancement, tenure security, and leadership and candidate selection in the PJ are also poorly routinized. Peronism lacks a bureaucratic hierarchy or stable career paths, and as a result, movement into, up, and out of the party hierarchy is fluid. According to Menemist activist Ernesto Storino,

> One of the great things about Peronism is that...any new member can reach the highest level if the opportunity is right or personal qualities permit it. You don't have to go through a long process. In other parties, like the UCR, you have to go through a kind of hierarchical structure within the party. Not in Peronism. With us, if you are an Argentine citizen, you can be a Peronist leader or candidate.[81]

Thus, just as Juan Manuel Abal Medina could be named the general secretary of the Superior Council in 1972 without having ever joined the party, and just as Isabel Perón could rise to the party presidency simply by virtue of being Perón's widow, Peronist leaders continue to "parachute" into party leadership positions without rising through the party bureaucracy. For example, José Maria Vernet, a former UOM advisor with no career in the party, was elected governor of Santa Fe in 1983. A year later, he was elevated to the National Council, where he was briefly named acting party president – the first party post he had ever held.[82] Parachute cases in the 1990s include those of automobile racer Carlos Reutemann and pop singer Ramon "Palito" Ortega, two outsiders who were elected governor of Santa Fe and Tucumán, respectively, in 1991. Both Reutemann and Ortega were elected president of their respective provincial branches just months after joining the party in 1993. Two years later, Reutemann was

---

[80] On AD, see Martz (1966) and Coppedge (1994). On the PT, see Mainwaring (1999: 165–7). On the PRI, see Langston (2001).
[81] Author's interview, March 4, 1997.
[82] *Clarín*, December 16, 1984, p. 6. Similarly, Eduardo Menem, a long-time conservative who joined the PJ in 1982, was elected to the National Council in 1987 and became the acting party president in 1990.

named to the National Council, and he became a party vice president soon afterward.[83]

Just as leaders may rise rapidly through party ranks, they may also be easily removed. No tenure security exists in party posts. Despite the fact that the party charter prescribes four-year terms in the party's national leadership bodies, these mandates are rarely respected. The party presidency changed hands six times between 1983 and 1990, and the first four acting presidents elected after the 1983 democratic transition – Lorenzo Miguel, José María Vernet, Vicente Saadi, and Antonio Cafiero – were forced to step down before their mandates had expired. The situation hardly stabilized in the 1990s; between 1990 and 1998, the party presidency passed through the hands of six leaders: Cafiero, Eduardo Menem, Roberto García, Ruben Marín, Eduardo Duhalde, and Carlos Menem.

Specific rules and procedures regulating leadership and candidate selection processes are also weakly routinized. For example, in most provinces, party statutes stipulate that candidates for public office must have been party members and residents of the district for at least two years. Whenever the party lacks an attractive candidate, however, these rules are circumvented. In the Federal Capital, for example, the party recruited conservative non-Peronist Avelino Porto as its senate candidate in 1992, passing a resolution in the party congress that lifted the party membership requirement and canceled internal elections. The party congress passed similar resolutions in 1993 and 1997, allowing Erman Gonzalez, a La Rioja resident who until 1990 had belonged to the Christian Democratic Party, and Daniel Scioli, a boating champion who had never belonged to a party, to head the party's lists for Congress.[84]

Even internal elections, which are often said to have been routinized under the Renovation, are frequently circumvented by means of "unity lists" imposed by party bosses. As one party activist put it, "internal democracy exists only when it serves the interests of the party leadership. When it does not serve the interests of the leadership, there is no internal democracy."[85] Indeed, a majority of the PJ's provincial branches failed to hold competitive elections in 1997. In five provinces (Formosa, La Pampa, Misiones, San Luis, and Santiago del Estero), not a single competitive intraparty election was held between 1989 and 1997, and in three others (Salta, San Juan,

---

[83] Ortega was the PJ's vice presidential candidate in the 1999 elections.

[84] Local parties also frequently violate their own "incompatibility clauses," which state that public office holders cannot simultaneously hold positions in the party leadership. For example, despite the fact that the Federal Capital branch introduced such a clause in 1986 (*Clarín*, May 3, 1986, p. 6; May 4, 1986, pp. 6–7), all of its presidents between 1986 and 1998 – Carlos Grosso, Carlos Ruckauf, Eduardo Vaca, Claudia Bello, and Raul Granillo Ocampo – simultaneously held public office. According to PJ legal representative Ricardo Morato, the party charter "is simply ignored on this matter.... It sounds absurd, but it's true" (author's interview, September 26, 1997).

[85] Author's interview with Ernesto Duhalde, May 19, 1997.

and Santa Cruz), no competitive elections were held after 1993. In some cases, internal elections are canceled entirely and candidates are simply "proclaimed" by the local party congress.[86] In other instances, party bosses modify winning lists after internal elections.[87] Finally, in some cases, candidates are imposed via the intervention of the national leadership. This was the case in Catamarca, Corrientes, Santa Fe, Tierra del Fuego, and Tucumán in 1991, Corrientes and Tucumán in 1993, Córdoba, Santiago del Estero, and Tucumán in 1994, Córdoba and San Juan in 1995, and the Federal Capital in 1997 and 1999.[88]

Competitive elections are even rarer at the national level. The highly competitive 1988 presidential primary, which is often cited as an indicator of PJ's internal democratization, proved to be more the exception than the rule. Despite the introduction in 1987 of direct internal elections to select the party's national leadership, no such election has ever been held. The first Renovation leadership was a unity list that the party congress "proclaimed" into existence. Menem gained control of the PJ presidency in 1990 after Cafiero resigned, and in both 1991 and 1995, the leadership lists were drawn "in the government house" by a handful of top government officials[89] and later "proclaimed" by the party congress. Hence, twenty-five years after Perón's death and more than a decade after the Renovation process, the PJ leadership had still never changed hands by routinized means. Indeed, it had arguably never changed hands in the same way twice. The party leadership was "inherited" by Isabel Perón in 1974, taken, de facto, by the "62"–Orthodox coalition in 1983, taken over by the Renovators through the creation of a parallel leadership in 1987, and surrendered to the Menemists via resignation in 1990.

The fluidity of the PJ hierarchy contrasts sharply with other Latin American labor-based parties, including AD, APRA, the Brazilian Workers Party, the Chilean Communist Party, and – to a lesser extent – the Chilean

---

[86] Such was the case with Domingo Cavallo's Congressional nomination in Córdoba in 1987, Ortega's 1991 gubernatorial nomination in Tucumán, Porto's 1992 Senate nomination in 1992, and Duhalde's gubernatorial nomination in Buenos Aires 1995. In this last case, the provincial party congress gave Duhalde a "special mandate" to nominate Congressional candidates as well (*Clarín*, December 18, 1994, pp. 12–13).

[87] In Buenos Aires in 1993, for example, Governor Duhalde modified seven of the top twenty positions on the parliamentary after the primary election had been held (*Clarín*, August 18, 1993, p. 5).

[88] In the capital in 1997, an internal election was held, but various steps were taken to ensure the victory of President Menem's candidate, Scioli.

[89] Author's interviews with former acting party president Roberto García (June 23, 1997), former Interior Ministers Gustavo Béliz (July 21, 1997) and José Luis Manzano (December 5, 1997), and Senator José Manuel De la Sota (November 17, 1997). In many cases, party leaders learn of their nomination to the National Council through government operators such as Eduardo Bauza (author's interviews with Senators Daniel Baum (November 19, 1997) and José Manuel De la Sota (November 17, 1997)).

Socialist Party. In these parties, it is rare for outsiders to enter the upper ranks of the party hierarchy or rise quickly into top leadership positions, and old-guard leaders tend to be difficult to remove from the hierarchy.[90] Although the UCR is hardly a bureaucratic party, it, too, maintained important filters in the 1990s, including a prohibition against outsider candidates.

The Party-Union Linkage

A third area of weak routinization, which is examined in greater detail in Chapter 5, is the party–union linkage. Most labor-based parties, both in Europe and in Latin America, are characterized by a relatively stable and taken-for-granted set of rules and procedures governing trade union participation. Party–union linkages may take various forms. Parties may have union branches, or bodies that guarantee a quota of power in the leadership, as in AD's Labor Bureau or the PRI's labor sector. They may also have formal or informal rules and procedures guaranteeing unions a bloc of votes in leadership and/or candidate selection process, as the British Labour Party traditionally had. They may also have established norms of consultation, such as the Scandinavian *remiss* system (Compston 1995).

The PJ-union linkage is strikingly different. Although trade unions were an important member of the Peronist coalition through the late 1980s, the party–union linkage was never well routinized. Efforts to routinize this linkage, such as the Labor Party in the 1940s and the Vandorista project in the 1960s, were derailed by Perón, and although the unions enjoyed a near-hegemonic role in the party leadership between 1975 and 1985, this power was largely de facto. From the early 1960s until the mid-1980s, labor participation was channeled through two informal corporatist mechanisms: the "62" Organizations, which served as the body representing labor within the party leadership, and the *tercio* system, through which the unions held the right to name a third of party candidacies and leadership posts. Neither of these mechanisms was mentioned in party statutes, and neither was rigorously respected.

The "62" Organizations functioned as a collective body representing labor within Peronism. Its origins lie in a September 1957 CGT congress in which an alliance of forty-three Peronist and nineteen communist unions wrested control of the confederation from military-backed unions. When the communists left the group several months later, Peronist unionists began calling it the "political arm of Peronist labor" (Cavarozzi 1984: 83–6; McGuire 1993: 181). Though it lacked formal legal status, headquarters, a budget,

---

[90] The Mexican PRI is more similar to the PJ in this regard, as changes in presidential administrations historically generated thorough housecleanings of the party hierarchy and at times permitted relative outsiders (such as Luis Donaldo Colosio in the 1990s) to ascend to top leadership positions.

or regularized meetings and leadership rotation (McGuire 1997: 99),[91] the "62" became the unions' primary organizational linkage to Peronism, establishing a de facto monopoly over Peronist labor representation. By the early 1960s, the "62" was widely recognized by unionists, politicians, and even Perón himself as the authoritative representative of Peronist labor. As the PJ's "labor branch," the "62" held the right to nominate the union candidates for party leadership posts and elected office.

Despite the fact that it was never formally written down in the party statutes, the "62's" status as Peronism's "labor branch" was at least partially routinized in the 1960s and 1970s. Even labor factions that opposed the UOM-dominated "62" leadership, such as the New Current of Opinion in the late 1960s or the Group of "25" in the late 1970s, never renounced their membership in the "62" (Zorrilla 1983a: 127).[92] Indeed, when divisions occurred in the labor movement, leaders of defecting factions created parallel "62s" rather than establishing a new political linkage to Peronism.[93] Beginning in 1983, however, the "62's" informal status as the PJ's "labor branch" began to erode.

The *tercio* system, like the "62" Organizations, was never written down in party statutes. Yet according to Peronist tradition, candidacies and leadership positions are to be divided into thirds, with the political branch, the women's branch, and the labor branch each naming a third. The origins of this system are disputed. Whereas many labor leaders claim that the *tercio* system was invented by Perón and was respected "like a law" during the first Perón government,[94] others view it as a "retrospectively created myth" that was "more folklore than reality."[95] Although there is little evidence that the *tercio* system was ever applied with rigor, many Peronists in the 1960s and 1970s accepted the idea that union leaders, based on their corporate position, enjoyed a right to a certain quota of candidacies and leadership positions. It was, in one former union leader's words, "an unwritten rule that was respected."[96] The *tercio* was employed – though not rigorously – by

---

[91] McGuire (1997: 98) describes the "62" as an "intermittent assembly of 'notable' Peronist union leaders."

[92] According to Raul Feuermann of the Federal Capital branch of the telephone workers union (FOETRA), "The internal struggle was all within the "62." We fought, even exchanged gunfire, but we were all inside the "62" (author's interview, April 4, 1997).

[93] For example, when José Alonso and Andres Framini left the Vandor-dominated "62" in 1965, they created the "62 de Pie Junto a Perón" ("Standing Up beside Perón").

[94] Author's interview with Jorge Lobais, organization secretary of the textile workers union, December 11, 1997.

[95] Author's interviews with Congressional Deputies Juan Carlos Maqueda (September 11, 1997) and Lorenzo Dominguez (September 25, 1997).

[96] Author's interview with former "25" leader Gustavo Morato, June 13, 1997. Similarly, cemetery workers' union leader Domingo Petrecca describes the *tercio* as "a practice that was respected ... without an obligation and without a law" (author's interview, October 15, 1997).

neo-Peronist parties in 1965 (James 1988: 179) and by the PJ in 1973 and 1983. Nevertheless, some political leaders always questioned it, and it was routinely ignored in peripheral provinces. Hence, respect for the union *tercio* was always more a product of union power than of taken-for-grantedness.

In sum, notwithstanding the post-1983 "partyization" process and the democratizing reforms carried out by the Renovators, the PJ remained an informal and weakly routinized mass party at the onset of the 1990s. Despite maintaining a powerful mass organization, the PJ never developed an effective central bureaucracy that either integrated subunits vertically or linked them together horizontally. As a result, the contemporary PJ remained informal, segmented and decentralized. Moreover, the authority of party leadership bodies remained contested, the rules of the game for selecting and removing leaders remained fluid, and no stable mechanisms of labor participation were established.

THE EFFECTS OF LOW ROUTINIZATION: CHAOS AND FLEXIBILITY

Low levels of routinization are generally thought to have negative implications for parties. To a significant extent, this is true of Peronism. The PJ's weakly routinized structure results in a substantial degree of organizational inefficiency and, not infrequently, chaos. Particularly when it is out of power, the PJ suffers frequent institutional crises, including contested authority structures, parallel leaderships with competing claims to authority, and prolonged conflicts over internal rules of the game. At the national level, the PJ suffered contested party congresses every year between 1983 and 1987, and again in 1998. The PJ was formally split between December 1984 and July 1985, and it remained divided, de facto, through November 1987. The PJ also suffers frequent institutional crises at the provincial level. Failures to reach agreement on rules of the game for leadership and candidate selection routinely produce party schisms, and as a result, two or more Peronist parties often compete in a given election. Such splits occurred in five districts in the 1985,[97] seven districts in 1987,[98] two districts in 1989,[99] five districts in 1991,[100] two districts in 1993,[101] and four districts in 1995–6.[102] In several districts, including Corrientes, San Juan, and Santiago del Estero, two or more Peronist parties competed for several years.[103] As a result of this

---

[97] Buenos Aires, Corrientes, Jujuy, Rio Negro, and Salta.
[98] Catamarca, Corrientes, Jujuy, Neuquén, San Luis, Santiago del Estero, and Tucumán.
[99] Corrientes and Santiago del Estero.
[100] The Federal Capital, Buenos Aires, Catamarca, Corrientes, and Santiago del Estero.
[101] San Juan and Santiago del Estero.
[102] The Federal Capital, Rio Negro, San Juan, and Santiago del Estero.
[103] Although conflicts over the rules of the game became less frequent in the late 1990s, they did not disappear. In Córdoba, for example, the party split into parallel provincial councils in 1993, provoking a National Council intervention. In the Federal Capital, likewise, the

internal chaos, party leaders must devote a substantial amount of time and energy to resolving intraparty conflicts and creating ad hoc rules to structure authority relations. During the 1990s, this entailed dozens of costly interventions into provincial branches, the organization of multiple party congresses to resolve conflicts from earlier disputed congresses, occasional court battles when party authorities failed to resolve conflicts to the satisfaction of all factions, and frequent frenzied, last-minute negotiations so that "normal" institutional processes – such as party congresses and elections – could take place. These negotiations often resulted in modifications of the party charter to "legalize" ad hoc solutions to crises.

Weak routinization also undermined internal accountability and undermined the quality and effectiveness of Peronist party representation. As McGuire (1997) has argued, weak institutionalization has historically limited the PJ's capacity to represent organized labor. In the absence of taken-for-granted party structures to channel union demands, powerful unions often pursued their interests outside of the partisan and electoral arenas – with negative consequences for democracy.

Yet low routinization also yields a striking degree of flexibility. The PJ is flexible in two senses. First, its entrenched mass base provides it with a relatively stable reservoir of support that allows it to innovate – and make strategic mistakes – without suffering massive short-term electoral defections. The PJ's electorate of belonging, or what Ostiguy (1998: 339–56) calls the Peronist "hardcore," has been estimated at 30–5 percent of the electorate.[104] Hardcore Peronist voters tend to remain loyal to the PJ in the short to medium term even if they disagree with the party's candidates or policies (Ostiguy 1998). Although this reservoir of support is by no means infinitely deep,[105] the strength of the Peronist identity can be understood to raise the threshold at which hardcore voters choose to abandon the party. This electoral cushion yields important advantages. To use Sani and Sartori's (1983: 330) terms, the size of the PJ's "domain of identification" reduces the degree to which it must venture into the "domain of competition." Whereas the UCR and other parties must win the bulk of their votes in the domain of competition, the PJ must only add an additional 10–5 percent to its floor to ensure electoral victory.

PJ divided over the mayoral nomination in 1996, with Gustavo Beliz and the Green List leaving the party. A similar split nearly occurred a year later in anticipation of the 1997 legislative elections, as opposing factions called parallel congresses that each claimed a quorum. The party was unified only by a National Council intervention. And in La Rioja, warring party factions were so unable to agree upon rules of the game to compete for power that the party was governed by a National Council intervention throughout most of the 1990s.

[104] See Di Tella (1968: 65), Kirkpatrick (1971: 90), O'Donnell (1973: 172), Gervasoni (1998b: 2), and Ostiguy (1998: 346).

[105] As the electoral collapse of APRA in Peru and AD in Venezuela in the 1990s demonstrates, a sufficiently poor performance in government may cause even hardcore voters to defect.

Yet unlike mass parties discussed in the literature, the PJ's stable mass base is not accompanied by strategic inflexibility. Rather, the party's informal and weakly routinized structure provides it with a striking degree of innovative capacity. Specifically, three aspects of the PJ party structure provide it with a degree of strategic flexibility that is generally not found in mass bureaucratic parties: (1) structural flexibility; (2) bureaucratic fluidity; and (3) mutual autonomy between higher- and lower-level bodies.

Structural Flexibility

First, key features of the PJ organizational structure are easily modified. In highly routinized parties, the structure of the organization tends to be "sticky," or difficult to change. Organizational features such as the form of subunits, the structure of the party bureaucracy, or the party's linkages to ancillary organizations such as unions have been in place for many years and are often widely taken for granted. To the extent that these structures are taken as "relative fixtures" within the party, efforts to search for or introduce alternative structures are limited. In the PJ, by contrast, few pieces of the party organization are well entrenched, and a result, the party structure tends to be far less "sticky." Virtually no aspect of the PJ organization is widely taken for granted or reinforced by powerful vested interests. As a result, they may be easily modified or even removed without substantial resistance from within. Thus, instead of being sticky, the PJ organization is relatively pliant, changing more or less in line with the short-term goals of dominant party actors. Rather than attaching themselves to particular organizational forms, local and national party leaders are open to, and indeed routinely experiment with, new ones. A clear example is the base unit. Local leaders and activists routinely abandon base units in favor of alternative organizational forms, such as soup kitchens, community centers, and informal "working groups." Another example is the party–labor linkage. As Chapter 5 will show, the PJ's traditional mechanisms of union participation, the "62" Organizations and the *tercio* system, were rather easily dismantled once unions lost the power to enforce them.

Bureaucratic Fluidity

Second, in contrast to most mass bureaucratic parties, the PJ hierarchy is characterized by substantial fluidity, which permits rapid and thorough leadership change. Thus, peripheral leaders such as Cesar Arias, Eduardo Bauza, Gustavo Beliz, and Alberto Kohan, as well as outsiders such as Carlos Reutemann, could "parachute" directly into the National Council's Executive Board in the early 1990s. Just as leaders may rise quickly through party ranks, they may also be easily removed. Indeed, PJ leadership changes frequently entail virtual "housecleanings" that remove the entire old-guard leadership from the National Council. Such housecleanings occurred in 1985, when more than 80 percent of the Executive Board was replaced, and in 1987, when more than 90 percent of the Executive Board was replaced. Unlike many other mass parties, then, the PJ experiences high rates of leadership turnover. Between 1983 and 1987, turnover in the National Council Executive Board was a full 100 percent. Although the turnover rate declined somewhat after 1987, it remained relatively high. Between 1990 and 1995, turnover in the Executive Board was 63 percent. To place these figures in comparative perspective, in his study of French parties in the 1960s and 1970s, William Schonfeld (1981: 223–5) found average turnover rates ranging from a low of 19 percent (the Communist Party) to a high of 44 percent (Gaullism).

As important as housecleanings is the *threat* of housecleaning. Because old-guard leaders lack tenure security in the party hierarchy, maintaining those positions requires that they remain in the good graces of those with "real" power in the party – generally those who hold high public offices. Thus, the PJ often experiences a "bandwagoning" phenomenon,[106] in which members of defeated factions defect to the winning faction in an effort to avoid losing their positions in the leadership. Because Peronists find bandwagoning to be a safer strategy than holding out, one rarely finds "entrenched bureaucrats" in the PJ. Rather than being Downs' (1967) "conservers," PJ officials become converts.[107]

Mutual Autonomy of Higher- and Lower-Level Bodies

Third, PJ leaders – particularly office-holding leaders – enjoy substantial autonomy from the party hierarchy. This autonomy has two sources. First, the PJ's formal leadership bodies lack taken-for-granted authority, and the bureaucracy lacks both the resources that politicians need to advance their careers and the stable career paths and tenure security needed to preserve them. As a result, when the PJ is in power, it tends to be vulnerable to office-based cooptation. To a significant extent, "control of the state means control of the party."[108]

Second, the segmented nature of the PJ organization enhances leadership autonomy. Organizational theorists have argued that strong horizontal ties among structurally equivalent actors are likely to produce a "cohesive group" with a "common understanding about their collective interests" (Knoke 1990: 11–12; also Duverger 1954/1963: 48–50). In the absence of

---

[106] Corrales (1996b: 206) uses the term "bandwagoning" in a similar fashion. McGuire (1997: 27) uses the term to describe the strategic behavior of Peronist unions.
[107] Although such political conversions are often viewed as an example of the lack of principle of Peronist leaders, given the institutional structure of Peronism, they may also be understood as rational efforts at political survival.
[108] Author's interview with former Congressional Deputy Jorge Arguello, May 19, 1997.

such horizontal links, actors may fall into a hub-and-spokes relationship with central leaderships. When these leaderships control needed resources, they can play secondary leaders against each other, maintaining centralized authority via a "divide and conquer" strategy (Knoke 1990: 12). Applying these ideas to political parties, Ansell and Fish (1999) argue that centralized leaderships often emerge in parties that are both ideologically and geographically fragmented, and in which a single leader establishes a multiplicity of ties to subgroups that cross-cut the party's internal cleavages. Although Ansell and Fish do not link such "non-charismatic personalism" to a particular party organizational form, hub-and-spokes relationships are arguably much more likely to emerge in parties that lack effective structures to link secondary leaders horizontally and bring them together in a regularized way. The PJ is a clear example of such a hub-and-spokes phenomenon. In the absence of strong horizontal links, secondary Peronist leaders have difficulty acting collectively to check the power of office-holding leaders. Consequently, office-holding leaders tend to enjoy substantial room to maneuver when developing and carrying out strategies.

Yet leadership autonomy should not be conflated with centralized or autocratic leadership. Although the PJ's segmented structure provides leaders with substantial autonomy vis-á-vis secondary leaders, this autonomy works both ways. Party leaders – even office-holding leaders – lack effective mechanisms with which to impose discipline on party subunits. According to PJ legislator Fernando Maurette,

> In other parties, everything one does has to be approved by the party hierarchy.... Your discourse has to conform to certain party standards. In Peronism, none of that is true. You can do or say whatever you want.[109]

Local autonomy is reinforced by Argentina's federal structure, which allows local and provincial office holders to establish independent patronage bases. Thus, unlike centralized mass parties such as AD or the French and Chilean Communist parties, in which subunits must strictly adhere to the national party line or face expulsion, the PJ exhibits a striking degree of internal tolerance and diversity. Indeed, the PJ functions like an organizational "big tent," containing within it divergent and often contradictory elements. During the 1990s, the party's neoliberal national leadership coexisted with subunits that were nationalist, traditional populist, social democratic, and even socialist.[110] Similar patterns of mutual autonomy, described by American political scientist Samuel Eldersveld as "stratarchy" (1964: 9–10), have been

---

[109] Author's interview, July 4, 1997.
[110] This organizational tolerance runs counter to conventional understandings of the movement as "verticalist" or authoritarian. For example, *La Prensa* observed in 1990 that the PJ "displays a curious degree of intra-party tolerance... that few of the other [parties] exhibit" (February 7, 1990, p. 4).

observed in U.S. parties (see Key 1949; Mayhew 1986). They have also been observed in other Latin American parties, such as the leading nonleftist parties in Brazil (Mainwaring 1999).

Mutual autonomy is critical to the PJ's adaptive capacity. Ian McAllister (1991) has argued that the existence of ideologically diverse factions contributed to the Australian Labor Party's (ALP) programmatic adaptation in the 1980s by providing an "institutional mechanism for accommodating the divergent beliefs of activists" (1991: 208). According to McAllister, the ALP's programmatic shift entailed policies that were "notably unpopular within the party" (1991: 211), but organized factions

> absorbed the dissatisfaction of traditional activists, unhappy with the changing appeal of the party. As they have seen the party's ideological raison d'être weakened by new policies, the faction provides a party in miniature into which they can retreat (1991: 223).

The PJ's decentralized system of *agrupaciones* serves a similar function, for it provides arenas in which activists can practice their own form of Peronism despite substantial disagreements with the national party. Thus, whereas activists in centralized bureaucratic parties must often choose between carrying out the national party strategy and leaving (or being expelled from) the party, Peronist activists can largely avoid that choice.

This disjuncture between the leadership and base organizations provides the PJ with an important advantage in electoral competition, for it allows the leadership to pursue "outward-oriented" electoral strategies aimed at independent voters (such as the nomination of attractive nonparty candidates, the formation of electoral alliances with ideologically dissimilar parties, and the pursuit of policies that diverge from the traditional program) while base-level organizations continue to look inward, targeting traditional Peronist votes. In other words, while Peronist base organizations attend to the domain of identification, PJ leaders are relatively free to pursue votes in the domain of competition.

In sum, the PJ exhibits a substantial degree of organizational fluidity. Whereas the organizational structures and programs of routinized or bureaucratic parties tend to be "sticky," PJ leaders are often able to modify both the party's structure and its strategy in response to environmental challenges. When party rules or organizational forms are perceived to hinder the pursuit of short-term party goals, they can be modified or dismantled without extensive debate. When the composition of formal leadership bodies does not correspond to the real balance of power in the party, they may be circumvented through informal parallel organizations, or they can be quickly recomposed in line with the real balance of power in the party. And when aspects of the party program are perceived to undermine the party's ability either to govern or win votes, office-holding leaders are relatively unconstrained by old-guard leaders or entrenched decision rules when they seek to modify or abandon them. Although a fluid internal structure does not guarantee that PJ leaders will choose appropriate adaptive strategies, it does facilitate the search for and implementation of such strategies. The chapters that follow demonstrate how such organizational adaptation took place in practice between 1983 and 1999.

CHAPTER 4

Populism in Crisis: Environmental Change and Party Failure, 1983–1985

On the evening of October 30, 1983, as the polls closed on the first election of Argentina's new democratic era, Peronists who gathered at the party headquarters were in a state of shock. Anxious party leaders repeatedly asked one another the same question: "When do the votes from the industrial belt come in?"[1] It soon became clear that those votes would not arrive, and that for the first time in its history, the PJ would lose a free election. The election night scene highlights one of two environmental challenges that Peronism confronted during the 1980s. Changes in Argentina's social structure had eroded the PJ's industrial working-class base, weakening the unions that had traditionally linked the party to its urban base and creating new groups of voters with weaker ties to the Peronist organization and subculture. Over the course of the decade, changing economic conditions presented the PJ with a second challenge: The debt crisis and the collapse of the inward-oriented economic model fundamentally altered national policy-making parameters, limiting the viability of the traditional Peronist program. The PJ's survival as a major political force hinged on its capacity to adapt to these environmental changes.

This chapter examines the electoral and economic challenges that confronted the PJ in the 1980s, as well as the strategic choices that party leaders faced in responding to them. It begins with a brief description of the PJ coalition and program at the outset of the contemporary period. It argues that the PJ was a de facto labor party in the immediate postdictatorship period. Unions served as the primary linkage to the party's urban base, and union bosses played a hegemonic role in the party leadership. The chapter then examines the environmental challenges facing the PJ in the post-1983 period. It argues that de facto laborism was a poor fit with an environment characterized by deindustrialization and working-class decline, and that this

---

[1] Taken from Beliz (1988: 74).

mismatch was a major cause of the party's unprecedented electoral defeats in 1983 and 1985.

PARTY AND LABOR IN 1983

The PJ emerged from military rule in 1983 as a de facto labor party. Trade unions played a hegemonic role in the party leadership, dominating decision-making and leadership and candidate selection processes. However, union influence was not channeled through institutional mechanisms, but rather was the de facto product of the raw power of the unions and the weakness of the party's political wing.

De facto laborism was rooted in the proscription period. After Perón's overthrow, unions became the "chief organizing force and institutional expression of Peronism" (James 1988: 76). With Perón in exile and the party banned, organized labor was "the only political instrument Peronism had," and as a result, union leaders "were transformed into the political representatives of Peronism."[2] In urban areas, Peronist politicians and activists depended so heavily on the unions that party and union came to be viewed as "two sides of the same coin."[3] Although Perón retained substantial authority over the labor movement while he lived, his death in 1974 created an enormous leadership vacuum in the PJ. Because the party lacked a stable territorial structure or a substantial number of leaders with independent support bases, the unions, whose organizational and mobilization power dwarfed that of the political wing, were well positioned to take over the party leadership (Torre 1983: 120–2). After defeating López Rega in 1975, Peronist labor "reached the highest point of corporative power it had ever achieved" (Delich 1982: 136), as the "62" virtually imposed Antonio Cafiero as economic minister and Carlos Ruckauf as labor minister. Labor hegemony was reinforced during the 1976–83 military dictatorship. With party activity repressed and much of the Peronist leadership in prison or exile, the unions again became hubs of PJ activity, providing office space, money, printing presses, and jobs. Peronist politics "was done in the union halls,"[4] as PJ leaders who escaped repression took jobs as union lawyers, accountants, or advisors.[5] Even acting president Deolindo Bittel relied on the unions to finance his activities.[6]

---

[2] Author's interview with former PJ leader Carlos Grosso, November 28, 1997.
[3] Author's interview with former "62" leader Miguel Gazzera, May 30, 1997.
[4] Author's interview with José Pedraza, general secretary of the railway workers union, July 10, 1997.
[5] Post-1983 party leaders who worked in unions during the dictatorships include Vice Presidents Eduardo Duhalde and Carlos Ruckauf, Governors Antonio Cafiero, Vicente Joga, Ruben Marín, and Jose Maria Vernet, and dozens of legislators.
[6] A resident of the distant province of Chaco, Bittel lived in a hotel paid for by the glass workers union when he was in the capital (author's interview with Deolindo Bittel, November 13, 1996).

The PJ thus entered the 1983 transition dominated by organized labor. The primary source of labor hegemony was control over financial and organizational resources. The unions' control over workers' health insurance programs and access to leading industrialists[7] placed them in a far better position than PJ politicians to finance political activity. Unions sponsored the bulk of the PJ's urban infrastructure. They provided locales for campaign headquarters, printed campaign materials, contributed scores of activists, and carried out most of the party's fund raising (Cordeu et al. 1985: 61–3).[8] Presidential candidate Italo Luder's main offices were provided by the metal workers union (UOM),[9] and the PJ's major campaign rallies were organized "almost exclusively" by labor.[10]

The unions used their organizational strength to gain a virtual hegemony over the PJ leadership. The unions dominated the party at the local and provincial levels. In the Federal Capital, where two of the three largest party factions were labor-based,[11] the "62" used its control of the local party congress to dominate the leadership and candidate selection process. As a result, unionists gained fifteen of twenty-eight seats in the PJ leadership, both senate candidacies, and five of the top seven spots on the list for the Chamber of Deputies (Cordeu et al. 1985: 152–3; Palermo 1986a: 99). In Santa Fe, union bosses imposed the gubernatorial ticket of UOM accountant José Maria Vernet and food workers union leader Carlos Martinez (Fernandez 1993: 36), and became the "power behind the throne" during the initial years of the Vernet government.[12] In Buenos Aires, "62" support was critical to Herminio Iglesias' gubernatorial nomination,[13] and in exchange, the "62" received a third of the party's Chamber of Deputies seats. In Córdoba, the "62" leader Alejo Simó gained the vice gubernatorial nomination, and in Santa Cruz, unionists secured two of the three top positions on the party's legislative list.[14]

---

[7] For example, oil workers union leader Diego Ibañez raised money in the oil sector, while paper workers union leader Fernando Donaires acquired paper donations to cover much of the party's flier production (Cordeu et al. 1985: 61–3).

[8] According to one activist, "I was with the MUSO faction, which means we depended on the tobacco employees union. I had nothing to do with the union, but that's where we held our student meetings, and that's where we were sent whenever we had to print up more fliers" (author's interview with Mariano Cabello, October 16, 1996).

[9] *Clarín*, August 7, 1983, p. 15.

[10] *Clarín*, October 18, 1983, pp. 2–3.

[11] These were the Metropolitan Political-Labor Bloc, which was sponsored by the "62," and 30 de Marzo, which was backed by the "25" labor faction. The only major faction without a labor ally was the Peronist Unity Front (FUP).

[12] Author's interview with plastic workers union leader Vicente Mastecola, October 7, 1997.

[13] *Clarín*, August 21, 1983, pp. 2–3; August 31, 1983, p. 6; and September 1, 1983, p. 16.

[14] Unionists were also elected to Congress in Catamarca, Formosa, Mendoza, La Rioja, Salta, San Luis, and Tucuman.

The unions also established hegemony over the national party. Although they initially held no formal position in the PJ leadership, union leaders such as Lorenzo Miguel (UOM) and Diego Ibañez (oil workers union) dominated party decision making. During the democratic transition, it was the union leadership, and not acting party president Bittel, that represented the PJ in secret negotiations with the military (Munck 1998: 150–3).[15] During the PJ's first posttransition congress in March, Miguel's makeshift office in a nearby union hall was "was converted into a kind of Mecca, where groups of delegates went in search of advice."[16] Presidential hopefuls such as Bittel, Luder, and Cafiero competed for the support of the "62," and factions without ties to the "62" found themselves marginalized from the centers of decision making. The Luder-Bittel presidential ticket was "chosen by Miguel and Ibañez"[17] after a series of back room meetings that were organized and run by the "62" (Cordeu et al. 1985: 27–30), and the party platform was drawn up by a committee selected by the "62."[18] The "62" converted its de facto power into formal power in the September 1983 party congress, during which Miguel was elected acting party president. Labor gained 29 of the PJ's 111 seats in the Chamber of Deputies in 1983, and Ibañez was elected president of the legislative bloc.

THE ENVIRONMENTAL CHALLENGE

De facto laborism was a poor fit with the political and economic environment that Peronism confronted at the outset of the contemporary democratic period. The PJ faced a twofold environmental challenge in the 1980s. On the one hand, deindustrialization had weakened the labor movement and changes in the structure and preferences of the electorate eroded the foundations of the PJ's traditional electoral base. At the same time, new constraints imposed by the domestic and international economic context reduced the viability of the PJ's traditional program.

The Coalitional Challenge: Deindustrialization and Working-Class Decline

The social bases of Argentine politics changed substantially between 1974 and 1990. Although this transformation was in part due to long-term trends

---

[15] When military leaders invited Bittel to negotiations on the terms of the democratic transition in February, Bittel had to travel to a beach resort to consult with Miguel before responding (*Clarín*, February 16, 1983, p. 3). Shortly afterward, military leaders bypassed Bittel entirely and began secret negotiations with Miguel and other union leaders (*Clarín*, April 3, 1983, pp. 10–11; April 9, 1983, p. 2; April 10, 1983, p. 10).
[16] *Clarín*, March 6, 1983, p. 6.
[17] Author's interview with railway workers leader José Pedraza, July 10, 1997.
[18] *Clarín*, September 7, 1983, p. 5.

toward a more service-based economy, it was also a product of the policies carried out under the 1976–83 dictatorship. Through a combination of repression and economic restructuring, the military government had sought to destroy the social bases of populism (Canitrot 1980; Villarreal 1987). In large measure, it succeeded. Trade liberalization, together with the deep economic crisis of the 1980s, decimated the manufacturing sector. Approximately fifteen thousand industrial firms went bankrupt during the decade that followed the 1976 coup (Lewis 1990: 470). The industrial sector contracted at an average rate of 4.7 percent a year between 1977 and 1981, falling from more than 29 percent of GDP in 1974 to just 22 percent in 1981 (Smith 1989: 253). At the same time, the commercial, financial, and service sectors boomed.

Deindustrialization decimated the industrial working class. Employment in the manufacturing sector declined by 26 percent between 1975 and 1980, and by more than a third between 1970 and 1990 (Smith 1989: 264; Powers 1995: 91–2). The working class also became more geographically dispersed. Employment in factories of more than one thousand workers fell by 48 percent between 1974 and 1985, while employment in factories of more than four hundred workers fell by 34 percent (Palomino 1987: 104; Beliz 1988: 73). Moreover, areas of industrial concentration, such as the Federal Capital, Greater Buenos Aires, Córdoba, and Rosario, lost thousands of manufacturing jobs as industry spread to the peripheral provinces (Palomino 1987: 108–9; Quintar 1990: 226).

Working-class decline produced a dual transformation of the urban popular sectors. On the one hand, the erosion of the blue-collar sector was accompanied by the vigorous growth of the retail and service sectors. This growth was part of a longer-term trend toward the white and pink collarization of the Argentine workforce. Between 1960 and 1980, employment in the retail and service sectors had expanded by 54 percent, increasing from 37.8 percent of the economically active population (EAP) to 49.1 percent of the EAP (Palomino 1987: 207). By contrast, employment in industry and transportation declined by 5.3 percent during that period. According to another analysis, the salaried working class declined from 45.8 percent of the EAP in 1947 to 34.4 percent in 1980, while the salaried middle class expanded from 18.7 percent of the EAP in 1947 to 30.0 percent in 1980 (Torrado 1992: 146). This process was accelerated during the military dictatorship. More than 75 percent of the formal sector jobs created during the 1970s were located in the white-collar, retail, or personal service sectors (Palomino 1987: 40).

At the same time, deindustrialization swelled the ranks of the urban poor. Hundreds of thousands of unemployed and underemployed workers entered the urban informal economy in the 1970s and 1980s. The informal sector expanded from 15.6 percent of the EAP in 1970 to 28.5 percent of EAP in 1990 (Tokman 1996: 72), reaching as high as 40 percent in deindustrialized zones such as Greater Buenos Aires (Orsatti 1991: 173–4). By the mid-1980s, then, the industrial working class was smaller, and the urban popular sectors more heterogeneous and fragmented, than at any time since the 1930s. Whereas in 1973 one of every eight voters had been a factory worker, a decade later, only one in fourteen voters was a factory worker (Ranis 1995: 8).

These social structural changes threatened the PJ's coalitional bases in two ways. First, they eroded the party's union-based linkages to its urban base. Deindustrialization decimated the unions that been the core of the Peronist coalition. Membership in industrial unions fell by 23 percent between 1973 and 1984 (Abós 1986: 187–8). Traditionally powerful unions such as the auto workers (SMATA), the textile workers (AOT), and the UOM suffered even heavier losses: SMATA membership fell from 121,000 in 1973 to 54,000 in 1984; AOT membership fell from 150,000 in 1979 to 74,000 in 1984; and UOM membership fell from 304,000 in 1970 to 170,000 in the early 1990s (Abós 1986: 187–8).[19] At the same time, membership in service sector unions increased by 17 percent (Abós 1986: 187–8). Between 1973 and 1984, retail workers union membership increased from 280,000 to 408,000, bank workers union membership increased from 84,000 to 186,000, restaurant workers union membership increased from 55,000 to 80,000, and sports referees union membership increased from 16,000 to 60,000 (Abós 1986: 187–8). These changes produced an important recomposition of the labor movement (see Table 4.1). Whereas industrial and transportation unions represented 67 percent of overall union membership in 1945, by the mid-1980s, they represented only 41 percent of union membership. During the same period, commercial and service sector unions expanded from 27 percent to 51 percent of total union membership (Godio 1991b: 372). By 1983, then, industrial unions were a minority presence within the labor movement. Only one of the country's ten largest unions – the UOM – was from the manufacturing sector, and the retail workers union surpassed the UOM as the largest single union.

Because industrial unions had historically been Peronism's primary linkage to the urban working class, the weakening of these unions threatened to erode the party's organizational base, mobilizational capacity, and overall presence in working- and lower-class society. Although service sector unions grew considerably, they were unlikely to serve as effective linkages to the Peronist base. Due to the deconcentrated nature of the work in many retail and service industries, unions such as the retail workers, restaurant workers, custodians, sports referees, and private security guards have little mobilizational capacity, rarely engage in collective action, and tend not to forge strong collective identities.[20] Rather, most of them focus primarily on

---

[19] UOM figures are based on the author's interview with UOM General Secretary Lorenzo Miguel, June 15, 1997.

[20] Bank workers unions, state employees unions, and teachers unions are exceptions in this regard.

TABLE 4.1. *Changes in the Sectoral Composition of the Argentine Labor Movement (Percentage of Overall Union Membership)*

Sector	1945	1965	1984/1986
Industry/mining/gas/electricity	36	38	31
Transportation/communication	31	17	10
Retail	10	13	15
Services	17	28	36
Construction	4	1	6
Agriculture	2	3	2

Source: Godio (1991b: 372).

the distribution of selective incentives such as health care. Workers in these unions tend to have weaker class identities – and to be less Peronist – than blue-collar workers (Godio and Palomino 1987: 46; Palomino 1987: 72).

Second, deindustrialization threatened the PJ's traditional electoral base. Because voters in the growing service and informal sectors had little contact with industrial unions, the influence – in terms of both electoral campaigns and long-term political socialization – that union-based party organizations could exercise over them (and their families) was limited. Moreover, the identities and interests of these new voters differed from those of traditional working-class voters. The decline of the industrial working-class created two new groups of voters: a "new urban poor," based in the urban informal sector, and a "new middle class," based in the retail and service sectors. The new urban poor tend to be "organically disconnected from union activities" and other forms of class-based organization (Villarreal 1987: 85). Although informal sector workers are often poorer than their blue-collar counterparts, the heterogeneous and geographically dispersed nature of their work weakens collective identities, creating "objective interests not easily articulable with those of wage workers" (Villarreal 1987: 85). The growth of this sector thus posed a potential electoral threat for the PJ. Whereas industrial unions had to a large extent fused Peronist and working-class identities, in the context of an eroding union-based linkage and weakening class identities, it was far from certain that the urban poor would remain solidly Peronist.

The new middle class also differed from the PJ's traditional electorate. Though often unionized, these white-collar workers shared little in common with manual workers in terms of their work, living, and educational experiences.[21] Generally better educated, more socially and geographically mobile,

---

[21] As Godio and Palomino (1987: 46) write, "Teachers, bank workers, state employees, hospital workers, [and] retail salespeople have in common with industrial workers the fact that their existence depends on their salary.... But the social location, work experiences, skills, and education and training backgrounds differ considerably from those of blue collar workers. And possibly their values and social and political identities differ as well."

and less attached to traditional party identities than their working- and lower-class counterparts, these voters – particularly younger ones – swelled the ranks of the independent electorate. This emerging group of younger, more independent voters constituted a "new center" of the Argentine electorate. This sector was new in that its voters' attachments to established parties were weaker and their electoral preferences more unstable. It constituted a center not in left-right terms but in terms of the Peronist–anti-Peronist cleavage that had dominated Argentine politics since the 1940s (Ostiguy 1998). Although most new middle-class voters did not identify themselves as Peronist, many of them did not share the deep antipathy toward Peronism that characterized many traditional socialist, Radical, and conservative voters. Indeed, many of them came from Peronist families. Hence, the "new center" bloc constituted a domain of competition (Sani and Sartori 1983: 330), or a bloc of independent voters who were available for both Peronist and non-Peronist appeals.

Unattached voters were also mobilized by a new set of issues in the post-1983 period. The Argentine electorate shifted in a more socially and politically liberal direction in the 1980s. As in the advanced industrialized countries, younger, better educated middle-class voters tended to be more liberal on social issues such as divorce or the role of the Catholic Church, less nationalistic, and more concerned about human and civil rights (Catterberg 1991: 83). Although this shift was partly a product of long-term sociological developments such as increased education, wealth, and social mobility, the salience of human rights was also a product of the experience of the 1970s. The violence and chaos of the 1973–6 period and the brutal repression of the military dictatorship left a powerful mark on the electorate, leading voters to place a greater emphasis on democratic institutions and the protection of human rights (Catterberg 1985: 266; 1991: 82–4).[22]

The Party System: Incentives for Capturing the Center

If changes in the structure of the electorate expanded the "domain of competition" by creating a larger independent electorate, party system dynamics created a strong incentive for the PJ to pursue those voters. Optimal labor-based party strategies may be expected to vary based on the degree of competition that they face on the left and in the center (Kitschelt 1994a: 117–25). Parties facing an emerging challenge on the left may opt to forego Downsian strategies in favor of "oligopolistic competition," or an effort to defeat the competitor on their own flank (Kitschelt 1994a: 128–30; 144–6).

---

[22] According to Edgardo Catterberg, "the freedom to speak, to have an opinion, and to express oneself were salient political beliefs" in the aftermath of the dictatorship, and these values "were especially strong among the younger population" (1991: 83).

By contrast, parties that continue to monopolize the vote within their own electoral bloc have a stronger incentive to capture the center or pivot of the party system (Kitschelt 1994a: 144).[23]

The dynamics of party competition in the 1980s created a strong incentive for the PJ to pursue the latter strategy. Post-1945 Argentine politics was structured by a class-based Peronism/anti-Peronism cleavage (Ostiguy 1998).[24] The party system divided into Peronist and anti-Peronist blocs, with Peronism representing the working and lower classes and the centrist UCR and a handful of small socialist, conservative, and provincial parties competing within the (predominantly middle- and upper-middle-class) anti-Peronist space (Ostiguy 1998). Despite the proscription of Peronism and repeated interruptions of electoral politics, the post-1945 party system developed a relatively stable bipolar dynamic. In 1983, the PJ and UCR accounted for 92 percent of the presidential vote, and in 1989, they accounted for 86 percent of the presidential vote. Although these figures fell slightly in midterm elections,[25] most analysts continued to characterize the party system as a predominantly two-party system (Catterberg 1991: 50; McGuire 1995: 224–6; Jones 1997: 264–9).

In such a context, an optimal vote-maximizing strategy would be to capture the emerging center between Peronism and anti-Peronism. This incentive was reinforced by the absence of intrabloc competition on the PJ's working- and lower-class flank. Since 1945, no political force had effectively challenged Peronism's electoral hegemony over the working and lower classes. The two significant national parties that emerged in the 1980s, the center-left Intransigent Party (PI) and the conservative Center Democratic Union (UCeDe), posed little threat to the PJ's traditional electorate. Although they differed on left-right issues, the PI and UCeDe were both middle- and upper-middle-class-based parties whose voters tended to be anti-Peronist. Indeed, the modest electoral inroads that each of these parties made in the

---

[23] Kitschelt's distinction between office-seeking and vote-seeking strategies is not made here because in two-party presidential systems (such as Argentina's during the 1980s and 1990s) in which the party that wins a plurality of the vote generally governs alone, vote-seeking strategies are virtually identical to office-seeking strategies. On the distinction between these two strategies in parliamentary systems, see Strom (1990a, 1990b).

[24] Although the Peronist/anti-Peronist cleavage resembled Western European cleavages in that it was class-based, it differed from the European cases in that the cleavage corresponded primarily to sociocultural, rather than left–right, differences (Ostiguy 1998). Ostiguy (1998) calls this sociocultural dimension the "high–low" axis, with "high" referring to the culturally *bien educado* (or "proper") and "low" referring to the culturally *popular*. Rather than becoming the Argentine left, Ostiguy (1998) argues, Peronism became the "low," or the sociocultural representative of the lower and working classes. At the same time, non-Peronist parties came to represent the "high," or the sociocultural patterns of the middle and upper classes.

[25] The two major parties accounted for 78 percent of the vote in 1985 and 81 percent of the vote in 1987.

1980s were limited to wealthy urban centers such as the Federal Capital.[26] Neither party performed well in Peronist strongholds such as the poor districts of Greater Buenos Aires or the northern provinces. Hence, the PJ's pursuit of new middle-class votes could be expected to have relatively low costs in terms of defections on its own flank.

The Programmatic Challenge: ISI Exhaustion, the Debt Crisis, and Neoliberalism

Since the advent of the debt crisis of 1982, the external economic environment and domestic economic crises have imposed considerable constraints on governing parties in Latin America. In Argentina, the statist, inward-oriented economic model that emerged in the 1930s and was consolidated under Perón had entered into crisis in the 1960s (O'Donnell 1973). Efforts by the military governments led by Juan Carlos Onganía (1966–70) and Jorge Videla (1976–81) to restructure Argentine capitalism achieved only partial and short-lived successes (Smith 1989; Lewis 1990). Under Videla, Economic Minister José Martinez de Hoz implemented an orthodox stabilization program and liberalized the country's trade and investment regimes. However, Martinez de Hoz's program did not fully dismantle the ISI state. Indeed, it used an influx of cheap foreign loans to prop up and even expand the country's inefficient state firms and bloated bureaucracy. Consequently, the foreign debt increased from $6.6 billion in 1976 to $32.2 billion in 1983 (Smith 1989: 261). The military's project began to unravel in 1980 when a wave of bankruptcies, currency speculation, and capital flight brought the financial sector to the brink of collapse, triggering a massive economic contraction. GDP declined by 6.2 percent in 1981 and another 5.2 percent in 1982. To make matters worse, the advent of the debt crisis plunged the country into a deep fiscal crisis. Whereas the net transfer of new loans and debt payments had constituted an inflow of $3.1 billion a year between 1980 and 1982, between 1983 and 1986 it constituted an *outflow* of $2.25 billion a year (Smith 1989: 284). It was in this context that the military government launched its ill-fated invasion of the Falklands/Malvinas Islands in April 1982, which led to Argentina's defeat in a war with Great Britain and, shortly thereafter, the collapse of the authoritarian regime (Munck 1998).

The government of Raúl Alfonsín thus inherited a profound economic crisis when it took office in 1983. Elected on the heels of a failed right-wing dictatorship and facing a powerful opposition labor movement, the Radical government was both unwilling and unable to implement the kinds of orthodox policies that were increasingly being called for by international

---

[26] For example, while the UCeDe and PI gained 10.4 percent and 7.9 percent, respectively, in the capital, they each won less than 1 percent of the vote in peripheral provinces such as Chaco, Corrientes, Formosa, Jujuy, and Salta.

lending institutions. In 1984, the new government challenged the IMF by suspending debt payment and implementing Keynesian pump-priming policies to "reinvigorate the economy and establish an equitable distribution of income."[27] The Keynesian strategy failed, and by early 1985, inflation had reached nearly 25 percent a month (Smith 1989: 272-4). Although the crisis compelled Alfonsín to implement stabilization policies, the government's "shock" package was heterodox, not orthodox. The June 1985 Austral Plan, which sought to control inflation through temporary wage and price controls, scored some initial successes but ultimately fell victim to distributional conflicts among powerful labor and business groups (Smith 1990). The resurgence of inflation forced the government to adopt increasingly orthodox policies in 1987 and 1988, but business and labor opposition, together with the UCR's crushing defeat in the 1987 midterm elections, weakened the government, eroded its credibility, and eventually sent the economy into a spiral of recession and hyperinflation. GDP contracted in both 1988 and 1989, foreign reserves were dangerously depleted, and in early 1989, both the IMF and World Bank suspended new payments to Argentina due to the government's failure to meet its payment obligations. To make matters worse, as the specter of a Peronist victory in the 1989 elections grew, capital flight and financial speculation soared, culminating in a massive run on the dollar in February 1989. The so-called market coup set off a hyperinflationary burst that brought the economy to the point of collapse; inflation reached 3,620 percent between August 1988 and July 1989 (Smith 1990: 29).

Carlos Menem thus took office in July 1989 in the context of an unprecedented economic crisis. Inflation had reached 197 percent a month, badly weakening the state's capacity to implement policy or mediate social conflict. GDP had descended to its 1974 level (Smith 1992: 48), the fiscal deficit stood at 12 percent of GDP, and the foreign debt had risen to $58.6 billion.[28] With its foreign reserves dwindling and without access to foreign credit, Argentina was virtually bankrupt. The hyperinflationary crisis, together with the longer-term constraints of the debt crisis and an increasingly competitive and liberalized global economy, raised the costs of the redistributive policies that had been at the core of the Peronist program. For any government, the questions of economic stabilization and reestablishment of ties to the international financial community would necessarily be at the top of the agenda.

The Strategic Choices Facing Peronist Leaders

Party adaptation and survival in this new context arguably required the reconfiguration, if not the very destruction, of the labor-based populist

---

[27] Economic Minister Bernardo Grinspun, quoted in Smith (1989: 272).
[28] *Latin American Weekly Report*, July 27, 1989, p. 4.

coalition that Peronism had represented since the 1940s. In the electoral realm, the erosion of Peronism's traditional base and the expansion of the independent electorate meant that the PJ would have to adapt in two ways. First, it would have to reconfigure its linkages to the urban working and lower classes. In an increasingly deindustrialized context, unions were a less effective means of mobilizing urban voters. Maintaining the support of a fragmented, heterogeneous, and nonunionized urban poor sector required that the party deemphasize traditional corporate, union-based linkages in favor of territorial-based linkages. Second, the PJ would have to win a portion of the emerging independent electorate. Winning such votes entailed a deemphasis of class-based appeals and traditional Peronist language and symbols, as well as a rethinking of the party's profile with respect to democracy, human rights, and other "new middle-class" issues. It also entailed a move away from inward-oriented, union- and activist-based campaigns toward more outward-oriented, media-based strategies.

In the programmatic realm, adaptation to the constraints posed by economic crisis and a liberalizing international political economy required that the PJ rethink its traditional statist program. In the post-1982 political economic setting, the party's capacity to pursue the kinds of statist, redistributive, and pro-union policies that it had historically espoused would be limited. However, because pressure for programmatic adaptation was most acute for *governing* labor-based parties, the PJ could continue to oppose market-oriented policies while in opposition between 1983 and 1989. Hence, while Peronism was forced to confront changes in the electoral environment as early as 1983, it was largely shielded from changes in the economic environment until it assumed control of the national government in 1989.

Both coalitional and programmatic adaptation would require a reconfiguration of the PJ's relationship with organized labor. An increased reliance on middle-class and independent voters and the creation of territorial, rather than corporate, linkages to the urban base necessarily entailed a reduction of union influence. Moreover, because union bosses were widely associated with the violence of the 1970s and were thus perceived as unattractive to independent voters, their removal from the party leadership was considered critical to the PJ's capacity to capture such votes. A market-oriented strategy also posed a direct challenge to the party-labor alliance, as industrial unions would be among the biggest losers under neoliberalism. Because union leaders could be expected to oppose these strategic changes, the PJ's successful adaptation hinged to a significant extent on its capacity to divorce itself from its union allies. Such a divorce was, of course, fraught with political risks. For one, the pursuit of middle-class votes risked further eroding the party's traditional identity. Moreover, abandoning the party's traditional program would likely alienate the unionists and working-class activists who had traditionally provided the party with its extraordinary base-level strength. If the

PJ lost this support, its electoral hegemony among the working and lower classes would potentially be imperiled.

NONADAPTATION AND PARTY CRISIS, 1983–5

The PJ did not adapt in either the coalitional or the programmatic realm during the 1983–5 period. In the coalitional realm, the party turned inward, choosing leaders and candidates from its political and union old guard. Although leaders such as Isabel Perón, Lorenzo Miguel, Diego Ibañez, Vicente Saadi, and Herminio Iglesias maintained a degree of support among party activists and core PJ voters, they were unpopular among the larger electorate. Indeed, Peronist union leaders were consistently found at the bottom of public opinion polls – below business leaders, politicians, and even the military (Catterberg 1991: 56; Palermo 1994: 331). Although PJ presidential candidate Italo Luder was not a unionist, he "could not free himself from the image of a man controlled by the union leadership."[29]

The PJ adopted an inward-oriented electoral appeal in 1983, appealing primarily to Peronist voters (Waisbord 1995: 30–2).[30] Party strategy was "aimed at party activists" in an effort to "reinforce loyalties" rather than win independent votes (Waisbord 1995: 31). As Peronist intellectual Alvaro Abós observed, the PJ leadership "seemed to understand politics as a continuation of 1975," immersing itself in the "doctrinal fetishisms of Peronism" (1986: 81). The electoral campaign thus became a "ritual of identity" (Palermo and Novaro 1996: 184) in which party leaders Peronist leaders glorified the unpopular Isabel Perón and employed language and symbols that evoked the often violent Peronist–anti-Peronist conflicts of the past. Buenos Aires gubernatorial candidate Herminio Iglesias' burning of a coffin labeled "UCR" at the PJ's final campaign rally in 1983, which was captured on television for millions to see, was perhaps the best-known example of such behavior.

Moreover, on critical issues related to democracy, human rights, and foreign policy, the PJ repeatedly took positions that alienated new middle-class voters. For example, many top PJ and union leaders maintained close ties with leaders of the outgoing military regime in 1983, permitting Radical candidate Alfonsín to denounce the existence of a "military-labor pact." During the 1983–5 period, top Peronist leaders opposed the creation of the National Commission on Disappeared People (CONADEP) (Cerruti

---

[29] *Clarín*, November 1, 1983, p. 13.
[30] According to Waisbord, the PJ "believed the old political and cultural identities that allowed it to win every electoral battle for four decades were still intact" (1995: 32). Indeed, PJ presidential candidate Italo Luder later recognized that PJ leaders "directed their discourse toward Peronists, naively believing that to be sufficient" (quoted in Waisbord 1995: 30).

1993: 186), refused to attend President Alfonsín's March for Democracy amid coup rumors in April 1985,[31] and publicly criticized the 1985 trial of top military leaders implicated in human rights violations during the *Proceso*.[32] The Peronist leadership's opposition to legislation liberalizing divorce and the leadership's staunch nationalist opposition to the Beagle Channel treaty with Chile (which was overwhelmingly approved in a November 1984 referendum)[33] further distanced the party from younger, independent, and middle-class voters.

Finally, the PJ made virtually no use of the mass media or other campaign technologies that might have helped it reach middle-class voters. The party's 1983 campaign, which was run primarily out of the unions, centered almost entirely around activist-oriented events, mass rallies of supporters, and intense base-level work (Waisbord 1995: 31, 181). The union-dominated leadership rejected the use of polling and television as means of appealing to a broader electorate (Waisbord 1995: 68, 87). According to one source, Luder appeared on television only three times during the 1983 campaign (Cordeu et al. 1985: 59).

In the programmatic realm, the PJ maintained its traditional statist and populist platform during the 1983–5 period. The "62" played a central role in developing the party platform in both 1983 and 1985,[34] and the PJ leadership consulted the CGT on all major legislative issues. The 1983 party platform described the state as an "essential pillar" in the economy (Partido Justicialista 1983: 85) and declared that "capital must be at the service of the national economy" (1983: 83). It called for extensive economic planning (1983: 86–7), nationalizing much of the financial system (1983: 91), state ownership of "basic and strategic sectors" of the economy (1983: 90), and an incomes policy aimed at the "sustained growth of real salaries" (1983: 87). It also promised a renegotiation of the foreign debt (1983: 85), that trade be would be "guided, promoted, and overseen by the state" (1983: 103), and that foreign investment would be permitted "only to the extent that it contributes to meeting the sovereign objectives set by the Nation" (1983: 90–1).

During the first two years of the Alfonsín administration, the PJ consistently opposed the government from the left on socioeconomic issues. The bulk of the PJ leadership opposed the government's negotiations with

---

[31] *Clarín*, April 26, 1985, p. 8.
[32] *Clarín*, October 15, 1985, p. 12, and October 19, 1985, p. 12. In their testimonies at the trials, Peronist union leaders Jorge Triaca and Juan Rachini denied any knowledge of cases of torture or disappearances during the dictatorship, and Triaca said he received "exemplary treatment" during his imprisonment under the military regime (*Clarín*, April 25, 1985, pp. 2–3, and May 6, 1985, p. 4).
[33] PJ Senate leader Vicente Saadi described the treaty as "treason" (*Clarin*, November 16, 1984, p. 8), and the PJ boycotted the referendum.
[34] *Clarin*, September 7, 1983, p. 5; and September 3, 1985, p. 13.

the IMF,[35] rejected the heterodox Austral Plan, and supported every one of the CGT's general strikes.[36] During the 1985 electoral campaign, PJ candidates called for full-employment policies and accused Alfonsín of "putting the planning of the national economy in the hands of the IMF."[37] Finally, PJ leaders joined the CGT in calling for a moratorium on debt payments, sent a delegation to Cuba's 1985 antidebt conference, and enthusiastically supported Peruvian President Alan García's decision to limit Peru's debt payments.[38]

The PJ's inward-oriented strategy had devastating electoral consequences. The UCR stunned the PJ in the October 1983 presidential elections by a margin of 52 percent to 40 percent. Two years later, the UCR easily defeated the PJ in midterm legislative elections, and the Peronists saw their vote share fall to just 34.9 percent. In both elections, the independent and new middle-class electorate voted overwhelmingly against the PJ, providing the UCR's margin of victory (Jorrat 1986: 111; Catterberg 1991: 81–2). Indeed, the PJ suffered its worst defeats in the most economically developed districts (the Federal Capital, Buenos Aires, Cordoba, Mendoza, and – to a lesser extent – Santa Fe[39]), where these sectors were largest (Mora y Araujo 1988: 173).

A major cause of the PJ's defeats in 1983 and 1985 was its failure to adapt to changes in the electorate. Whereas the UCR explicitly and successfully targeted the new center, making issues such as democracy and human rights the centerpiece of its campaign and associating Peronism with "union gangsters" and the outgoing military regime (Cordeu et al. 1985: 48–51; Catterberg 1991: 83), the PJ "directed its message to a quasi group that had diminished in size" (Catterberg 1991: 83). According to Catterberg, such a strategy was "more appropriate to the context in which Peronism emerged in the 1940s than to Argentine society 40 years later" (1991: 82). Although Peronism largely retained its traditional electorate, particularly among the poorest and least educated voters (Gonzales Esteves and Llorente 1985: 45; Cantón 1986: 48–9; Ostiguy 1998: 353–5), it failed to capture a significant portion of middle-class, white-collar, or youth votes (Gonzáles Esteves and Llorente 1985; Cantón 1986: 48–9; 164; Catterberg 1991: 82). According to one survey, the UCR defeated the PJ by 67 percent to 25 percent among

---

[35] In August 1985, for example, the National Council declared that it "rejects, together with the CGT, any plan that means the subordination of Argentine development to the enslaving measures of the IMF" (*Clarín*, August 14, 1985, p. 6).

[36] *Clarín*, August 14, 1985, p. 6.

[37] Herminio Iglesias, quoted in *Clarín*, September 9, 1985, p. 2.

[38] *Clarín*, July 30, 1985, p. 8. PJ president Vicente Saadi traveled to Peru in October 1985 to express the PJ's solidarity with García, declaring that Argentina should not make debt payments "while there is hunger among our people" (*Clarín*, October 3, 1983, p. 10; and October 4, 1985, p. 10).

[39] The PJ won the governorship of Santa Fe in 1983, as the middle-class vote was divided between the UCR and center-right Progressive Democratic Party.

middle-class voters, 60 percent to 30 percent among white-collar employees, 71 percent to 22 percent among professionals, and 61 percent to 19 percent among students (Catterberg 1991: 82). Similarly, a Federal Capital survey by Cantón (1986: 48–9) found that the UCR defeated the PJ by 65 percent to 13 percent among self-described middle-class voters, 61 percent to 16 percent among white-collar employees, and 66 percent to 10 percent among those who had completed secondary school.[40]

It should be noted that the PJ's statist economic program was *not* a major cause of its defeats in 1983 and 1985. Indeed, the UCR also positioned itself on the center-left in the 1983–5 period, adopting a redistributionist, "social democratic" program that did not differ substantially from the Peronist platform. Moreover, the Renovation faction that led the PJ to victory in 1987 did not break substantially with Peronism's traditional pro-labor economic program. Thus, while laborist Peronism's electoral failures in 1983 and 1985 were clearly attributable to its inability to make a multiclass appeal, it was not the party's programmatic strategy that cost it middle-class votes.

In sum, Peronism confronted a profound political crisis in the early and mid-1980s. The PJ's links to industrial unions tied it to an increasingly narrow stratum of society and limited its capacity to make broader electoral appeals. Although the party's powerful mass organization and entrenched identity allowed it to maintain its electorate of belonging, this core electorate was insufficient to win elections in Argentina's predominantly two-party system. The PJ failed to capture the vast majority of new and independent voters, effectively ceding this terrain to the UCR and new parties such as the PI and the UCeDe. As a result, the PJ's electoral coalition was largely reduced to its working- and lower-class core.

[40] Cantón found similar tendencies in Greater Buenos Aires (1986: 53–4).

CHAPTER 5

From Labor Politics to Machine Politics: The Transformation of the Peronist Party–Union Linkage

We beat the unions. We took the party from them.
– Renovation leader José Luis Manzano[1]

Where is Peronism if not in the unions?
– Peronist union leader[2]

The PJ underwent a striking coalitional change after 1983, transforming itself, in less than a decade, from a de facto labor party into a predominantly patronage-based party. At the national level, reformers removed old-guard unionists from the party leadership, dismantled traditional mechanisms of labor participation, and broadened the party's appeal to attract middle-class and independent voters. At the base level, PJ politicians used their access to public offices to build patronage-based support networks at the margins of the unions. Over time, patronage networks replaced unions as the PJ's primary linkage to its working- and lower-class base. As a result of these changes, organized labor's influence in the party declined precipitously. This process of deunionization contributed in an important way to the PJ's electoral success in an increasingly postindustrial electoral environment. It permitted the party simultaneously to appeal to a new constituency (new middle-class and independent voters) and find a new basis – clientelism – on which to maintain its old one (the urban poor). Moreover, by weakening a major opponent of neoliberal reforms and eroding the class basis of the urban Peronist identity, deunionization facilitated the PJ's programmatic shift to the right under Carlos Menem.

This chapter examines urban Peronism's transition from de facto laborism to machine politics. The chapter argues that the speed and extent of the PJ's deunionization is explained by two factors: the weakly routinized nature of

[1] Author's interview, December 5, 1997.
[2] Quoted in *Clarín*, August 25, 1985.

the party–union linkage and a substantial change in the balance of resources between party and union leaders. Notwithstanding labor's central role in the Peronist coalition, traditional mechanisms of union participation were neither formalized in party statutes nor widely taken for granted. This left the party–union linkage vulnerable to changes in the distribution of power and preferences in the party. Such a change took place in the years following the 1983 democratic transition. The PJ's access to public office fundamentally altered the balance of resource dependence between party and union leaders. As party leaders gained positions in local and provincial governments, they substituted state resources for union resources, building patronage-based organizations at the margins of the unions. Patronage networks provided the organizational bases for a reformist challenge to labor's privileged position in the party. When reformers gained control of the party in 1987, Peronism's weakly routinized mechanisms of union participation collapsed like a house of cards. The dismantling of the "62" and the *tercio* left the PJ without any mechanisms of union participation, which paved the way for the consolidation of machine politics in the 1990s.

THE RISE OF THE RENOVATION AND THE COLLAPSE
OF THE TRADITIONAL PARTY–UNION LINKAGE

The PJ's 1983 defeat sparked the emergence of the Renovation, a heterogeneous movement that included progressive urban politicians, provincial bosses, and the left-of-center "25" union faction.[3] Renovation leaders converged around two central goals, both of which entailed an assault on the unions. First, they sought to broaden the PJ's electoral appeal. Convinced that the PJ had lost the 1983 election because it had "confused the country of 1983 with the country of 1946,"[4] and that the party's "plebeian Peronism" and "primitive authoritarianism" had scared away middle-class voters (Abós 1986: 82–4), the Renovators warned that "Peronism will not be a majority again ... if it does not open its arms and take in other sectors of national life."[5] To win middle-class votes, the Renovators argued, the PJ would have to loosen its ties to labor, deemphasize traditional party symbols and rhetoric, make better use of mass media technologies, and shed its authoritarian and socially conservative image in favor of a more progressive platform. Second, the Renovators sought to democratize the PJ internally and strengthen its territorial structure. This entailed replacing the PJ's traditional corporatist structure with a "pure territorial organization" (Abós 1986: 86–7). Thus, the *tercio* system would be replaced with a system of direct primaries to

---

[3] The '25' included the railway workers, pharmacy workers, auto workers, state workers, teachers, mine workers, rubber workers, truckers, naval workers, and shipyard workers.
[4] Carlos Grosso interview in García and Montenegro (1986: 63–4).
[5] Grosso interview in García and Montenegro (1986: 63–4).

select leaders and candidates. The "territorialization" of Peronism would enable the PJ to "differentiate itself institutionally from the labor movement" (Alvarez 1987: 19) and develop a "global project" in which union demands would be "redefined through a partisan logic" (Palermo 1986b: 84).

The Organizational Bases of the Renovation: Public Office, Patronage, and Informal Party Building

The rise and eventual triumph of the Renovation is usually presented in terms of elite politics. According to the elite-level story, Renovation leaders such as Antonio Cafiero, José Manuel De la Sota, Carlos Grosso, and Carlos Menem challenged the "62"-backed Orthodox faction's control of the party beginning in 1984, and after overcoming the old-guard leadership's authoritarian efforts to cling to power in 1985 and 1986, finally gained control of the national party in 1987. Yet this elite-level outcome was made possible by important changes at the base level. When the Renovators failed in their efforts to take over the national leadership in the 1984 and 1985 party congresses, they were forced to battle their way to power at the local and provincial levels. It was only after Cafiero, De la Sota, Grosso, and other reformers had defeated Orthodox factions in the large urban districts that the Renovation was able to take over the national party leadership.

These local victories were made possible by a fundamental change in the distribution of resources between the party's political and union wings. Reintegrated into electoral politics after 1983, PJ politicians began to replace union-based resources with alternative sources of funding. The most important of these sources was the state.[6] Although the PJ lost the presidency in 1983, it won twelve governorships, hundreds of mayoralties and provincial legislative seats, and thousands of city council seats. Holders of these offices gained immediate access to patronage resources. Local *punteros* who had previously gone to the unions for resources now turned to PJ government officials. PJ office holders built alliances with these *punteros*, creating *agrupaciones* whose principal bases were patronage, rather than unions. The *agrupaciones* became alternative party organizations, created at the margins of both the unions and the party bureaucracy. In stitching together the *agrupaciones* into larger, territorially based factions, party leaders essentially built "parties

---

[6] Renovation leaders also gained access to external sources of finance. For example, financial support from business leaders – particularly industrialist Francisco Macri – was crucial to the organization-building efforts of Renovators such as Grosso, De la Sota, and José Octavio Bordón. In addition, several top Renovators, including Cafiero, De la Sota, Grosso, and José Luis Manzano, established ties to foreign political party organizations and international ideological organizations such as International Christian Democracy and the Socialist International.

on the side," or informal organizations with which they would compete for power within Peronism. Upon gaining control of local parties, these informal organizations *became* the party organization, replacing the unions entirely.

The construction of patronage-based support networks was easiest for the newly elected governors, who had provincial governments at their disposal. Governors such as Carlos Juarez of Santiago del Estero, Ruben Marín of La Pampa, Carlos Menem of La Rioja, and Adolfo Rodriguez Saa of San Luis quickly built patronage-based machines that limited their dependence on the unions. Hence, it is not surprising that Juarez, Marín, and Menem were among the first to challenge the "62"-backed party leadership in late 1983 and early 1984. In the industrialized districts, where unions were stronger and (with the exception of Santa Fe) the PJ did not control the governorship, the construction of territorial organizations was a slower and more decentralized process. In these districts, the Renovation emerged as a patchwork of smaller organizations built up by individual city council members, mayors, and national and provincial legislators. In the Federal Capital, for example, the Renovation was initially a loose network of city council members and *punteros* called *Cabildo Abierto* (Open Town Meeting). Although many *Cabildo Abierto* members shared neither the urbane style nor the center-left ideology of local Renovation leader Grosso, they were territorial leaders who stood to benefit from an elections-based candidate selection system. Thus, they led the opposition to the "62"-dominated leadership throughout 1984, laying the foundation for the Renovation in the capital. The Renovation also emerged out of the city council in Quilmes. Council members such as Eduardo Camaaño, Federico Scarabino, and Transito Saucedo built patronage-based territorial structures in opposition to Orthodox leader Roberto Morguen. By 1987, they had won over the bulk of the city's *punteros*, turning the formal party leadership into "an empty shell."[7]

Together with unions from the "25" faction, these emerging territorial structures provided Renovation leaders with the human and organizational resources to compete with union-backed Orthodox factions in the large industrialized districts. In the Federal Capital, the Renovation campaign was led by Grosso, who brought *Cabildo Abierto* and several other *agrupaciones* together in mid-1985 to form the Front for Peronist Victory (VP). VP aligned with another powerful *puntero* network, the Peronist Unity Front, and the "25" union faction to oppose the "62" in internal elections in 1985. The Renovators won by a nearly two-to-one margin, and Grosso was elected party president. In Buenos Aires, the Renovation was led by territorial leaders whose reform efforts had been violently rebuffed by Orthodox boss

---

[7] Author's interview with José Luis Saluzzi, Quilmes director of public entities, September 4, 1997.

Herminio Iglesias. Unable to force Iglesias to hold internal elections, the Renovators, led by Cafiero, temporarily abandoned the party in 1985 to form the Renovation Front. The organizational strength of the Front was provided by emerging *agrupaciones* led by mayors such as Eduardo Duhalde and Julio Carpinetti, as well as by the "25." The Renovation Front outpolled the Iglesias-led PJ by a three-to-one margin, and a year later, Cafiero was elected party president. Similar processes allowed Renovators to defeat Orthodox factions in Córdoba and Rio Negro. These victories enabled the Renovators to win control of the national party leadership in 1987.

The Institutional Weakness of Traditional Mechanisms of Union Participation

If the Renovation challenge was made possible by a fundamental change in the balance of resources within the PJ, the party's radical deunionization was a product of the weakly routinized nature of the party-union linkage. As Chapter 3 argued, the informal mechanisms that had traditionally linked Peronist unions to the party – the "62" and the *tercio* – were never formalized in party statutes or broadly accepted and adhered to within the movement. Although the *tercio* was largely respected in 1983, its maintenance was not the product of routinization. Rather, it was either explicitly enforced or negotiated by union bosses. As the unions lost power between 1983 and 1987, the fragile consensus behind the "62" and the *tercio* eroded, leaving the PJ without any agreed upon rules of the game for union participation.

The "62" Organizations: From Labor Branch to Labor Faction

Between 1983 and 1987, the "62" lost its informal status as the PJ's encompassing "labor branch" and instead came to be viewed by Peronists as one of several labor factions. The "62" had maintained its national-level monopoly over Peronist labor in 1983, as all major union factions, including the left-of-center "25," recognized it as labor's umbrella organization. Thus, when unions from the collaborationist CGT-Azopardo temporarily broke with the Lorenzo Miguel-led "62," they created a parallel "62-Azopardo" rather than an alternative labor organization.[8]

The "62's" status as the PJ's official labor branch eroded rapidly after 1983. This outcome was partly a product of Renovation strategy. The

---

[8] The short-lived CGT-Azopardo represented a group of unions that had maintained close ties to the military government during the *Proceso*. The "62's" hegemony was questioned in some provinces, however. In Mendoza, for example, the Group of the East union faction broke with the "62" and, in alliance with a provincial faction called the Green List, defeated the "62"-backed Peronist Unity list in internal elections.

Renovators initially worked within the "62,"[9] seeking to replace the body's Orthodox leadership with allies from the "25" and *Gestión y Trabajo* (GyT) union factions. These efforts failed, however, when Miguel forged an alliance with GyT, thereby ensuring his reelection as "62" general secretary.[10] With their control over the "62" intact, orthodox unions successfully defended the body's monopoly over labor representation at the PJ's July 1985 party congress. A "25" proposal to allow each labor faction to name unionists to the party leadership was rejected, and instead, the "62" named all eighteen union representatives to the National Council.[11] Excluded from the "62," the Renovators opted to oppose it *as an institution*, and to treat the "25" as an alternative labor branch. In the 1985 elections, for example, Renovation leaders in the Federal Capital and Buenos Aires allowed the "25," rather than the "62," to nominate union candidates for parliamentary lists. In the capital, where the Renovation defeated a "62"-backed faction in the primaries, Renovation leader Grosso ignored Orthodox claims that it was "the right of the 62 Organizations to name [union] candidates,"[12] and instead placed "25" member Roberto Digón on the PJ's parliamentary list. Similar events unfolded in Buenos Aires. The Renovators, forced by Herminio Iglesias' authoritarian tactics to run outside the PJ, awarded the right to nominate union candidates to the "25."

The Renovation's 1985 victories constituted the "nail in the coffin of the 62 Organizations' traditional hegemony."[13] Pronouncing the "62" "finished as the political arm of Peronist labor,"[14] the "25" opened a think tank, launched a newspaper, and established regional organizations throughout the country. The Renovators adopted a similar position, describing the "62" as "an historical artifact" that "no longer globally represents Peronist labor,"[15] and electing "25" member Roberto Digón, rather than a "62" member, as vice president of the Renovation-dominated legislative faction. Orthodox leaders made a last-ditch effort to enforce the "62" monopoly during the 1986–7 leadership and candidate selection process. Thus, the "62"-backed National Council formally recognized the "62" as the "exclusive political representative" of Peronist labor, and party president Vicente Saadi ordered provincial branches to "guarantee" the "62's" "traditional representation"

---

[9] The 1985 Renovation congress at Rio Hondo recognized the "62" as labor's "institutional representative." Renovation leaders declared that the "62" was "the only political arm of Peronist workers, and for that reason, we seek its normalization, without exclusions, to achieve the full organic participation of the movement" (*Clarín*, January 10, 1986, p. 10, and March 19, 1985, p. 10).

[10] *Clarín*, May 22, 1985, p. 8.

[11] *Clarín*, July 5, 1985, p. 6; July 8, 1985, pp. 2–3; July 9, 1985, p. 8.

[12] *Clarín*, August 29, 1985, p. 6.

[13] *Clarín*, August 26, 1985, p. 7.

[14] *Clarín*, 20 December, 1985, p. 11; 23 December, 1985, p. 17; 2 July, 1986, p. 7.

[15] Antonio Cafiero, quoted in *Clarín*, June 19, 1986, p. 12, and June 22, 1986, p. 7.

on party lists.[16] These efforts were widely ignored, however, as Renovation-led party branches awarded their union candidacies to the "25."[17] In this context, new union political factions, such as the *Ubaldinistas* (supporters of the CGT General Secretary Saúl Ubaldini), emerged, which further undermined the "62's" claim to be the encompassing representative of Peronist labor. By 1987, then, the "62" had ceased to function as the PJ's "labor branch" and had instead been converted into one of several union factions. As a result, unions were left without even an informal body to represent them in the party leadership.

The Erosion of the Union Tercio

The union *tercio*, rooted in the corporatist notion that labor leaders possessed a right to a certain number of party candidacies and leadership posts, was already contested in 1983. Whereas top party leaders such as Cafiero defended the *tercio* as "unmodifiable,"[18] others, such as Angel Robledo, Raul Matera, and the Peronist Convergence faction, called for its replacement with a system of direct elections.[19] Although the traditional *tercio* system was generally complied with, it was hardly a taken-for-granted procedure. Rather, it was generally a product of direct enforcement by the unions or an explicit exchange between party and union leaders. As one union leader put it, "the *tercio* was a concession, not something the politicians wanted."[20] In some districts, such as the Federal Capital, Santa Cruz, and Santa Fe, the *tercio* was imposed by a dominant "62"-backed faction. In many other districts, it was a product of a negotiated exchange between union and party leaders, and in some cases, party leaders acceded to the *tercio* only after intense lobbying from the "62." In Tucumán, for example, party boss Fernando Riera initially refused to include a union leader on the PJ's parliamentary list and agreed to include unionist Julio Miranda only after being subjected to heavy pressure by the national "62" leadership.[21] Mendoza party leaders also rejected the *tercio*, arguing that it made sense only while Perón lived.[22] When the dominant Green List faction ignored union demands for representation in the local party leadership, the national "62" sent a representative to negotiate

---

[16] *Clarín*, March 18, 1986, p. 10; March 20, 1986, pp. 14–15; March 25, 1986, pp. 8–9.

[17] In the Federal Capital, for example, Carlos Grosso rejected pleas by the "62" to recognize its right to nominate labor's candidates, placing "25" leader Roberto García on the party's legislative list instead. In Mendoza, when the "62" announced a boycott of the party primaries to protest the dominant Orange List's failure to recognize its labor monopoly, a group of unions called the Renovation Bloc ignored it and aligned with Orange List (*Los Andes*, October 21, 1986, p. 16; November 15, 1986, p. 8; November 23, 1986, p. 11).

[18] *Clarín*, April 11, 1983, p. 7.

[19] *Clarín*, April 12, 1983, p. 6; April 14, 1983, p. 10; April 26, 1983, pp. 6–7; June 9, 1983, p. 12.

[20] Author's interview with former "25" leader Roberto García, June 23, 1997.

[21] Author's interview with Julio Miranda, December 4, 1997.

[22] *Clarín*, April 27, 1983, p. 8.

the inclusion of three unionists in the party's nine-member provincial council.[23] Finally, in peripheral provinces in which unions were weak, respect for the *tercio* depended on the good will of party bosses. Thus, provincial bosses in Catamarca, Formosa, and La Rioja respected the *tercio*, whereas those in Corrientes and Santiago del Estero ignored it.

The Renovation challenge eroded the last vestiges of legitimacy behind the *tercio*. Viewing the corporatist branch system as a thinly veiled mechanism to maintain labor hegemony (Palermo 1986b: 83–4), the Renovators sought to replace it with a system of direct elections. Similarly, the "25" called for an "end to percentages in the distribution of candidacies" (Movimiento Sindical Peronista Renovador 1986: 15), arguing that unions would have to gain power "in the political arena by competing in internal elections."[24] The "62," by contrast, defended the *tercio* as a "creation of Perón"[25] and a practice that was "in the rules of Justicialism."[26] Orthodox union leaders attacked the direct election of party leaders and candidates as a "liberal fiction" that would violate Peronism's "movementist tradition" and "convert Peronism into just another political party."[27]

The Renovation's initial proposals with respect to the *tercio* were ambiguous. At the same time that they called for direct elections, the Renovators pledged to preserve Peronism's "movementist character."[28] For example, although the Renovators-led congress in Rio Hondo called for the direct election of the party leadership, it also included a stipulation that a unionist be one of the four representatives elected from each district (Gutierrez 1998: 18). Yet as they gained strength, the Renovators grew increasingly critical of the *tercio*. The Renovators' 1985 victories in the capital and Buenos Aires convinced them that direct elections were not only their road to power in the party, but also a primary source of legitimacy in their battle against the Orthodox leadership. Thus, Renovators began to call for the party to "do away with the absurd labor percentage" (Bárbaro 1985: 151) on the grounds that it "impedes the free decision of the membership."[29] Moreover, the first major Renovation assembly held after the 1985 election produced a document calling for direct elections without any kind of clause to ensure union representation (Gutierrez 1998: 22–3).

Orthodox party and union leaders responded to attacks on the *tercio* by attempting formally to enforce the old system. In March 1986, the

---

[23] *Los Andes,* April 10, 1983, p. 8.
[24] Author's interview with former "25" leader José Luis Castillo, July 2, 1997.
[25] Lorenzo Miguel, quoted in *El Litoral*, October 1, 1988, p. 1.
[26] *Clarín*, July 15, 1986, p. 13.
[27] Oil workers union leader Diego Ibañez, quoted in *Clarín*, July 20, 1986, p. 7.
[28] *Clarín*, November 21, 1984, p. 11; December 1, 1985, pp. 2–3. According to Grosso, the Renovators sought to transform the PJ into a "corporative-political party, along the lines of the German parties" (author's interview, November 28, 1997).
[29] José Manuel De la Sota, quoted in *Clarín*, July 11, 1986, p. 12.

"62"-backed National Council officially ratified the *tercio*, and party president Saadi declared it to be a "common law right, where the custom is the law."[30] Using its power to intervene provincial parties, the National Council sought – unsuccessfully – to legislate the *tercio* in major districts. In Córdoba, the Orthodox party leadership modified the party statutes to reserve eight of twenty-six seats in the party leadership for the labor and women's branches.[31] Only a few months later, however, the Renovators won control of the party and replaced the quota system with direct elections. In Mendoza, where the Renovation-led party branch refused to employ the *tercio*, the national party leadership sent an official "observer," who threatened to take over the local party if it did not "ensure the institutional participation of the labor and women's branches."[32] Local party leaders ignored these threats, however, insisting that they would "maintain the principle of the direct vote for all party posts."[33] Efforts to enforce the *tercio* thus failed, and by 1987, the idea that the unions held a legitimate right to name candidates had virtually disappeared.

The Renovation Triumph and the Rupture of the Party–Labor Linkage

The Renovators gained control of the party leadership in November 1987, ushering in a brief period of what might be described as de facto social democracy. Despite their opposition to both the old-guard union leadership and corporatist mechanisms of labor participation, the Renovators neither sought, nor immediately brought about, the deunionization of Peronism.[34] Rather, they sought a party–labor linkage along the lines of European social democracy, in which labor would play a central, yet subordinate, role. Such a party, Renovator Guido Di Tella argued, would be "comparable to ... British Labour, the German Social Democratic Party, and the Spanish Socialist Workers Party."[35] Indeed, the "25" remained an important member of the dominant coalition in the Renovation-led PJ. "25" leader Roberto García was named party vice president, and "25" leaders participated in

---

[30] *Clarín*, March 18, 1986, p. 10; March 19, 1986, p. 7; March 20, 1986, pp. 14–15; March 25, 1986, p. 8.
[31] *Clarín*, July 10, 1986, p. 8; July 11, 1986, p. 12.
[32] *Los Andes*, September 21, 1986, p. 12; September 29, 1986, p. 5; *Clarín*, October 6, 1986, p. 10.
[33] *Los Andes*, September 29, 1986, p. 5.
[34] Grosso, for example, claims that the Renovators never sought "a purely political party left in the hands of professional politicians.... It was not that we didn't want labor within Peronism. We just didn't want to be employees of the labor leaders" (author's interview, November 28, 1997). Similarly, José Manuel De la Sota claims, "I don't believe in a party run by the unions, but I also do not believe in a party without unions.... It was never our intention to eliminate the unions" (author's interview, November 17, 1997).
[35] *La Prensa*, September 13, 1987, p. 4.

most national-level decision-making processes. Moreover, the Renovators respected the union *tercio* in each of the major electoral districts in 1987.³⁶ Yet as Renovation intellectual Hugo Chumbita observed at the time, in the process of reforming and democratizing the party, the Renovators were "throwing out the baby with the bath water" in terms of the party's relationship with labor (1987: 70).³⁷ In doing away with the "62" and the *tercio* and creating no alternative institutional arrangements to replace them, the Renovation left labor without any (formal or informal) mechanism of participation.

A major reason for this outcome was the failure of party and union leaders to converge around new rules of the game to structure union participation. On the one hand, orthodox unionists remained wedded to the old corporatist rules of the game, declaring that

> The 62 Organizations are going to ensure that the stipulations of the party charter, which establish that it is this – and no other – union organization that has the right to designate the union tercio of representation within the party, are complied with.³⁸

On the other hand, "25" leaders did not seek *any* kind of institutional linkage to the party. According to "25" leader José Pedraza, there was "no serious debate" within the "25" on establishing new rules for labor participation, and the "25" "never even discussed the possibility of demanding a *tercio*."³⁹ Confident that the Renovation takeover would ensure them a place in the party leadership, "25" leaders did not concern themselves with creating institutional arrangements to guarantee labor participation in the

---

[36] According to Cafiero, the Renovators "continued to respect the *tercio*. Maybe not a third, but we put union leaders on our candidate lists. We weren't forced to do so by the party charter, but we did it" (author's interview, October 3, 1997). Indeed, in the Federal Capital, García gained the second spot on the PJ chamber of deputies list. In Buenos Aires, five unionists were placed on the party's legislative list, and "25" leader José Luis Castillo was elected president of the party congress. In Santa Fe, auto workers leader Ruben Cardozo was elected to Congress, and labor gained key appointments in the cabinet of new governor, Victor Reviglio. In Mendoza, oil workers leader Antonio Cassia was elected to the Chamber of Deputies, and in Córdoba, eight unionists gained spots on the party's list for the provincial legislature. Only in San Juan did a rupture occur between Renovation leaders and labor.

[37] According to Chumbita, the Renovators' displacement of union influence "went too far, and without constructing alternative channels of communication with workers.... In their effort to throw out the thugs, they have thrown out labor; in removing the old guard, they have excluded virtually the entire labor movement" (1987: 70–1).

[38] Meat packers union leader Lesio Romero, quoted in *La Prensa*, October 17, 1987, p. 4. In addition to being factually inaccurate, the defense of the *tercio* system was out of line with dominant sentiments in the party. As "62" member Juan José Zanola later recognized, "Our error was in not realizing that a change was needed.... The old characteristics that the PJ may have had in Perón's era were no longer applicable.... We still operated with a Vandorist vision, in which the political sector had to be subordinated to union power – a closed and corporatist vision that generated internal opposition. This was the greatest error we made" (author's interview, October 22, 1997).

[39] Author's interview, July 10, 1997.

future.⁴⁰ In the words of ex-"25" member Gustavo Morato,

> We did not seek a special institution, labor party style, that guaranteed union participation in the party.... We expected that with our leaders participating in the Renovation leadership, we would have no problem.... We didn't think about what would happen if we lost, or if our leaders weren't there. We should have found some kind of mechanism for union participation, like in Venezuela or in European social democracy. But in the struggle for internal democracy, we forgot all about that.⁴¹

The "62" was revived prior to the 1987 party congress, providing what may have been the last opportunity to reestablish an encompassing trade union body in the party leadership. In October 1987, orthodox unionists organized a "62" congress to select labor's representatives to the party leadership. In an effort to avoid what they viewed as the "anarchization of the labor movement,"⁴² they called on all union factions – including the "25" – to attend the congress and work within the "62." Renovation leaders were also interested in a unified labor body, although they insisted that such a body be under Renovation control.⁴³ The "25," however, rejected the proposal, declaring that the "62" had "passed into history and has no relevance in a modern society."⁴⁴ Thus, "25" leaders refused to attend the "62" congress and opposed the incorporation of the "62" into the party leadership.⁴⁵ Six months later, "25" and *Ubaldinista* unions would form the *Mesa de Enlace Sindical*, an organization they hoped would serve as the "labor branch of Peronism" under the Renovation-led PJ.⁴⁶

Divided and without a common project for labor participation in the party, the unions exercised little influence in the November 1987 congress. The Renovation-led congress did away with the *tercio* system and replaced it with a system of direct elections, which placed power in the hands of those who controlled votes. No alternative mechanisms were created to guarantee labor a role in the candidate and leadership selection process. The congress also failed to establish a body to represent labor collectively within the party. Although the new party charter reserved 17 of 110 seats in the National Council for labor, it did not specify who would choose these

---

⁴⁰ According to former "25" leader García, "We didn't realize that we were not always going to be powerful. We didn't realize that we might lose the tremendous power that we had for so long. So we didn't bother to create anything to ensure our participation. It's like an inheritance from your grandfather. You spend and spend and before you realize it, you are down to your last dollar. That's what happened to us. We thought labor would continue to be powerful, to continue to be able to place candidates. But that was not to be" (author's interview, June 23, 1997).
⁴¹ Author's interview, June 13, 1997.
⁴² Armando Cavalieri, quoted in *La Prensa*, November 22, 1987, p. 5.
⁴³ Author's interview with Antonio Cafiero, October 3, 1997.
⁴⁴ *La Prensa*, October 25, 1987, p. 5.
⁴⁵ *La Prensa*, October 22, 1987, p. 4; November 25, 1987, p. 11.
⁴⁶ *Clarín*, May 30, 1988, p. 9; June 4, 1988, p. 8.

union representatives or how they would be chosen. In the absence of a "62"-like body to choose these representatives, the selection of union representatives for party leadership and legislative lists fell into the hands of the political bosses who drew up the party's leadership lists. Hence, the new institutional arrangement meant that labor "accepted, de facto, the right of political leaders to choose... which union leaders would go on the lists."[47]

Labor's weakness vis-á-vis the political sector was seen in the negotiations to select the seventeen union representatives in the new National Council. Whereas the "62" insisted that "the union representatives must come out of the '62' congress,"[48] the "25" and *Ubaldinista* factions claimed the right to name these representatives based on their alliance with the Renovation.[49] Ultimately, it was the party leadership, rather than any of the union factions, which selected the union representatives. The Renovation leadership ultimately gave ten positions to pro-Renovation unionists (including a vice presidency) and seven to the "62" (Beliz 1988: 211).

The Electoral Success of Renovation Peronism

The Renovation leadership used its new autonomy from the unions to redefine the PJ's image and electoral strategy in an effort to appeal to independent and middle-class voters. This strategy had several components. First, although the PJ did not break with the unions, it kept them at arm's length and, perhaps more importantly, out of the public eye. Thus, while the "25" remained an important ally of the Renovation-led PJ, none of the top figures in the new party leadership were unionists. Second, the Renovators abandoned the PJ's inward orientation in favor of catch-all campaign strategies that entailed playing down traditional Peronist language and symbols and explicitly targeting independent and middle-class voters. In predominantly middle-class districts such as the Federal Capital, Córdoba, and Mendoza, PJ leaders created a more professional image, earning the label "jacket and tie Peronism." This outward-oriented strategy was accompanied by the use of new campaign techniques that would facilitate appeals to independent voters, such as professional polling, marketing consultants, and mass media advertising (Waisbord 1995: 68–9, 87). The Renovation-led PJ also adopted

---

[47] Author's interview with former "25" leader José Pedraza, July 10, 1997. Although "25" leaders supported the direct vote system, many of them, including Roberto García, later concluded that this strategy was "a terrible mistake. We should have fought for a legal *tercio*. We were left with nothing" (author's interview, June 23, 1997). Similarly, former "25" leader Gustavo Morato claims that "Direct elections broke us. They leave you without a means of participation. We have become completely detached from the party. It was a great error on our part, which we are paying for under Menem" (author's interview, June 13, 1997).
[48] Lorenzo Miguel, quoted in *La Prensa*, October 17, 1987, p. 4.
[49] *La Prensa*, September 26, 1987, p. 4; October 9, 1987, p. 3.

a politically liberal and socially progressive profile. The Renovators adopted a clear position in defense of democracy and human rights, strongly backing the trial of military leaders responsible for repression during the dictatorship, and opposing legislation – such as the *Punto Final* and *Obedencia Debida* – that limited the scope of such prosecutions. Whereas some Orthodox leaders reacted ambiguously to the April 1987 military uprising, Renovation leaders harshly condemned it and appeared in public with President Alfonsín to defend the democratic regime. The Renovators were also careful to present an image as democratic in internal party politics, contrasting their "New Democratic Peronism"[50] with the "thug" politics of the old party leadership.[51]

The Renovation's middle-class appeal was not accompanied by a substantial shift on the left–right axis, however. The Renovation Peronist program was neither antilabor nor market-oriented. Renovation leaders described themselves as "center-left" and "social democratic,"[52] and they publicly converged with organized labor on all major socioeconomic issues in 1987 and 1988. Thus, they rejected Alfonsín's heterodox stabilization program as "monetarist,"[53] opposed the government's timid privatization proposals as a "surrender of our national patrimony,"[54] and called on the government to "stand up to the IMF"[55] and declare a moratorium on debt payments.[56] Finally, the Renovation-led PJ supported every general strike led by the CGT, and Peronist legislators worked with the CGT in passing both a new labor law and legislation returning the administration of health insurance funds to the unions.[57]

The strategic changes carried out by the Renovation proved successful. As Table 5.1 shows, the PJ's electoral performance improved markedly in 1987 and 1989. The PJ decisively won the 1987 midterm elections, capturing seventeen of twenty-two governorships. The party made striking gains in the largest and most industrialized provinces, winning the governorships in

---

[50] José Manuel De la Sota, quoted in *Clarín*, March 31, 1987, p. 9.
[51] The Renovation-led PJ also adopted more liberal or progressive positions on social and cultural issues. For example, whereas Orthodox Peronists had worked with the Catholic Church to oppose legislation to legalize divorce, top Renovators supported the bill and helped pass it into law (*Clarín*, June 22, 1986, p. 7; June 25, 1986, p. 6; July 3, 1986, p. 21; August 12, 1986, p. 14; August 15, 1986, p. 3; August 20, 1986, pp. 2–3).
[52] Author's interviews with former Renovation leaders Jose Octavio Bordón, Antonio Cafiero, José Manuel De la Sota, Carlos Grosso, José Luis Manzano, and Miguel Angel Toma.
[53] *Clarín*, March 17, 1986, p. 11; July 21, 1987, pp. 2–3; August 24, 1988, p. 4.
[54] Carlos Grosso, quoted in *Clarín*, February 23, 1986, p. 6. In August, 1988, Renovation leaders participated in an antiprivatization march organized by the PJ-Federal Capital (*Clarín*, August 18, 1988, p. 6).
[55] *Clarín*, February 25, 1986, p. 6; October 6, 1986, p. 10; October 17, 1986, p. 16.
[56] *Clarín*, July 10, 1987, p. 8; March 9, 1987, p. 7.
[57] *Clarín*, February 9, 1987, pp. 2–3; February 16, 1987, pp. 2–3; January 13, 1988, p. 4; January 14, 1988, p. 6.

TABLE 5.1. *Presidential and Legislative Electoral Results, 1983–9, Percentage of Valid Vote*

Party	1983 (P)	1983 (L)	1985 (L)	1987 (L)	1989 (P)	1989 (L)
Justicialista Party (PJ)	40.1	38.6	34.9	41.5	47.3	44.7
Radical Civic Union (UCR)	51.7	48.0	43.6	37.2	32.4	28.8
Democratic Center Union (UCeDe)	0.1	1.2	2.9	5.8	6.2	9.6
Intransigent Party (PI)	2.3	2.8	6.1	2.0	—	—
Minor and provincial parties	5.8	9.4	12.5	13.5	14.1	16.9
TOTAL	100.0	100.0	100.0	100.0	100.0	100.0

Notes: (P) = Presidential election.
(L) = Chamber of Deputies election.
Sources: Fraga (1995), McGuire (1995), Jones (1997), and www.mivoto.com.

Buenos Aires and Mendoza, retaining the governorship in Santa Fe, and nearly winning it in the Radical stronghold of Córdoba. Two years later, Carlos Menem captured the presidency and the PJ raised its share of the legislative vote to 45 percent.

Critical to the PJ's electoral success in 1987 and 1989 were its gains among middle-class voters. Survey data suggest that whereas the UCR defeated the PJ by a two-to-one margin among white-collar employees and a nearly three-to-one margin among students in 1983, in 1989 the PJ split the white-collar vote and nearly split the student vote (Catterberg and Braun 1989: 372; Gervasoni 1998b: 27, 29). According to Catterberg and Braun, the PJ increased its support among students from 19 percent to 36 percent and among white-collar employees from 30 to 40 percent (1989: 372). Moreover, whereas the UCR easily defeated the PJ among housewives and self-employed workers in 1983, in 1989 the PJ won decisively among these voters (Catterberg and Braun 1989: 372). Although Peronism clearly benefited from a sharp decline in popular support for the Radical government, the PJ's electoral gains were made possible by its renewed capacity to appeal to independent and middle-class voters. The fact that the PJ faced competition for middle-class votes from the center-left PI and the conservative UCeDe – both of which emerged as viable "third parties" in the 1980s – demonstrates that the PJ was more than simply a default option for many middle-class voters.

The Legacies of the Renovation

Between 1985 and 1989, then, the Renovators succeeded both in democratizing the PJ and in broadening its electoral base. To a significant extent, these successes came at the cost of the PJ's traditional party–union linkage. Paradoxically, the Renovators did not intend to eliminate labor's role in the party. Although they subordinated the unions and broadened the PJ's appeal, the Renovators themselves neither deunionized the party nor shifted it decisively toward a market-oriented program. Unions from the "25" remained important – if junior – partners in the PJ leadership during the late 1980s. Yet the Renovators and their union allies failed to create new mechanisms of labor participation, and as a result, labor's position in the PJ remained highly vulnerable to changes in the distribution of power and preferences within the party.

Such a change occurred with Carlos Menem's defeat of Cafiero in the July 1988 presidential primaries. Menem's victory was initially perceived to strengthen Orthodox labor. Menem had run an explicitly "movementist" campaign that embraced the "62" as "the backbone of the Justicialista movement."[58] He declared

> We don't want to turn Peronism into another liberal democratic party.... We won't renounce our movementist conception.... The four vital branches – political, union, women's, and youth – must be represented in the party leadership.[59]

Orthodox unionists, who had been marginalized by the Renovation leadership, flocked to Menem.[60] The financial and organizational resources provided by the "62" and other orthodox unions were critical to Menem's victory in the primaries, for they helped to compensate for Cafiero's control over the bulk of the party apparatus (Wainfeld 1988: 19). Buoyed by Menem's victory, Orthodox unionists called a "62" congress aimed at reestablishing the organization as "the single totalizing expression" of Peronist labor.[61]

Yet Menem neither needed nor intended to restore preexisting mechanisms of labor participation. Rather than work through the "62," Menem created an alternative labor organization: the Menem for President Labor Roundtable. Founded in March 1988 by restaurant workers union leader Luis Barrionuevo, the Labor Roundtable "acted as a *de facto* parallel '62,'" contributing vast financial and organizational resources to Menem's campaign.[62] In February 1989, Menemist unions replaced the Labor

---

[58] *Clarín*, March 23, 1988, p. 8.
[59] Quoted in McGuire (1997: 212).
[60] *Clarín*, March 13, 1988, p. 19; March 14, 1988, p. 13; April 6, 1988, p. 6. The breaking point between the "62" and the Renovators was Cafiero's choice of Renovator De la Sota, rather than "62" ally José María Vernet, as his running mate. According to former "25" member Gustavo Morato, "25" leaders were unwilling to relinquish the position of power they had achieved through the Renovation takeover and thus "pushed to the death for an ultra-Renovation ticket that would do away with the '62'.... We were the ones responsible for De la Sota.... We convinced Cafiero that we could win with De la Sota. And if we won with De la Sota, bingo! It would be the end of the '62'" (author's interview, June 13, 1997).
[61] *Clarín*, July 11, 1988, p. 6; July 17, 1988, p. 13; August 2, 1988, p. 18; August 26, 1988, p. 10.
[62] *Clarín*, August 8, 1988, p. 13; October 17, 1988, p. 15. For example, the Labor Roundtable was the major force behind Menem's highly successful closing rally in the River Plate soccer stadium (*Clarín*, June 10, 1988, p. 4; June 26, 1988, p. 5; June 30, 1988, p. 17).

Roundtable with yet another labor branch: the *Mesa de Enlace Sindical*. The *Mesa de Enlace* served as the primary mediator between Menem and labor during the first year of the Menem government, and Barrionuevo declared that it would "come to play the role that the 62 Organizations played in the past."[63]

The emergence of the Labor Roundtable and the *Mesa de Enlace* completed the deroutinization process that had begun with the "25's" challenge. Despite repeated efforts to "relaunch" itself, the "62" never again managed to encompass the bulk of Peronist labor. Although most union leaders still claimed to belong to the "62," the organization became an "empty name"[64] that "no one pays any attention to."[65] By the mid-1990s, the once hegemonic labor organization represented only a handful of unions.[66] No organization replaced the "62" as the encompassing representative of Peronist labor. Rather, labor fragmented into competing political factions, which undermined their negotiating power vis-á-vis party bosses. Lacking a labor branch with the right to name candidates and unable to act collectively to demand a seat at the table where lists were drawn up, the unions effectively ceded the authority to nominate union candidates to the party bosses who put together the lists.

This shift was clearly seen in the candidate selection process for the 1989 elections. In the Federal Capital, the "62," "25," and *Ubaldinistas* all backed the parliamentary list presented by party leader Grosso, which permitted Grosso to play these factions against each other. The support of the "62" reduced Grosso's dependence on the "25," enabling him to "betray" his erstwhile allies by placing Roberto Monteverde of the "62," rather than "25" leader Roberto Digón, on the PJ list. A similar situation unfolded in Córdoba, where both the "25" and the "62" backed the unity list headed by De la Sota. Unionists gained few positions in the provincial party leadership, and the fourth spot on the parliamentary list, which had been expected to go to a unionist, was given to a Menemist politician.[67] In Mendoza, the "62," the "25," and the Group of the East all negotiated alliances with the dominant Orange List, and although each gained some representation on the party's lists, union leaders complained that the

---

[63] *La Prensa*, October 28, 1989, p. 5. Nevertheless, the Mesa Sindical also failed to bring together the entire labor movement, as oppositionist unions from the "25" and *Ubaldinismo*, as well as a group of orthodox unions linked to Miguel, refused to join it.

[64] Author's interview with Lorenzo Minichielo, general secretary of the Quilmes section of the auto workers union (SMATA), May 15, 1997.

[65] Author's interview with former CGT General Secretary Oscar Lescano, October 27, 1997.

[66] Seven unions actively participated in the "62" in 1996: the UOM, taxi drivers, rural workers, service station workers, food workers, cemetery workers, and ceramic workers.

[67] *La Voz del Interior*, October 15, 1988, p. 4; October 16, 1988, p. 6; October 18, 1988, p. 4.

party leadership had "not respected what has historically corresponded to us."[68]

In sum, Renovation Peronism might be described as a de facto social democratic party. The Renovators never envisioned a deunionized PJ, and while they controlled the party, the "25" remained an important partner in the party's dominant coalition. Had Renovation and union leaders reached a consensus on a new role for labor, they might have converted this "social democratic moment" into a routinized labor-based party. Yet like the labor-dominated arrangement that preceded it, the Renovation's party-labor alliance was entirely de facto. In dismantling the last vestiges of the traditional party–union linkage and failing to replace them with new mechanisms of labor participation, the Renovators created the conditions under which deunionization was not only possible, but likely. Hence, although the Renovators themselves did not oversee the PJ's deunionization during the 1987–9 period, they paved the way for such an outcome in the 1990s.

THE CONSOLIDATION OF MACHINE POLITICS: PARTY AND LABOR IN THE 1990S

Union influence in the PJ declined precipitously in the 1990s. Whereas labor had played an important, if junior, role under the Renovation, it was largely excluded from the party leadership after 1989. The erosion of union influence was accompanied by the consolidation of machine politics,[69] which may be defined as an informal pattern of political organization in which state resources, particularly government jobs, are the primary currency of political exchange between higher- and lower-level party actors. The consolidation of machine politics was facilitated by two legacies of the Renovation period: (1) a pure electoral regime for selecting leaders and candidates; and (2) the political–organizational fragmentation of labor. First, by

---

[68] *Los Andes*, June 5, 1988, p. 15. Only two union leaders were named to the provincial party leadership, and for the first time, no unionists were placed on the PJ's legislative list. In Buenos Aires, a Menemist-Renovation unity list was put together by a mixed committee with no union representatives. Although unionists received five of the top twenty spots on the list, the positions were divided up among the "25," the Labor Roundtable, and the *Ubaldinistas* (the "62" was left out entirely), and union leaders exercised little influence over the selection process (*Clarín*, September 6, 1988, p. 9 and November 23, 1988, p. 9). Only in Santa Fe did labor maintain a central role in the nomination process. In that province, unpopular Governor Victor Reviglio was unable to consolidate control over the party and was challenged in an internal election by Menemist Vice Governor Antonio Vanrell. Vanrell's challenge forced Reviglio to rely more heavily on labor, which allowed the unions gain two of five positions on the party's Chamber of Deputies list.

[69] This term is taken from Wolfinger (1972: 374–5). As Ansell and Burris (1997: 4) point out, machine politics should be distinguished from "political machines," in which power is relatively concentrated in a single leadership. Machine politics, by contrast, includes cases in which a power is relatively fragmented and decentralized.

replacing the *tercio* system with internal elections, and by failing to create either new mechanisms for union participation or an effective party bureaucracy, the Renovators left an organizational void that was filled by patronage politics. Internal elections placed increased importance on the delivery of votes, which created an incentive for both leaders and activists to organize around patronage distribution. Due to their access to state resources, public office holders enjoyed a great advantage in the patronage game. As patronage-based leaderships consolidated, state resources became the primary linkage between activists and the party. If in the 1980s such organizations served as "parties on the side" that enabled PJ politicians to reduce their dependence on the unions, in the 1990s they became the only game in town.

A second Renovation legacy that contributed to the consolidation of machine politics was the political–organizational fragmentation of labor. With the demise of the "62," Peronist labor fell into a state of atomization. National union factions disintegrated, and each union began to "play its own game"[70] in the political arena, either by negotiating individual alliances with party bosses or by creating its own political *agrupación*. Thus, unions from the "25" "continued working politically, but as individuals, not as the '25.'"[71] In the Federal Capital, for example, the tobacco employees, telephone workers, state workers, pasta workers, and custodians unions each created their own *agrupaciones*, while in Buenos Aires province, the rubber workers, ship captains, and auto workers unions created individual *agrupaciones*. Efforts to reconstruct an encompassing labor organization, such as the Convocation of Peronist Workers in 1994 and the Duhalde for President Labor Roundtable in 1996, repeatedly failed. Because no centralized authority existed to enforce compliance among unions, these crosssectoral organizations never managed to encompass more than a single labor faction.

The absence of an encompassing labor organization limited the unions' leverage vis-á-vis the party leadership, for it allowed party bosses to play unions against one another as they competed for positions on candidate lists. As a La Matanza textile workers union leader put it:

Each union tries to seek out the best solution for its own organization, and union leaders go with the political leader who pays best.... It's easier for political leaders to negotiate with single unions than to negotiate with labor as a whole. They give a post to the UOM here, to the municipal workers there, and then they have labor divided and it doesn't bother them anymore. It would be different if the labor movement were united, say in the 62 Organizations, negotiating as a single entity.[72]

---

[70] Author's interview with textile workers union leader Hugo Benítez, April 11, 1997.
[71] Author's interview with former "25" leader José Luis Castillo, July 2, 1997.
[72] Author's interview with Hugo Benítez, former general secretary of La Matanza branch of the textile workers union, April 11, 1997.

The Transformation of the Party–Union Linkage

Labor's atomization, combined with the concentration of power in the hands of local and provincial bosses, effectively removed the unions from the leadership and candidate selection process. Increasingly, unionists who made it onto candidate lists did so "through the goodwill of the politicians in power."[73] According to former CGT General Secretary Saúl Ubaldini,

> We participate only if the governors say we can participate...the "62" disappeared. The *tercio* disappeared. And logically, with their disappearance, no one is going to come looking for us.... Today labor does not even have the power to say "we want to impose some candidacies." We published a communiqué the day before the lists were made [this year], but none of the governors, none of the list-makers, paid any attention to it.[74]

Three Cases of Machine Consolidation

The consolidation of machine politics and the subsequent decline in union influence can be seen in the cases of two large industrialized municipalities, the Federal Capital and La Matanza, and the country's largest and most industrialized province, Buenos Aires. In each of these cases, office-holding party bosses used their control over state resources to coopt the vast majority of local leaders and neighborhood *punteros*, thereby ensuring victory in internal elections. This left the unions with little to offer in exchange for candidacies or party leadership posts.[75] Lacking an encompassing organization, labor fragmented in each district, and unions were reduced to competing among themselves for positions on party lists. It is not a coincidence that in all three of these cases, successful machine builders were Renovators. In their struggle to defeat union-backed Orthodox factions in the mid-1980s, urban Renovators such as Eduardo Duhalde (Buenos Aires), Carlos Grosso (Federal Capital), and Alberto Pierri (La Matanza) developed sophisticated organizational techniques. These included the use of polling, the media, and outside consultants, but they also included patronage-based financing schemes that were both quantitatively and qualitatively different from those employed by their Orthodox opponents. The regularized distribution of jobs and other material resources as a payoff for political loyalty had not been possible during Peronism's proscription, and although the unionists and Orthodox leaders who dominated the party in the 1983–5 period certainly distributed

---

[73] Author's interview with Juan José Zanola, general secretary of the bank workers association, October 22, 1997.
[74] Author's interview, October 3, 1997.
[75] According to Quilmes UOM leader and city council member Juan Carlos Chumen, "They don't need us any more. The political sector does and undoes. The governor prepares the party lists as he wants. And who is going to confront the governor?...If we can't offer anything in exchange, how can we enter into an alliance? They'll laugh us out of there. All we can do is support the party's candidate in the next election" (author's interview, May 15, 1997).

patronage, these exchanges were never very systematic. Indeed, Orthodox leaders relied as much on union activists and solidarity incentives as on the distribution of material payoffs. It was the Renovators who, in need of a means of competing with orthodox unions, routinized such practices.

The Federal Capital: The Rise and Fall of the "System"

The machine that emerged in the capital centered around Carlos Grosso. Grosso, who was elected president of the local PJ after the Renovation won control of the party in 1985, was appointed mayor of the city of Buenos Aires by President Menem in 1989. During his mayoral term, which lasted until his resignation amid corruption charges in 1992, Grosso consolidated a patronage-based coalition known as the "System." The origins of the System lie in the Renovation coalition that defeated the "62" in 1985, which consisted of two powerful *puntero* networks: Peronist Victory (VP) and the Peronist Unity Front (FUP). The System began to take form in 1987, when eight VP members were elected to the city council. The new city council members became "professionals of patronage," building followings through a system of "paid activism."[76] The increased availability of patronage jobs (each city council member was allocated twenty staff positions) produced an "explosion of base units" as activists flocked to the emerging *agrupaciones*. By the late 1980s, "the neighborhoods, which were once controlled by the unions, were dominated by the city council members."[77]

When Grosso was appointed mayor in 1989, VP and FUP divided up the city government, vastly increasing the number of activists on the government payroll.[78] The *agrupaciones* "municipalized Peronism, converting the party activists into city employees."[79] The city council, over which the PJ gained control in 1989, was another important source of patronage. The city council payroll grew from 1,771 in 1985 to over 5,000 in 1991 (Carnota and Talpone 1995: 54–5). Still other patronage jobs were found in the national government, particularly in the Ministry of the Interior. By the early 1990s, the vast majority of the city's roughly four hundred base units were run by activists with government jobs. As *punteros* joined pro-System *agrupaciones* in search of patronage, power became increasingly concentrated in the hands of Grosso and top VP and FUP leaders. *Agrupaciones* that opposed the System were marginalized, as Grosso lists won the 1988 and 1991 internal elections with more than 70 percent of the vote. Although Grosso was forced to resign in 1992, the System remained largely intact under mayors Saúl Bouer and

---

[76] Author's interview with PJ activist Juan Carlos Castro, September 30, 1997.
[77] Author's interview with PJ activist Carlos Racedo, March 15, 1997.
[78] According to FUP leader Eduardo Rollano, the initial takeover of city hall was accompanied by a "massive distribution of patronage" (author's interview, June 24, 1997).
[79] Author's interview with Salvador Corraro, former city council member and president of the PJ-Federal Capital congress, October 13, 1997.

Jorge Domínguez between 1992 and 1995. Although its corrupt image hurt the local PJ electorally,[80] the System remained unbeatable in internal elections through 1996. Indeed, it took the election of Radical Mayor Fernando De la Rua in 1996 and an intervention of the local party by the national PJ leadership in 1997 to effectively destroy it.

The consolidation of the System was accompanied by the marginalization of organized labor. Labor fragmented in the 1990s, with individual unions such as the oil workers (ex-"62"), public administration workers (ex-*Ubaldinista*), custodians (ex-"25"), tobacco employees (ex-"25"), and pasta workers (ex-"25") creating individual *agrupaciones*, and the UOM (ex-"62") and the city workers union largely negotiating on their own. As a result, labor's negotiating leverage vis-á-vis Grosso eroded, and the number of union candidacies for higher office dwindled. Whereas unionists gained two spots on the party's Chamber of Deputies list in 1989, they received one spot in 1991 and 1993 and were excluded entirely after that.

La Matanza: "Business Peronism"

La Matanza Peronism was dominated by Chamber of Deputies President Alberto Pierri in the 1990s. A businessperson who had never participated in politics, Pierri joined the PJ in 1985, reportedly gaining a spot on the Renovation's extraparty parliamentary list in exchange for a substantial campaign contribution (López Echague 1996: 87–9). Pierri established his political base in La Matanza, where he owned a paper factory, and formed the *agrupación* Peronist Militancy and Renovation (MyRP). At the time, city politics was dominated by Mayor Federico Russo, a traditional boss backed by Orthodox and labor sectors. Pierri brought an entirely different style of politics to La Matanza. Whereas Russo's governing style was based on personal loyalties and long-term friendship networks, Pierri "treated Peronism like a business,"[81] paying activists regular stipends and "giving jobs to those who had always worked for nothing in their neighborhoods."[82] Although Pierri lost to Russo in the 1987 mayoral primary, he built a powerful base. In 1989, Pierri was elected president of the Chamber of Deputies, which gave him control of hundreds of patronage jobs. Using these jobs and his own money, Pierri bought off dozens of Russo's *punteros*, and in 1991, he defeated Russo for control of the party and imposed his former accountant, Hector Cozzi, as mayor. Once in control of the local government, Pierri used city jobs and an annual $12.5 million of "reserved funds" in the city budget[83]

---

[80] The PJ vote fell from 32 percent in the 1993 Congressional elections to 17 percent in the 1995 Senate elections.
[81] Author's interview with Nedda Abella, secretary of women in the PJ-La Matanza party council, May 16, 1997.
[82] Author's interview with Gloria Rodriguez, La Matanza secretary of culture, April 8, 1997.
[83] Author's interview with city council member Abraham Delgado, November 21, 1997.

to transform the MyRP into a massive enterprise capable of financing 480 base units. Control over state resources enabled Pierri to coopt all major *agrupaciones* into "unity lists" for the 1993 and 1995 elections.

Labor influence diminished significantly under Pierri. The UOM, municipal workers, and other major unions had aligned with Russo in both 1983 and 1987, getting unionists elected to city council each year.[84] Although Pierri was initially backed by the "25," unions were never an important part of the *Pierrista* coalition. Moreover, labor was so fragmented by the 1990s that it enjoyed little leverage in negotiating with the Pierri machine. Several unions, including the rubber workers, auto workers, retail workers, and doormen, established individual *agrupaciones*. Two other unions, the wood workers and the plastic workers, aligned with the Work and Production *agrupación*. Still others – including the UOM, auto workers, and city workers – worked individually, generally negotiating alliances with Pierri. They were largely ineffective. No unionists gained positions in the city council after 1991. In 1997, former "25" leader Osvaldo Borda was unable to gain re-election to Congress, and the local branch of the UOM failed to place its general secretary, Carlos G'Dansky, on the PJ's legislative list.

The Province of Buenos Aires: The Duhaldista *Machine*

In Buenos Aires, Eduardo Duhalde built a powerful machine after leaving the vice presidency to run for governor in 1991. Duhalde began to build a provincial base in 1990, when he created the Federal League, which was based on a network of local party and union leaders who opposed then-Governor Cafiero. The well-financed League won over a large number of local Cafiero supporters, weakening Cafiero's Buenos Aires Peronist Front (FREPEBO) to such an extent that it gave up its aspirations for retaining the governorship and backed Duhalde. Duhalde sealed the Federal League-FREPEBO alliance by offering the vice governorship to *Cafierista* Rafael Romá. This coalition gave Duhalde the majority he needed to gain control of the party.

After winning the governorship, Duhalde built a broad coalition based on an alliance between the League and the ex-*Cafieristas*, who had organized the Buenos Aires Peronist League (LIPEBO). LIPEBO, which included a large number of mayors and progressive Renovators, allowed Duhalde to maintain the support of many traditional and left-of-center Peronists. The coalition was cemented with patronage. The Federal League was given control of the public works ministry (held by Hugo Toledo), which, together with the presidency of the national Congress (held by League member Pierri), served as the basis for that faction's patronage distribution. LIPEBO controlled the provincial legislature, which provided assembly president Osvaldo Mercuri with a

---

[84] Author's interview with Carlos G'Dansky, general secretary of UOM-La Matanza, December 2, 1996.

reported $90 million a year and hundreds of jobs with which to maintain his organization.[85] Duhalde also made political use of the Suburban Reparation Fund, an arrangement that diverted 10 percent of federal tax revenues to Greater Buenos Aires for public works. The Fund invested $1.6 billion on more than twelve hundred public works projects between 1992 and 1995 (López Echague 1996: 173–5). This money was allocated according to a clear political logic, with pro-Duhalde mayors getting the largest share (López Echague 1996: 167–173). Finally, Duhalde created the Family Council, which, under the guidance of his wife, was given control over the bulk of the province's social programs. The largest of these programs, the Life Plan, had an annual budget of $200 million and used ten thousand female volunteers – called *Manzaneras* – to deliver milk, eggs, and other basic goods to more than half a million people.[86]

Control over patronage permitted Duhalde to establish "total hegemony" over Buenos Aires Peronism.[87] Although the province's two dominant factions, the Federal League and LIPEBO, competed against each other at the local level, they both supported Duhalde at the provincial level.[88] In the 1993 primaries, the Federal League–LIPEBO coalition defeated a Menemist faction with an astounding 93 percent of the vote.[89] In 1995, the party congress canceled the gubernatorial and legislative primaries altogether, authorizing Duhalde to make the lists.[90] In 1997, Duhalde again imposed a unity list, this time headed by his wife.

Union influence in Buenos Aires Peronism declined significantly in the 1990s. In 1991, when Duhalde needed union support in his bid for the gubernatorial nomination, labor was able to place four unionists on the PJ's parliamentary list. In 1993, Duhalde placed three unionists on the PJ legislative list, and in 1995, after hinting that he might not name any unionists, Duhalde named two.[91] In 1997, labor again received two candidacies, and in 1999, it received one candidacy. Thus, although Duhalde continued to nominate unionists in the late 1990s, the nature of nomination process had changed dramatically. As former "25" leader José Pedraza put it,

If two unionists get on the list, it is because Duhalde says so. It is he who decides who the union candidates are and how many there will be. That is what remains of union participation in politics.[92]

---

[85] *Clarín*, November 14, 1997, p. 24.
[86] *Página/12*, August 30, 1996, pp. 12–13; *El Bonaerense*, January 1997, p. 14.
[87] Author's interview with former provincial senator José Maria Rocca, May 19, 1997.
[88] Duhalde described the Federal League and LIPEBO as "two legs. They don't fight against each other" (N.C.O., May 16, 1997, p. 5).
[89] *Clarín*, June 7, 1993, p. 5.
[90] *Clarín*, December 18, 1994, pp. 12–13.
[91] *Clarín*, November 8, 1994, p. 17.
[92] Author's interview, July 10, 1997.

Similar machines emerged in other provinces in the late 1980s and early 1990s. In Santa Fe, for example, Governors José Maria Vernet and Victor Reviglio built a patronage-based coalition that came to be known as the "Cooperative," which dominated the provincial party until it collapsed due to a series of corruption scandals in 1991. In Mendoza, the Orange List faction established a powerful patronage-based structure during the governorships of José Octavio Bordón, Rodolfo Gabrielli, and Arturo LaFalla. In La Pampa, San Luis, and Santa Cruz, multiterm governors built powerful machines and dominated politics in their provinces throughout the decade. Stable machines also emerged in Formosa, Misiones, and Salta. Although no stable machines emerged in provinces where the PJ remained out of power (such as Chubut, Córdoba, Neuquén, and Rio Negro), machine politics nevertheless became widespread. In all of these cases, the rise of machine politics was accompanied by a decline in union influence.

Union Responses to Machine Politics

Unions pursued three different strategies in response to the consolidation of machine politics. First, the UOM and a few other orthodox unions maintained a corporatist strategy.[93] These unions invested little in territorial politics and avoided, whenever possible, competing in internal elections. Instead, they sought to obtain influence via direct exchanges with party bosses, offering union resources in exchange for candidacies. Although the UOM was able to negotiate Congressional candidacies in every election through 1993, by the early-1990s, the strength of local machines had greatly reduced its negotiating power. The UOM failed to gain candidacies in 1995 and 1997, and when Naldo Brunelli's term expired at the end of 1997, the union was left without legislative representation for the first time since the dictatorship.

A second strategy was to use union resources to finance territorial *agrupaciones*. This strategy was widely pursued by unions from the "25" in the 1990s.[94] In the Federal Capital, for example, tobacco employees leader Roberto Digón created an *agrupación* called Solidarity, a union-financed organization that sponsored dozens of UBs and helped him win a seat

---

[93] Other unions that may be said to have followed this strategy include the textile workers, Federal Capital municipal workers, light and power workers, cemetery workers, and to a lesser extent, the bank workers.

[94] According to restaurant workers union leader (and Beratazegui city council member) Angentino Geneiro, "the days of union quotas are over. The politicians are not going to come to us. They hardly need us anymore. We have to compete in the political terrain.... We have to form *agrupaciones* and compete in elections. If we don't, we'll be left on the outside" (author's interview, May 22, 1997). Similarly, according to tobacco workers union leader Antonio Cortes, "we realized that being a union leader was no longer sufficient to gain influence in politics, and that we had to deepen our work in the neighborhoods" (author's interview, October 13, 1997).

in Congress in 1993. Custodians' union leader José Maria Santamaría "territorialized" his union by placing a local union hall in each of the city's twenty-eight wards. During election campaigns, the union halls served as UBs, transforming themselves into the "October 2" *agrupación*. "October 2" helped elect Santamaria to two terms in the city council. Another ex-"25" member, Juan Manuel Pico of the pasta workers union, built a powerful base in the city's twenty-fifth ward, which he used as a springboard to the city council presidency. In Greater Buenos Aires, Osvaldo Borda (rubber workers) and José Luis Castillo (ship captains) created *agrupaciones* in La Matanza and Avellaneda, respectively. Both were elected to three terms in Congress, and Castillo was elected president of his local party. Several non- "25" union leaders also created *agrupaciones* in the 1990s. For example, restaurant workers union leader Luis Barrionuevo used resources from his union to build a powerful political organization in Greater Buenos Aires, which helped him elect both his wife and brother-in-law to Congress. In Tucumán, private oil workers leader Julio Miranda, who was originally elected to Congress as a member of the "62," created the *agrupación* Peronism of Hope in 1992. The *agrupación* became one of the leading factions in Tucumán, helping to elect Miranda senator in 1992 and governor in 1999. The success of these entrepreneurs induced other union leaders to follow their example, and dozens more union-based *agrupaciones* appeared in the late 1990s.[95]

Although territorial *agrupaciones* have at times been effective in electing union leaders to higher office, this strategy faces two important limitations. First, because *agrupaciones* are almost always based on single unions, and frequently on local branches of those unions, they tend to be highly fragmented. This weakens labor's collective power, enabling party bosses to play unions against each other. According to La Matanza textile workers union leader Hugo Benítez,

> it does us no good when the metal workers make their deal, the auto workers make their deal, and the textile workers make their deal. It serves individual leaders, but it does not serve organized labor as a whole.[96]

Union-financed *agrupaciones* have become fixed investments, entrenching this system of fragmented union politics and making the construction of crosssectoral union political projects even more difficult.

[95] These included the Federal Capital–based White Peronism, which drew the bulk of the activists from the public administration workers union (UPCN), and the Quilmes-based Peronist Commitment, which was led by private security workers union leader Alberto García.

[96] Author's interview, April 11, 1997. According to former "25" leader Roberto García, unions "were right to open up base units, like the politicians, but we should have done it collectively, as a single organization. We ignored this and it cost us terribly" (author's interview, June 23, 1997).

Second, in building territorial bases and competing in internal elections, union leaders are compelled to act according to the same logic as their non-union counterparts. Their primary objectives become winning over *punteros* and negotiating alliances with local bosses,[97] and when they are elected, they owe more to their territorial bases and party bosses than to their unions. Thus, Congressional Deputy Juan José Chica Rodriguez, who is general secretary of San Juan branch of the light and power workers union, "didn't run for office as a union representative," but rather "as a citizen and a party member."[98] Chica Rodriguez claims that he "didn't even consult the union" when he decided to enter politics.[99] Not surprisingly, the behavior of territorially based union legislators tends to be similar to that of nonunion legislators. Indeed, many union leaders who build territorial bases eventually leave their unions and become full-time politicians. Such was the case with Angel Abasto, a member of Congress who was originally elected to the Quilmes city council as leader of the local textile workers union, and railway workers union leaders Lorenzo Pepe and Oraldo Britos, both of whom left the union for long careers in Congress.

In an effort to limit fragmentation and hold elected unionists accountable to labor as a whole, some union leaders opted for a third strategy during the 1990s: the creation of "labor roundtables." Modeled on the Menem for President Labor Roundtable, labor roundtables brought various unions together into a single body, generally in support of a particular faction or candidate. This enabled the unions to negotiate as a bloc, thereby preventing party bosses from playing them against one another. Scores of labor roundtables emerged at the local and provincial levels in the mid-1990s. In La Matanza, for example, unions formed two labor roundtables in preparation for the 1997 legislative elections: the LIPEBO Labor Roundtable and the Federal League Labor Roundtable. The LIPEBO Labor Roundtable was formed by eight unions seeking to "regain the influence we have lost" and "get one or two of our *compañeros*" into the city government.[100] Offering human and organizational resources collected among the participating unions, the group hoped to defeat incumbent PJ Mayor Hector Cozzi, whom it viewed as antilabor. It also began to define a programmatic agenda for the local labor movement, including a plan to develop an industrial

---

[97] According to former "25" leader José Castillo, "I have my own *punteros*, just like everyone else" (author's interview, July 2, 1997).

[98] Author's interview, September 23, 1997. Similarly, tobacco workers union leader and Federal Capital city council member Antonio Cortes claims that "I don't get elected these days as a unionist. I get elected because of my political base" (author's interview, October 13, 1997).

[99] Author's interview, September 23, 1997.

[100] Author's interview with Mario Ortiz, general secretary of the La Matanza branch of the textile workers union, April 8, 1997. Participating unions included the auto workers, textile workers, custodians, wood workers, chemical workers, and plastic workers.

park.[101] The twenty-seven-member Federal League Labor Roundtable, which backed Cozzi, sought to create a "permanent labor organization" and "win back a seat at the table" in the local PJ leadership.[102] In the province of Buenos Aires, a group of unions formed the Duhalde for President Labor Roundtable in 1996 in an effort to "build up a little strength to be able to influence some decisions and include some of our candidates on the lists."[103] Although the roundtable initially brought together an impressive number of unions, it divided along political factional lines and was "captured" by Federal League unions. Duhalde ignored the roundtable in drawing up the party's 1997 legislative lists, and the organization subsequently collapsed.

Labor roundtables are unlikely to function as effective crosssectoral organizations because they lack the resources necessary to discipline member unions or to act on their behalf. Union leaders are thus free to prioritize their own interests over those of the roundtable, and as a result, roundtables routinely collapse as member unions negotiate individual deals with party bosses. At best, then, labor roundtables can be expected to function as short-lived coalitions of unions that converge around a single candidacy and then dissolve.

The Decline of Union Influence

The consolidation of machine politics brought a precipitous decline in labor influence in the PJ. Because local and provincial party bosses controlled powerful patronage-based organizations, they no longer needed union support in either internal primaries or general elections. As a result, unionists were increasingly excluded from party leaderships. The erosion of union influence can be seen in the change in the number of unionists represented in the national PJ leadership and the Chamber of Deputies. Table 5.2 charts the decline in union representation in the PJ National Council. Although the 1987 party charter guaranteed the unions seventeen representatives in the 110 member National Council, the number of unionists in positions of power declined considerably. In the National Council's Executive Board, for example, union representation fell from more than a third (37.5 percent) in 1983 to a quarter in 1990 to an eighth (12.5 percent) in 1995.

[101] Author's interviews with Carlos Coma, general secretary of the plastic workers union, April 4, 1997, and Ricardo Pignanelli, general secretary of the La Matanza branch of the auto workers union, May 7, 1997.
[102] Author's interview with Pablo Gonzales, adjunct secretary of the La Matanza branch of the construction workers union and member of the Federal League Labor Roundtable, June 11, 1997. Participating unions included the construction workers, restaurant workers, railway workers, rubber workers, and light and power workers.
[103] Author's interview with hospital workers union leader Carlos West Ocampo, October 13, 1997.

TABLE 5.2. *The Erosion of Union Representation in the PJ National Council, 1983–95*

	1983	1990	1995
Party executive[a]	Acting president	1st vice president	None
Executive Board[b] (percentage of total)	37.5	25.0	12.5
Full National Council (percentage of total)	30.8	15.5	15.5

Notes:
[a] Includes the party presidency and vice presidencies.
[b] Includes party executive and party secretaries. The Executive Board had eight members in 1983, twenty-four members in 1990, and thirty-two members in 1995.

TABLE 5.3. *PJ Trade Unionists Elected to the Chamber of Deputies in the Five Largest Industrialized Districts, 1983–2001*

District	1983	1985	1987	1989	1991	1993	1995	1997	1999	2001
Federal Capital	3	1	1	2	1	1	0	0	0	0
Buenos Aires	10	3	6	4	4	3	2	2	1	1
Córdoba	1	1	0	1	0	0	0	0	0	0
Mendoza	1	0	1	0	0	0	0	0	0	0
Santa Fe	4	2	1	2	0	0	0	0	0	0
TOTAL	19	7	9	9	5	4	2	2	1	1

Source: Author's own count.

A second indicator of the decline of union influence is the steady reduction in the number of unionists elected to congress. Table 5.3 shows this decline for the major urban districts.[104] Whereas in the mid-1980s union members were regularly elected in all of the major industrialized districts, a decade later they were only being elected in Buenos Aires. Table 5.4 shows the overall decline in union representation in the Chamber of Deputies. The number of Peronist union representatives declined steadily between 1985 and 1995, despite the fact that the overall size of the PJ bloc increased substantially during that period. Whereas unionists constituted more than a quarter of the PJ bloc in the mid-1980s, a decade later they constituted less than 5 percent.[105] By the end of the decade, the percentage of unionists in the PJ bloc was lower than that of the opposition Front

---

[104] The 1983 figure is inflated due to the fact that all Chamber of Deputies seats were filled in that year, as opposed to half in subsequent elections.

[105] In 1994, not a single unionist was elected to the PJ bloc in the Constituent Assembly, while three unionists were elected on the opposition Big Front ticket.

TABLE 5.4. *The Erosion of Peronist Union Representation in the Chamber of Deputies, 1983–2001*

	1983	1985	1987	1989	1991	1993	1995	1997	1999	2001
Number of union members in PJ bloc	29	28	22	24	18	10	6	5	4	3
Overall size of PJ bloc	111	101	105	120	120	128	130	119	99	118
Percentage of PJ bloc belonging to union	26.1	27.7	21.0	20.0	15.0	7.8	4.6	4.2	4.0	2.5

Source: Gutierrez (1998: 41–4) and author's own count.

for a Country in Solidarity (FREPASO),[106] which was hardly a labor-based party.

There was also a qualitative change in the relationship between the unions and their legislative representatives. With the "62's" decline and the strengthening of territorial machines, the unionists elected to Congress increasingly owed their seats to political bosses, rather than their unions or labor as a whole. As a result, the CGT "has no control over them whatsoever."[107] According to Oscar Lescano, who served as CGT general secretary in 1992 and 1993,

> In the past, the CGT and "62" placed men on the lists, so these men depended on the labor movement. Now the unionists... are sent there by political bosses.... There is no centralized power, either in the CGT or the 62 Organizations.[108]

The CGT's difficulties in controlling union deputies became manifest in the latter half of 1991, when the dominant labor factions began to shift from a strategy of unconditional support for the Menem government to one of critical, or negotiated, support. In June 1991, when union deputies helped block a government bill to postpone payments of Christmas bonuses, seventeen of twenty-four union deputies joined the various CGT factions in opposing the bill, while seven unionists backed the Menem-Duhalde position in favor of the bill.[109] The CGT's influence over labor deputies further eroded during the following Congressional term. In September 1992, when Oscar Lescano threatened to order labor deputies to boycott a session dedicated to

---

[106] Four of FREPASO's thirty-eight congressional deputies (10.5 percent) were unionists in 1997.
[107] Author's interview with former CGT General Secretary Naldo Brunelli, July 22, 1997.
[108] Author's interview, October 27, 1997.
[109] *Clarín*, June 21, 1991, p. 10.

privatizing the state oil company (thereby preventing a quorum) as leverage in negotiations to pass collective bargaining legislation, only five of fifteen union deputies heeded his call.[110] After a meeting with government officials, the other ten union deputies opted to attend the session and vote for the bill.[111] The following year, Labor Minister Enrique Rodriguez secured a commitment from six of the ten labor deputies to respect "party discipline" and act independently of the CGT on legislation to flexibilize labor markets.[112] The labor deputies eventually split on the moderate (CGT-backed) flexibilization bill that was passed in 1995, with a slight majority voting for the package.[113] During the 1995–7 Congressional period, four of the six union legislators – Alfredo Atanasoff, Osvaldo Borda, José Luis Castillo, and Juan José Chica Rodriguez – regularly voted in line with their governors. Only Naldo Brunelli of the UOM consistently voted a union line.[114]

Union influence over party strategy declined as well. Whereas union leaders had largely imposed party strategy in 1983 and party and union leaders continued to converge on programmatic issues during the Renovation period, in the early 1990s, *Clarín* described labor as "scarcely a spectator" within the party.[115] According to pharmacy workers union leader José Azcurra, a former member of the National Council who attended virtually all of the National Council meetings between 1989 and 1991, "no one listened" to him and other union leaders who spoke out against the government's economic policies.[116] Although the CGT continued to back the PJ throughout the decade, its relationship to the party was closer to that of a friendly lobbyist than a partner.[117] To the extent that labor was able to influence government policy, as it did in the areas of health insurance deregulation, labor market reforms, and social security reform, it did so via direct negotiations with the government or government-sponsored tripartite negotiations (Etchemendy and Palermo 1998). Rarely were unions able to

---

[110] Author's interview with Oscar Lescano, October 27, 1997; also *Clarín*, September 17, 1992, pp. 4–5; September 24, 1992, p. 4.

[111] *Clarín*, September 24, 1992, p. 4. According to one CGT leader, "In my presence one of [the labor deputies] talked to [government official Eduardo] Bauza by telephone to tell him that if they solved a problem in his union, he would take the floor" (*Clarín*, September 28, 1997, pp. 8–9).

[112] *Ambito Financiero*, September 15, 1993, p. 3.

[113] *Clarín*, March 8, 1995, p. 8; March 9, 1995, p. 2.

[114] Author's interviews with Naldo Brunelli, July 22, 1997, and CGT General Secretary Rodolfo Daer, October 2, 1997. Another unionist, Roberto Digón, maintained a territorial base in a district without a powerful party boss (the Federal Capital) and was thus relatively independent.

[115] *Clarín*, September 28, 1991, p. 14.

[116] Author's interview, October 20, 1997.

[117] Indeed, CGT leader and National Council member Carlos West Ocampo declared in 1997 that the PJ was "more closely aligned with big business today than it is with the CGT" (author's interview, October 13, 1997).

channel their demands through the party. For example, when labor leaders lobbied the National Council to oppose the government's plan to deregulate the union-administered health insurance system, they were unable to get the body even to debate the issue.[118] When the CGT carried out its first general strike against the government in November 1992, the PJ publicly opposed it as "without motive."[119] This marked the first time since the return to democracy that the PJ had opposed a CGT strike.

Labor's influence in the PJ remained low after Menem left office. The party's top leaders in the post-1999 period, such as Governors José Manuel De la Sota, Carlos Reutemann, and Carlos Ruckauf, maintained few ties to the unions and rarely consulted them when formulating their positions on key issues. In 2000, for example, De la Sota, Reutemann, and other PJ governors supported Radical President Fernando De la Rua's efforts to liberalize labor markets (despite intense opposition from sectors of the Peronist labor movement) and opposed the CGT's first general strike against the De la Rua government.

The erosion of union influence in the PJ generated an unprecedented debate in the labor movement over the value of maintaining the party-labor alliance. Within the CGT leadership, discussions began to take place over whether or not to "break with the party, like in Spain."[120] In 1992, a handful of white-collar unions, including the state workers (ATE) and teachers (CTERA) unions, left the CGT to form the Argentine Workers Congress (CTA), which adopted an autonomous position vis-á-vis political parties. A few other unions, including the paper workers, beer workers, pharmacy workers, and bus drivers unions, remained Peronist but largely detached themselves from party activity in the 1990s. Many of these unions joined the Argentine Workers Movement (MTA), which remained within the CGT but adopted a dissident profile.

Yet the vast majority of unions continued to participate in Peronist party politics throughout the 1990s.[121] They campaigned for particular factions in primary elections, contributed financial, organizational, and human resources to general election campaigns, and lobbied to place unionists on candidate lists and in party and government offices. A survey of thirty-six local unions in the Federal Capital, La Matanza, and Quilmes found that thirty-three of them, or 92 percent, participated in party activity in 1997 (Table 5.5). Thirty-one unions contributed financial or organizational resources to internal or general election campaigns. When asked whether they supported the idea of continued participation in the PJ, thirty union leaders

---

[118] *Clarín*, January 23, 1992, p. 3; February 19, 1992, p. 13.
[119] *Clarín*, November 5, 1992, p. 11.
[120] Author's interview with CGT General Secretary Rodolfo Daer, October 2, 1997.
[121] For an analysis of why the CGT remained wedded to the PJ alliance, see Levitsky and Way (1998).

TABLE 5.5. *Local Union Participation in the PJ in the 1990s*[a]

Question	Responses	Number	Percent
Did the union participate in PJ politics in 1997?	Yes, actively	25	69.4
	Yes, minimally	8	22.2
	No	3	8.3
Did the union provide support to a PJ faction in 1997?	Yes	31	86.1
	No	5	13.9
Has a union member held a post in the local party or government since 1990?	Yes	15	41.7
	No	21	58.3
How has the union's participation in the PJ changed over the last 10 years?	Increased	3	9.7
	Unchanged	15	48.4
	Decreased	13	41.9
Does the union favor continued participation in the PJ?	Yes	30	83.3
	Only if PJ changes	2	5.6
	No	4	11.1

Note:
[a] Based on author's survey of leaders of thirty-six local unions in the Federal Capital, La Matanza, and Quilmes.

said yes and only four said no. A survey of national-level unions produced similar results (Table 5.6). Thirty-three of thirty-nine unions reported having participated in Peronist party activity in 1997, and twenty-four unions reported having placed a member of their leadership in an elected, appointed, or party office since 1990. Although a majority reported that their union's political participation had declined over the last ten years, only three of thirty-nine opposed continued participation in the party.

This evidence suggests that McGuire's (1995: 237–8; 1997: 281) concern that the PJ's continued low level of institutionalization in the 1990s reinforced the party's historical failure to commit unions to party – and hence democratic – politics may be unfounded. Union leaders remained highly involved in PJ politics through the end of the 1990s, particularly at the local and provincial levels. As such, they are likely to have developed a significant stake in the continuation of party activity.

Why, given the clear decline in labor's influence, did individual unions continue to participate actively in the PJ in the 1990s? One was the existence of a long history of union participation in Peronist politics, as well as the persistence of strong interpersonal ties between party and union leaders. Indeed, most Argentine unions were still dominated by unionists whose formative experiences occurred during the late 1960s and 1970s. This generation of union leaders, many of whom suffered acute persecution for their Peronist activities, was highly unlikely to abandon the party. However, another reason why individual unions continued to engage in party politics in the 1990s is that despite the rather meager collective result of labor's

TABLE 5.6. *National Union Participation in the PJ in the 1990s*[a]

Question	Responses	Number	Percent
Did the union participate in PJ politics in 1997?	Yes, national and local	14	35.9
	Yes, local level only	19	48.7
	No	6	15.4
Has a union member held a post in the party or government since 1990?	Yes	24	61.5
	No	15	38.5
Approximately how many members of local union branches hold positions in provincial party leaderships or governments?	More than 10	6	16.7
	Between 3 and 10	14	38.9
	Between 1 and 3	3	8.3
	None	13	36.1
How has the union's participation in the PJ changed over the last 10 years?	Increased	7	20.0
	Unchanged	8	22.9
	Decreased	20	57.1
Does the union favor continued participation in the PJ?	Yes	31	79.5
	Only if PJ changes	5	12.8
	No	3	7.7

Note:
[a] Based on author's survey of leaders of thirty-nine national unions in 1997.

political activity, individual union leaders continued to find party participation worthwhile. Unions remain an important springboard for political careers in the PJ, particularly at the local level. Most unions continue to possess substantial financial and organizational resources that entrepreneurial union leaders may use in launching political careers. Union leaders who invest in politics have a reasonable chance to be elected to city council or the provincial legislature, from which they may later build patronage-based organizations.

ASSESSING THE PJ'S COALITIONAL SHIFT: DEUNIONIZATION AS SUCCESSFUL ADAPTATION?

In less than a decade, then, the PJ transformed from a de facto labor party into a predominantly patronage-based party in which organized labor exerted only marginal influence. Whereas trade unions had held a near-hegemonic position in the party leadership in 1983 and had been junior partners in the Renovation leadership in 1987, by the early 1990s, they were excluded from the party's dominant coalition. Moreover, unions had ceased to be the primary organizational linkage between the PJ leadership and its urban base.[122]

[122] Of the base units surveyed for this study, only 14 percent maintained even minimal ties to a union.

Although the transition from laborism to machine politics had important costs from the perspective of organized labor, it arguably benefited the PJ in at least two ways. First, it facilitated the PJ's adaptation to an increasingly "postindustrial" electoral environment by allowing it both to appeal to a new constituency (the new middle class) and to find a new basis on which to maintain its old constituency (the urban working and lower classes). On the one hand, the reduction in union influence allowed PJ leaders to broaden the party's electoral appeal, which allowed the Peronists to make important inroads among middle-class and independent voters. In 1987 and 1989, these were largely progressive, left-of-center voters. During the 1990s, as we shall see, they were largely conservative voters.

At the same time, the territorially based *agrupación* system created new bases upon which the PJ could sustain its linkages to the urban working and lower classes. Clientelistic linkages are better suited than unions to organize – and win votes among – the fragmented and heterogeneous strata of urban unemployed, self-employed, and informal sector workers generated by deindustrialization. In urban zones characterized by high structural unemployment, unions tend to be marginal or nonexistent, and corporate channels of representation are therefore likely to be ineffective. A territorial organization, and especially one based on the distribution of particularistic benefits, can be far more effective in such a context. As Chapter 7 shows, territorial *puntero* networks became the hub of Peronist activity in the 1990s, providing access to jobs, neighborhood services, and basic items such as food and medicine to people who had been marginalized from the formal economy and even the state.

The transition from union-based politics to machine politics may also have facilitated the programmatic shift undertaken by the Menem government in the 1990s. Coalitional change does not, of course, necessitate programmatic change. Indeed, as Martin Shefter has shown in the case of the Tammany Hall machine in New York City, machine politics may be quite compatible with pro-union policies (1986: 267).[123] Nevertheless, patronage-based organizations tend to be more pragmatic than class-based organizations (Scott 1969; Wilson 1973/1995: 37–8). Primarily concerned with local, particularistic needs, machines are generally more willing than class-based parties to accommodate elite economic interests.

The PJ's shift from laborism to machine politics facilitated the party's neoliberal turn in two ways. First, it largely eliminated an important source of potential intraparty opposition to the Menem program. Peronist union leaders tended to be more critical of the Menem government's neoliberal program than nonunion party leaders. Table 5.7 shows the responses of

---

[123] According to Shefter, the Tammany Hall machine reached an "accommodation" with organized labor and in fact helped push important pro-labor legislation through the state legislature (1986: 267).

nonunion National Council members, unionist National Council members, and Peronist union leaders to a 1997 survey on the Menem government's economic program. Respondents were asked which of the following four statements most closely described their view of the government's economic policies: (1) The neoliberal reforms were necessary and should be continued; (2) neoliberal policies were initially necessary but should have been modified after the crisis ended; (3) some kind of economic reform was necessary, but the Menem government went too fast or too far; (4) the neoliberal reforms should not have been carried out. Those who chose the first response were labeled *neoliberals*; those who chose the second response were labeled *pragmatists*; those who chose the third response were labeled *critics*; and those who chose the fourth response were labeled *opponents*. As can be seen in Table 5.7, union leaders were less likely to be neoliberals and more likely to be critics or opponents. Whereas only about a third of political leaders on the National Council could be classified as critics or opponents, about two-thirds of national union leaders fell into those categories.

Table 5.8 applies the same questions to local union and party leaders from the Federal Capital, La Matanza, and Quilmes.[124] While local leaders are generally more critical of the reforms than are national leaders (thereby reducing the difference between political and union leaders), one still finds union leaders slightly less likely to be neoliberals and slightly more likely to be critics or opponents. Indeed, nearly a third (31.4 percent) of local unionists fully opposed the reform process, compared to only 16.7 percent of local political leaders. Thus, deunionization may have eroded an important source of potential intraparty opposition to the Menem program.

Second, the shift from union-based politics to machine politics may have helped to dampen popular sector opposition to neoliberalism. Research by Javier Auyero (1998, 2000) suggests that the consolidation of clientelistic linkages began to change the way working- and lower-class Peronists relate to the party. During the 1960s and 1970s, when the Peronist party was proscribed, trade unions represented Peronist workers both economically and politically. Unions thus played a fundamental role in the formation and reproduction of Peronist identities, infusing the movement with a class character (Torre 1983: 12; James 1988: 18). This identity changed significantly in the 1980s and 1990s. As Auyero (2000) argues, in poor urban zones, Peronist identities are now closer to those of "clients" than of workers. Although the Peronist identity had always been ambiguous and contested, and although "social work" and "giving away things" have always formed part of the Peronist subculture (Auyero 2000: 140–8), these elements now clearly predominate over the "oppositionist" or "heretical" culture that had been

---

[124] The sample included members of the local party council, city council members, and leaders of major *agrupaciones*.

TABLE 5.7. *National Party and Union Leaders' Views of the Menem Economic Program (Percentages)*

Category	National Council nonunion members (n = 25)	National Council union members (n = 14)	National union leaders (n = 37)
Neoliberals			
Reforms were necessary and should be continued	20.0 (5)	21.4 (3)	8.1 (3)
Pragmatists			
Reforms initially necessary but should have been modified after the crisis ended	48.0 (12)	28.6 (4)	21.6 (8)
Critics			
Some reforms were necessary, but the Menem government went too far/too fast	32.0 (8)	35.7 (5)	48.6 (18)
Opponents			
Reforms should not have been undertaken	0.0 (0)	14.3 (2)	21.6 (8)
TOTAL	100 (25)	100 (14)	100 (37)

TABLE 5.8. *Local Party and Union Leaders' Views of the Menem Economic Program (Percentages)*

Category	Nonunion party leaders (n = 48)	Unionist local party leaders (n = 27)	Local union leader (n = 35)
Neoliberals			
Reforms were necessary and should be continued	25.0 (12)	11.1 (3)	8.6 (3)
Pragmatists			
Reforms initially necessary but should have been modified after end of crisis	14.6 (7)	25.9 (7)	17.1 (6)
Critics			
Some reforms necessary, but Menem government went too far/too fast	43.8 (21)	59.3 (16)	42.9 (15)
Opponents			
Reforms should not have been undertaken	16.7 (8)	3.7 (1)	31.4 (11)
TOTAL	100 (25)	100 (14)	100 (37)

once been a central feature of urban Peronism (James 1988; Auyero 2000: 188–200). According to Auyero,

> In the context of deproletarianization, widespread material deprivation, and symbolic rejection...Peronism is not a heretical voice, a challenge to sociocultural boundaries, but a promise of food that holds no one responsible for its scarcity. Amid an

undeclared war on the poor, the (Peronist) problem-solving networks are now the most important webs of relations in which the remains of a strong Peronist identity are kept alive (2000: 204).

By the late 1990s, Peronist activists tended to view the PJ as a "party based on social work,"[125] rather than a party of workers. As an activist in La Matanza put it,

Peronism is about helping poor people, and that's what we are doing here. The economic situation is terrible and people are needy. So we give them bags of food, medicine, maybe even a job. That's what Peronism is all about.[126]

Such an understanding of Peronism is more compatible with a neoliberal project than the "oppositionist" identity associated with class-based Peronist organizations of the past.[127]

In sum, the PJ that entered the 1990s was profoundly different from that which emerged from authoritarian rule in 1983. Labor was a relatively marginal player in the Peronist coalition, and patronage-based organizations had largely replaced unions as the PJ's primary linkage to its working- and lower-class base. Whereas the urban Peronist base had once been composed largely of workers, in the 1990s it was increasingly made up of clients. These changes facilitated the programmatic adaptation undertaken by the Menem leadership in the 1990s. Peronist unions, which opposed many features of the Menem government's neoliberal program, were less influential in party decision making, less necessary in terms of resources and the delivery of votes, and less influential over the Peronist rank and file.

Yet if the Menem government benefited from the erosion of labor's power in the party, it is worth noting that the PJ's deunionization was largely *not* a product of Menemism. The policy changes associated with neoliberalism often create an incentive for labor-based party leaders to loosen their ties to organized labor (Taylor 1993; McCarthy 1997; Burgess 1999, 2000). However, in the Peronist case, there is little evidence that President Menem actively sought to reduce labor's influence in the party in the 1990s. Rather, as this chapter has shown, the organizational and institutional changes that were most responsible for the erosion of union influence, such as the dismantling of the "62" and the *tercio* and the rise of machine politics, occurred *before* Menem took office. Thus, deunionization was not a product of the PJ's shift to the right. Rather, it preceded – and almost certainly facilitated – the party's neoliberal turn. This programmatic transformation is the subject of Chapter 6.

---

[125] Author's interview with a PJ activist, April 8, 1997.
[126] Author's interview, August 26, 1997.
[127] In the words of another activist, "These days ... what we do is try to solve people's problems. We meet people's needs. They need clothes, medicines, a job. That's what Peronism is today. Let's be honest. Idealism has ended" (author's interview with Juan Carlos Scirica, PJ-Federal Capital activist, July 3, 1997).

CHAPTER 6

Menemism and Neoliberalism: Programmatic Adaptation in the 1990s

In the contemporary period, what the electoral platforms say is of no use.
– Carlos Menem[1]

Beginning in 1989, under the leadership of newly elected President Carlos Menem, the PJ underwent a stunning about-face. Despite having been elected on a populist platform, the Menem government abandoned the PJ's traditional program and embarked upon a set of neoliberal reforms that have been characterized as the most far-reaching in Latin America in the 1990s (Gwartney et al. 1996: 113; Inter-American Development Bank 1997: 96). The reform program was carried out with striking political success. Although many PJ leaders and activists were critical of the neoliberal turn, Menem confronted surprisingly little intraparty opposition.

This chapter seeks to explain the Menem leadership's capacity to sell a radical neoliberal project to the PJ. Although several factors, including the depth of the economic crisis and the skilled leadership of Menem himself, contributed to Menem's success, the chapter argues that this process was greatly facilitated by the Peronist party structure. Many party leaders and activists had serious doubts about the neoliberal strategy, but the weakly routinized nature of the PJ organization left them with few opportunities, and little incentive, to challenge Menem. The PJ's organizational structure enhanced Menem's strategic autonomy in three ways. First, in the absence of a stable bureaucracy with established career paths and secure tenure patterns, many non-Menemist party leaders bandwagoned to Menemism in an effort to preserve or advance their careers. Second, the weakness of the PJ's authority structures allowed Menem either to ignore the formal party leadership (as he did between 1989 and 1990) or to stack it with government officials (as he did between 1990 and 1999). Third, the absence of horizontal links undermined

---

[1] Quoted in *La Prensa*, September 24, 1989, p. 4.

the capacity of internal critics to build intraparty coalitions. Secondary party leaders fell into a hub-and-spokes relationship with the executive branch, which left internal opposition coalitions vulnerable to cooptation.

Yet if the PJ's segmented structure provided President Menem with substantial autonomy vis-á-vis secondary leaders, it also limited his capacity to impose strategies on lower-level branches. Indeed, local branches routinely rejected – or ignored – instructions from the national leadership and followed strategies that often had little to do with either Menem or his neoliberal program. Consequently, while the Menemist leadership undertook radical neoliberal reforms at the national level, local and provincial Peronist branches remained remarkably "un-Menemized."

THE MENEM REFORMS

After winning the presidency on a populist platform that promised a *salariazo* (big wage hike) and a limit on debt payments, Menem responded to the 1989 hyperinflationary crisis with a stunning political reversal. He named an executive of Argentina's largest multinational company, Bunge y Born, as his economic minister and filled his government with market-oriented technocrats, reserving few top posts for Peronists.[2] He also forged an alliance with the right-wing UCeDe, named UCeDe leader Alvaro Alsogaray as his debt advisor,[3] and signed a "programmatic pact" with the UCeDe that called for the "substitution of a statist, inflationary economy with a free economy."[4] From the beginning, Menem eschewed incremental reform in favor of an "all or nothing" strategy (Palermo and Torre 1992; Palermo 1994: 322). Within days of taking office, Menem announced a "tough, costly, and severe adjustment" that he likened to "surgery without anesthesia."[5] Empowered by two sweeping reform bills – the Economic Emergency Law and the State Reform Law – approved by the legislature in August 1989, the Menem government proceeded to dismantle the statist, inward-oriented economic model to which Peronism had long been wedded.[6] It eliminated a variety of regulations, price controls, industrial subsidies, and restrictions on foreign investment, lowered tariff barriers, privatized virtually all of the country's state enterprises (including the pension system and the petroleum sector), and launched a state restructuring program that would cut nearly seven hundred thousand jobs

---

[2] So few party leaders were given top government posts that observers joked that a party called the PDR (Peronistas de Repente, or Sudden Peronists) had taken office (*La Prensa*, June 23, 1989, p. 9).

[3] In 1983, Menem had described Alsogaray as "sinister.... When he was minister he starved the people" (Cerruti 1993: 155).

[4] *Clarín*, February 28, 1992, p. 15; March 5, 1992, p. 24).

[5] *La Prensa*, July 10, 1989, p. 5.

[6] For a detailed analysis of the politics of the Menem reforms, see Palermo and Novaro (1996).

from the federal bureaucracy (Gibson and Calvo 2000: 40–1).[7] The rapidity of the initial reforms, which earned Menem cheers of "Long Live Carlitos!" on the floor of the Buenos Aires stock exchange,[8] stunned politicians and analysts alike. As one business leader put it, Menem "did in 20 days what others were unable to do in six years."[9]

A central component of the Menem program was the Convertibility Law. Designed by Economic Minister Domingo Cavallo in 1991, the Convertibility Law made the Argentine peso freely convertible with the dollar, essentially reducing the Central Bank to a currency board (Gerchunoff and Torre 1996: 745). The government maintained the Convertibility Law through the end of the decade, resisting calls by party leaders to "Peronize" the economic model. Indeed, when the 1994 Mexican peso crisis threatened the post-1991 stability, Menem announced – in the middle of a reelection campaign – a severe austerity program that included further privatization, a reduction in some public sector salaries, and a billion dollars in spending cuts.[10] The Convertibility Law succeeded in ending hyperinflation and restoring economic growth. Inflation fell from 27 percent in February 1991 to 0.4 percent in November 1991, and the GDP expanded by an average rate of 7.7 percent between 1991 and 1994. At the same time, however, unemployment crept steadily upward, increasing from 8.1 percent in 1989 to an unprecedented 18.4 percent in 1995.

The neoliberal program ran counter to the perceived interests of many of the PJ's traditional constituencies, including organized labor.[11] State reform and trade liberalization decimated many public sector and industrial unions. Between 1989 and 1997, UOM membership fell from nearly 300,000 to 170,000, railway workers union membership fell from 67,000 to 14,000, oil workers union membership fell from 35,000 to 2,000, and textile workers union membership fell from 74,000 to 44,000.[12] Although labor market reforms lagged behind other reforms (Etchemendy 1995; Etchemendy and Palermo 1998), unions were adversely affected by decrees that regulated public sector strikes and severely restricted collective bargaining,[13] as well

---

[7] As Gibson and Calvo note, however, provincial government payrolls remained largely intact during Menem's first term in office (2000: 40–1).
[8] *Clarín*, May 16, 1990; p. 2.
[9] *Latin American Weekly Report*, September 7, 1989, p. 4.
[10] *Clarín*, February 26, 1995, p. 2; February 28, 1995, pp. 2–3.
[11] For analyses of state–labor relations in the Menem period, and of union responses to the Menem reforms, see Murillo (1997, 2001), Etchemendy and Palermo (1998), and Levitsky and Way (1998).
[12] Data provided to the author by the unions.
[13] In July 1991, the government issued a decree prohibiting collective contracts that include wage increases not demonstrably linked to increases in productivity (*Clarín*, July 16, 1991, p. 8.). For many unions, including the UOM, this entailed a de facto multiyear wage freeze.

as legislation that "flexibilized" labor contracts.[14] The government also took a hard line on labor protest, crushing strikes in the railroad, telecommunications, and banking sectors during its first year in office.

Menem also antagonized traditional party activists. Not only did he abandon cherished Peronist principles on a range of issues, but he did so in a way that highlighted, rather than downplayed, the contradictions with the traditional party program. Menem publicly embraced his conversion, making use of grand gestures that were particularly jarring for party leaders and activists. For example, the government not only abandoned Peronism's nationalist foreign policy in favor of staunchly pro-U.S. orientation, but also sent troops to fight alongside the United States in the Gulf War and even spoke of "carnal relations" with the United States.[15] Similarly, Menem stunned activists with his public embrace of Admiral Isaac Rojas, who had been responsible for the brutal repression of Peronists after the 1955 coup, and his 1990 pardon of military officers responsible for repression of the 1976–82 Dirty War. On economic issues, Menem called on Peronists to "revise and rethink everything,"[16] insisting that economic recovery required "solutions that have nothing to do with the Peronism of the 1940s or the 1970s."[17] He declared that Peronists had "gotten used to living almost without working,"[18] and dismissed intraparty opponents as "stuck in 1945."[19] Although this public embrace of radical change enhanced the government's credibility with investors and lenders, it did not sit well with many activists. As one dissident Peronist intellectual wrote, the Menem government

> exceeds many limits. Not only does it negotiate with the enemy; it negotiates badly. It brings it into the government. It adopts its jargon.... It's not just that an adjustment was undertaken. It's that it was undertaken with the program of the others.... Peronism handed over power to Bunge y Born while it commissioned its best men to destroy the CGT (Wainfeld 1990: 7–10).

Similarly, a PJ city council member from the Federal Capital complained that

> Menem is not even ambiguous. He is solidly aligned with the economic centers of power. If he at least fought for us a little, if we could say he was fighting for us in

---

[14] In March 1995, the Congress passed a bill that permitted short-term contracts with reduced benefits, limited indemnity payments, made it easier to hire and fire workers, and flexibilized workers' hours and vacation schedules for firms with forty or fewer employees (*Clarín*, March 16, 1995, p. 13).
[15] Foreign Minister Guido Di Tella, quoted in *Clarín*, November 9, 1991, p. 7.
[16] Speech to the Congress, "Peronist Mobilization for Political and Doctrinal Updating," Cervantes Theater, Federal Capital, March 16, 1991.
[17] *Clarín*, March 11, 1990, p. 16.
[18] Quoted in Palermo 1994: 315.
[19] *Clarín*, June 21, 1990, pp. 2–3.

his meetings with business leaders, then I could say to my base, "hang in there for a while longer, he is fighting for us." But he is not doing that at all.[20]

Few PJ leaders shared Menem's neoliberal strategy. Party president Antonio Cafiero, for example, sought a "less drastic" reform and an economic model that maintained "a degree of state intervention" and "greater social equity."[21] Most of the party's urban leaders, including Carlos Grosso,[22] José Manuel De la Sota,[23] and José Octavio Bordón,[24] preferred a more moderate or "social democratic" approach. In the interior, provincial bosses such as Ramon Saadi of Catamarca[25] and Vicente Joga of Formosa[26] were critics of neoliberalism. Doubts about neoliberalism also pervaded the legislative bloc. According to former bloc president José Luis Manzano, "very few" PJ legislators supported the neoliberal strategy.[27] Indeed, many of the party's top legislators, such as Marcelo López Arias, Oraldo Britos, Lorenzo Pepe, Humberto Roggero, and Eduardo Vaca, were strong critics of neoliberalism. As ex-legislator Roberto García put it,

We went crazy when they told us they were going to privatize everything. To us, a strong state was the only Peronism we knew. This was Perón.... I voted for laws with one hand and cursed them with the other.[28]

Even top cabinet members such as Eduardo Bauza and Vice President Eduardo Duhalde initially viewed the adjustment as a short-term policy that

[20] Author's interview with PJ city council member Victor Pandolfi, June 5, 1997.
[21] Author's interview with Antonio Cafiero, October 3, 1997.
[22] Grosso preferred "a social democratic neoliberalism, like that of Felipe Gonzalez," to what he describes as Menem's "Thatcherite" policies (author's interview, November 28, 1997). Grosso and his allies leaders sought a "European-style state" that played a "greater role in promoting industry and redistributing wealth" (author's interview with former national deputy Jorge Arguello, a Grosso ally, May 19, 1997).
[23] De la Sota described himself as a social democrat who "does not believe in Menem's idea of an ultraliberal state," and who sought reforms that were "more just and consensual." According to De la Sota, the Renovators "would have modernized Argentina, but we would have it differently, maintaining the roots of Perón" (author's interview, November 17, 1997). According to Senator Juan Carlos Maqueda, a De la Sota ally, the Renovators sought an "active state" with a "more profound social welfare role" (author's interview, September 11, 1997).
[24] Bordón describes himself as a "Keynesian...a U.S.-style liberal" (author's interview, November 26, 1997).
[25] Saadi rejected privatization in favor of the "Argentinization" of the economy and the "mixed" control of state enterprises (*Clarín*, February 22, 1990, p. 4; *La Prensa*, April 2, 1990, p. 5).
[26] Joga opposed the alliance with the United States as "degrading," rejected neoliberalism as "unjust," and described Menemism as "a liberal sector that infected the Peronist movement" (author's interview, December 17, 1997).
[27] Author's interview with José Luis Manzano, December 5, 1997.
[28] Author's interview, June 23, 1997.

would be followed by a "Peronization" of the economic program (Palermo and Novaro 1996: 269).²⁹

Nevertheless, Menem's neoliberal strategy faced surprisingly little intra-party resistance. The PJ made no effort to develop an alternative program, and proposals by National Council members such as De la Sota and José Azcurra for a more "Keynesian" approach went unheeded by the party leadership.³⁰ Indeed, *not once* did the National Council publicly oppose a position taken by President Menem. In the legislature, the bulk of the reform program – including the general framework for privatization and state reform (1989), the Convertibility Law (1991), and petroleum and pension privatizations (1993) – was approved with near-unanimous Peronist support (Corrales 1996b: 265–70). Although PJ legislators substantially modified many post-1991 reform bills (Llanos 2001),³¹ they rarely rejected them outright during the 1989–95 period. In other words, Peronists exerted real influence over individual pieces of legislation, but the policy agenda was set entirely by the government. Indeed, with the partial exception of labor market flexibilization,³² Menem was able to push through all of the major pieces of his reform program. Efforts to build anti-Menemist coalitions repeatedly failed during the 1990s. Despite controlling both the party hierarchy and the legislative bloc, the Renovation faction disintegrated soon after Menem took office, and subsequent efforts to build non-Menemist factions failed to take hold. As a result, Menem enjoyed substantial autonomy in carrying out his neoliberal strategy.

EXPLAINING MENEM'S SUCCESS: ALTERNATIVE APPROACHES

Explaining why President Menem chose a radical adaptive strategy is relatively straightforward. As Chapter 4 argued, the domestic and international economic environment left the new government with little room for maneuver.³³ The constraints were both economic and political-institutional. Not

---

²⁹ Duhalde is said to have had serious differences with the Menem economic program, reportedly preferring a price freeze, rather than monetarist policies, as a means of combating inflation (*Clarín*, March 11, 1990, p. 13; March 18, 1990, p. 12).
³⁰ Author's interview with José Azcurra, October 20, 1997.
³¹ For example, the PJ bloc made substantial modifications in the government's social security privatization bill. Whereas the government sought a purely private system, Peronist deputies added a clause that allowed Argentines to remain in the state-run pension system. They also facilitated unions' entry into the private social security market. PJ legislators were also able to negotiate modifications – often to benefit provincial interests – in the privatizations of the gas and petroleum sectors. See Llanos (2001).
³² Between 1990 and 1998, PJ legislators repeatedly blocked government efforts to pass legislation flexibilizing labor markets, ultimately forcing the government to accept a more limited set of reforms (Etchemendy 1995; Etchemendy and Palermo 1998).
³³ The neoliberal program was almost certainly developed as a response to the 1989 hyperinflationary crisis. There is little evidence that Menem planned the shift prior to 1989 (Palermo and Novaro 1996: 128).

only did extreme fiscal crisis virtually compel the new government to adopt orthodox austerity measures, but the near-total erosion of the state's institutional capacity in the face of hyperinflation and bureaucratic inefficiency was such that a policy that surrendered resource allocation to the market was increasingly seen as "the only option" (Palermo and Novaro 1996: 143). This idea was reinforced by both the market-oriented ideas flowing from international lending institutions, foreign consultants, and U.S.-trained technocrats, and the negative examples provided by the failure of heterodox reform attempts in Argentina and other Latin American countries in the 1980s (Palermo and Novaro 1996: 145). Finally, the extreme nature of the Menem strategy can be attributed to the "credibility gap" that the government faced with respect to domestic and foreign investors and lenders (Gerchunoff and Torre 1996: 736; Palermo and Novaro 1996: 135–9). To send a clear signal to investors that a president from a populist party was committed to reform, Menem was compelled to "go the extra yard" in terms of both his policies and his public postures.

What is more puzzling than Menem's decision to pursue a radical adaptive strategy was his capacity to get away with it. The PJ was, after all, a predominantly working- and lower-class party with a longstanding commitment to a statist, redistributionist, and nationalist program. Hence, it could be expected that a radical adaptive strategy would generate significant intraparty resistance. This is precisely what occurred under the government of Carlos Andres Pérez in Venezuela in the late 1980s and early 1990s (Corrales 2000, 2002).

How Peronists Viewed the Neoliberal Program: Some Survey Evidence

One possible explanation of Menem's ability to get away with a radical neoliberal strategy is that such a strategy enjoyed widespread support within the party. If the bulk of Peronist leaders and activists agreed with the neoliberal program, then party cooperation is easily explained. To examine this hypothesis, the following section presents results from surveys of national party leaders, local leaders, and *punteros* carried out by the author in 1997, as well as two surveys of party members carried out by Hugo Haime and Associates. The results suggest that a large percentage of the PJ leadership and base held serious doubts about the neoliberal program, and that, notwithstanding the successes of the Convertibility Plan, these doubts persisted into the mid-1990s.

Two methodological caveats should be mentioned regarding the survey results. First, because many party dissidents were weeded out (either through defection or a failure to be renominated for party leadership or legislative posts) in the 1989–97 period, the sample is more Menemist than a sample drawn from the 1989–91 period would have been. Second, respondents' reports of their view of the economic program may differ from the positions

TABLE 6.1. *National Party Leaders' Views of the Menem Economic Program (Percentages)*

Category	PJ National Council members[a] (n = 39)	PJ legislators[b] (n = 87)
Neoliberals		
Reforms were necessary and should be continued	20.5 (8)	21.8 (19)
Pragmatists		
Reforms initially necessary but should have been modified after end of crisis	41.0 (16)	39.1 (34)
Critics		
Some reform necessary, but Menem government went too far/too fast	33.3 (13)	35.6 (31)
Opponents		
Reforms should not have been undertaken	5.1 (2)	3.4 (3)
TOTAL	100.0 (39)	100.0 (87)

Notes:
[a] Based on author's 1997 survey of thirty-nine National Council members. All had been members of the National Council at some point between 1995 and 1997.
[b] Based on author's 1997 survey of eighty-seven members of the Senate and the Chamber of Deputies.

they actually held at the time of the reforms. For example, the success of the Convertibility Law may have led respondents to offer a more positive view of the reforms than they actually held in 1991. On the other hand, because increased unemployment led to greater public dissatisfaction with the economic program in the late 1990s, respondents may also offer a more negative view of the reforms than they had actually held. Overall, it is reasonable to suggest that the data presented here are biased in a slightly pro-Menem direction.

Respondents were asked to place themselves in one of four categories with respect to the Menem government's economic policies: (1) those who believed that neoliberal reforms were necessary and should be continued, whom I label *neoliberals*; (2) those who believed that neoliberal reforms were initially necessary to combat the hyperinflationary crisis, but that they should have been discontinued, or at least substantially modified, during Menem's second term (*pragmatists*); (3) those who believed that some economic reform was necessary, but that the Menem government's neoliberal reforms were too rapid and/or went too far (*critics*); and (4) those who believed that neoliberal reforms should never have been undertaken (*opponents*).

Table 6.1 shows the results of a 1997 survey of thirty-nine PJ National Council members and eighty-seven national PJ legislators. Both surveys suggest that a majority of national party leaders initially accepted the Menem

TABLE 6.2. *Local Party Leaders' Views of the Menem Economic Program (Percentages)*

Category	Local party leaders[a] (n = 75)	PJ *punteros*[b] (n = 100)
Neoliberals		
Reforms were necessary and should be continued	20.0 (15)	19.0 (19)
Pragmatists		
Reforms initially necessary but should have been modified after end of crisis	36.0 (37)	29.0 (29)
Critics		
Some reform necessary, but Menem government went too far/too fast	32.0 (24)	29.0 (29)
Opponents		
Reforms should not have been undertaken	12.0 (9)	23.0 (23)
TOTAL	100.0 (75)	100.0 (100)

Notes:
[a] Based on author's 1997 survey of seventy-five local PJ leaders in the Federal Capital, La Matanza, and Quilmes. The sample includes city council members, party council members, and leaders of major *agrupaciones*.
[b] Based on author's 1997 survey of the leaders of 112 base units in the Federal Capital, La Matanza, and Quilmes. Twelve *punteros* did not answer this question and were excluded from the sample.

reforms, and that very few (less than 10 percent of each sample) opposed them outright. Yet they also suggest that relatively few leaders (around 20 percent of the sample) were neoliberals. Rather, the largest group in the sample was that of the pragmatists, or those who viewed neoliberal policies as a necessary evil to overcome the crisis, but who then sought some form of "Peronization" of policy – such as increased social spending and state promotion of national industry – in the postcrisis period. Many others were critics, in that they viewed the reforms as necessary but preferred either a more limited or more gradual reform.

Opposition was somewhat more pronounced at the local level. Table 6.2 shows the results of 1997 surveys of seventy-five local party leaders and one hundred *punteros* from the Federal Capital, La Matanza, and Quilmes. As with the national survey, a majority (56 percent) of local leaders accepted the initial reforms, but few (20 percent) could be described as converts to neoliberalism. Again, the largest group (36 percent) was that of the pragmatists. Although the number of opponents remained low (12 percent), the percentage of local leaders who were highly critical of the Menem program (critics and opponents) was substantial (44 percent). Among the surveyed *punteros*, the percentage of neoliberals remains roughly the same (19 percent), but the

Programmatic Adaptation in the 1990s   153

TABLE 6.3. *Party Members' Views of the Menem Economic Program (1992)[a]* (Percentages)

Statement	Agree	Disagree
The government should privatize public enterprises	46	42
The government should make state firms more efficient rather than privatize	56	32
It is necessary to prioritize stabilization even if it entails social costs	42	48
The current economic policy has been designed for a country of the few	45	46
Agree with state reform	69	20
Agree with the government's social policies	27	61
Agree with the government's policies toward the IMF	44	40
Agree with the government's alliance with the U.S.	44	38

How close should the government be to...	Very close	Somewhat close	Not close
The United States	37	53	10
The UCeDe	9	45	45
Business	48	48	4
Unions	55	38	7
Workers	89	10	0

How valid are the following elements of the traditional Peronist program today?	Totally valid	Still valid, but must be updated	No longer valid
Social pact with labor	49	35	11
Nonalignment	25	36	34
Economic independence	43	41	15
Social justice	68	23	8

Note:
[a] 1992 survey of PJ members in the Federal Capital and Greater Buenos Aires carried out by Hugo Haime and Associates.

percentage of opponents rises, and critics and opponents constitute a majority (52 percent).

To assess the views of party members, I use surveys of the PJ membership carried out by Haime and Associates in 1992 and 1996.[34] The 1992 survey (Table 6.3), conducted when the Convertibility Plan was at the peak of its

[34] Data provided to the author by Hugo Haime and Associates. All surveys were carried out in the Federal Capital and Greater Buenos Aires.

TABLE 6.4. *Party Members' Views of the Menem Economic Program, by Income Level (1996)[a] (Percentages)*

How is your own economic situation compared to 1991?	Lower-income	Middle-income	Upper-income
Better	19	24	24
Same	24	19	24
Worse	55	56	49
Overall opinion of the Menem government's economic policies	Lower-income	Middle-income	Upper-income
Approve	33	38	43
Neutral	5	4	4
Disapprove	60	57	50

Note:
[a] 1996 survey of PJ members in the Federal Capital and Greater Buenos Aires carried out by Hugo Haime and Associates.

popularity, found the membership strongly in support of state reform and evenly split on issues such as privatization and the government's policies toward the IMF and the United States. Yet it also found that a majority preferred making state firms more efficient rather than privatizing and that a plurality rejected stabilization if it entailed "social costs." It also found strong opposition to the government's social policies and the military pardon, as well as greater support for an alliance with workers and unions than with the UCeDe, business, or the United States. Finally, the survey found a mixed response with respect to the validity of the traditional Peronist program. The vast majority (68 percent) believed that "social justice" was still a "totally valid" goal, while pluralities found "economic independence" and a "social pact with labor" to be valid. In a second survey of party members carried out four years later,[35] Haime and Associates found even greater opposition to the Menem program. As Table 6.4 shows, a majority of party members opposed the economic program and believed that their economic situation had *worsened* since 1991.

Several conclusions may be drawn from these data. First, many Peronists accepted the initial reforms, and few of them rejected the reforms outright. Second, although the bulk of the party leadership acquiesced to the Menem reforms, few could be considered neoliberal converts. Most were pragmatists who viewed the policies as a necessary – and temporary – evil. Third, particularly when we take into account the fact that many dissidents had

---

[35] Survey of party members in the Federal Capital and Greater Buenos Aires, conducted by Hugo Haime and Associates, April 24, 1996. Data provided to the author by Hugo Haime and Associates.

already been weeded out at the time of the 1997 sample, it is clear that an important sector of the party opposed much of the Menem program throughout the 1989–97 period. At the local and neighborhood levels, this sector may have been a majority. Indeed, according to Haime, "the bulk of the party ... was always opposed to the process of transformation carried out by Menem and Cavallo."[36] Thus, the question of why doubts about the Menem program were not translated into active opposition or effective pressure to moderate or "Peronize" economic policy after stabilization had been achieved remains to be answered.

The Impact of Economic Crisis and Leadership

Scholars have frequently pointed to two factors that contributed to President Menem's capacity to develop and sustain a neoliberal strategy within a party whose members had serious doubts about such a program. The first was the 1989 hyperinflationary crisis, together with the government's success in both resolving the crisis and compensating reform "losers" in the post-1991 period (Palermo and Torre 1992; Gerchunoff and Torre 1996; Palermo and Novaro 1996). The hyperinflationary crisis convinced many PJ leaders that there was no alternative to neoliberalism, and that efforts to pursue an alternative risked disaster (Palermo and Novaro 1996: 217).[37] According to PJ legislator Miguel Angel Toma,

> There was an unbelievable sense of urgency due to the hyperinflation. We sensed that the choice was between hyperinflation and chaos. And as a result, we did not debate much about the longer-term effects of the model.[38]

Thus, a week after Menem took office, PJ president Antonio Cafiero declared that "given the depth of the crisis, the only option we have is to comply with the measures that the government is announcing."[39]

After 1991, party cooperation was facilitated by both the success of the reforms and the government's capacity to compensate potential dissidents with material benefits (Gerchunoff and Torre 1996; Palermo and Novaro 1996; Gibson and Calvo 2000; Etchemendy 2001). The economic success of the Convertibility Plan, together with the PJ's victories in the 1991 and 1993 elections, convinced many Peronists that the Menem program was economically and politically viable. Moreover, the three-year boom triggered by the

---

[36] Interview in *El Colorado*, November 6, 1996, p. 3.
[37] Palermo and Novaro write that "the hyperinflationary crisis affected not only Peronist voters ... but also union leaders, middle level leaders, legislators, and government officials. Aware that an internal conflict could lead everyone to disaster, very few dared ... to block presidential decisions" (1996: 217).
[38] Author's interview, July 10, 1997.
[39] Quoted in *La Prensa*, July 12, 1989, p. 5.

Convertibility Law provided the government with the resources to carry out a range of "compensation schemes" to buy off those who remained unconvinced (Gerchunoff and Torre 1996: 751). Thus, to maintain trade union support, the government postponed plans to flexibilize labor markets and to deregulate the union-run health insurance system, granted unions a share of newly privatized industries, and allowed the unions to participate in the new private pension market (Etchemendy and Palermo 1998). The support of provincial party bosses was obtained by means of a "compromise between patrimonialism and market reforms" (Palermo and Novaro 1996: 356), by which the national government did not force provincial governments to carry out economic adjustments in line with those being implemented at the national level. Thus, provincial banks were allowed to continue financing government deficits, and provincial payrolls, which served as the foundation for local patronage organizations, were virtually untouched (Gerchunoff and Torre 1996: 757; Gibson 1997; Gibson and Calvo 2000).

Although the hyperinflationary crisis and effective compensation schemes powerfully shaped Peronist responses to the Menem program, they do not fully explain PJ cooperation. As Javier Corrales (1996b: 135–6) has argued, reform programs have often been blocked in the context of deep economic crisis (Brazil, Russia), and cooperation has often taken place in the absence of crisis (Spain, Costa Rica). Nor does the post-1991 economic success fully explain Menem's capacity to stay the course. Stabilization often generates increased pressure for redistribution. Moreover, although it is true that the post-1991 compensation schemes were crucial to maintaining the Peronist coalition, it remains to be explained why poststabilization demand making was limited to particularistic benefits rather than collective pressure for programmatic change. Hence, a crisis and compensation explanation must be complemented by an examination of intraparty dynamics.

A second factor behind PJ cooperation was the leadership and strategies of President Menem himself. In his insightful comparison of economic reform programs in Argentina and Venezuela, Corrales (1996b, 2002) focuses on these strategies. According to Corrales, Menem gained the PJ's support via a "party-conforming" strategy that included increased party participation in the government (1996b: 213), a "major effort to seduce the legislative branch" (1996b: 216), and a "vigorous campaign" to convince party leaders of the need for reform. This last strategy included a "massive party congress" in March 1991, in which Menem depicted liberalizing reforms as "compatible with the party's ideology" (1996b: 214–15), as well as Economic Ministry efforts to "train" PJ candidates in selling the reforms during the 1991 electoral campaign (1996b: 217). As a result of this campaign, the PJ's "loyalty toward the president solidified," and the government "obtained a negotiated permit from the ruling party to proceed with the reforms" (1996b: 219). Thus, the government's party-conforming strategy "succeeded in turning the

PJ into its principal public relations instrument" (1996b: 217), and the party even "began to campaign on behalf of the reforms" (1996b: 342).

Although Corrales' work provides an important corrective to accounts that portray the PJ as marginal to the reform process, it overstates both the extent to which Menem invested in winning the party's support and the degree to which Peronists actively supported the neoliberal program. There is little evidence that Menem invested heavily in winning over the party, or that the strategies pointed to by Corrales were particularly influential toward this end. According to former Minister of the Interior Gustavo Beliz, who helped organize the March 1991 congress, the event was "just an isolated incident," and the government in fact "made very little effort" to sell the reform strategy to the party.[40] Indeed, of the more than three hundred Peronists interviewed for this study, not a single one mentioned the 1991 speech or Ministry of the Economy "training" as having shaped their orientation toward the economic program.[41] Corrales also overstates the degree to which the party leadership was brought into the decision-making process. Most party leaders claim that the national party become *less*, rather than more, active after 1989.[42] Hence, although Corrales is correct in observing that Peronist leaders cooperated with the Menem program, his causal argument, which centers on Menem's leadership, appears to be somewhat off the mark.

This chapter offers an alternative explanation of party cooperation. It argues that Peronist acquiescence to the Menem reforms is better understood as a response to the opportunities and constraints posed by the PJ party structure than as a product of Menem's "party-conforming" strategies. Although Menem may indeed have carried out more effective strategies than Carlos Andres Pérez in Venezuela, this leadership was exercised in an institutional context that was more facilitative of radical strategic change than was AD's more bureaucratized structure.

PARTY WEAKNESS AND PRESIDENTIAL AUTONOMY: AN ORGANIZATIONAL EXPLANATION

To understand PJ leaders' responses to the Menem reforms, one must examine how the PJ's organizational structure mediated their strategies. The argument presented here suggests that although many party leaders and activists had serious doubts about the neoliberal strategy, the weakly routinized

---

[40] Author's interview, July 21, 1997.
[41] According to PJ pollster Haime, "the government never explained...to the middle level leadership where the model was going" (interview in *El Colorado*, November 6, 1996, p. 3).
[42] Of the thirty-one National Council members surveyed for this study, only three (9.7 percent) responded that the party "functions as it should" under Menem, while 28 (90.3 percent) said it did not.

nature of the PJ organization left them with little incentive, and few opportunities, to challenge President Menem.

This section examines the relationship between President Menem and the party between 1989 and 1999. It argues that the PJ's organizational structure enhanced Menem's strategic autonomy in three ways. First, in the absence of established career paths and secure tenure patterns, many Renovators and other Menem critics bandwagoned to Menemism in an effort to preserve their careers. Second, the weakness of the PJ's authority structures allowed the government to ignore, and later to colonize, the party's formal party leadership. Third, the absence of horizontal links undermined the capacity of Menem critics to build intraparty coalitions. Secondary party leaders fell into a hub-and-spokes relationship with the president, which left opposition coalitions vulnerable to cooptation.

Bandwagoning and the Collapse of the Renovation Faction, 1988–9

After Menem won the presidential nomination in 1988, his position in the party was strengthened by a process of intraparty bandwagoning. In mid-1988, two-thirds of National Council members, more than 60 percent of the National Council Executive Board (including President Cafiero), and 68 of the 103 members of the PJ legislative bloc (including bloc president José Luis Manzano) belonged to the center-left Renovation faction.[43] However, Menem's victory triggered a wave of defections to the Menem camp that led to the disintegration of the Renovation faction. This bandwagoning process was widely interpreted as opportunistic behavior rooted in Peronism's "power-seeking" political culture. Peronists, it was argued, are "creatures of power,"[44] and the PJ is a "party of government."[45]

Yet Peronist bandwagoning might also be understood in more structural terms. Rather than a product of weak loyalties or the government's "open arms" strategy, bandwagoning may be viewed as a strategic response to the risks and opportunities presented by the PJ party structure. From this perspective, the collapse of the Renovation faction was a product of the strategies of individual Renovation leaders who calculated that an alliance with Menem was the best way to protect or advance their careers.[46] Because the party hierarchy lacks secure tenure patterns and routinized career paths, and because the state, rather than the party, is the primary route to positions of power and prestige, PJ leaders seeking to preserve or advance their careers

---

[43] *Clarín*, July 14, 1988, pp. 2, 15; July 29, 1988, p. 7.
[44] Author's interview with Victor Pandolfi, a PJ city council member in the Federal Capital, June 5, 1997.
[45] Mario Wainfeld, personal communication. Even Corrales, whose argument centers on Menem's "open arms policy" (1996b: 206) toward the Renovators, claims that the Renovators "simply did not have entrenched loyalties" (1996b: 320).
[46] Palermo and Novaro (1996: 217, 223) make a similar argument.

must remain on good terms with party leaders who control public office. Consequently, when opposing factions win public office, Peronists have a strong incentive to jump to the winning side.[47] In such a context, the failure to bandwagon may have severe consequences for one's political career. Thus, whereas conservatism may be a rational career-preserving strategy in a bureaucratic context (Downs 1967: 96–100), bandwagoning strategies – or opportunism – may be more rational in the PJ.

This incentive structure was clearly at work in 1988 and 1989. Given that the party bureaucracy could offer neither tenure security nor access to positions of power and prestige, Renovators found that remaining in the non-Menemist camp posed a serious threat to their careers. Party leaders such as Cafiero, Vice Presidents José Maria Vernet and Roberto García, legislative bloc president José Luis Manzano, Federal Capital leader (and mayoral aspirant) Carlos Grosso, and Córdoba leader (and gubernatorial aspirant) José Manuel De la Sota lacked office-based support structures and thus needed Menem's backing to retain their party posts.[48] Immediately after the primaries, these leaders found their positions threatened by Menem loyalists who sought a housecleaning of the party hierarchy. Menemists called on Cafiero and other party leaders to resign (despite the fact that their terms did not expire until 1991), declaring that "the guillotine is ready and the heads selected."[49] They also sought Manzano's removal as president of the legislative bloc.[50] Because there existed a clear precedent for removing party authorities before their mandates expired, these calls for a housecleaning posed a credible threat. In the face of this threat, many Renovators concluded that an alliance with Menem was the best means of assuring their political survival. As one local party leader put it, "everyone ran to Menem because they were afraid of losing what they had."[51]

Menem's 1988 victory thus triggered a large-scale bandwagoning process. Led by Manzano and García, a large fraction of ex-Renovators joined the ranks of Menemism. Many ex-Renovators were given positions in the government,[52] and some, such as Manzano and Carlos Corach, found their way into Menem's inner circle. Others became the core of the new dominant

---

[47] As Armada and Wainfeld put it, "given a choice between working in the party or working in the state, no one chooses the party" (1990: 21).
[48] Cafiero possessed an independent power base as governor of Buenos Aires, but he stood to lose it when his term expired in 1991.
[49] *Clarín*, July 17, 1988, p. 14. Also *Clarín*, July 11, 1988, pp. 2–3, 7; July 14, 1988, pp. 14–15; July 15, 1988, p. 4; July 18, 1988, p. 8.
[50] *Clarín*, July 11, 1988, p. 7; July 14, 1988, pp. 2, 15; July 17, 1988, p. 5; July 19, 1988, pp. 7, 9.
[51] Author's interview with Reinaldo Mendoza, former PJ city council member in the Federal Capital, April 4, 1997.
[52] These included Eduardo Amadeo, Raul Carignano, Eduardo Cevallo, Carlos Corach, Miguel D'Allesandro, Rodolfo Diaz, Guido Di Tella, Oscar Fappiano, Juan Carlos Mazzon, and Luis Prol.

faction in the legislature.[53] According to Corrales, this bandwagoning process was "far more encompassing" than that which occurred in AD under Pérez (1996b: 320).

Although De la Sota and a handful of other Renovators attempted to maintain the Renovation as an organized faction,[54] top Renovation leaders, apparently convinced that such a project would fail, opposed the move. According to Cafiero,

> Experience told me that such a faction would be devoured by power. If we won the 1989 election, then surely all the Renovators, or a large number of them, were going to emigrate to Menem's side.... I wasn't going to be able to stop this process.... Many of my Renovation friends had already begun to look for positions in the new government.... Although we had an ideological program, it wasn't strong enough to resist the temptation of power. And power had passed into Menem's hands.[55]

Similarly, Grosso argues that a Renovation faction

> would have been impossible to maintain. Menemism would have used all of the structures of power to make such a faction disappear. Coopting some, destroying others. It was inevitable.[56]

Indeed, as *Clarín* observed, most Renovators seemed "more interested in negotiating positions in the next Peronist government than in forming an internal current," and many had "already reached accords with Menemism" at the time De la Sota launched his project.[57] Consequently, the project collapsed, and the Renovation ceased to exist.[58] The "25" underwent a similar process of disintegration, as union leaders such as García, Guerino Andreoni, Osvaldo Borda, José Luis Castillo, and José Pedraza rejected a proposal by state workers union leader Victor De Gennaro to maintain a critical posture toward the government in favor of individual alliances with Menemism.[59]

---

[53] Key members of this group were Oscar Lamberto, who chaired the Budget Committee, Osvaldo Borda, who chaired the Labor Committee, Miguel Angel Toma, who chaired the Defense Committee and became a leading spokesperson for the government, and Jorge Matzkin, who took over as bloc president when Manzano was named minister of the interior in 1991.

[54] Author's interview with José Manuel De la Sota, November 17, 1997. De la Sota proposed the creation of a Renovation National Coordinating Board, which would allow the faction to "maintain its structure" and "facilitate debate" within the party (*Clarín*, March 4, 1989, pp. 10–11; March 5, 1989, p. 10; March 15, 1989, p. 16).

[55] Author's interview, October 3, 1997.

[56] Author's interview, November 28, 1997.

[57] *Clarín*, March 13, 1989, p. 12.

[58] According to De la Sota, "We were half the party.... If the Renovation faction had continued to exist, we would have been able to avoid many errors that the Menem government committed. For example, we could have built a better bridge between Peronism's past and its present.... But we did not seek to maintain ourselves as an internal line. Many just jumped into the circus" (author's interview, November 17, 1997).

[59] Author's interviews with former "25" leaders Roberto Digón (July 1, 1997) and Roberto García (June 23, 1997).

The Renovation defectors, who came to be known as "neo-Menemists," brought about a critical realignment in the PJ, enabling Menem to establish a new dominant coalition. The incorporation of the neo-Menemists broadened the Menemist coalition so that it included an important fraction of the PJ's center-left wing. Inside the government, the neo-Menemists aligned with the *Celeste* faction,[60] which positioned itself as a counterweight to the orthodox Menemist *Rojo Punzó* faction.[61] Although relations between the *Celestes* and *Rojo Punzó* were often stormy, their ability to bridge the party's two main factions provided Menem with a broad base of intraparty support. In the Chamber of Deputies, Manzano built an alliance between orthodox Menemists and approximately thirty ex-Renovators who offered their "unrestricted support for the government's policies."[62] This new coalition, which ranged from sixty to eighty of the PJ's 120 deputies, gave Menem control of the legislative bloc and allowed for the relatively smooth passage of the bulk of the government's legislative agenda.[63]

The Institutional Weakness of Party Leadership Bodies

President Menem's strategic autonomy was further enhanced by the weakly routinized nature of the PJ's leadership bodies, as internal critics were largely unable to use these organs as vehicles for questioning, modifying, or slowing down the neoliberal strategy. As Chapter 3 argued, the authority of the party congress, the National Council, and other leadership bodies is not widely taken for granted by Peronists. Indeed, they are rarely taken seriously as arenas for collective action. Thus, the National Council "lacks an institutional life of its own," and party decision making tends to be "a product of the momentary balance of power at any given time."[64] This means that when the PJ in is power, the formal party leadership lacks autonomous authority vis-á-vis office-holding leaders. In other words, "control of the state means control of the party."[65]

This dynamic was clearly at work in the Menem government. Despite the fact that Renovation leaders controlled the National Council's Executive Board in 1989 and 1990, the National Council exerted little autonomous

---

[60] *Celeste* leaders included Eduardo Bauza, Carlos Corach, José Luis Manzano, and Eduardo Menem. Miguel Angel Toma, a *Celeste* ally, describes the *Celeste* as "an alliance of the most progressive sectors of Menemism.... It was the meeting place between the Renovators and the most rational Menemists" (author's interview, July 10, 1997).

[61] *Rojo Punzó* leaders included Luis Barrionuevo, Alberto Kohan, and Julio Mera Figueroa.

[62] *La Prensa*, March 24, 1990, p. 4.

[63] According to neo-Menemist Congressional Deputy Miguel Angel Toma, the ex-Renovators "made the Congress work. Without us, nothing would have passed" (author's interview, July 10, 1997).

[64] Author's interview with National Deputy Lorenzo Dominguez, September 25, 1997.

[65] Author's interview with former Congressional Deputy Jorge Arguello, May 19, 1997.

authority vis-á-vis Menem. When the party leadership diverged from the positions taken by the government, Menem simply ignored it. In 1990, top Renovators were removed from the National Council, and the Menem government began to colonize the party leadership from the state. After 1990, the National Council was largely controlled by the government. At no time, then, could the party leadership be used to limit Menem's strategic autonomy.

Party Circumvention (1988–90)
Between 1988 and 1990, the National Council remained in the hands of the Renovation. Although several top party leaders, including Cafiero, Vice President Vernet, and Political Secretary De la Sota, were critical of the Menem program, the National Council lacked sufficient authority to influence the president's strategy. As Vice President Eduardo Duhalde put it, "no one cares who the president of the party is. The conductor of the movement is Carlos Menem."[66]

Menem began to circumvent the party leadership as soon as he won the presidential nomination. Although the National Council "bubbled over with projects and teams"[67] during the 1989 electoral campaign, Menem routinely ignored it. When the National Council produced a three-hundred-page platform, Menem published a separate platform called "The Productive Revolution." The party congress approved a program that combined the two versions,[68] but Menem immediately distanced himself from this platform as well, telling the press that it was not "written in stone" and that he would not be bound by it.[69] Rather than working through the National Council, Menem worked through his inner circle, known as the Twelve Apostles,[70] and an informal body called the Commission of Ten. The Commission of Ten functioned as a parallel National Council, developing campaign strategies, mediating intraparty conflicts, and negotiating candidate lists.[71] After his May 1989 election, Menem ignored the advisory councils created by the National Council to discuss options in different policy areas in preparation for taking office,[72] and during the initial weeks of the Menem government, party leaders complained that they were learning about government appointments through the newspapers.[73] The alliance with

---

[66] *Clarín*, June 8, 1990, p. 5.
[67] *La Prensa*, March 15, 1989, p. 1.
[68] *Clarín*, February 26, 1989, pp. 2–4.
[69] *La Prensa*, February 27, 1989, p. 5.
[70] These were Augusto Alasino, Cesar Arias, Luis Barrionuevo, Eduardo Bauza, Ruben Cardozo, Julio Corzo, Alberto Kohan, Julio Mera Figueroa, Eduardo Menem, Alberto Pierri, Juan Carlos Rousselot, and Antonio Vanrell.
[71] *Clarín*, August 30, 1988, p. 3; September 21, 1988, p. 6; October 4, 1988, p. 7; October 5, 1988, p. 16; November 10, 1988, p. 18.
[72] *Clarín*, May 4, 1989, p. 11.
[73] *Clarín*, July 16, 1989, p. 23; July 17, 1989, p. 7.

Bunge y Born was never approved by the party, and in fact was opposed by Cafiero.[74]

The Cafiero-led National Council did not share Menem's neoliberal strategy. While the body expressed its "categorical support" for the Menem program, it also expressed "concern" over the socioeconomic costs of neoliberal policies and the "advances of Bunge y Born within the government."[75] Cafiero defended the PJ's "commitment to social justice,... equality of opportunity, and the social-political role of the state" as a "non-substitutable... part of our ideological and political identity,"[76] and warned against the "infiltration of the conservative right."[77] When the initial stabilization plan faltered in late 1989, Cafiero announced that the National Council was "prepared to offer its collaboration" with the government in developing an "alternative economic plan."[78] When the government opted instead for a monetarist approach, Cafiero declared that it would be "difficult to ask the people for more sacrifice,"[79] and that "free markets become perverse... when they are not accompanied by social sensibility."[80] After a series of internal debates,[81] the National Council released a document that, while expressing its "unwavering solidarity" with the government, rejected "liberal-conservative" ideas and opposed efforts to "lead Argentina toward crude and dehumanized efficientism."[82] Three months later, the National Council issued a document that criticized "liberal capitalism" and called for a "mixed market economy" and "social equity brought about by state action."[83]

These positions had virtually no influence over the Menem government. Notwithstanding Cafiero's insistence that the National Council would "institutionally link" government decision making to the party,[84] the body's declarations and proposals consistently went unheeded. Although he continued to meet weekly with Cafiero, Menem privately dismissed the National Council as "non-existent," and Cafiero complained privately that the party was not being consulted.[85] The daily newspaper *Clarín* observed that Menem enjoyed "absolute autonomy" from the PJ,[86] and that the National Council's

[74] Author's interview with Antonio Cafiero, October 3, 1997.
[75] *Clarín*, July 26, 1989, p. 6; October 31, 1989, p. 5.
[76] *Clarín*, November 19, 1989, p. 7.
[77] *Clarín*, May 28, 1990, p. 3. Cafiero described Alvaro Alsogaray and other liberals in the government as "enemies of Peronism."
[78] *La Prensa*, February 21, 1990, p. 8.
[79] *La Prensa*, March 28, 1990, p. 4.
[80] *Clarín*, March 10, 1990, p. 11.
[81] *Clarín*, February 20, 1990, p. 2; March 10, 1990, p. 11.
[82] *Clarín*, April 3, 1990, p. 2; *La Prensa*, April 3, 1990, p. 5; April 4, 1990, p. 7.
[83] *Clarín*, July 14, 1990, p. 6.
[84] *La Prensa*, August 1, 1989, p. 5.
[85] *Clarín*, November 16, 1989, p. 14.
[86] *Clarín*, April 8, 1990, p. 13.

"influence over Menem is almost nil."[87] Cafiero offers a similar assessment, claiming that Menem broke a "gentleman's agreement" in which he agreed to consult the party:

> We had made an agreement to share power, Menem as candidate and me as president of the party. Menem said yes to everything and then complied with none of it.... He took off on his own. He did not consult with anyone, and he did not share power.... He and I met regularly, but the meetings were over smaller things. We never dealt with any important issues.... There was no way to make him see the existence of another authority at his side.[88]

According to Cafiero, the National Council had "no role" in policy making in 1989 and 1990:

> We met every week, and we kept minutes and other records.... But influence over the government? No.... I was producing reports and documents whose terms contradicted what the government was doing. So we were ignored.[89]

Although the National Council rarely took positions that directly contradicted the government line, when the party's stances differed from that of the government, it was generally ignored. For example, the government pardoned top military officers jailed for human rights violations despite the fact that the National Council had previously made public its opposition to the measure,[90] and the government pushed through Congress a bill expanding the Supreme Court from five to nine members despite the fact that Cafiero had negotiated a bipartisan reform with the UCR that would have expanded the court to seven.[91]

Rather than working with the National Council, Menem relied on an unstable coalition of Menemist government officials – the orthodox *Rojo Punzó* and "neo-Menemist" *Celestes* – to manage the relationship between the government and the party. For example, it was *Rojo Punzó* and Menemist union leaders, rather than the National Council, who mobilized people for the successful pro-reform "Plaza del Sí" rally in April 1990.[92] Similarly, *Celeste* leaders, rather than the National Council, organized a May 1990 "summit" in Cosquín, Córdoba, to debate the "refoundation" of Peronism.[93] In effect, the summit was an informal party congress. Although Cafiero and other

---

[87] *Clarín*, June 24, 1990, p. 13.
[88] Author's interview, October 3, 1997.
[89] Author's interview, October 3, 1997.
[90] *Clarín*, December 27, 1989, p. 12.
[91] *Clarín*, April 8, 1990, p. 13.
[92] Because several non-Peronists, including television commentator Bernardo Neustadt, played a leading role in calling for the Plaza del Sí, the rally is often portrayed as having bypassed the party (Palermo and Novaro 1996: 231). This was not the case. Although the National Council was indeed bypassed, the main organizing forces behind the event, such as Luis Barrionuevo and the Menem for President Labor Roundtable, were Peronist.
[93] *Clarín*, May 18, 1990, p. 6; May 26, 1990, pp. 2–3; May 27, 1990, pp. 2–3.

The Government Takeover of the Party Leadership (1990–9)

In August 1990, after losing a Buenos Aires referendum that would have permitted his reelection as governor, Cafiero succumbed to internal pressure and resigned as party president – a year and a half before his term expired. Party vice president Vernet, a Cafiero ally, also resigned. After a series of back room negotiations, Menem was named party president, his brother Eduardo was named vice president, and neo-Menemist Roberto García was named first vice president.[94] Carlos Menem, and later Eduardo Menem, took a leave of absence, which meant that García would serve as acting party president. The "Menemization" of the National Council closed the gap between the formal party leadership and the real balance of power in the PJ by essentially "unifying the government and the party."[95] The leadership change also represented a major step toward the "governmentalization" of the National Council. Although García was not a member of the government, the rest of the new leadership consisted of government officials. Not surprisingly, then, Eduardo Menem announced that the PJ leadership would shift from a position of "critical support" for the government to one of "unconditional support."[96] Similarly, new Interior Minister José Luis Manzano declared,

> With this leadership composition, the party will be able to support the government's work with greater fluidity, without the necessity of a permanent state of deliberation each time a decision needs to be made.[97]

Although the National Council maintained an organizational life of its own under García between 1990 and 1992, it was largely run by *Celeste* leaders such as Manzano, Minister of the Presidency Eduardo Bauza, and Eduardo Menem. García always met with either Bauza or Eduardo Menem before presiding over National Council meetings, and all intraparty conflicts "were worked out in Bauza's office before the meetings."[98] The March 1991 party congress, which was dedicated to "updating" the PJ program, was organized by Bauza, Manzano, and other *Celeste* officials,[99] and the party's strategies for the 1991 midterm elections and 1992 Senate elections

---

[94] National Council members Jorge Yoma and José Azcurra insisted – in vain – that the new leadership be selected by the entire 110-member National Council. After the selection process, National Council member José Ramos complained that council members had "found out about it in the newspapers" (*Clarín*, August 11, 1990, pp. 4–5).
[95] *Clarín*, August 9, 1990, p. 4.
[96] *Clarín*, August 11, 1990, p. 5.
[97] Quoted in *Clarín*, August 9, 1990, p. 10.
[98] Author's interview with Raul Roa, treasurer of the Federal Capital party branch, July 7, 1997.
[99] *Clarín*, March 13, 1991, p. 4; March 15, 1991, p. 5.

were developed by Bauza, Manzano, and Eduardo Menem.[100] The situation reached such an extreme in mid-1991 that García threatened to resign, claiming that the Interior Ministry was running the PJ's campaign.[101] Finally, when the National Council's mandate expired in 1991, Bauza and Manzano drew up the new party leadership list in the presidential palace.[102]

The García-led National Council exerted little influence over government policy making. Indeed, party leaders continued to complain that they were "finding out about the government's initiatives in the newspapers."[103] According to one former National Council member, the body largely "ratified decisions that had already been made by the executive branch."[104] In the few cases in which the National Council took a position at odds with the executive branch, such as when the body opposed the government's decision to withdraw from the Non-Aligned Movement,[105] the executive branch ignored it.

Post-1990 party organs thus functioned more as government mouthpieces than as channels for party demands. For example, despite the fact that the 1991 Convertibility Law generated sharp criticism within the party,[106] the National Council never gave voice to these criticisms. Indeed, the September 1991 party congress expressed its "unrestricted support" for the government's economic plan, and in early 1992, the National Council launched a public campaign in defense of the plan.[107] The party leadership also refused to question President Menem's decision to send troops to fight in the Persian Gulf War, despite the fact that much of the party leadership opposed the move.[108] Beginning in 1992, government officials used the National Council to push for a constitutional reform to permit Menem's reelection.[109] Finally,

---

[100] Author's interview with José Luis Manzano, December 5, 1997.
[101] *Clarín*, June 26, 1991, p. 9.
[102] Author's interviews with José Luis Manzano (December 5, 1997) and Roberto García (June 23, 1997). According to De la Sota, "I was there when Manzano and Bauza were putting together the new leadership. Manzano asked me if I wanted to be on it. I said, 'No. This party is so unimportant that you can be here putting it together by yourself. If it were important, there would be a thousand people at the door trying to get in. This is clearly not going to be any good for anything, so I don't want to be on it'" (author's interview, November 17, 1997).
[103] Oraldo Britos, quoted in *Clarín*, January 24, 1992, p. 9.
[104] Author's interview with former National Council member Juan José Zanola, October 22, 1997.
[105] *Clarín*, May 2, 1991, p. 13.
[106] *Clarín*, February 14, 1991, p. 4.
[107] *La Voz del Interior*, September 21, 1991, p. 4a; *Clarín*, January 9, 1992, p. 6; January 22, 1992, p. 4.
[108] According to *Clarín*, fifteen of the PJ's twenty-five senators opposed Menem's decision (September 19, 1990, pp. 2–3; September 20, 1990, pp. 4–5).
[109] In June 1992, the National Council – under pressure from Bauza and Eduardo Menem – declared its support for Menem's reelection and began to campaign for the reform (*Clarín*, March 8, 1992, p. 6; May 17, 1992, p. 10; June 7, 1992, p. 6; June 24, 1992, p. 8).

Programmatic Adaptation in the 1990s

the National Council sided with the government in its conflicts with organized labor. In January 1992, the National Council refused to take up CGT leader (and council member) Carlos West Ocampo's request to debate the deregulation of union-administered health insurance funds.[110] A year later, the party issued a communiqué – "without holding any meeting whatsoever" – supporting the government's deregulation policy.[111] And in November 1992, the National Council joined the government in opposing the CGT's first general strike against Menem.[112] Although CGT General Secretary Oscar Lescano claimed the declaration was "not a statement from the party, but rather from a group of government officials,"[113] in reality, the two had become virtually one and the same.

In late 1992, when ex-Renovators Grosso and Manzano were forced to resign their posts as Federal Capital mayor and interior minister, respectively,[114] the balance of power in the party shifted from the *Celestes* to a loose coalition of Menemists and PJ governors, particularly Buenos Aires Governor Duhalde. Because the Executive Board remained in the hands of the *Celestes*, President Menem reverted to a party-circumventing strategy. Rather than work through the National Council, government officials organized an informal, parallel party summit in Mar del Plata to develop the PJ's electoral strategies for the 1993 elections.[115] They also created an informal "electoral command" that would operate at the margins of the formal party leadership.[116] Marginalized, Grosso, Manzano, and eventually García resigned their positions in the party leadership. García later claimed that there were

> three phases in my presidency. In the first phase, I drew up the party communiqués and got them approved by the government before signing them. In the second phase, the government sent me the communiqués and I revised them and signed them. In the third phase, I read about the party communiqués in the newspapers. That's when I knew it was time to quit.[117]

The departing neo-Menemists were replaced in the National Council Executive Board by government ministers Eduardo Bauza and Gustavo Beliz, and La Pampa Governor Ruben Marín replaced García as acting president.

---

[110] *Clarín*, January 23, 1992, p. 3.
[111] Paper workers union leader and National Council member Blas Alari, quoted in *Página/12*, March 25, 1993, p. 10. Alari resigned from the National Council in protest.
[112] *Clarín*, November 5, 1992, p. 11.
[113] *Clarín*, November 5, 1992, p. 11.
[114] Grosso resigned as mayor of the Federal Capital, amidst allegations of corruption, in October 1992. Manzano resigned as interior minister – also amidst corruption allegations – in December 1992.
[115] *Clarín*, February 4, 1993, p. 10.
[116] *Clarín*, February 7, 1993, pp. 4–5; *Página/12*, March 31, 1993, p. 5.
[117] Author's interview, June 23, 1997.

Once again, the new leadership was drawn up – in Bauza's office – by top government officials.[118]

The 1993 leadership change again allowed the government to close the gap between the formal party leadership and the real balance of power in the party. Although the new Executive Board included independent governors such as Marín, Vicente Joga, and Nestor Kirchner, its overall composition reflected the new Menemist–Duhaldist coalition. After this recomposition, Menem again began to govern through the party. The Mar del Plata summit was canceled and replaced by a National Council assembly,[119] and the National Council took control of the "electoral command."[120]

García's removal completed a process that legislator Rodolfo Gazia described as the "substitution of the government for the party."[121] Beginning in May 1993, all of the members of the top leadership were either members of the national government or governors. As a result, the National Council ceased to operate as an even minimally autonomous entity. Party decisions were "made in the government house,"[122] and party leaders "carried out the policies of the government."[123] According to Carlos West Ocampo, the party leadership became

a government appendage, a government office.... I don't even attend party meetings because they are just meetings of government officials. They are managed by Bauza and Eduardo Menem.[124]

In 1993 and 1994, the bulk of party activity was aimed at a constitutional reform that would permit Menem's reelection.[125]

After Menem's reelection, National Council activity was "restricted to the point where one could say it exists only formally."[126] For example, during the 1997 midterm elections, the PJ's national campaign was run largely out of the Interior Ministry.[127] In this context, party and government positions were indistinguishable. For example, in December 1995, the National Council offered rubber stamp support for Menem's entire

---

[118] *Clarín*, May 12, 1993, p. 8; May 13, 1993, p. 6.
[119] *Clarín*, March 17, 1993, p. 10.
[120] *Clarín*, June 28, 1993, p. 10; July 7, 1993, p. 12; July 15, 1993, p. 15.
[121] Author's interview, December 5, 1997. According to Congressional Deputy Mario Das Neves, the PJ began to "confuse party leaders with government officials. We go to a party debate and we find [conservative non-Peronist cabinet members] Roque Fernandez and Maria Julia Alsogaray giving orders" (author's interview, November 20, 1997).
[122] Author's interview with Senator José Luis Gioja, September 18, 1997.
[123] Author's interview with Senator Omar Vaquir, September 24, 1997.
[124] Author's interview, October 13, 1997.
[125] *Clarín*, August 13, 1993, pp. 10–11; October 12, 1993, pp. 4–5; October 25, 1993, p. 4.
[126] Author's interview with Congressional Deputy Juan Carlos Suarez, September 16, 1997. Even acting party president Ruben Marín recognized that the National Council "meets very little" (*Clarín*, April 7, 1997, p. 7).
[127] *Página/12*, August 29, 1997, p. 5.

postelection legislative agenda, including the granting of extraordinary legislative powers to Economic Minister Domingo Cavallo.[128] In 1998, Menem successfully pressured the party congress to declare its support for his bid for a third term in office – despite its clear unconstitutionality.

The Failure of Internal Challenges

President Menem's strategic autonomy was further enhanced by his capacity to maintain a hub-and-spokes relationship with secondary party leaders. Menem's internal critics confronted a difficult collective action problem. Had they united, they might have had the capacity to force the president to moderate his reform strategy, for their collective opposition could have inflicted heavy political costs on Menem. As one former "25" leader put it,

> If the ex-Renovators and union leaders... had been united, the reform process would not have taken place like this. There would have been a degree of rationality to the process. By 1993, we would have been able to say "stop," and we would have been able to leave the Convertibility by 1994.[129]

However, intraparty coalition-building efforts repeatedly failed between 1989 and 1999. Secondary leaders fell into a hub-and-spokes relationship with the president, leaving them vulnerable to cooptation. This dynamic had two roots. The first was the absence of effective horizontal linkages within the PJ. As Chapter 3 argued, the PJ lacks an effective party bureaucracy or other mechanism to bring secondary leaders together in a regularized way. The absence of such horizontal linkages makes it more difficult for secondary leaders to form a "cohesive group" with a "common understanding about their collective interests" (Knoke 1990: 11–12).

Second, the hub-and-spokes dynamic was reinforced by Menem's skillful positioning within Peronism's complex system of internal networks. As Padgett and Ansell (1993) and Ansell and Fish (1999) have shown, centralized authority relations often emerge in fragmented organizations in which a leader is able to establish a multiplicity of ties to subgroups that cross-cut internal cleavages. In this way, the leader becomes an "indispensable" hub within the organization. Such a dynamic emerged in the PJ in the 1990s. Over the course of his political career, Menem undertook a series of alliance shifts that took him from the far left of the party to the far right.[130] Although

---

[128] *Clarín*, December 3, 1995, p. 22. According to Congressional Deputy José López, the National Council "doesn't function. There is no debate. There aren't even any meetings.... The party is run by the government. Menem's policies become the policies of the party" (author's interview, May 15, 1997).
[129] Author's interview with Gustavo Morato, June 13, 1997.
[130] In the 1980s, Corrientes boss Julio Romero observed that Menem "is always jumping from side to side, and it is difficult to figure him out" (*La Prensa*, December 1, 1987, p. 6).

his political roots lay in Orthodox Peronism, Menem was a founder of the Renovation in the mid-1980s. Yet in his quest for the 1988 presidential nomination, Menem abandoned the Renovators and, in a strategy that was described as "Operation Ambulance," appealed to a range of Peronists who had been marginalized by the Renovation. Thus, he built a coalition of "the political cadavers of Peronism" (Santoro 1994: 190), including old-guard unionists, Orthodox leaders, and rump cadre organizations of the left (Montoneros) *and* right (Iron Guard, C de O). Although this strategy earned Menem a reputation for opportunism,[131] it allowed him to establish a set of crossfactional ties that few leaders possessed.

Upon winning the presidential nomination, Menem reestablished ties to hardline Renovators. Thus, alliances with Renovators such as José Luis Manzano and Carlos Corach and "25" leaders such as Roberto García and Guerino Andreoni cemented his position at the hub of the party's alliance system. The first Menem administration was divided between ultra-Menemist (*Rojo Punzó*) and ex-Renovation (*Celeste*) factions. As *Clarín* observed, the two factions were "united only by their personal loyalty to the president."[132] *Rojo Punzó* members described the *Celestes* as "social democratic infiltrators,"[133] while the *Celestes* described *Rojo Punzó* as a "gang of delinquents" who were "profoundly authoritarian."[134] Although conflicts between these two factions were often viewed as a source of weakness (Corrales 1996b: 208), their coexistence was also a source of strength, for they allowed Menem to maintain ties to all major party factions. While *Rojo Punzó* leaders such as Cesar Arias, Luis Barrionuevo, and Julio Mera Figueroa maintained close ties to the ex-Orthodox wing, *Celeste* leaders such as Manzano, Corach, and Bauza maintained close ties to ex-Renovators. Together, the two factions represented virtually the entire array of Peronist forces.[135]

Lacking an effective party bureaucracy or other mechanism to bring them together in a regularized way, and often sharing less in common with each other than with Menem, secondary leaders fell into a hub-and-spokes relationship with Menem. This allowed Menem to play non-Menemists against each other, thereby undermining their efforts to act collectively. Because Menem could inflict much more damage on individual leaders than they, by themselves, could inflict on him, critics repeatedly backed down from

---

[131] Cafiero called Menem a "Renodox," or a hybrid of Renovator and Orthodox (*Clarín*, June 9, 1986, p. 8; June 10, 1986, p. 11).
[132] September 16, 1990, p. 10.
[133] *Clarín*, January 4, 1989, p. 9.
[134] Author's interview with Miguel Angel Toma, July 10, 1997.
[135] Manzano describes the Menemist coalition as "a Persian Bazaar. He had everyone inside. There was no black or white. No good or bad. Everyone was inside: Renovators, Carapintadas, intellectuals, Montoneros, thieves, whores..." (author's interview, December 5, 1997).

potential confrontations with the president.¹³⁶ Defections repeatedly undermined efforts to build non-Menemist coalitions, leading many internal critics to conclude that it was "impossible to challenge Menem from within."¹³⁷ According to one former Renovator,

Everyone will tell you, "I surrendered because the others surrendered. What do you want me to do, go it alone?".... People were frightened of losing what they had. So they negotiated individually. Each one negotiated his own deal.¹³⁸

As a result of this hub-and-spokes dynamic, efforts to act collectively to moderate or oppose the Menem program repeatedly broke down in the 1990s. This was clearly seen, for example, during the initial eighteen months of the Menem presidency, when the government's failure to resolve the economic crisis led to a considerable decline in political support. As Menem's public approval fell from nearly 80 percent in mid-1989 to just 24 percent in March 1990,¹³⁹ the reform program came to be widely questioned within the party. PJ legislators denounced the program as "not Peronist," and called for a "return to our roots,"¹⁴⁰ and a group of influential senators began to call for price controls and Keynesian reactivation policies.¹⁴¹ In this context, two internal opposition factions emerged. The first was a group of left-of-center Renovators called the Group of Eight. The Group of Eight opposed the bulk of the Menem reforms, including state reform and privatization, characterizing them as "betrayal of the popular vote."¹⁴² In early 1990, the Group of Eight had the support of about twenty-five Congressional deputies, as well as a handful of public sector unions.¹⁴³ The second group was Peronist Militancy, an Orthodox faction, led by Catamarca Governor Ramon Saadi, that included about twenty Congressional deputies from the northern peripheral provinces.¹⁴⁴ In early 1990, Saadi called on PJ governors to "unite against liberalism," and launched a campaign to "Peronize the government" and gain control of the party leadership.¹⁴⁵ At times, the Group of Eight, Peronist Militancy, non-Menemist unionists, and other loosely organized

---

¹³⁶ As one PJ leader put it, "If Menem calls us tomorrow and tells us, be quiet and you get this, everyone is going to grab it because on his own no one is strong enough on their own to resist" (Palermo and Novaro 1996: 221).
¹³⁷ Author's interview with Carlos Grosso, November 28, 1997.
¹³⁸ Author's interview with Gustavo Morato, June 13, 1997.
¹³⁹ *La Prensa*, August 26, 1989, p. 5, and Palermo (1994: 332).
¹⁴⁰ Senator Oraldo Britos, quoted in *La Prensa*, December 18, 1989, p. 4.
¹⁴¹ These included Oraldo Britos, Eduardo Vaca, Remo Constanzo, Ruben Marín, and Alberto Rodriguez Saa (*Clarín*, February 24, 1990, p. 4; February 26, 1990, p. 4; *La Prensa*, February 27, 1990, p. 8).
¹⁴² *Clarín*, March 1, 1990, p. 12; March 17, 1990, p. 7; June 17, 1990, p. 6.
¹⁴³ Author's interview with former Group of Eight leader Juan Pablo Cafiero, November 18, 1997. Also *Clarín*, December 15, 1989, p. 15.
¹⁴⁴ *La Prensa*, February 11, 1990, p. 5; May 17, 1990, p. 9; *Clarín*, April 15, 1990, p. 2.
¹⁴⁵ *Clarín*, February 11, 1990, p. 4; February 21, 1990, p. 4; February 22, 1990, p. 4.

groups of critics collectively represented a majority of the party leadership. In early 1990, for example, the Menemist coalition in the legislature was reduced to fewer than half of the party's 120 deputies.[146]

Yet non-Menemist factions repeatedly failed to unite into a single coalition. Orthodox provincial bosses like Saadi shared little in common with the urban progressives who led the Group of Eight. Moreover, powerful critics within the labor movement, such as Lorenzo Miguel, Diego Ibañez, and bank workers union leader Juan José Zanola, also maintained poor relations with the ex-Renovators in the legislature and the National Council. Consequently, cooperation across non-Menemist factions proved difficult. Rebellions against the Menem leadership repeatedly failed, and each of the opposition factions proved short-lived. Thus, despite attempts to build alliances with former Renovators such as De la Sota, Duhalde, and José Octavio Bordón,[147] Peronist Militancy was unable to expand beyond its Orthodox and northwestern provincial base. Saadi-led efforts to remove Manzano from the legislative leadership in June and November of 1990 failed when erstwhile critics such as the Federal Parliamentary Group and allies of Vice President Duhalde struck deals with the neo-Menemists.[148] When a corruption scandal forced Saadi out of office in 1991, the faction collapsed. Similarly, the Group of Eight "slowly dwindled down to eight," and by late 1990, it was isolated within the party.[149] According to Group of Eight leader Carlos "Chacho" Alvarez,

> In private, 90 percent of the bloc criticized Menem from top to bottom. But in public they didn't say a thing.... They would all come up to me and say they were sympathetic with my positions, but that it was a shame I didn't fight from within.... They were all coopted.... It was a question of raw power.[150]

The Group of Eight left the PJ in late 1990 in the hope of creating an alternative Peronist party. Few Peronists followed them.

The success of the Convertibility Plan and the PJ's victory in the 1991 midterm elections left Menem virtually unchallenged in the party through much of 1992. However, by early 1993, an initial lame duck effect – Menem's

---

[146] *Clarín*, March 1, 1990, p. 10; June 3, 1990, p. 6. In March of that year, Manzano could only gather fifty legislators to make a public declaration of support for Menem (*Clarín*, March 9, 1990, p. 2).

[147] *Clarín*, December 26, 1989, p. 6; April 15, 1990, p. 2; May 31, 1990, p. 15; July 2, 1990, p. 9.

[148] *Clarín*, June 9, 1990, p. 7; November 27, 1990, p. 10; November 29, 1990, p. 13.

[149] Author's interview with Juan Pablo Cafiero, November 18, 1997.

[150] Author's interview, July 29, 1997. Similarly, former Group of Eight leader Juan Pablo Cafiero claims that "there were many dissident voices in the party, but when Menem entered the room they all quieted down, because the government is the place where positions of power are distributed.... We could not fight from within, because the PJ is a party of power, and you don't fight from within in a party of power.... You can create the fiction of debate, of a party congress, but it's just a parody" (author's interview, November 18, 1997).

term expired in 1995 and the constitution prohibited reelection – opened the door to several "post-Menemist" challengers. Because UCR opposition to a constitutional reform appeared to make Menem's reelection unlikely, Peronists began to rethink their internal alliances. Although Menem's popularity and control of the state created a strong incentive for cooperation, PJ leaders were forced to weigh that incentive against the cost of missing the opportunity for an alliance with the PJ's future candidate.

Several post-Menemist projects emerged in late 1992 and early 1993. An abortive effort was launched by Federal Capital Mayor Carlos Grosso, who called for a "re-Peronization" of economic policy before a corruption scandal forced him to resign in late 1992. In early 1993, Cafiero declared his intention to launch a "post-Menemist current" composed of a group of "rebel" Peronist senators.[151] At the same time, De la Sota, who was at odds with Menem over the National Council's intervention in the Córdoba party branch, began to call for a "new Renovation."[152] De la Sota declared himself an opponent of Menemism, and insisted that "Justicialism must be capable of accumulating wealth with policies of redistribution and social welfare."[153] Buenos Aires Governor Duhalde also distanced himself from Menem, describing himself as a "Peronist, not a Menemist."[154] The most important challenge, however, came from Mendoza Senator (and presidential hopeful) José Octavio Bordón. Although Bordón did not oppose the Convertibility Law, he insisted that "stability by itself is not going to guarantee growth and social justice."[155] Bordón compared the government's social policies to the "anti-social policies of the 1930s,"[156] criticized the government's "excessive dependence on foreign capital inflows,"[157] and accused Menem of "converting Justicialism into a party of the rich."[158] He also sought an alliance with organized labor and opposed the government's efforts to "flexibilize" labor markets.[159] By mid-1993, Bordón appeared to have the support of Cafiero, De la Sota, Duhalde, Lorenzo Miguel, and other key party leaders.[160]

[151] These included José Octavio Bordón, Oraldo Britos, Remo Constanzo, Cesar MacKarthey, Alberto Rodriguez Saa, and Eduardo Vaca (*Clarín*, April 22, 1992, pp. 2–3; *Página/12*, May 11, 1993, p. 7).
[152] *Clarín*, January 24, 1993, p. 4.
[153] *Clarín*, February 26, 1993, p. 6; July 30, 1993, p. 8; *Página/12*, March 23, 1993, p. 12.
[154] *Clarín*, April 5, 1993, p. 8; *Ambito Financiero*, September 6, 1993, p. 21; September 27, 1993, p. 5.
[155] *Clarín*, June 11, 1993, p. 16.
[156] *Clarín*, May 31, 1993, p. 8.
[157] *Página/12*, March 24, 1993, p. 14.
[158] *Clarín*, August 5, 1994, p. 15.
[159] *Clarín*, October 18, 1992, p. 7; October 26, 1992, p. 7; May 6, 1993, p. 10; May 7, 1993, pp. 4–5.
[160] *Página/12*, March 23, 1993, p. 12; May 11, 1993, p. 7; *Clarín*, May 9, 1993, p. 16; May 11, 1993, p. 11; May 13, 1993, p. 6; June 9, 1993, p. 8; July 8, 1993, p. 13.

However, the *Bordonista* project soon collapsed. In large part, the project was buried by the November 1993 Olivos Pact, which assured Menem's reelection. In obtaining the possibility of reelection and thus putting to rest any potential lame duck effect, Menem altered the strategic calculus of Peronist leaders. With Menem likely to retain control of the presidency through 1999, few PJ leaders were willing to oppose him. Thus, Duhalde, who had been in conflict with Menem in early 1993, realigned with the president, and Cafiero, a Duhalde ally, never joined the Bordón camp. Expected support from key provincial party bosses never materialized. Even De la Sota, who had publicly backed Bordón, began to call for Menem's reelection. By late 1993, Bordón was "ostracized" within the party,[161] and he could gain the support of only a handful of secondary party leaders and dissident unions. Marginalized, Bordón left the PJ in September 1994, joining the ex–Group of Eight to form the center-left Front for a Country in Solidarity (FREPASO). Only four of the PJ's 128 Congressional deputies left with Bordón.

Several ex-Renovators later came to view Bordón's challenge as a missed opportunity. According to De la Sota,

Had it not been Bordón alone, but rather Bordón, [La Pampa Governor Ruben] Marín, [former Extre Rios Governor Jorge] Busti, De la Sota . . . who had put forth a non-Menemist project, the possibilities would have been many.[162]

Similarly, Grosso claimed that a *Bordonista* coalition would have "changed the balance of power in Peronism. It would have forced Menem to confront a real opposition."[163] However, the absence of effective horizontal links made such a coalition extremely difficult to sustain.

Bordonismo represented the last serious internal challenge during Menem's first term. Although increased unemployment and social discontent led several PJ governors to call for a "social face" to the economic model,[164] internal critics were unable to establish an "alternative pole of power to organize the protest and push the party in a new direction." Rather, the opposition remained confined to "isolated leaders expressing their anguish."[165] Thus, the Federal Current, which was created by Governors Rodolfo Gabrielli and Nestor Kirchner in an effort to "correct Menemism from within," could not be sustained beyond an initial meeting with progressive Congressional deputies,[166] and although Duhalde was able to veto the vice presidential

---

[161] *Ambito Financiero*, September 13, 1993, p. 12.
[162] Author's interview, November 17, 1997.
[163] Author's interview, November 28, 1997.
[164] These governors included Rodolfo Gabrielli (Mendoza), Vicente Joga (Formosa), Nestor Kirchner (Santa Cruz), Ruben Marín (La Pampa), and Mario Moine (Entre Rios) (*Clarín*, February 24, 1994, p. 5; May 5, 1994, p. 8; May 6, 1994, pp. 2–3; June 19, 1994, pp. 6–7; July 4, 1994, p. 11).
[165] Author's interview with Congressional Deputy Julio César Díaz Lozano, October 1, 1997.
[166] *Clarín*, September 14, 1994, p. 8; December 23, 1994, p. 11.

candidacy of rival Palito Ortega in favor of ally Carlos Ruckauf, his effort to broaden his Buenos Aires–based Federal League into a national faction failed, as potential allies such as Governors Gabrielli, Kirchner, Vicente Joga, and Ruben Marin refused to join.[167]

The hub-and-spokes pattern continued after Menem's reelection. Due to a recession that elevated the unemployment rate to an unprecedented 18.6 percent, Menem's public support fell to less than 20 percent in 1996 and 1997.[168] In this context, several PJ governors began to call for more "active" state policies to combat unemployment,[169] and the government's efforts to "deepen" the reform process through labor market flexibilization and further privatization encountered substantial resistance in the legislature. Several non-Menemist factions emerged in 1996 and 1997. One was a loose confederation of provincial leaders headed by Formosa party boss Joga. This faction came to be known as Great North. Great North encompassed approximately twenty legislators from northern provinces such as Catamarca, Formosa, Jujuy, Salta, and Tucumán.[170] Most of these leaders were critical of the neoliberal model, preferring more protectionist and redistributive state policies.[171] A second non-Menemist faction was the Peronist Current, which was created by Santa Cruz Governor Kirchner. Seeking to establish itself as a national representative of "progressive Justicialism,"[172] the Peronist Current adopted a "markedly anti-Menemist profile."[173] In 1997, the Peronist Current joined with Entre Rios Governor Jorge Busti and Buenos Aires Vice Governor Rafael Romá to form the Progressive Current.

These projects failed to take hold. Great North remained confined to the northern interior, and the Peronist Current failed to gain the support of other governors and soon collapsed. Even Duhalde, who would eventually be the party's presidential nominee in 1999, failed in his efforts to build a national faction. Overwhelmingly reelected as governor of Buenos Aires in 1995, Duhalde could count on disciplined *Duhaldista* factions in the party congress and the legislature. Through his thirty-seven legislative representatives, Duhalde exercised a virtual veto power over legislation in the 1995–9 period. Yet Duhalde's efforts to build a national-level coalition of provincial party bosses repeatedly failed. For example, in early 1997, Duhalde launched the Federal Union, which was expected to include Cafiero, De la

---

[167] *Clarín*, October 9, 1994, p. 3; October 13, 1994, p. 3.
[168] *Ambito Financiero*, March 12, 1997, p. 10.
[169] *Clarín*, July 23, 1995, pp. 2–3.
[170] Author's interview with Congressional Deputy Vicente Joga, December 17, 1997.
[171] Author's interviews with Great North Congressional Deputies Adriana Bogado (November 26, 1997), Julio César Díaz Lozano (October 1, 1997), Jorge Díaz Martinez (November 26, 1997), and Joga (December 17, 1997).
[172] Nestor Kirchner, quoted in *Página/12*, May 15, 1997, p. 8.
[173] Author's interview with PJ city council member and Peronist Current member Victor Pandolfi, June 5, 1997.

Sota, Chamber of Deputies president Alberto Pierri, and several governors and labor leaders.[174] Had Duhalde sustained such a coalition, he would have enjoyed a clear majority in the party. Yet party bosses refused to commit to the Federal Union, and the project was abandoned.

The causes of these failures were similar to those that undermined non-Menemist coalitions in the 1989–95 period. First of all, the party remained fragmented, both geographically and ideologically. Whereas Great North was based in the country's poor northern provinces and consisted largely of leaders with Orthodox or nationalist backgrounds, the Peronist Current was based in the Patagonia region and the Federal Capital and consisted largely of progressive ex-Renovators. And although *Duhaldismo* called itself "federal," it was in fact concentrated in Buenos Aires. Second, President Menem effectively used state resources to reinforce this hub-and-spokes relationship and coopt potential opponents.[175] Finally, Menem avoided a lame duck syndrome (which would likely have triggered a process of bandwagoning toward Duhalde) by repeatedly raising the specter of another reelection. Despite its clear unconstitutionality, Menem loyalists pursued "re-reelection" through several avenues. In early 1997, Menemist Senator Jorge Yoma introduced legislation to call a plebiscite on whether Menem should be permitted to run for a third term. Other Menemists appealed the ban on a third term in the courts. And in July 1998, in a questionable party congress that was boycotted by *Duhaldistas*, Menem gained the party's official support for re-reelection. Although public disapproval and the opposition of both Duhalde and the major political parties made Menem's reelection a virtual impossibility, these efforts created enough uncertainty among Peronists that most preferred to adopt a wait-and-see attitude rather than make a premature jump to Duhalde.[176]

In sum, PJ leaders fell into a hub-and-spokes relationship with President Menem during the 1989–99 period, which permitted Menem to use a

---

[174] *Clarín*, February 5, 1997, p. 9; February 9, 1997, p. 9; February 17, 1997, p. 8. The governors reportedly included Jorge Busti of Entre Rios, Arturo Lafalla of Mendoza, Ruben Marín of La Pampa, Jorge Obeid of Santa Fe, and Juan Carlos Romero of Salta.

[175] According to one Peronist Current leader, "Many governors, when you sit down with them, agree with you. They are very critical. But the provinces are so fragile economically, so dependent on the state, that they cannot afford to break with Menem.... It's always easier to make a deal" (author's interview with PJ city council member and Peronist Current member Victor Pandolfi, June 5, 1997).

[176] Key PJ leaders such as Jorge Busti, Arturo Lafalla, Jorge Obeid, and Juan Carlos Romero, who had initially backed Duhalde, shifted to a position of neutrality, while Cafiero, De la Sota, and Marín, all of whom needed Menem's support for 1999 gubernatorial bids, actively supported Menem's reelection effort. Cafiero gained Menem's support for his gubernatorial bid in Buenos Aires, in opposition to *Duhaldista* candidate Carlos Ruckauf. De la Sota used Menem's support to win the gubernatorial nomination in Córdoba. Marín gained Menem's support for a second consecutive constitutional reform in La Pampa, which allowed Marín to run for a third term in 1999.

combination of threats and cooptation to undermine non-Menemist coalitions. Unable to rely on stable horizontal linkages to other party leaders, potential critics often found themselves alone when confronting Menem. Because the costs of a conflict with Menem were far higher for individual secondary leaders than they were for Menem, these potential critics had a strong incentive to back down. Had the various non-Menemist factions united, they might have forced the Menem leadership to slow down or moderate its reform program. Yet because PJ leaders who were privately critical of Menem consistently refused to participate in public opposition efforts, internal opposition coalitions repeatedly broke down, and Menem's leadership and program went largely unchallenged from within.

MUTUAL AUTONOMY AND THE LIMITS OF MENEMISM

Menem's autonomy vis-á-vis the PJ did not mean he was able to impose his will on the party, however. It is often argued that the PJ's provincial organizations were subordinated to, and transformed by, the Menem leadership (Novaro 1994, 1995; Palermo and Novaro 1996; 370–6, 404; Yannuzzi 1995: 179–86). According to Marcos Novaro, the PJ "was completely reorganized, from the highest positions to each one of its local chapters" (1998: 12). From this perspective, the national party leadership "functioned as a...mechanism of control of provincial leaderships" (Palermo and Novaro 1996: 404), allowing Menem to routinely impose strategies on provincial branches and replace local party leaders and candidates with media-friendly "outsiders" (Novaro 1995: 60–2; Yannuzzi 1995: 179–86; McGuire 1997: 243–8). Indeed, the Menemist leadership imposed outsider candidates in several critical elections, including the 1991 gubernatorial candidacies of businessman Jorge Escobar (San Juan), pop singer Ramon "Palito" Ortega (Tucumán), and auto racer Carlos Reutemann (Santa Fe), the 1992 Senatorial candidacy of conservative Avelino Porto in the Federal Capital, and the legislative candidacies of Menem crony Erman Gonzales and boating champion Daniel Scioli in the Federal Capital in 1993 and 1997, respectively. In total, the National Council "intervened" in twelve of the party's twenty-four district-level branches – most for an average of about two years – during the 1989–99 period.[177]

Yet President Menem's influence over local and provincial party branches was less extensive than is often believed. Menem's autonomy vis-á-vis the PJ

---

[177] These were the Federal Capital, Catamarca, Córdoba, Corrientes, Jujuy, La Rioja, Santiago del Estero, Salta, San Juan, Santa Fe, Tierra del Fuego, and Tucumán. Most of these interventions occurred in the 1989–91 period, when deep fiscal crises and conflicts between traditional *caudillos* and emerging leaders generated severe disorder in many provincial branches. Only three interventions were carried out after 1993 (La Rioja in 1994, San Juan in 1995, and the Federal Capital in 1997), and as of 1999, only the La Rioja and the Federal Capital branches remained under intervention.

generally worked both ways. Because the PJ bureaucracy lacked mechanisms with which to discipline subunits, the Menem leadership's capacity to impose leaders or strategies on local and provincial branches was limited. Efforts to impose candidates or strategies on local branches frequently failed, and the national party leadership often found its strategies thwarted – or ignored – by local leaderships. In most provinces, Menem was forced to settle for a "live and let live" strategy, in which old-guard party leaderships and programs remained virtually intact. Indeed, the relationship between Menem and provincial party branches was closer to one of mutual autonomy than one of imposition.

The autonomy of local PJ leaders is largely rooted in their control over local party machines. As Chapter 3 showed, local organizations are responsible for the bulk of the PJ patronage distribution and activist mobilization, and they deliver a large percentage of the party vote. Control over these organizations is essential to winning internal elections. Because voting in primaries is voluntary and virtually all voters must be physically brought to the polling place, winning such elections requires an extensive activist-based organization. Due to Argentina's federal structure, these organizations generally fall under the control of local office holders, such as mayors and governors, who use public sector jobs and other state resources to coopt *agrupaciones* into municipal or provincial machines. Where such machines consolidate and local bosses gain a monopoly over the local activist base, outsiders – even those backed by the president – stand little chance of success in intraparty competition. Although the national party has the formal authority to intervene provincial branches, doing so in the face of a unified, office-based party is costly, for it risks dividing the party and losing the votes controlled by the local boss.

The persistence of strong local machines sharply limited President Menem's capacity to influence lower-level party branches. In 1989 and 1990, some "ultra-Menemist" government officials had envisioned a "Menemized" PJ in which neoliberals, business leaders, and pro-Menem "outsiders" would be wedded to the Peronist base through Menem's direct mass appeal,[178] and a few of them reportedly sought to take over all non-Menemist provincial branches and impose Menemist leaderships.[179] Menem himself spoke of creating a "League of Winners," suggesting in 1990 that he would back the gubernatorial candidacies of a range of non-Peronist outsiders, conservative provincial party leaders, and even ex-military officials who supported his economic program.[180]

---

[178] *Clarín*, November 3, 1991, p. 7.
[179] *Clarín*, August 15, 1990, p. 4. Other Menemists talked of creating a "Menemist party" that would break with the PJ and base itself entirely on Menem's personalistic appeal (*Clarín*, July 8, 1990, p. 14; September 11, 1990, p. 18).
[180] *Clarín*, November 5, 1990, p. 5.

Yet efforts to impose leaders and strategies upon provincial branches frequently failed. For example, when Menem instructed provincial branches to align with the right-wing UCeDe and other conservative parties in the 1991 elections, only a handful complied. Local leaderships in Salta, San Juan, and other districts openly rejected the order,[181] and many others simply ignored it. Similarly, in 1993, when Menem sought to impose a campaign strategy that centered on the government's economic program and Menem's reelection,[182] various party branches ignored the national campaign and maintained their own profiles. Indeed, Buenos Aires boss Duhalde ordered the "de-Menemization" of the provincial party's campaign.[183]

The Menem leadership was also limited in its capacity to impose candidates on provincial branches. Although "outsider" cases such as those of Ortega and Reutemann became well-known, they proved to be the exception rather than the rule. In fact, provincial party branches fiercely resisted the League of Winners strategy, ultimately forcing Menem to abandon nonparty candidacies in all but a few districts.[184] In Buenos Aires, Duhalde ignored Menem's request to place business leaders Carlos De la Vega and Guillermo Alchouran on the party's parliamentary list and included only two Menemists in the top twenty positions on the list.[185] In Mendoza, Menem's attempt to place "people of confidence"[186] on the legislative list was thwarted when non-Menemist party leaders created their own list and defeated a coalition of Menemist factions in internal elections.

Similarly, when government officials designed a strategy in 1992 to ensure that provincial branches nominated Menemist candidates for the Senate,[187] they managed – despite months of lobbying[188] – to obtain their preferred candidates in only three districts (the Federal Capital, Entre Rios, and Tucumán). In Catamarca, Jujuy, La Pampa, Salta, Santa Cruz, and Santa Fe, the national leadership's candidates were openly rejected by provincial party branches.[189] In Santa Fe, for example, despite intense pressure from Menem and other top government officials to reelect Senator Liliana Gurdulich,[190] the local party nominated Jorge Massat, an ally of Governor Reutemann. In La Pampa, where Menem sought to fill one of two vacant senate seats with ex-Governor Nestor Ahuad, provincial boss Ruben Marín imposed allies

---

[181] *Clarín*, June 29, 1990, p. 13; July 7, 1991, p. 13.
[182] *Página/12*, March 31, 1993, p. 5.
[183] *Clarín*, August 15, 1993, p. 11.
[184] *Clarín*, June 27, 1990, p. 14; June 28, 1990, pp. 9, 11; July 23, 1990, p. 7.
[185] *Clarín*, June 5, 1991, p. 13; June 26, 1991, p. 9; June 30, 1991, pp. 8–9; July 30, 1991, pp. 8–9.
[186] *Clarín*, October 19, 1990, p. 11.
[187] *Clarín*, March 5, 1992, p. 14; March 8, 1992, p. 2.
[188] *Clarín*, May 13, 1992, p. 6; June 3, 1992, p. 18; September 11, 1992, p. 9.
[189] *Clarín*, June 18, 1992, p. 7; September 6, 1992, p. 15.
[190] *El Litoral*, April 30, 1992, p. 12; May 6, 1992, p. 12; September 2, 1992, p. 12.

Esteban Martinez and Carlos Verna instead.[191] In Buenos Aires, Formosa, Mendoza, Misiones, and San Luis, the national leadership had so little influence that it ultimately decided not to propose a candidate.

The Menem leadership also failed to impose its preferred candidate in several key gubernatorial elections. In Mendoza, efforts by Bauza to bring the provincial party "fully in line with the national project of Justicialism"[192] and nominate non-Peronist businessman Carlos Pulenta for the 1995 gubernatorial candidacy failed when the local party nominated Menem critic Arturo Lafalla. In Tucumán, the provincial branch nominated old-guard leader Olijela Rivas for the governorship in 1995 despite Menen's public opposition and intense pressure from government officials.[193] Non-Menemists also won gubernatorial nominations in Buenos Aires, Entre Rios, Salta, Santa Cruz, San Luis, Santiago del Estero, and Santa Fe in 1995.

The national party leadership was able to intervene in provincial branches only in cases of deep internal crisis, in which the party was both deeply divided and unable to resolve internal conflicts by institutional means. Such crises occurred when corruption scandals discredited sitting governors (as in Santa Fe and Tucumán in 1991), deep internal conflicts led to the de facto rupture of the party (as in Corrientes, San Juan, Santiago del Estero, and Córdoba in the early 1990s), or the party – generally out of power – became highly fragmented (as in the Federal Capital). In such cases, important factions sought out the support of the national leadership, thereby providing the leadership with the organizational base it needed to intervene. For example, Ortega's candidacy in Tucumán emerged after the forced removal of PJ Governor José Domato had left the local party "divided and discredited."[194] With the party trailing badly in the polls, a group of PJ leaders led by Julio Miranda and Miguel Nacul lobbied successfully for the National Council to take over the local branch and impose Ortega as candidate. Similarly, Reutemann's candidacy in Santa Fe emerged after a series of corruption scandals in the government of Victor Reviglio (which landed two vice governors in prison) left the PJ "atomized and beaten up."[195] With Reviglio discredited and the PJ in third place in the polls, Peronism fragmented into six major factions and experienced "an avalanche of Fujimori-like candidates" for governor.[196] When the June 1991 party congress deadlocked, leaving the PJ without a mechanism for selecting candidates, local leaders lobbied, successfully, for a National Council

---

[191] *Clarín*, April 27, 1992, pp. 6–7.
[192] *Clarín*, March 11, 1994, p. 10.
[193] *Clarín*, February 15, 1995, p. 8; March 19, 1995, p. 4; March 22, 1995, p. 13.
[194] *Clarín*, March 29, 1990, pp. 12–13.
[195] *Clarín*, June 15, 1991, p. 9.
[196] *El Litoral*, March 17, 1991, p. 6; April 14, 1991, p. 6; May 3, 1991, p. 5.

intervention.[197] The intervening delegate suspended internal elections and backed the gubernatorial campaign of Reutemann, a well-known non-Peronist automobile racer. Interventions in the Federal Capital, Corrientes, San Juan, Salta, and Santiago del Estero occurred in the context of similar crises.

In districts in which provincial bosses consolidated stable machines, such as Buenos Aires, Entre Ríos, Formosa, La Pampa, Mendoza, Misiones, Salta, Santa Cruz, and San Luis, interventions did not occur. In each of these provinces, party leaders and candidates were consistently selected from within the local organization, and attempts by the Menem leadership to impose leaders or strategies were generally rebuffed. In almost all of these cases, provincial branches retained traditional Peronist – rather than neoliberal – profiles.

Even where interventions occurred, they rarely produced long-term changes in provincial parties. In most cases, externally imposed leaderships failed to consolidate control of the party, and in many intervened districts, old-guard leaders soon regained power. For example, a National Council intervention failed to dislodge Catamarca boss Ramon Saadi in 1991, and Menemist efforts to replace Santiago del Estero boss Carlos Juarez with a group of outsiders and technocrats failed when the old *caudillo* easily won back the governorship in 1995. Similarly, in Tucuman, Ortega quickly alienated the local party leadership, and by 1995, old-guard sectors had regained control of the party. And in Córdoba, efforts to replace Renovation leader De la Sota with allies of Economic Minister Domingo Cavallo failed when De la Sota won back the party leadership in 1996.

Contrary to many conventional accounts, then, the Menem leadership's capacity to transform local and provincial Peronist branches proved limited. To a significant extent, traditional Peronism remained intact at the local and provincial levels at the end of the 1990s. With few exceptions, the organizations that ran the PJ's campaigns, recruited and developed its leaders, and selected its national legislators had become neither Menemist nor neoliberal. Indeed, in 1999, a full decade after Menem took office, only four of the PJ's twenty-four districts were controlled by Menemists: the Federal Capital, La Rioja, Neuquén, and San Juan. These districts represented just 15 percent of the overall electorate. By contrast, fourteen districts,[198] representing more than two-thirds of the electorate, were controlled by non-Menemists. In

---

[197] *Clarín*, June 16, 1991, 10; *El Litoral*, June 16, 1991, p. 7; June 22, 1991, p. 5; June 23, 1991, p. 5; *El Litoral*, June 16, 1991, p. 7. National Council member Cesar Arias argued that the intervention was due to "growing atomization" and the "exaggerated proliferation of candidacies, which made leadership impossible" (quoted in *El Litoral*, June 21, 1991, p. 6).

[198] These were Buenos Aires, Catamarca, Chubut, Córdoba, Entre Rios, Formosa, La Pampa, Mendoza, Misiones, Salta, San Luis, Santa Cruz, Santiago del Estero, and Tucumán. The remaining six districts (Chaco, Corrientes, Jujuy, Rio Negro, Santa Fe, and Tierra del Fuego) were mixed cases.

TABLE 6.5. *Argentine Electoral Results, 1991–9 (Percentage of Valid Vote)*

Party[a]	1991 (L)	1993 (L)	1994 (C)	1995 (P)	1995 (L)	1997 (L)	1999 (P)	1999 (L)
Justicialista Party (PJ)	40.2	42.5	38.5	49.9	43.0	36.3	38.3	33.0
Radical Civic Union (UCR)	29.0	30.2	20.5	17.0	21.7	–	–	–
Democratic Center Union (UCeDe)	5.2	2.6	1.5	–	3.2	0.6	–	–
Front for a Country in Solidarity (FREPASO)[b]	–	2.5	13.6	29.2	20.7	–	–	–
Movement for Dignity and Independence (MODIN)	–	5.8	9.2	1.7	1.7	0.9	–	–
Alliance for Jobs, Justice, and Education[c]	–	–	–	–	–	45.7[d]	48.4	45.5
Action for the Republic	–	–	–	–	–	3.9	10.2	8.0
Minor and provincial parties	25.6	16.4	16.7	2.2	9.7	12.6	3.1	13.5
TOTAL	100	100	100	100	100	100	100	100

Notes:
[a] (P) Presidential election; (L) lower house election; (C) Constituent Assembly election.
[b] Big Front (FG) in 1993 and 1994.
[c] UCR and FREPASO.
[d] Total includes vote for the UCR and FREPASO in districts in which these parties ran separately.
Sources: Fraga (1995), McGuire (1995); Gervasoni (1997); www.mivoto.com.

several of these districts, party branches were controlled by traditional party sectors that had dominated the party – in some cases, with interruptions – since 1983.[199]

THE ELECTORAL SUCCESS OF MENEMIST PERONISM

The PJ was highly successful in electoral terms in the 1990s, winning four straight national elections after the Menem government's neoliberal turn (see Table 6.5). In the 1991 midterm elections, which were held during the first months of the Convertibility Plan, the PJ scored a major victory, defeating the second place UCR by 40 percent to 29 percent and retaining key governorships in Buenos Aires, Mendoza, and Santa Fe. The victory, which was widely interpreted as a vote of support for the Convertibility Plan, provided Menem with a clear mandate to proceed with the reform

---

[199] These include Catamarca, Formosa, Misiones, Santiago del Estero, San Luis, Salta, and Tucumán.

process. The PJ again defeated the UCR in the 1993 legislative elections, this time by 43 percent to 30 percent. This second victory, which included unprecedented wins in Radical bastions such as the Federal Capital, was sufficiently decisive to convince ex-President Raúl Alfonsín to negotiate the UCR's support – via the November 1993 Olivos Pact – for a constitutional reform permitting Menem to run for reelection in 1995 (Acuña 1995). In 1994, the PJ finished first in elections for the new Constituent Assembly, nearly doubling the vote total of the second place Radicals, and in 1995, Menem was overwhelmingly reelected with 50 percent of the vote, compared to 29 percent for FREPASO candidate Bordón and 17 percent for UCR candidate Horacio Massaccessi. Although the PJ was defeated by the Alliance for Jobs, Justice, and Education – a coalition of the UCR and FREPASO – in the 1997 midterm elections and the 1999 presidential elections, it retained control of nearly two-thirds of the country's governorships (including those of the three largest provinces) and easily remained the largest party in Argentina.

The PJ's electoral success in the 1990s was based on a dualistic electoral coalition. One component, which might be called the Menemist vote, was made up of traditionally non-Peronist voters who backed the PJ out of support for the government's economic program. Most of these votes were drawn from the middle and upper-middle sectors and were ideologically right of center (Gervasoni 1998a: 15). A substantial number of them migrated from the conservative UCeDe, which declined from nearly 10 percent of the Chamber of Deputies vote in 1989 to just 2.6 percent in 1993 and virtually disappeared from the political map shortly thereafter (Gibson 1996: 186–97; Gervasoni 1998a: 11–17). Others were drawn from conservative provincial parties, the UCR, and the growing pool of new and independent voters. Although these "tactical Menemist" voters were critical to the PJ's electoral success in the 1991–5 period (Gervasoni 1998b), they probably never constituted more than a quarter of the overall Peronist vote (Gervasoni 1998b: 21).

By far the largest group of PJ voters in the 1990s was that of traditional Peronists, or voters who had consistently supported the PJ *before* the party's programmatic shift to the right (Gervasoni 1998b; Ostiguy 1998: 357–69). Evidence that the PJ largely retained its traditional electoral base in the 1990s comes from a variety of sources. Carlos Gervasoni, using 1989 and 1995 preelection surveys carried out by Mora y Araujo, Noguera, and Associates, found that the PJ retained 67 percent of its 1989 electorate in the 1995 presidential election (1998b: 19), and that those who defected from the PJ in 1995 tended to be better educated and more independent voters rather than traditional Peronists (1998b: 35–6). Gervasoni also found that 71 percent of respondents who had voted Peronist in 1983 also voted for the PJ in 1989 and 1995 (1998b: 41–2). Ecological and survey data suggest that this "captive" vote remained concentrated in lower-income sectors. Throughout the 1990s, the PJ vote remained highest in the poorest districts of the country (Adrogúe 1995; Burdman 1997; Ostiguy 1998; Escolar 2001: 161), and surveys consistently found support for the PJ to be highest among poorer and less educated voters (Ostiguy 1998: 357–8; Gervasoni 1998b: 24–9).[200] These patterns were consistent with Peronist voting patterns between the 1940s and 1970s (Kirkpatrick 1971; Mora y Aruajo and Llorente 1980; Schoultz 1983; Cantón 1986; Ostiguy 1998).

The motivations underlying the stability of the Peronist vote were varied. Although the success of the Convertibility Plan contributed to the PJ's success among its traditional electorate (Palermo and Novaro 1996: 309–24; Gervasoni 1997), it was clearly not the only factor. Many traditional Peronists were critical of the government's economic program (Ostiguy 1998: 165, 464–6). For example, Gervasoni found that nearly 50 percent of pro-Menem voters adhered to "statist" and "redistributive" economic views in 1995 (1998b: 32 – 3), and surveys carried out in 1994 and 1995 found that between 40 and 60 percent of PJ voters were either neutral to or opposed to the Menem economic program.[201] These votes can be attributed to factors – such as strong partisan loyalties (Ostiguy 1998) and the delivery of clientelistic benefits (Gibson 1997; Gibson and Calvo 2000) – that were not directly related to the success of the Convertibility Plan. Rather, they are better understood as products of the PJ's social and organizational rootedness in working- and lower-class zones.

An important caveat is in order. Although the PJ's capacity to retain its traditional electorate in the 1990s cannot be directly attributed to the Menem government's economic program, the reforms nevertheless had an indirect effect in at least two ways. First, the economic growth of the 1991–5 period provided the Menem government with the resources to continue to finance – and in many cases, expand – the powerful provincial-level clientelist machines run by Peronist governors (Gerchunoff and Torre 1996; Gibson and Calvo 2000). Patronage machines were most effective in lower-income districts such as Formosa, La Rioja, Misiones, and San Luis, but as Chapter 5 showed, they also they took on increased importance in industrialized provinces such as Buenos Aires. Second, although the Menem reforms were not the primary reason that many traditional Peronists voted PJ in the

---

[200] For example, preelection surveys in 1995 found support for Menem to be more than 60 percent among the lower sectors, compared to less than 40 percent among the middle and upper sectors (Gervasoni 1998b: 25).

[201] April 5, 1994 survey of voters in the Federal Capital and Greater Buenos Aires, provided to the author by Haime and Associates; and June 1995 survey in the Federal Capital and Greater Buenos Aires, provided to the author by the Centro de Estudios Union Para la Nueva Mayoria. Similarly, in his survey of lower-class voters in Greater Buenos Aires, Ostiguy (1998: 464–5) found that the majority of respondents "reject the economic policies of the Menem government," and "prefer a different set of policies, closer to the redistributionism and nationalism of Peronism."

1990s, it is reasonable to make the following counterfactual claim: Had the Menem government failed to stabilize the economy, the PJ would likely have lost a large number of even its core supporters.[202]

The PJ's electoral success in the 1990s was thus a product of both change and continuity. On the one hand, the Menem reforms were critical to the party's success in two senses. First, the reforms attracted a substantial share of the independent and conservative vote, which provided the party's margin of victory in 1991, 1993, and 1995. Second, in stabilizing the economy, the reforms helped the PJ avoid the kind of electoral collapse suffered by AD and APRA in the 1990s. At the same time, however, the PJ benefited enormously from the stability of its traditional electoral base. Most traditional Peronists continued to vote PJ throughout the 1990s, despite the fact that a large number of them were critical of neoliberal economic policies. Although this outcome cannot be understood independently of the government's economic successes, it had more to do with the PJ's social and organizational rootedness than with neoliberalism. Hence, the PJ's electoral success in the 1990s drew upon two distinct sources: the Menem leadership's capacity to undertake radical programmatic change *and* the PJ's capacity to retain the support of long-time Peronists, many of whom disliked the government's macroeconomic program. Understanding this second outcome requires a closer look at the front line of the PJ's traditional vote-getting efforts: its base-level organization. Chapter 7 thus moves to the base level, asking how party activists and local Peronist organizations responded to the Menem government's neoliberal turn.

[202] Examples of parties that experienced such a rapid erosion of support include Peru's APRA and, to a lesser extent, AD in Venezuela. Although APRA's electoral base was never as massive as that of the PJ, it was widely believed to have the loyalty of somewhere between a quarter and a third of the electorate. Nevertheless, due in large part to the García government's economic failures in the late 1980s, APRA saw its share of the electorate plummet from a high of 53 percent of the valid vote in the 1985 presidential election to just 4 percent in the 1995 presidential election.

CHAPTER 7

A View from Below: Party Activists and the Transformation of Base-Level Peronism

This chapter examines the relationship between the PJ and its activist base in the context of the Menem government's neoliberal turn. Activists are often believed to be more ideologically driven than party leaders (May 1973; Koelble 1992, 1996; Ware 1992). If that is the case, then we should expect that Peronist activists, who have historically been almost uniformly antiliberal, would have either actively opposed Menemism or abandoned the party in droves in the 1990s. Yet as Chapter 6 showed, the Menem leadership confronted little intraparty resistance in the 1990s. And although Peronist activists did tend to be critical of the Menem program, relatively few of them left the party. In fact, the PJ's activist base remained quite vibrant, and this base-level activism contributed in an important way to the government's political success.

The chapter attributes the PJ's capacity to maintain its activist base to two factors: (1) increased access to state resources and (2) a decentralized party structure. The combination of state resources and local autonomy allowed activists who were critical of Menem to continue to engage in traditional Peronist practices even as the national party abandoned them. Yet if the PJ's mass linkages persisted through the 1990s, they were transformed in important ways. As state resources became the primary currency of exchange among activists, the personal, ideological, and union-based ties that had long sustained local Peronist organizations began to erode. This transformation left the PJ more dependent on state resources than at any time since 1955, and it threatened to erode the party's social and cultural presence in working- and lower-class society.

THE ROLE OF PARTY ACTIVISTS IN THE 1990S

In recent years, scholars have noted a generalized decline in the importance of local party organizations.[1] As capital-intensive, media-based campaigns have

---

[1] See Panebianco (1988: 262–74); Katz (1990); Katz and Mair (1994, 1995); Perelli et al. (1995).

replaced labor-intensive campaigns, parties have become "organizations of leaders rather than citizens," and activists have become "less necessary" and even "a nuisance" to party leaders (Katz 1990: 145–6). A similar trend has been observed in Argentina (Novaro 1994, 1995; Landi 1995; Waisbord 1995). According to Novaro, "it is now an accepted fact that... image building is much more important than the organization of activists" (1995: 58). Novaro claims that Peronist leaders "reduced the role of the party organization to a minimum" in the 1990s, and that the contemporary PJ "no longer maintains a privileged link with the old mass organizations" (1995: 59–60).

Yet claims about the erosion of mass organizations should not be overstated. As Alan Ware has argued, even in the advanced industrialized countries, the "vast majority of political parties... still require labor to conduct a variety of activities," and in some cases, established parties even shifted back in the direction of grassroots organization-building in the 1980s (1992: 73–5; also Scarrow 1996). Such caution is particularly warranted in the Peronist case. Although a trend away from mass organization and toward media-based politics is clearly observable in Argentina (Waisbord 1995), this process started later, and has advanced less far, than in many European cases. Outside of the Federal Capital and a few other metropolitan centers, local party organizations continued to weigh heavily in politics in the 1990s (Waisbord 1995: 61–2).[2] Indeed, there is little evidence that the PJ's mass linkages were substantially eroded during this period. Party membership levels remained stable, and although there are no figures for the number of base units, many activists claimed that the number of UBs *increased* over the course of the decade.[3]

The PJ's vast infrastructure of UBs, unions, soup kitchens, clubs, and informal personal networks linked rank-and-file Peronists to the party and the state in a variety of ways in the 1990s. For example, PJ activists played a major role in delivering social assistance in lower income neighborhoods. Of the base units surveyed for this study in 1997, 96 percent engaged in some form of social assistance. Although scholarly and journalistic accounts of this material goods distribution tend to portray it as naked clientelism (Lawton 1994; López Echague 1996; Otero 1997),[4] virtually no research has been done on what UBs actually do. Indeed, as recent work by Javier Auyero (2000) demonstrates, the picture is somewhat more complex. Much Peronist base-level social assistance is in fact clientelistic. As Table 7.1

---

[2] Thus, it is no coincidence that while the media-based FREPASO scored striking electoral victories in major metropolitan centers such as the Federal Capital and Rosario in the 1990s, it fared poorly in peripheral districts.

[3] Of the Greater Buenos Aires activists surveyed for this study, more than three-quarters said the number of activists either *increased* (68 percent) or remained the same (8 percent) in the 1990s.

[4] See also *Página/12*, October 6, 1996, p. 14.

TABLE 7.1. *Social Welfare Activities of Surveyed Base Units*[a]

Activity	Number (n = 112)	Percentage
General social assistance	107	95.5
Direct distribution of food or medicine	78	69.6
Regular delivery of particularistic favors	67	59.8
Programs for children	63	56.3
Neighborhood social and cultural events	59	52.7
Neighborhood improvement	48	42.9
Programs for the elderly	51	45.5
Legal assistance	29	25.9
Provision of government jobs	25	22.3

Note:
[a] Based on the author's 1997 survey of 112 base units in the Federal Capital, La Matanza, and Quilmes.

shows, more than two-thirds (69.6 percent) of the UBs surveyed for this study engaged in the direct distribution of food or medicine, and nearly a quarter (22.3 percent) of the UBs regularly provided jobs for their constituents.

Yet UBs also provided a range of other social welfare services – including medical and legal services, child care, job training, and programs for the elderly – that were less directly tied to a political exchange. For example, the "Reconquest" UB in the Federal Capital offered school tutoring for children, computer classes and a job location program for adults, and a retirees center for the elderly; the "October 3" UB in Quilmes ran a health clinic and provided school uniforms for a local school; and the "Juan Manuel de Rosas" UB in La Matanza founded a child care center, organized a neighborhood youth soccer team, and ran a retirees center. Of the UBs surveyed for this study, 56.3 percent provided regular activities for children, 45.5 percent offered programs for the elderly, and 25.9 percent provided free legal assistance for low-income residents.

UBs also engaged in a variety of social and cultural activities in the 1990s. For example, the Nelson Calvi Peronist House in the capital ran a youth soccer program, held monthly parties to celebrate neighbors' birthdays, and threw a well-attended annual Children's Day party; the "Ramon Carillo" UB in Quilmes organized barbecues for workers from a nearby factory; and the "Menem Leadership" UB in La Matanza offered martial arts, movie nights, and dance lessons for teenagers. Overall, 52.7 percent of the UBs surveyed regularly organized social and cultural activities in their neighborhoods.

A smaller number of base units organized specifically Peronist cultural activities. About a third of the UBs (35.7 percent) surveyed sponsored Peronist cultural events such as annual masses for Evita and the celebration of Peronist holidays such as Evita's birthday, October 17, and the "Day of the Activist."[5] For example, the "Companions" UB in the Federal Capital organized a campaign to "reactivate the memory" of Evita in 1997, and the "Juan Manuel de Rosas" UB organized an Evita Day, in which women were invited to discuss "what Evita means to me." A few UBs (6.3 percent) continued to teach Peronist "doctrine," either through classes, reading groups, or the distribution of Perón's writings.

Peronist base organizations played a critical role in linking working- and lower-class citizens to the state in the 1990s. Many UBs participated directly in implementing government social programs. Although such politicization is often viewed as a corrupt and inefficient distortion of state policy,[6] in many lower-class areas, the state bureaucracy was so weak that party networks may well have been a more effective means of reaching the population. An example is the Pierri Law in Greater Buenos Aires, through which tens of thousands of families received legal titles for their properties. Because many residents were unaware of the program's requirements, and because local governments lacked the resources to carry out an extensive grassroots campaign, Peronist activists frequently provided the legwork, going door to door and helping residents to fill out the necessary forms. Another example is the Life Plan, which distributed a daily ration of eggs, milk, and other basic goods to nearly four hundred thousand people through a network of ten thousand volunteer *manzaneras*, or block workers.[7] Of the Greater Buenos Aires UBs surveyed for this study, 59.6 percent participated in the implementation of at least one government social program. About a quarter (25.5 percent) participated in the implementation of the Pierri Law, and 17 percent participated in the Life Plan.

PJ activists also played an important role from below in providing residents of lower-class neighborhoods with access to the state. Where the PJ controls the local government, activists use their ties to public officials to act as a "nexus between the neighborhood and the city government."[8] Thus, local PJ organizations serve as "problem solving networks" (Auyero 2000), obtaining wheelchairs, disability pensions, scholarships, funeral expenses, and odd jobs for working- and lower-class residents who lack

---

[5] The Day of the Activist, November 17, marks the day on which Perón returned from exile in 1972.

[6] See, for example, the various publications of the Instituto Bonaerense de Análisis y Proyectos (IBAP), as well as López Echague (1996: 161–74).

[7] Although the program is officially nonpartisan (*manzaneras* are chosen through community organizations), the vast majority of *manzaneras* are Peronist, and most are linked to the party through informal Peronist networks. For example, in his research in a Lanus shantytown, Auyero found that twenty of the zone's twenty-three *manzaneras* were recruited from Peronist networks (Auyero 1997: 123). In La Matanza, local Life Plan director Mario Ferreri acknowledged that a "majority" of the nongovernmental organizations from which *manzaneras* are selected are "run by Peronists" (author's interview, September 19, 1997).

[8] Author's interview with La Matanza activist Tina Blanco, May 31, 1997.

alternative sources of social assistance. Although most problem-solving networks are particularistic, activists also employ them to obtain collective goods and services for their neighborhoods. In La Matanza, for example, the "Perón and Evita" UB played a major role in bringing street lights, paved roads, and bus service to a neighboring squatter settlement. In the capital, the "October 8" UB brought a child care center, a gymnasium, and a computer-equipped job training center to the Ciudad Oculta (Hidden City) shantytown; the Nelson Calvi Peronist House helped bring a sewage system to the Soldati neighborhood; and the "United or Dominated" UB began teenage pregnancy and battered women's programs in the city's first ward. Overall, 42.9 percent of the UBs surveyed for this study engaged in such collective neighborhood improvement work (see Table 7.1).

Peronist activists also engage in political fights in defense of neighborhood interests. In La Matanza, for example, the "Perón and Evita" UB represented local residents when the regional electric company sought to collect back debts that they could not pay. In the capital, the "United or Dominated" UB defended a nearby squatter settlement against city government efforts to remove it. In Quilmes, UBs from the Loyalty faction organized protests that forced the regional water company to restore service to the neighborhood after it had been cut off for nonpayment, successfully pressured the city government to increase police patrols in the neighborhood, and led a petition drive to pressure the provincial government to take action to prevent flooding from a nearby river.

Finally, a minority of UBs functioned as channels of grassroots participation by creating arenas for debate or holding regular meetings with local politicians. In Quilmes, for example, the "Cooperativism and Social Justice" UB organized a day-long workshop in which women from poor neighborhoods discussed their economic problems with local leaders. In the Federal Capital, the "Hour of the People" UB held monthly public lectures on issues such as the future of the government's economic program, social policy, and labor market reform. Also in the capital, the Justicialista Victory UB held well-attended weekly political meetings with city council member Kelly Olmos. Overall, 39.4 percent of the surveyed UBs showed evidence of some kind of purposive or issue-oriented political activity, and 15.8 percent showed evidence of high and sustained levels of such activity.

In sum, PJ activism remained high in the 1990s, as rank-and-file Peronists engaged in a variety of activities that linked working- and lower-class Argentines to the party and the state. By providing channels for patronage distribution, policy implementation, social and cultural contact, and political demand making, Peronism's grassroots activist networks thus served as critical mediators between the national government and the PJ's working- and lower-class base. Although the political impact of this activity is difficult to measure, it almost certainly helped to sustain the Peronist subculture and identity (Auyero 2000) and very likely helped the PJ retain support among its traditional working- and lower-class base.

EXPLAINING PERONIST ACTIVISM IN THE 1990S

The persistence of a relatively high level of Peronist activism in the 1990s presents somewhat of a puzzle. It is often argued that activists are more ideologically driven than party leaders (May 1973; Strom 1990b; Koelble 1992, 1996; Ware 1992).[9] Although activists' goals vary significantly (Wilson 1973; Panebianco 1988; Kitschelt 1989a, 1989b; Seyd and Whiteley 1992), a substantial number of them are generally characterized as "believers" (Panebianco 1988: 26–30) or "ideologues" (Kitschelt 1989a: 50). Peronist "believers" are a diverse group: some are leftist, others are nationalist, and still others can be considered traditional or "orthodox" Peronists. Notwithstanding this diversity, however, Peronists historically converged in their opposition to free market economics. Hence, they should have opposed the Menem government's neoliberal program. Indeed, data from a 1997 survey of PJ activists suggest that they were in fact quite critical of the Menem program. As Tables 7.2 and 7.3 show, more than two-thirds of surveyed activists said they opposed either a substantial part (49.1 percent) or all (19.5 percent) of the Menem program. Moreover, large majorities believed the government's policies to be "too favorable" to business (70.4 percent) and "too unfavorable" to workers (67.8 percent). On the question of what economic policies a future PJ government should carry out, 42.1 percent sought to "return to the roots of Peronism."

Despite this base-level opposition to neoliberalism, there is little evidence that the PJ suffered a substantial erosion of its activist base in the 1990s. First, few activists joined other parties or followed PJ defectors out of the party in the 1990s. Although the Group of Eight had hoped to bring a substantial number of left-of-center activists out of the party with them in 1990, very few joined them.[10] José Octavio Bordón similarly failed to coax large numbers of activists out of the party when he left in 1994. Moreover, despite the emergence of the nationalist Movement for Dignity and Independence (MODIN) and the center-left FREPASO as serious political alternatives in early 1990s, there is no evidence that either of these parties attracted a large number of Peronist activists.

---

[9] Kitschelt (1989a: 44–55) critiques this view.
[10] In the words of one of the group's advisors, "no one came with us – not even our wives" (author's interview with Mario Wainfeld, June 29, 1994). According to Group of Eight leader Chacho Alvarez, the defectors were left "like seven shipwreck victims on a desert island." Alvarez claims that approximately two hundred to three hundred activists – primarily from the Federal Capital and Greater Buenos Aires – joined the group (author's interview, July 29, 1997).

TABLE 7.2. *Activists' Views of the Menem Economic Program*[a]

View of the government's economic policies	Percentage
Agree with the Menem program	10.2
Disagree with the Menem program but back the government out of party loyalty	10.5
Disagree with the neoliberal program but believe that no other option existed	10.7
Disagree with key aspects of the Menem program and believe other options existed	49.1
Oppose the Menem program as a betrayal of Peronist ideals	19.5
TOTAL	100.0

Note:
[a] Based on the author's survey of 611 PJ activists in the Federal Capital, La Matanza, and Quilmes in 1997.

TABLE 7.3. *Activists' Views of Government Policies toward Business, Unions, and Workers*[a]

View	Business	Unions	Workers
Too favorable	70.4	7.4	0.7
Correct	26.3	45.4	31.3
Too unfavorable	2.9	47.1	67.8
TOTAL	100.0	100.0	100.0

The next Peronist government should…	Percentage
Continue the Menem program	5.5
Continue the Menem program, but with more social justice	52.4
Return to the roots of Peronism	42.1

Note:
[a] Based on the author's survey of 611 PJ activists in the Federal Capital, La Matanza, and Quilmes in 1997.

Although it is difficult to measure the number of activists who simply quit politics in the 1990s, there is little evidence that the activist base was substantially depleted. Indeed, more than three-quarters of surveyed activists in Greater Buenos Aires said the number of activists either *increased* (68 percent) or remained the same (8 percent) in the 1990s. Moreover, the relatively high level of PJ activism in the 1990s appears not to have been a product of an influx of new – perhaps pro-Menem – members. The results of the survey suggest that the composition of the activist base did not change substantially in the 1990s. Table 7.4 shows the distribution of *punteros* and activists in terms of when they began their party activity.

TABLE 7.4. *Peronist Punteros and Activists, by Year of Entry into Party Politics*[a]
(Percentages)

	Pre-1967	1967–82	1983–9	1990–5	1996–7
Punteros (n = 105)	16.2	32.4	38.1	8.6	4.8
Activists (n = 494)	13.6	26.7	32.6	21.1	6.1

Note:
[a] Based on the author's 1997 survey of PJ activists in the Federal Capital, La Matanza, and Quilmes.

Among *punteros*, only 13.3 percent began their careers after 1989. Almost half of the *punteros* surveyed (48.6 percent) began their careers before the 1976 coup, and another 38.1 percent entered the party in the 1983–9 period. Although a slightly larger number of activists (27.2 percent) entered the party after 1989, the vast majority were active in the party long before the Menem presidency. Hence, notwithstanding the widely reported entry of UCeDe activists in the early 1990s,[11] the composition of the activist base in 1997 was not substantially different from that which existed when Menem took office. Nearly three quarters of party activists (73 percent) and almost nine-tenths of *punteros* (87 percent) began their careers before 1989.

There is also little evidence that activists joined the PJ after 1989 out of ideological agreement with the Menem program. As Table 7.5 shows, surveyed activists who entered the party after 1989 were not more likely to support neoliberal policies than old-guard activists. Indeed, to the extent that differences exist across cohorts, newer activists appear to be more critical of the Menem program than veteran activists.

It is also clear that the PJ lacked the kinds of participatory channels that are said to be an important currency of party-activist exchange in European parties (Strom 1990b; Ware 1992). The survey of base units carried out for this study revealed low levels of democratic participation and purposive, or issue-based, political activity. For example, only 4.8 percent of the base units showed evidence of regular leadership turnover, whereas 73.4 percent of UBs showed no evidence of internal elections at all. Similarly, only 15.8 percent of the base units showed evidence of regular purposive political activity, whereas 60.6 percent showed no evidence of purposive political activity at all.

Hence, not only did a substantial number of PJ activists disagree with the Menem government's neoliberal policies, but these activists enjoyed

---

[11] Reportedly, at least six hundred UCeDe activists joined the PJ in the early 1990s (*La Nación*, June 6, 1994). According to former UCeDe activist Oscar Giménez, the bulk of the UCeDe youth, and perhaps half of the party's overall membership, defected to the PJ (author's interview, June 14, 1994).

TABLE 7.5. *Activists' Views of the Menem Program, by Year of Entry into the Party*[a] *(Percentages)*

View	Pre-1967 (n = 64)	1967–82 (n = 124)	1983–9 (n = 144)	1990–7 (n = 130)	Total (n = 462)
Agree with the Menem program	12.5	9.7	9.0	12.3	10.6
Disagree with the Menem program but back the government out of loyalty	20.3	10.5	13.2	5.4	11.3
Disagree with the Menem program but believe no other option existed	4.7	12.1	12.5	15.4	11.5
Disagree with key aspects of Menem program; believe other options existed	40.6	50.8	56.9	45.4	49.8
Oppose the Menem program as a betrayal of Peronist ideals	21.9	16.9	17.4	23.8	19.7

The government's policies toward unions are...	Pre-1967 (n = 59)	1967–82 (n = 122)	1983–9 (n = 151)	1990–7 (n = 116)	Total
Too favorable	6.8	3.3	11.9	6.0	7.4
Correct	47.5	46.7	44.4	44.0	45.3
Too unfavorable	45.8	50.0	43.7	50.0	47.3

The next Peronist government should...	Pre-1967 (n = 65)	1967–82 (n = 124)	1983–9 (n = 152)	1990–7 (n = 131)	Total
Continue the Menem program	12.3	1.6	5.9	5.3	5.5
Continue the Menem program, *but* with more social justice	46.2	55.6	57.9	49.6	53.4
Return to the roots of Peronism	41.5	42.7	36.2	45.0	41.1

Note:
[a] Based on the author's 1997 survey of PJ activists in the Federal Capital, La Matanza, and Quilmes.

few participatory channels through which to try to change those policies. What, then, enabled the PJ to maintain its activist base in the neoliberal era? Two factors kept anti-Menemist activists in the party: (1) access to state resources and (2) substantial base-level autonomy from the national leadership.

TABLE 7.6. *Patronage Distribution in PJ Base Units*[a]

Base units according to level of patronage (number of state jobs)	Number	Percentage
High (*puntero* and two or more activists)	37	34.3
Medium (*puntero* and 0 or 1 activists)	37	34.3
Low (no patronage jobs)	34	31.5
TOTAL	108	100.0
Sources of base unit finance	Number	Percentage
State-based *agrupación*	84	75.7
Union-based *agrupación*	15	13.5
Self- or privately financed	12	10.8
TOTAL	111	100.0

Note:
[a] Based on the author's survey of 112 base units in the Federal Capital, La Matanza, and Quilmes in 1997.

Access to State Resources

Scholars have long noted that activists may be linked to parties through selective material incentives, as in the case of machine politics (Banfield and Wilson 1963; Scott 1969). Because such material exchanges are not based on purposive or issue-based commitments, patronage-based parties are said to enjoy a greater degree of programmatic flexibility than other parties (Banfield and Wilson 1963: 115–17; Scott 1969: 143–4; Wilson 1973/1995: 37). Although Peronist activism had been based largely on nonmaterial incentives between 1955 and 1983, access to public office beginning in 1983 dramatically altered the incentive structures facing party leaders and activists. By the early 1990s, patronage resources had become a primary currency of intraparty exchange. As Table 7.6 shows, more than two thirds (68.6 percent) of the base units surveyed for this study were run by activists with government jobs, and in more than a third (34.3 percent) of the base units, at least two other activists also held government jobs. Also, three-quarters (75.6 percent) of the base units surveyed were financed by *agrupaciones* with positions in the government, while only a handful of base units were financed by unions (13.5 percent) or financed themselves (9 percent). In some areas, patronage politics was so prevalent that the line between party and government offices became somewhat blurred.[12]

The increased supply of patronage was accompanied by a sharp increase in demand (Auyero 2000). In the mid-1990s, unemployment rates surpassed

---

[12] For example, one La Matanza activist claimed that her base unit "is the government. What does it depend on economically? How does it subsist? The government, of course!" (author's interview, August 28, 1997).

20 percent in many working- and lower-class zones. As a result, patronage resources took on enormous importance among activists. As one Greater Buenos Aires activist put it,

> I'm 50 years old and I have no job. They call me because I can write a little and they throw some money at me. With that I buy food for my family. This may seem disappointing after having just laid out a nice package of concepts and ideology on the table. But that's the way it is.... I have a wife and two older children, all without work.... This doesn't mean I don't believe in anything.[13]

Activists also sought access to the state as a means of obtaining collective goods for their neighborhoods. Indeed, in lower-class areas, many Peronists entered party activity as a means of gaining material benefits for their neighborhoods, such as the pavement of roads and sidewalks, the installation of street lights, or the construction of a school, child care center, or health clinic. For example, the Children of the Future Mothers' Commission in Quilmes was created to address problems of flooding from a nearby river. Although they had never been involved in party politics before, the Commission's leaders established ties with PJ city council member Hugo Guerreño, who "helped open doors for us" in the provincial government.[14] Later, the Commission joined Guerreño's Loyalty *agrupación* in order to maintain access to the state. Similarly, the Barrio Eucalyptus Mothers Association joined Loyalty after Guerreño helped the organization bring the Life Plan to the neighborhood,[15] and Cecilia Fernandez, who ran a health care clinic in a lower class-neighborhood in Quilmes, joined the Federal League *agrupación* to gain access to government programs that distribute food and medicine to the elderly.[16]

In the 1990s, then, a substantial number of party activists depended in some form or another on state resources. This resource dependence powerfully shaped activist responses to the Menem government's shift to the right. Particularly in lower-class zones, where Peronism was politically the "only game in town," leaving the party entailed giving up critical resources. For many Peronists, staying in the party was a matter of preserving their jobs. As one La Matanza activist put it, many activists did not leave the party "because if they left, they would be fired. And they need to feed their

---

[13] Interview with Carlos Torres in *El Colorado*, November 8, 1996, p. 4. A Quilmes activist (who was considering switching from a left-wing *agrupación* to a Menemist *agrupacion*) made a similar point: "I just want a job for myself and for my people.... What does loyalty get me? Nothing! You can't feed your kids with loyalty. You need to get something. No one works for nothing. Not when you have kids to feed" (author's interview, June 10, 1997).
[14] Author's interview with members of the Children of the Future Mothers' Commission, June 10, 1997.
[15] Author's interview with members of the Barrio Eucalyptus Mothers Association, June 10, 1997.
[16] Author's interview with Cecilia Fernandez, September 21, 1997.

families."[17] Dependence on the state also limited the degree to which activists could challenge the Menem government. According to a local party leader in La Matanza,

> We have to swallow a lot. We have to accept a lot of things that we don't agree with. But we have to fight from the inside.... We can't be isolated.... People don't come here anymore out of love, like we used to. They come here out of need. If we can't offer them anything, they won't work with us.[18]

This resource dependence helps to explain why opposition parties such as the center-left FREPASO had difficulty convincing even left-of-center Peronist activists to leave the party. One left-leaning shantytown activist who was recruited by FREPASO in the mid-1990s claimed that he refused to join because

> FREPASO has no organization and no power.... FREPASO has built up a team of journalists and people who denounce corruption, which is fine. But what good does that do us here in the shantytown? We need access to real things.[19]

Local Autonomy

Yet the stability of the PJ activist base cannot be attributed solely to patronage. Between 1955 and 1983, nonunion Peronist activism had been based almost entirely on social and ideological linkages. As late as 1997, nearly one-third of surveyed UBs (31.4 percent) had no access to patronage at all, and in a majority of UBs, patronage benefits did not extend beyond one or two activists. Hence, a substantial number of activists continued to participate despite having little or no access to state resources.

Moreover, the fact that UBs enjoy access to patronage resources does not mean that such resources are the primary incentive behind activist

---

[17] Author's interview, March 20, 1997.
[18] Author's interview, April 8, 1997. Similarly, a Federal Capital activist declared, "I'm not a Menemist. I am critical of Menem's economic policies. Most of us don't agree with Menem. But we can't act against Menem because we would lose our jobs in the Interior Ministry. We belong to the Liberators [agrupación]. Liberators depends on the Interior Ministry. And the Interior Ministry depends on Menem" (author's interview, May 31, 1997).
[19] Author's interview with Ernesto Duhalde, July 8, 1997. Similarly, according to Alberto Pérez, a PJ activist from Greater Buenos Aires who joined FREPASO in 1994, many Peronists remain in the party "due to their personal economic situations. If they leave, they lose the possibility of collecting a municipal or provincial paycheck.... It is a completely realistic assessment. They tell me, 'You people are right, but if we leave we lose what we have. Can you guarantee that we won't lose this?' No, we can't guarantee that. In their current position, activists have at least something. Some kind of a job. But if they join FREPASO, they would automatically be fired from the city government. They would be told, 'you joined FREPASO? Good bye'" (author's interview, October 7, 1996).

participation. Nonunion activists may be linked to UBs in three different ways: (1) via material benefits (*machine* UBs); (2) via kinship ties or longstanding personal loyalties (*traditional* UBs); or (3) via shared ideological commitments and/or horizontal social ties (*modern-amateur* UBs). Although activists in traditional and modern-amateur UBs may (and often do) receive material benefits, such exchanges supplement or reinforce longer-term relationships based on other ties. Of the base units surveyed for this study, 38.6 percent could be characterized as machine UBs, in that the bulk of their activists were recruited and retained via the distribution of selective material benefits.[20] At the same time, 40.6 percent could be characterized as traditional, and 21.8 percent were modern-amateur. Hence, although the vast majority of base units enjoyed access to material resources, such resources were the *primary incentive for participation* in less than half of the surveyed UBs. For a substantial number of activists, then, party work continued to take the form of "gifts" (Ware 1992: 78–80), or participation based on nonmaterial incentives.

Critical to keeping many of these activists in the party is the base-level autonomy created by the PJ's segmented and decentralized structure. Unlike centralized mass parties such as the French and Chilean communists or the Venezuelan AD, in which subunits must strictly adhere to the national party line or face expulsion, the PJ's decentralized structure allowed activists to avoid making a stark choice between adhering to the national party line and leaving (or being expelled from) the party. Rather, "each *agrupación* does what it wants, behaving in its own way."[21] This organizational "big tent" was critical to retaining party activists in the 1990s, for it provided alternative channels of participation to Peronists who disliked the party's national profile. Indeed, throughout the 1990s, nationalist, traditional populist, social democratic, and even socialist *agrupaciones* coexisted with Menemism, providing arenas in which local cadres and activists could continue to practice their own forms of Peronism in spite of disagreement with the direction taken by the national party.

Such subunits were found in each of the districts covered in this study. An example of a nationalist subgroup is C de O, which transformed into

---

[20] Scorings are the author's judgment, based on visits to the UBs and interviews with both *punteros* and activists. UBs in which a substantial number of activists obtained material benefits from the *puntero*, and in which there was little evidence of personal or ideological ties between activists and the *puntero*, were labeled machine UBs. UBs in which a substantial number of activists were linked to the *puntero* through longstanding personal or family ties that appeared to trump material incentives (for example, activists turned down offers to join UBs with more resources) were labeled traditional. UBs in which core activists exhibited clear evidence of shared ideology and/or longstanding friendships (e.g., dating back to university activism) were labeled modern-amateur. In 11 of 112 base units, the author lacked sufficient information to make a judgment.

[21] Author's interview with former legislator Roberto Fernández, May 16, 1997.

an *agrupación* in La Matanza in the 1980s. Though no longer a paramilitary group, C de O continued to engage in nationalist activities in the 1990s,[22] including regular events to protest the British occupation of the Falklands/Malvinas Islands and to commemorate the 1982 war over the islands. In 1997, as part of its battle against "cultural imperialism,"[23] C de O organized protests against the screening of the (foreign-made) movie *Evita*. In the Federal Capital, many nationalists belonged to either Doctrinal Peronism or FUMPE, both of which led protests against *Evita* and sponsored a range of other nationalist activities in 1997.[24]

An example of a left-wing *agrupación* is "March 11"[25] in Quilmes. Founded in 1985 by a group of leftist activists and ex-guerrillas, "March 11" grew into the largest *agrupación* in Quilmes in the 1990s, with approximately three hundred activists. "March 11" leaders described themselves as "socialist" and shared a commitment to "deepening democracy" through grassroots organization.[26] They participated in a variety of left-wing political activities in the 1990s, including benefits to raise money for Cuba and an annual party to celebrate the fall of Saigon. Several "March 11" members occupied posts in the Quilmes Secretariat of Culture, which they used to take the city's cultural programs "out of the hands of the artistic elite" by creating cultural centers in lower-class neighborhoods that provided free access to theater, music, art, and poetry classes.[27] "March 11" clearly attracted left-wing activists. Nearly half (48 percent) of the "March 11" members surveyed for this study fully rejected the government's economic reforms, compared to 19.5 percent of the overall sample, and a full 80 percent (compared to 42.1 percent of the overall sample) believed that the next PJ government should "return to the roots of Peronism."

Several left-of-center *agrupaciones* existed in the Federal Capital in the 1990s. For example, former JP leader Juan Carlos Dante Gullo's Peronism for Everyone *agrupación* maintained a small but committed core of leftist activists, many of whom were ex-Montoneros.[28] Peronism for Everyone claimed to uphold the Peronist left's "national and popular revolutionary discourse," and regularly supported strikes and other protests against the

---

[22] C de O's headquarters are filled with posters that read "Defend the Malvinas Islands!" and "Long Live the Argentine Army."
[23] Author's interview with C de O leader Alberto Brito Lima, April 8, 1997.
[24] For example, Doctrinal Peronism carried out a campaign to uncover those responsible for digging up Perón's remains – and cutting off his hands – in the mid-1980s.
[25] March 11, 1973 is the date on which Hector Cámpora, a close ally of the Peronist left, was elected president.
[26] Author's interviews with "March 11" leaders Mario Scalisi (May 28, 1997), Eduardo Schiavo (April 9, 1997), and Oscar Vega (April 2, 1997).
[27] Author's interview with "March 11" leader Mario Scalisi, May 28, 1997.
[28] Author's interviews with Juan Carlos Dante Gullo (December 11, 1997) and Oscar Nievas (December 7, 1997).

Menem government.²⁹ A more moderate left-of-center *agrupación* was the Peronist Unity Front (FUP). FUP maintained a selective recruitment process in which only "Peronists, not Menemists," were accepted.³⁰ Many of its UBs served as arenas for participation for progressive Peronists. Examples include the Hour of the People UB, which held a speaker series in which activists debated issues such as the social costs of the neoliberal model and alternatives to neoliberalism, and the United or Dominated base unit, which is run by a group of self-described "progressive" activists who are committed to issues of women's rights, squatters' rights, and poverty alleviation. A third left-of-center *agrupación* in the Federal Capital was Solidarity, which was led by ex-"25" leader Roberto Digón. Activists in one Solidarity UB backed the Cuban revolution and were critical of the IMF and the "savage capitalist system."³¹ One activist described Solidarity as "the last place I have here in Peronism."³²

Finally, many *agrupaciones* and base units provide arenas for participation for traditional or orthodox Peronists. These activists tend to be strongly attached to both the traditional Peronist program and to Peronist symbols and practices. An example of a traditional Peronist *agrupación* is Peronist Loyalty in La Matanza, which was run by former mayor Federico Russo. The second largest *agrupación* in La Matanza in the mid-1990s, Peronist Loyalty, contained dozens of old-guard orthodox activists, many of whom had worked for Russo since the 1970s. Most of these activists strongly opposed the neoliberal model. For example, long-time Russo supporter Juanita Pocovic, a self-described "nostalgic Peronist," claimed that Menem

> is not Peronist. A Peronist cannot become president and immediately bring in all the capitalists to govern us, as he did with Bunge y Born. I wanted to die. I don't understand it at all.... It's sad to say, but I hate Menem. I hate him because he is starving our people.³³

In the late 1990s, Peronist Loyalty was one of the few PJ *agrupaciones* that maintained active women's and youth branches and continued to engage in "doctrinal training." Russo carefully maintained the image of a traditional Peronist *caudillo*. His wife Pocha played an Evita-like role, heading the

---

[29] Author's interviews with Juan Carlos Dante Gullo (December 11, 1997) and Oscar Nievas (December 7, 1997). Although Dante Gullo remained at the margins of PJ politics, he claimed that he could "do and say what I want and no one does anything to me."

[30] Author's interview with FUP leader and Congressional Deputy Eduardo Rollano (June 24, 1997). This was confirmed by several PJ activists, both within and outside of FUP.

[31] Author's interviews with activists in the Tabare de Paula/Primera Junta Neighbors' Center, October 17, 1997.

[32] Author's interview, October 17, 1997.

[33] Author's interview, November 19, 1996. According to another Peronist Loyalty activist, "Peronism is about social justice. It is the creation of jobs. That's what we want to return to" (author's interview, August 29, 1997).

TABLE 7.7. *Activist Responses to the Question, "What Level of Party Activity Is Most Important to You?"*[a]

	Federal capital (n = 255)	Greater Buenos Aires (n = 235)	Total (n = 490)
Agrupación	25.5	40.0	32.4
Local/provincial party	10.6	22.6	16.3
National party	63.9	37.4	51.2

Note:
[a] Based on the author's 1997 survey of PJ activists in the Federal Capital, La Matanza, and Quilmes.

TABLE 7.8. *Comparing Neoliberal and Opposition Activists' Views of What Level of Party Activity Is Most Important*[a]

	Neoliberals (n = 48)	Opponents (n = 86)	All activists (n = 490)
Agrupación	18.8	45.3	32.4
Local/provincial party	6.3	16.3	16.3
National party	75.0	38.4	51.2

Note:
[a] Based on the author's 1997 survey of PJ activists in the Federal Capital, La Matanza, and Quilmes.

"women's branch." In the faction's meetings, both Russo and his wife repeatedly insisted that the PJ must "retake the cause of social justice."

The PJ's decentralized and segmented *agrupación* system thus provided outlets for scores of Peronist "believers," allowing them to continue to carry out forms of Peronism that had little to do with – and in many cases contradicted – the programmatic agenda of the Menem government. Data from the activist survey suggest that this base-level autonomy may have affected the decision of more ideological activists to stay inside the party. Table 7.7 shows activists' responses to the question, "What level of party activity is most important to you?" Overall, about a third of the activists surveyed (32.4 percent) said their *agrupación* was most important, and another 16.3 percent chose their local or provincial party. In Greater Buenos Aires, nearly two-thirds of the activists said their *agrupación* (40.0 percent) or local party (22.6 percent) was more important to them than the national party. The survey results also suggest that anti-Menem activists were more likely to prioritize their *agrupación* than were other activists. As Table 7.8 shows, nearly half (45.3 percent) of the activists classified as opponents of the government's economic policy responded that their *agrupación* was most important, compared to 18.8 percent of neoliberals and 32.4 percent of the overall sample. Taken together, these data suggest that a substantial number of activists who were critical of the Menem program took shelter in their *agrupaciones* in the post-1989 period, prioritizing their local work and, to some extent, detaching themselves from national party activity.

Rather than leaving the party, many activists appear to have retreated into a kind of "micro-Peronism," in which they pursued "social justice" – both real and symbolic – in their neighborhoods rather than pursuing objectives at the macro level.[34] As one local leader put it,

> I can't make a difference at the national level. I know that at the national level we have a regressive recipe imposed, for the most part, by the international financial institutions. But I don't think about that level. I can only make a difference at the local level. Here, I can change things.[35]

Activists' focus on base-level social work raises questions about the frequently made distinction between patronage-based and ideology-based activism. In the Peronist case, the two are clearly somewhat blurred. Without question, patronage became a primary currency of exchange for an increasing number of Peronist activists in the 1990s, overriding both personal ties and ideology. Yet state resources also helped the party retain many ideological activists, for those resources enabled activists to continue engaging in their own form of Peronist activism – from organizing Malvinas protests and Evita masses to building neighborhood health clinics and providing food, clothing, and medicine to the poor – at the base level.

To a significant extent, then, the PJ's segmented structure allowed traditional Peronism to survive at the grassroots level despite the Menem's government's right-wing turn. Notwithstanding Menem's takeover of the national party, activists continued to do their own form of Peronism at the base level. For a relatively small but committed minority, channels existed for the continued expression of leftist, nationalist, or orthodox Peronist beliefs. For a larger group of activists, who were less ideological but nonetheless uncomfortable with the neoliberal turn, the persistence of semi-autonomous local organizations allowed them to continue to practice their own style of Peronism at the grassroots level rather than face a stark choice between Menemism and leaving the party.

MACHINE POLITICS AND THE EROSION OF THE PJ'S WORKING-CLASS LINKAGES

Yet if decentralization and access to state resources helped the PJ maintain its activist base in the 1990s, they also generated important costs for the party. Historically, Peronism's linkages to working- and lower-class society

---

[34] For an insightful discussion of how base-level Peronist identities are changing in this regard, see Auyero (1998, 2000).
[35] Author's interview with Hector Drewes, June 16, 1997.

were both deeply rooted and diverse. Peronists were linked to the movement through unions, family and friendship networks, neighborhood clubs, and in some cases, ideological *agrupaciones*. Although patronage was never absent from the movement,[36] between 1955 and 1983, such material exchanges were rarely primary. Rather, they supplemented personal, social, ideological, and union-based linkages. In the 1990s, however, this began to change. As state-based material resources became the dominant currency of exchange, both between local leaders and *punteros* and between *punteros* and voters, local organizations based on nonmaterial linkages – such as personal ties or ideology – found it increasingly difficult to compete. As these organizations died off, the personal networks that had linked the PJ to working- and lower-class neighborhoods throughout years of proscription and repression began to erode.

The Predominance of Material Exchange in the 1990s

The PJ's sustained access to state resources in the 1990s led to a profound transformation of its base-level linkages, as an increasing number of party activists abandoned traditional forms of base-level organization in favor of material exchange–based relationships. This transformation was a product of the incentive structures facing individual activists. To gain power in the party, local politicians must either win internal elections or demonstrate the capacity to do so (and then negotiate deals with party bosses). In the 1990s, an increasing number of political entrepreneurs concluded that strategies based on material exchange were the most efficient means of achieving these goals.

Exchange-based or machine organizations differ in important ways from traditional or modern-amateur ones. First, whereas traditional and modern-amateur UBs tend to be led by long-time activists, machine UBs are more likely to be created by political newcomers with purely office-related goals. In La Matanza, for example, the Citizen Participation UB was opened in 1995 by a non-Peronist businessman who planned to run for mayor, and the Immortal Evita *agrupación* was created in 1996 by a successful ham distributor who sought a seat in Congress.[37]

Second, unlike traditional UBs, in which *puntero*-activist relationships are rooted in long-term personal ties, or modern-amateur UBs, in which activists are linked by friendship and shared ideological goals, machine UBs are based

---

[36] Unions, which maintained ties to the state throughout the 1955–83 period, were always a source of patronage resources for some activists.

[37] Similarly, the Cooperativism and Social Justice UB in Quilmes was founded by a political novice who said her primary goal was "to get some kind of position for myself and a few of my people" (author's interview, December 12, 1996).

almost entirely on material exchange.³⁸ An example is the Ramos Mejia Study Center in La Matanza, where members describe themselves as "both activists and employees."³⁹ Local residents come to the base unit looking for work. Those who are accepted are put on a payroll and assigned regular hours, and they must sign in and out every day. Because activists work for material reward rather than out of personal loyalty or shared collective goals, they frequently switch UBs and *agrupaciones* in an effort to get a better deal.⁴⁰

Third, exchange-based organizations tend to focus almost entirely on vote-maximization strategies. Unlike traditional UBs, in which *punteros* devote considerable time and energy to maintaining personal relationships through face-to-face meetings, or modern-amateur UBs, which devote time and energy to internal procedures and issue-oriented political activity, machine UBs reduce political and organizational activities to those that are necessary to win votes in intraparty elections. Few meetings are held outside of electoral campaigns, and traditions such as women's and youth branches, doctrinal training, and the celebration of Peronist holidays tend to be neglected. Rather than opening their UBs every day, machine *punteros* generally open up a few weeks before an election. Indeed, as cellular phones have reduced the need for meetings and office hours in the UB, many machine *punteros* have opted to work out of their homes. Rather than spending evenings talking, playing cards, or drinking *mate* with neighbors, *punteros* invest almost all of their time and resources into direct vote-getting activities such as mass distribution of food and other material goods. For example, the Los Aromos UB, located in a lower-class public housing complex in La Matanza, operates out of the apartment of its *puntero* and is dedicated almost exclusively to food distribution. In 1997, the *puntero* distributed four hundred bags of food a month among local residents, in exchange for which he demanded party membership and a vote in the internal elections.⁴¹

Exchange-based *agrupaciones* have developed a variety of organizational innovations that have made them more efficient vote-getting machines. For one, many of them contract out much of their campaign activity. For

---

³⁸ As an activist in the Cooperativism and Social Justice base unit put it, "it's like this: if you don't pay me, I don't work for you" (author's interview, April 9, 1997).

³⁹ Author's interview, 26 August, 1997.

⁴⁰ According to one activist, such defections "used to be considered treason. Twenty years ago, an activist who did that would be shot. These days it is considered strategic" (author's interview with Gustavo Gaudino, June 24, 1997).

⁴¹ This "exchange" was observed firsthand by the author. While distributing bags of food two weeks before intraparty elections, the *puntero* told recipients, "Remember, you have to vote on June 29. If not, you are automatically crossed off the list!" When one woman who missed the food truck came to the *puntero*'s apartment literally to beg for food, the *puntero* told her, "you have to wait. There are party members who are going to vote. I have to attend to them first" (author's observation, June 16, 1997).

example, rather than relying on youth activists to paint campaign graffiti (an activity that is deeply rooted in Peronist tradition), in the late 1980s, emerging political entrepreneurs began to pay organized youth gangs to do it.[42] Although these gangs are usually Peronist, they do not belong to particular *agrupaciones* and may in fact work for various factions during a single campaign. Some have even evolved into small enterprises. In the Federal Capital, for example, wall painting is now done almost exclusively by four or five local gangs that charge up to $500 a day for their services. Poll watching is also contracted out. Due to the possibility of fraud in internal elections, competing factions must mobilize scores of people to serve as poll watchers on election day. Whereas this work was traditionally done by party activists, well-financed *agrupaciones* now regularly pay people up to $60 to serve as poll watchers. Finally, many *agrupaciones* regularly contract taxi services to bring people to the polls on election day, rather than rely on the activists themselves. In La Matanza, for example, the dominant Peronist Militancy and Renovation (MyRP) began renting hundreds of taxis to "get out the vote" in 1987.

Another innovation is centralized coordination. Finding Peronism's decentralized system of base units to be inefficient, many local PJ leaders have begun to centralize key areas of their activities. For example, several *agrupaciones* have centralized the delivery of social assistance by obtaining food and medicine in bulk and either distributing the goods from a central office or renting trucks to deliver the goods to their various base units. In La Matanza, for example, Hector Drewes' "August 22" *agrupación* gave away food to three thousand families a month in 1997, contracting trucks to deliver food bags to each of its base units.[43] Similarly, Universal Evita distributed six tons of vegetables every week out of its central office. Many *agrupaciones* have also centralized their campaign organizations. In La Matanza, for example, MyRP organized its 450 base units into twenty-six "subcommands," which are coordinated out of a central office called the Big House. Similarly, Hurlingham Mayor Juan José Alvarez attempted to consolidate his *agrupación's* twenty-seven base units into three central headquarters – one for each of the district's three major neighborhoods.[44] Finally, in some cases, PJ leaders have abandoned UBs entirely, preferring to work out of central offices. For example, when Adalberto "Tito" Dal Lago created his Universal Evita *agrupación*, he decided not to create any base units, but rather to work out of *punteros*' homes. According to Dal Lago, this arrangement is "more efficient. You don't have to pay the rent, and the activists are there all the time,

---

[42] As one La Matanza activist put it, "they discovered that it is easier to buy off a young gang from a local soccer club with money than it is to convince an activist through doctrine" (author's interview with Raul Tuncho, August 30, 1997).
[43] Author's interview with Hector Drewes, June 16, 1997.
[44] Author's interview with Hurlingham Mayor Juan José Alvarez, July 18, 1997.

TABLE 7.9. *Comparing Three Types of Base Units*[a] *(Percentages)*

	Traditional (n = 41)	Modern-amateur (n = 22)	Machine (n = 39)	Total (n = 101)
Core activists together since before 1990	95.1	81.8	68.4	82.2
Puntero is from the neighborhood	92.7	85.7	71.1	83.0
Distributes food and medicine	73.7	42.9	92.1	74.5
Maintains traditional base unit format	75.6	52.4	23.7	51.5
Celebrates Peronist holidays	67.6	21.1	21.1	39.8
Holds regular political meetings	28.9	80.0	23.7	37.5
Shares same ideology as the *agrupación*	46.4	76.2	13.2	42.3

Note:
[a] Based on author's survey of 112 base units in the Federal Capital, La Matanza, and Quilmes. Of these, eleven could not be easily categorized as traditional, modern-amateur, or machine UBs and were excluded.

rather than just a few hours a day."[45] Similarly, the "October 8" *agrupación* in Quilmes abandoned UBs because they "cost too much money."[46] In 1997, it ran a network of eighty *punteros* out of eight central offices.

Table 7.9 compares traditional, modern-amateur, and machine UBs on a range of dimensions. According to the survey of base units carried out for this study, entrepreneurial base units are less likely to be rooted in neighborhoods and long-established activist networks, and more likely to engage in clientelism, than are traditional and modern-amateur base units. They are less likely to engage in Peronist cultural activities than traditional UBs and less likely to be ideological or active in purposive political activity than modern-amateur UBs.

Pure exchange-based strategies began to win out over other organizational forms in the 1990s. To gain or maintain access to public office or state resources, local Peronists must win internal elections, and an increasing number of PJ leaders and activists concluded that exchange-based strategies maximized votes more efficiently. Whereas traditional *punteros* maintain close ties with a few dozen people in their neighborhoods, well-financed entrepreneurial *punteros* can buy hundreds of votes at election time. Moreover, such strategies do not require heavy investments in party traditions, personal

---

[45] Author's interview, May 23, 1997.
[46] Author's interview with "October 8" leader José Luis Saluzzi, September 4, 1997.

relationships, or purposive political activity. Peronists who maintain traditional organizational practices have difficulty competing against these machinelike methods, and thus are losing internal elections and becoming marginalized.

The increasing predominance of exchange-based organizational forms can be seen in La Matanza. Throughout the 1970s and much of the 1980s, La Matanza Peronism was dominated by traditional *caudillo* Federico Russo. Russo's Peronist Loyalty *agrupación* was based primarily on "friendship and loyalty."[47] Most of its *punteros* were long-time Russo allies who were fiercely loyal to him. Russo invested heavily in maintaining maintaining these personal ties, sending birthday cards to each of his activists and taking care to speak with each one individually before the *agrupación's* weekly assemblies. The *agrupación* also invested heavily in maintaining Peronist traditions. By the mid-1980s, however, many Peronists viewed Russo as an "anachronistic *caudillo*"[48] who "gave out political offices to friends and family, rather than to the activists who worked."[49] The anti-Russo movement was led by businessman and political neophyte Alberto Pierri. After gaining a seat in Congress in 1985, Pierri transformed his MyRP into a powerful patronage-based machine. MyRP employed a range of new organizing techniques, including paid campaign workers and the rental of hundreds of taxis to get out the vote during elections. Using his access to state resources, Pierri "bought off Russo's *punteros* left and right,"[50] and in 1991, MyRP defeated Peronist Loyalty and took over the party leadership. According one former Russo ally, "Russo trusted in his popularity and his charisma, but it wasn't enough. People had other needs, and Pierri met them."[51]

Upon gaining control of city hall, Pierri fired hundreds of Russo supporters and replaced them with his own *punteros*. Using its vast patronage resources, MyRP coopted dozens of *punteros* from traditional *agrupaciones* such as Peronist Loyalty. Both MyRP members and opponents described the organization as being "run like a business." While internal critics attacked Pierri for "commercializing" or "prostituting" Peronism,[52] his supporters described MyRP as a "meritocratic." According to one Pierri ally, whereas

---

[47] Author's interview with La Matanza Peronist leader Aníbal Stela, July 16, 1997.
[48] Author's interview with La Matanza Peronist leader Aníbal Stela, July 16, 1997.
[49] Author's interview with Nedda Abella, member of the La Matanza party council, May 16, 1997.
[50] Author's interview with local PJ leader Oscar Zarate, April 3, 1997.
[51] Author's interview with Miguel Pretto, April 8, 1997. According to Russo, Pierri "turned Peronism into a business.... If you go around with a ton of money and truck in tens of thousands of votes from all over the place, of course you can beat the activist who works with nothing. That's what Peronism has become in La Matanza" (author's interview, August 29, 1997).
[52] According to former provincial Senator José Maria Rocca, "Anyone who raises his head, Pierri finds his price, and he ends up working for Pierri" (author's interview, May 19, 1997).

Russo "gave out political offices to friends and family," in MyRP, "you know that if you work hard, they'll find a job for you."[53] Not surprisingly, MyRP was nonideological. According to one local leader, "No one agrees with Pierri ideologically. There is no such thing as an ideological *Pierrista*. They are with him out of economic need."[54]

The success of machine-style politics encouraged other outsiders to replicate this strategy. In La Matanza, for example, Tito Dal Lago, a local ham distributor who had never participated in politics, created the Universal Evita *agrupación* in 1995. According to Dal Lago, "I looked around and I said to myself: 'I can do this.' So I started my own *agrupación*."[55] Using his own money and donations from business friends, Dal Lago recruited nineteen *punteros*, through whom he distributed vegetables to five hundred families every week.[56] Similarly, Hector Drewes, an independently wealthy government official with close ties to the business community, created the "August 22" *agrupación* to lay the groundwork for a future mayoral bid. According to Drewes, he "started by himself" in 1996, going into poor zones and "looking for *punteros*" to establish base units from above.[57] In his first year of operations, Drewes spent $250,000 of his own money in recruiting *punteros* and establishing a vast food distribution network in the district.[58]

Faced with the success of machine politics, traditional and ideological Peronist organizations were forced to adopt similar tactics in order to survive. As one Federal Capital leader put it, "everywhere these days, base units are maintained with salaries and jobs. Those are the rules of the game. Everyone has to do it."[59] The effect of competition on organizational strategy can be seen in the case of the leftist "March 11" in Quilmes. "March 11" learned the effects of clientelistic politics the hard way in 1991, when its eighteen-month grassroots campaign was undermined by the opposition Federal League's massive distribution of patronage and clientelistic benefits one month prior to the party primaries. According to one "March 11" leader,

> We were naive enough to think that our model of politics could defeat their [clientelistic] model.... We encouraged participation, painted walls, talked to the people.... But with a lot of money, they stole the election from us.[60]

---

[53] Author's interview with Nedda Abella, May 16, 1997.
[54] Author's interview with local PJ leader Oscar Zarate, April 3, 1997.
[55] Author's interview with Adalberto Dal Lago, May 23, 1997.
[56] Author's interview with Dal Lago, May 23, 1997.
[57] Author's interview with Hector Drewes, June 16, 1997.
[58] Author's interview with Drewes, June 16, 1997.
[59] Author's interview with Raúl Roa, May 12, 1997. According to another Federal Capital leader, whose faction was defeated in 1997: "We spent $150,000 on posters. They spent their money on buying *punteros* and buying votes. And they won. What's the lesson? Next time everyone is going to go out and buy votes" (author's interview with Congressional Deputy Eduardo Rollano, June 24, 1997).
[60] Author's interview with Claudio Oliveras, May 22, 1997.

TABLE 7.10. *The Increasing Role of Selective Material Benefits in Fostering PJ Activist Participation*[a] *(Percentage of Surveyed Base Units)*

Primary incentive for activist participation	UB established before 1985 (n = 45)	UB established between 1985–95 (n = 39)	UB established after 1995 (n = 17)
Personal ties, social networks, or ideology	82.2	51.2	35.3
Selective material benefits	17.8	48.8	64.7

Note:
[a] Author's judgments, based on interviews with activists in each base unit. Eleven UBs could not be scored due to insufficient information.

Although "March 11" remained an ideological organization throughout the 1990s, it subsequently made extensive use of patronage to ensure that its activists did not defect.

Evidence from the survey of base units carried out for this study suggests that exchange-based organizations are becoming increasingly prevalent in the Federal Capital and Greater Buenos Aires. As Table 7.10 shows, of the surveyed base units that were established before 1985, 82.2 percent were held together primarily by personal ties, social networks, or shared ideology. In only 17.8 percent of the cases were selective material incentives clearly the dominant linkage between activists and the UB. Of the UBs created between 1985 and 1995, however, the percentage of cases in which selective material incentives predominated rose to 48.8 percent, and of the UBs that were established after 1995, the percentage rose to 64.7 percent. This evidence suggests that PJ activism is increasingly based on selective, rather than collective, incentives, and that the urban PJ is becoming less of a "community of values" (Panebianco 1988: 9) and more of a machinelike party.

The Costs of Machine Politics

Although entrepreneurial strategies may be optimal from the standpoint of individual politicians seeking to win internal elections, over time these strategies may have negative consequences for the PJ as a whole.[61] The consolidation of machine politics has been costly for the PJ in at least three ways. First, the party organization is more dependent on state resources than at any time since 1955. As long as purposive or solidary incentives predominated, as in 1955–83, controlling the state was not necessary to maintain the activist base. As material incentives replace personal, ideological, and union ties as

---

[61] Warner (1997: 544) makes a similar argument about the collective costs of patronage politics.

the primary glue linking activists to the party, however, the PJ organization has become more vulnerable to losing power. In the contemporary period, it is unclear how many activists would participate in the absence of patronage resources.[62]

Second, the consolidation of machine politics has left the PJ increasingly vulnerable to reformist electoral challenges. Machine politics are often associated with corruption, and the leaders they produce – the local bosses who control the votes – often prove to be unattractive to middle-class voters. To the extent that local party organizations are transformed into machines, then, they are vulnerable to reformist or "clean government" appeals by opposition parties. Reformist appeals can be particularly damaging in districts with large middle-class electorates. Indeed, the corruption issue badly hurt the PJ's electoral performance in wealthy urban centers such as the Federal Capital and Rosario. In the capital, which is the wealthiest and best-educated district in the country, the local PJ machine became widely associated with corruption during the 1990s. As a result, its share of the local electorate fell from 31 percent in the 1989 legislatives elections to just 9 percent a decade later.

Third, the consolidation of machine politics began to erode the PJ's long-established social and cultural linkages to working- and lower-class society. Over time, the spread of machine politics resulted in the defeat or marginalization of the "natural leaders" of the neighborhoods. In most cases, long-time activists were unable to compete with well-financed machine politicians in internal elections. In other cases, the party suffered what former PJ activist Luis D'Elia calls the "yuppification" of neighborhood *punteros*,[63] as local activists were drawn into the state or party machine and became increasingly detached from neighborhood politics. According to D'Elia, most PJ *punteros*

are now very well paid, and more and more they are hanging out in the cafes and bars with their cellular phones, rather than working in the neighborhoods. They have given up their role as social mediators. Consequently, many neighborhoods now lack *punteros* who are social mediators.[64]

Thus, whereas PJ base organizations were predominantly bottom-up in the 1980s, by the late 1990s, base-level organizations were increasingly top-down or "statized." Indeed, in many working- and lower-class neighborhoods, base-level Peronism "has come to function exactly like an old-time conservative party: pure and simple clientelism."[65]

---

[62] As one *puntero* put it, "If we are defeated in the next election, we run the risk of dissolution. We have lost our ideology. Now the only thing that unites us is 'business'" (quoted in Otero 1997: 67).
[63] Author's interview, October 23, 1996.
[64] Author's interview, October 23, 1996.
[65] Author's interview with PJ activist Ricardo Morato, September 22, 1997.

Party Activists and the Transformation of Peronism

The consolidation of machine politics also eroded the PJ's cultural linkages to its base. Pure machinelike organizational strategies tend to leave aside the traditions and cultural practices – such as Peronist holidays, youth *bombo* (drum) corps, wall-painting brigades, doctrinal training, and neighborhood "social work" – that have historically helped to sustain the Peronist subculture. To the extent that this subculture erodes, there will be increasingly less to differentiate the PJ from other parties. As one activist put it:

> The destruction of Peronist culture and tradition is even worse than the undoing of the traditional Peronist program. It is worse than the privatizations or the dismantling of the state because it undoes what makes us different from all the rest of the political forces. It does away with our comparative advantage, so to speak.[66]

Alternatives to Machine Politics

The costs of machine politics led some Peronists to search for alternative organizational strategies in the late 1990s. One strategy, which could be observed in predominantly middle-class districts, was to abandon base-level organization in favor of media-based, issue-oriented, or candidate-centered appeals. The shift away from territorial organization was most pronounced in the Federal Capital. Due to the high levels of wealth and education, as well as the powerful influence of national politics and the mass media, the Federal Capital electorate is more independent, issue-oriented, and volatile than anywhere else in the country. The city also has a large reform-oriented or "clean government" constituency, which is based primarily in the well-educated middle-class and upper-middle-class sectors. Compared to the national electorate as a whole, then, the Federal Capital is a relatively hostile environment for machine politics, and a relatively propitious environment for capital-intensive, media-based parties. This was made manifest by the rise of FREPASO, a media-based party that did not invest in party organization, but which nevertheless emerged out of nowhere to win the 1994 Constituent Assembly elections in the capital.

In this context, many PJ leaders and activists concluded that their investments in territorial organization were not paying off in the 1990s. As one local activist put it,

> It's not worth it, in a cost/benefit analysis, to finance base units. Having a base unit does not guarantee votes anymore. Here in the capital, two minutes on television can wipe out five years of work in the neighborhood.... *Punteros* tell you they need base units to work with the people. But "the people" turns out to be three guys who come over to *drink mate*.... There are four hundred base units in the capital and we are at 8 percent in the polls. Something clearly isn't working.[67]

---

[66] Author's interview with Rolando Smith, July 21, 1997.
[67] Author's interview with María Lenz, March 31, 1997. Even Carlos Grosso, who many view as the father of the local PJ machine, argues that "you don't need an organization to win in

Consequently, Federal Capital Peronists began to abandon labor-intensive, activist-based strategies in favor of capital-intensive, media-based strategies. As Congressional Deputy Javier Mouriño, a leader of the Liberators of America *agupación*, put it:

Maintaining base units is very expensive. How much does it cost to attract fifty thousand votes through television? Much less.... If you have a big *puntero* on your candidate list, you have fifteen hundred votes. But if you have a well-liked media figure on your list, you have seven thousand votes.... Sooner or later, the *punteros* are going to die off. My media figures are going to defeat your *punteros*.[68]

Given the capacity of inward-oriented, *puntero*-based factions to win internal elections, capital-intensive, media-based strategies initially required the external intervention of the national party. Thus, in both 1992 and 1993, the national leadership imposed nonparty candidates who were more attractive to middle-class, independent voters. The national leadership followed a similar strategy in 1997, taking over the Federal Capital branch to help outsider Daniel Scioli defeat the local machine to win the nomination for Congress. Scioli's campaign marked a major shift in organizational strategy. The Scioli team operated out of a centralized campaign headquarters, using hired staff rather than activists. Although Scioli did not forego the use of *punteros* entirely, he waged much of his campaign – both in the primaries and the general election – through the media.

As local leaders' investment in neighborhood organization dropped over the course of the 1990s, the PJ's activist base eroded. The survey of activists carried out for this study reflects this decline. Asked whether they thought that the number of PJ activists had increased, decreased, or remained the same over the course of the 1990s, 61.4 percent of Federal Capital activists responded that the number of activists had declined. By contrast, only 23 percent of activists in Greater Buenos Aires believed that the level of activism had declined, while a full two-thirds (68 percent) responded that the number of activists in the party had *increased*.

As the Peronist activist base eroded in the capital over the course of the 1990s, the PJ's Federal Capital branch increasingly took on features of a media-based and candidate-centered party. As a result, the PJ's electoral base in the capital became increasingly volatile. This volatility can be seen in Table 7.11. Although the party was capable of winning elections, as it did in 1993 when Menemist legislative candidate Erman Gonzalez successfully appealed to conservative voters, it also suffered electoral declines that were virtually unthinkable in other districts. Whereas the national party vote never fell below 33 percent in legislative elections, and the Peronist vote never fell

---

the capital anymore.... It's better to operate out of a television station than out of a base unit" (author's interview, November 28, 1997).

[68] Author's interview, July 1, 1997.

TABLE 7.11. *The Volatility of the Peronist Vote in the Federal Capital, 1989–99*[a]

	1989	1991	1993	1995	1997	1999
Federal capital PJ vote	31.1	28.2	31.9	23.3	18.0	9.2
National PJ vote	44.7	40.2	42.5	43.0	36.3	33.0

Note:
[a] Figures are from Chamber of Deputies elections.

below 45 percent in highly organized provincial branches such as La Rioja, San Luis, and Santiago del Estero, Peronism in the Federal Capital fell from 32 percent to just 18 percent in 1997 and a mere 9 percent in 1999.

In working- and lower-class areas, where local organization remained much more important in the 1990s, a few PJ leaders and activists experimented with what might be called a "collectivist" alternative to clientelism. Collectivist organizations are based on horizontal ties among activists, rather than vertical, patronage-based ties between neighborhood brokers and activists. The basis of such organizations is what Peronists call "social activism." Although they pursue material benefits, these benefits take the form of collective neighborhood goods such as paved roads, sewage systems, street lights, health clinics, and child care centers, rather than particularistic or clientelistic benefits. Proponents of the collectivist strategy view it as a means of maintaining a political presence in working- and lower-class society without resorting to clientelism.

An example of a collectivist strategy is the Mariano Llanos *agrupación* in the impoverished San Francisco de Solano section of Quilmes. Led by former union activist Marcelo Mayo, Mariano Llanos linked together several dozen Peronist social activists in the late 1990s. Most of the activists were women. They included Gladis, who ran a mothers' club and a Center for the Protection of Single Mothers; Cecilia, who ran a health care cooperative; Claudia, who created the My Little Star civil association, which was dedicated to assisting poor children; and Ana, who ran a Mothers' League. Although all of these women were life-long Peronists, few had participated actively in party work before the 1990s. In joining the *agrupación*, which was aligned with the powerful Federal League, they sought to increase their access to local Peronist officials.

Another example of a collectivist project is the Peronist Neighborhood Front (FREPEVE), which was created in 1995 by a group of Federal Capital shantytown leaders who had worked together since the 1970s. FREPEVE was based out of the Hidden City shantytown, although it also included a handful of soup kitchens and working groups from other working- and lower-class neighborhoods. The organization's primary goal was to gain collective material benefits for its neighborhoods. To obtain resources, FREPEVE negotiated with local PJ factions, exchanging its members' votes for social benefits, playing different factions against each other, and aligning with those that offered the best deal.[69] FREPEVE obtained a range of collective benefits in the 1990s, including a child care center and a gymnasium.

Although most collectivist organizations are confined to a single neighborhood, a few larger organizations could also be found in the late 1990s. One example is the leftist "March 11" in Quilmes. Having concluded that the PJ's base units had lost the capacity to foster popular participation, "March 11" opted to work out of cooperatives, soup kitchens, and squatters organizations.[70] "March 11" leaders sought out "people with a social activist background" who could "replace the old clientelistic practices" with a "different style of communication with the neighbors."[71] According to "March 11" leader Oscar Vega, such organizations are the only way to maintain a "participatory" territorial organization in urban poverty zones in which deindustrialization has led to the virtual disappearance of unions.[72]

Other Greater Buenos Aires *agrupaciones* pursued similar strategies in the second half of the 1990s. For example, Quilmes city council member Hugo Guerreño, convinced that base units had "lost credibility," ordered his thirty *punteros* to transform their UBs into civic associations in 1996.[73] His followers created a variety of new organizations, including cooperatives, community centers, women's groups, mothers' associations, children's rights groups, and professional associations. In Hurlingham, Mayor Juan José Alvarez pressured local PJ leaders to close down their base units and replace them with nonprofit organizations,[74] and in La Matanza, the "La Matanza Sports" *agrupación* established a "solidarity network" of ten "community centers" that "emphasize the social, rather than the political."[75] Although most of these innovations entailed little more than window dressing, in that the

---

[69] According to FREPEVE leader Mate Ocampo, "Before every election I write letters to all of the major faction leaders, outlining our latest project. Whoever delivers the goods, we back. The politicians use us and we use them.... My motto is, within the neighborhood, the greatest possible ethics; outside the neighborhood, pure mercenaries" (author's interview, March 22, 1997).

[70] Author's interview with "March 11" leader Eduardo Schiavo, April 9, 1997. For example, the organization's "October" *subagrupácion* includes a cultural center, a youth soccer club, a "friends of the plaza" neighborhood clean-up committee, and several neighborhood cooperatives.

[71] Author's interviews with "March 11" leaders Angel García (March 14, 1997) and Claudio Oliveres (May 22, 1997).

[72] Author's interview, April 2, 1997.

[73] According to Guerreño, he ordered this change because "it's better, politically speaking, to have civic associations as a base than to have base units. These days, base units are associated with patronage and cheap politics. With civic associations, I can avoid that" (author's interview, June 10, 1997).

[74] Author's interview with Juan José Alvarez, July 18, 1997.

[75] Author's interview with La Matanza Sports leader José Montenegro, August 26, 1997.

underlying organizational logic in many of these *agrupaciones* continued to be patronage-based, in a few cases, activists transformed their organizations into effective mechanisms for pressing local demands. In the case of Loyalty, for example, several of the new civic associations became increasingly mobilized around neighborhood issues – at times dragging Guerreño into local protests. For example, Loyalty activists organized a series of protests after the newly privatized water company cut off service to a lower-class Quilmes neighborhood, and Guerreño was eventually pressured to go to court to restore service. In a second case, after a wave of violent assaults in their neighborhood, Loyalty members organized a series of protests – which included blockading a local highway with burning tires – to demand better security measures in poor neighborhoods. Guerreño was again dragged into the protest, and the group eventually won an expansion of the police patrol for the zone.

Where they succeeded, collectivist organizations allowed the PJ to address activists' material needs while at the same time remaining embedded in working- and lower-class life. In areas where machine politics has eroded the party's image among middle- and working-class voters, this organizational form may be attractive from an electoral perspective as well. For this reason, some PJ leaders began to think about ways of generalizing the collectivist form to the party as a whole. For example, former Montonero leader Roberto Cirilo Perdía proposed replacing UBs with "community councils" made up of representatives of different neighborhood organizations.[76]

Yet collectivist organizations are unlikely to spread beyond scattered neighborhoods and leftist *agrupaciones*, for at least two reasons. First, collectivist organizations have difficulty competing against machine-based factions in internal elections. As long as patronage is deemed necessary to win internal elections, it is unlikely to be dispensed with entirely. Second, due to the PJ's weak bureaucracy and decentralized structure, it is virtually impossible to create collectivist organizations from above. The question of finding organizational alternatives to machine politics thus reveals the double-edged nature of the PJ's fluid and decentralized structure. On the one hand, the absence of a rigid bureaucracy makes it easy for politicians to experiment with new organizational forms, which enhances the prospects for organizational innovation. On the other hand, the PJ's decentralized structure makes it difficult to impose new organizational forms from above.

In sum, local Peronist organizations underwent an important transformation in the 1980s and 1990s. Increasingly, linkages based on social and ideological ties were replaced by material exchange–based linkages. Although such machinelike practices are more efficient in winning internal elections,

---

[76] Author's interview, June 3, 1997. In Quilmes in the late 1990s, Mayor Federico Scarabino pressured all of the districts *punteros* to work through civic associations by insisting that all government resources be distributed through civic associations rather than base units.

they may have important long-term electoral consequences for the party. As well-financed machine politicians defeat traditional neighborhood leaders, and as emerging PJ leaders forsake traditional Peronist rituals in favor of more efficient vote-maximizing techniques, both the PJ's embeddedness in working- and lower-class society and the subculture it fostered are being eroded. Consequently, even in areas where the PJ maintains a mass organization, the degree to which this organization can continue to encapsulate Peronist voters is increasingly uncertain.

CHAPTER 8

The Paradox of Menemism: Party Adaptation and Regime Stability in the 1990s

This book has argued that the PJ's capacity to adapt to the opportunities and constraints of the neoliberal era was critical to its survival as a major political force. The following chapter takes the argument a step further, making the case that the Peronist adaptation contributed in an important way to the performance and stability of Argentine democracy. Argentine democracy was surprisingly successful during the 1990s. Core democratic institutions such as free elections, the protection of civil liberties, and civilian control over the military became firmly established. Indeed, these institutions proved sufficiently robust to survive a hyperinflationary crisis, radical economic reform, and the abuses of the Menem government.

One of the keys to understanding this outcome lies in the transformation and survival of Peronism. The socioeconomic crisis of the 1980s and 1990s posed a fundamental threat to established parties and party systems in Latin America. This was particularly the case in what Roberts (1997a, 1998b) calls labor-mobilizing party systems, or party systems in which established labor-mobilizing parties are central actors. Where labor-mobilizing parties failed to adapt to the challenges posed by socioeconomic crisis and neoliberalism, as in Peru and Venezuela, party systems collapsed (Roberts 1997a). In theory, the collapse of established parties should lead to the emergence and consolidation of newer, more representative parties. In such a case, party decline would simply result in a realignment of the party system. In contemporary Latin America, however, the failure of established parties has more frequently led to party system fragmentation or decomposition. Due to long-term structural changes such as the erosion of class identities and the increased influence of mass media technologies, collapsed party systems in Latin America proved extremely difficult to reconstruct in the 1980s and 1990s. Indeed, outside of El Salvador and Mexico, weakened or failed parties generally gave way to personalistic vehicles or loosely organized "flash" parties, many of which disappeared after a single electoral cycle (Perelli et al. 1995).

Party system decomposition may pose a serious threat to the performance and even the stability of young democratic regimes. Parties structure voters' electoral choices, link class actors and other interest groups to the state, and facilitate the organization and functioning of legislatures. When they fail and party systems decompose, state–society linkages often break down and democratic governance becomes difficult. Party system decomposition may weaken democracies in two ways. First, it undermines governability. Inchoate or fragmented party systems have been associated with legislative gridlock, executive–legislative conflict, policy ineffectiveness, and failed economic reform (Mainwaring and Scully 1995; Mainwaring 1999). Second, party system decomposition often paves the way for the emergence of antisystem or "neopopulist," politicians, many of whom are weakly committed to representative institutions (Roberts 1995). This phenomenon was clearly seen in Peru and Venezuela, where the crisis of established populist or labor-based parties was accompanied by party system decomposition and the breakdown or near breakdown of democratic regimes.

The PJ's adaptation and survival helped to avoid such an outcome in Argentina, at least during the 1990s. Peronism's extensive working- and lower-class linkages helped the Menem government to end a regime-threatening hyperinflationary crisis by dampening popular sector mobilization against neoliberal reforms, reducing the space for antireform appeals, and providing Menem with an effective legislative majority. Moreover, the PJ's electoral success helped to stabilize a party system that in the early 1990s had showed clear signs of erosion, thereby helping to prevent the kind of governability crises and neopopulist "surge candidates" seen in countries such as Brazil, Peru, and Venezuela.

RETHINKING ARGENTINE DEMOCRACY IN THE 1990S

For most of the twentieth century, Argentina was one of the world's leading democratic underachievers. Despite the country's high levels of wealth and education, large middle class, relatively egalitarian social structure, and developed civil society, civilian regimes repeatedly broke down between 1930 and 1976. Beginning with the ill-fated second government of Hipólito Yrigoyen (1928–30), every civilian government that came to power through elections – including those of Juan Perón (1946–55), Arturo Frondizi (1958–62), Arturo Illia (1963–6), and Juan and Isabel Perón (1973–6) – ended in a military coup. In 1976, Argentina became the wealthiest country ever to suffer a military coup (Przeworski and Limongi 1997: 170).

The democratic regime that emerged from military rule in 1983 remained fragile. Although the Raúl Alfonsín government undertook important democratizing initiatives, particularly in the area of human rights, the governability crisis of the late 1980s suggested that many of the problems that had plagued previous civilian governments had persisted into the contemporary period. Severe distributional conflict, a series of military rebellions, and an eventual descent into hyperinflation forced Alfonsín to abandon the presidency six months before the end of his mandate and raised the specter of yet another military coup.

Although the Menem government put an end to the hyperinflationary crisis, its marginally constitutional efforts to concentrate power weakened the country's already fragile system of checks and balances, or what O'Donnell (1994) has called "horizontal accountability." During his first term, Menem made repeated use of his ambiguously constitutional authority to issue Decrees of Necessity and Urgency (NUDs) (Ferreira Rubio and Goretti 1998). Whereas Alfonsín issued just ten NUDs between 1983 and 1989, Menem issued 545 NUDs over the course of his presidency (Ferreira Rubio and Goretti 2000: 1, 4). Menem also assaulted the judicial branch. In 1990, the government pushed through legislation (over the objections of the opposition and with a contested quorum) expanding the Supreme Court from five to nine members, and then stacked it with Menem loyalists (Larkins 1998: 427–9). The new Supreme Court rarely ruled against the executive branch during Menem's first term (Larkins 1998; Helmke 2000b). Although the courts were never completely subordinated to the executive branch, the cozy relationship between many federal judges and the government seriously eroded the judiciary's legitimacy.[1] Finally, Menem's reckless efforts to reform the constitution – by virtually any means necessary – to allow his own reelection twice brought the country to the brink of an institutional crisis.[2]

In light of these abuses, scholars offered almost uniformly pessimistic accounts of Argentine democracy in the 1990s.[3] In a highly influential article, O'Donnell (1994) labeled Argentina a "delegative democracy," which he defined as a democratic regime in which horizontal accountability – and more generally, the liberal dimension of representative democracy – was weak. Other scholars described Argentina as a "democracy in turmoil" (De Riz 1996) and a "persistently unconsolidated democracy" (Schmitter 1995: 17), and some even raised concerns that the Menem government would not leave power peacefully (De Riz 1996: 165; Novaro 1998: 15).

Yet in many ways, Argentine democracy proved remarkably robust during the Menem period. Unlike in many other nominally democratic regimes in Latin America, Argentina's core democratic institutions were never seriously violated during the 1990s. At no time was the fairness of elections in doubt,

---

[1] Indeed, surveys found that as many as 80 percent of Argentines did not trust the judicial branch or believe it to be independent (Cardenas 1998: 155; Helmke 2000a: 13).
[2] In 1994, Menem bullied the UCR into accepting a constitutional reform permitting reelection by threatening to hold a plebiscite on the issue. Four years later, despite the clear unconstitutionality of running for a third term, Menem toyed publicly with the idea and even sought a court ruling permitting his candidacy.
[3] See O'Donnell (1994); De Riz (1996), Nino (1996), Ferreira Rubio and Goretti (1998), Larkins (1998), and Diamond (1999: 34–5). An exception is Palermo and Novaro (1996).

and political and civil liberties were broadly protected. There were no states of emergency, government opponents of all ideological stripes enjoyed substantial freedom, and press freedom remained among the most extensive in Latin America.[4] Moreover, civilian control over the armed forces was better established than at any time since 1930. After 1990, when the Menem government crushed a final military rebellion and issued a controversial pardon of top military officers convicted of human rights violations, the military's presence in politics was virtually nil. Unlike Brazil, Chile, Ecuador, or Peru, the military had no role in the government, military officers did not issue independent proclamations, and there were no military shows of force in the streets of the capital. Indeed, the armed forces were remarkably quiet as the Menem government reduced their size by a third, slashed their budget,[5] abolished the draft, and privatized military-owned enterprises. By the end of the decade, military spending was under the exclusive control of the Ministry of the Economy, responsibility for determining military missions and deployment was in the hands of the Foreign Ministry, and the "bulk of serious military effort" was being devoted to external peacekeeping missions (Trinkunas 2000: 100).

Even on the dimension of horizontal accountability, the Menem government's abuses were comparatively limited and short-lived. President Menem did not routinely bypass his party or the legislature after 1990. Congress approved the bulk of the government's post-1990 reform measures, and most of these involved arduous negotiations with Congressional leaders, governors, and business and labor leaders (Etchemendy and Palermo 1998; Corrales 2000; Llanos 2001). Many reform bills, including social security reform and bills to privatize the gas and petroleum sectors, were substantially modified by the legislature (Llanos 2001: 85–96). Others, such as labor market reforms, were blocked entirely. Menem's capacity to govern unilaterally was further reduced during his second term. Much of the government's post-1995 legislative agenda was bogged down in Congress (Llanos 2001: 92–5), and although Menem frequently threatened to impose key reforms by decree, these threats were generally not carried out. Indeed, the number of NUDs issued by the executive branch declined significantly over the course of the 1990s. Whereas Menem issued an average of sixty-eight NUDs a year between 1989 and 1993, he issued only thirty-six NUDs a year between 1994 and 1998 (Ferreira Rubio and Goretti 2000: 8). Judicial rulings against the

---

[4] Although government officials launched a handful of libel suits against journalists and media outlets, they lost the most important of these cases. In one of these cases, that of Joaquín Morales Solá, the Supreme Court invoked the U.S. Supreme Court's "real malice" doctrine, which requires that plaintiffs demonstrate that journalists who publish false information do so with malicious intent. Such legal norms are unusually liberal by Latin American standards.
[5] Military spending declined from 18.2 percent of government expenditure in 1989 to 10.6 percent in 1993 (Trinkunas 2000: 100).

government also increased during Menem's second term (Helmke 2000a: 21–2).[6]

The resilience of Argentina's democratic institutions was made manifest in 1998, when President Menem engaged in a reckless, if halfhearted, attempt to run for a third term. In contrast to 1994, Menem's "re-reelection" bid was opposed by a strong and united opposition, as well as by roughly half of his own Peronist party. Although Menem loyalists sought to obtain a favorable ruling from the Menemist-dominated Supreme Court, the justices quickly made it clear that they would take no such action (Helmke 2000a). As a result, Menem was left with no alternative but to hand over the presidency, as scheduled, in December 1999.

The robust nature of Argentine democracy becomes particularly striking when one takes into account the depth of the 1989–90 hyperinflationary crisis and the extent of the Menem government's economic reforms. Virtually none of the most radical economic reforms in post-1973 Latin America were undertaken in a context of full-fledged democracy. In Chile and Mexico, reforms were carried out under authoritarian regimes. In Peru, they were accompanied by an *autogolpe* in which the Congress and the judiciary were temporarily dissolved and the leading opponent of neoliberalism was forced into exile. Even in Bolivia, which is generally viewed as having maintained a democratic regime in the 1980s, orthodox stabilization was implemented via distinctly authoritarian mechanisms, including states of siege and harsh labor repression. By contrast, in democracies such as Costa Rica, Uruguay, Venezuela, and Brazil, economic reform was slower and less extensive. Placed in comparative perspective, then, Argentina combined radical reform and democracy in a way that was virtually unparalleled in Latin America: Among fully democratic cases, Argentina carried out the most rapid and far-reaching economic reforms; among cases of deep crisis and radical reform, Argentina was the most democratic.

PERONISM AND DEMOCRATIC GOVERNANCE

The relative success of Argentine democracy in the 1990s was rooted in a variety of factors.[7] Among these were the extraordinary failures of the 1976–83 dictatorship and the regime's collapse following the 1982 Falklands/Malvinas war, which broadly discredited military rule and weakened the armed forces vis-à-vis future civilian governments. A second factor was a fundamental change in elite and mass attitudes toward democracy. Prior to 1976, democracy had rarely, if ever, been the "only game in town" in

---

[6] In 1999, for example, the Supreme Court voted, for the first time, to limit executive discretion in issuing NUDs (Helmke 2000a: 21–2).
[7] For other explanations, see Palermo and Novaro (1996), Waisman (1999), and Peruzzotti (2001).

Argentina. Groups on both the right and the left had routinely flaunted democratic rules of the game, and at various times, conservative elites, Peronists, business leaders, and union bosses had all actively supported nondemocratic alternatives. In the post-1983 period, by contrast, an unprecedented elite consensus emerged around democratic rules of the game. Both the PJ and the CGT exhibited a steadfast commitment to democracy, particularly after the Renovation faction gained control of the party. Moreover, the disastrous military experience led many conservative and business elites to reassess the value of democracy, and for the first time in decades, many of them began to invest seriously in electoral politics (Gibson 1996). A similar change could be observed at the mass level. The violence and chaos of the 1973–6 period and the brutal repression of the dictatorship had a profound impact on mass attitudes toward democracy. Issues of human rights and democracy took on unprecedented salience among the electorate during the 1980s (Catterberg 1991: 82–4), and surveys found high levels of commitment to democracy throughout the 1990s (Lagos 2001: 139).

Yet Argentine democracy's capacity to survive both a hyperinflationary crisis and the implementation of radical economic reforms was also rooted in the continued political strength of Peronism. Given Peronism's historical association with regime instability, this outcome may seem somewhat surprising. Prior to the 1980s, key Peronist actors – including Perón himself – were weakly committed to liberal democratic institutions. Perhaps more importantly, Peronism and its labor allies were perceived as such a threat by economic and military elites that these elites resorted to proscribing Peronism from the electoral arena. This produced a highly unstable or "stalemated" party system dynamic (O'Donnell 1973: 166–97; Collier and Collier 1991: 721–42). Peronism's electoral strength was such that a lifting of the ban was almost certain to result in a Peronist victory, an outcome that key elite sectors found unacceptable. Yet Peronism's proscription proved to be equally destabilizing, for it left unions and the working class without representation in the party system. Consequently, labor and other Peronist groups frequently resorted to praetorian tactics – such as general strikes, large-scale protests, and factory takeovers – that undermined governability and at times threatened regimes (Cavarozzi 1986: 30–1; McGuire 1997). Without broad electoral bases or ties to labor, non-Peronist civilian governments tended to be weak. Governability was frequently undermined by labor protest, which left civilian governments vulnerable to military intervention (O'Donnell 1973, 1988; Collier and Collier 1991: 490–2, 738).

Peronism underwent two transformations after 1983 that fundamentally altered this dynamic. First, as noted previously, Peronist elites firmly committed themselves to democratic rules of the game. Second, as this book has shown, the PJ's subordination of organized labor and programmatic shift to the right allowed it to reconcile with the economic elite. Indeed, the Menem government's neoliberal policies gave business leaders an unprecedented stake in an elected – not to mention Peronist – government. As business magnate Jorge Born declared at the outset of the Menem presidency,

> For the first time in the century-old organization that I head, our destiny is linked tightly with that of the future government, or with the success or failure of a public administration.[8]

At the same time, the PJ maintained its alliance with organized labor. As Chapter 5 showed, the bulk of the labor movement continued to align itself with the PJ throughout the Menem presidency. Peronism's capacity to maintain labor support while at the same time protecting elite economic interests effectively ended the stalemated dynamic that had characterized Argentine politics since the 1940s. In essence, the party system was transformed from a stalemated system into an integrative system not unlike those of Mexico and Venezuela in the aftermath of labor incorporation (Collier and Collier 1991). Because such party systems have the capacity to represent (or control) organized labor and protect elite economic interest simultaneously, they have historically been associated with regime stability in Latin America (Collier and Collier 1991).

The shift from a stalemated to an integrative party system transformed the PJ from a source of regime instability into a source of regime stability. This could be seen in two ways in the 1990s. First, the PJ's strong working- and lower-class linkages facilitated the implementation of radical economic reforms that put an end to a regime-threatening hyperinflationary crisis. Second, the PJ's continued electoral success helped to stabilize the party system. Consequently, Argentina did not experience the kind of party system fragmentation, executive-legislative conflict, and neopopulist or antisystem candidacies seen in several other Latin American countries.

Party Strength and Economic Reform

During the 1990s, Argentina combined radical economic reform and democracy in a way that was virtually unparalleled in Latin America. The Menem government stabilized a hyperinflationary economy and carried out far-reaching liberalizing reforms without an authoritarian regime (as in Chile and Mexico), an *autogolpe* (as in Peru), or labor repression and states of siege (as in Bolivia). This outcome was made possible, in large part, by the PJ's linkages to the working and lower classes.[9] Peronism's capacity to maintain the support of many of the expected losers of neoliberal reforms was critical to successful reform implementation in a democratic context, for it

---

[8] Quoted in Chumbita (1989: 166).
[9] This argument has been made by Rodrik (1994), Cukierman and Tomassi (1998), and Levitsky and Way (1998). Rodrik (1994) calls this dynamic the "Nixon in China syndrome."

dampened antireform mobilization and limited those sectors' availability for antireform appeals.

The PJ's integrative capacity was most clearly seen with respect to organized labor. Labor mobilization had contributed to the failure of the Alfonsín government's "heterodox" stabilization policies in the 1980s. Yet the Menem government gained a remarkable degree of labor acquiescence to – and even cooperation with – a set of much more radical reforms (McGuire 1997: 226–41; Levitsky and Way 1998; Murillo 2000).[10] In stark contrast to the Alfonsín period, during which it led thirteen general strikes, the CGT did not lead a single general strike during Menem's first three and half years in office, and it led only one general strike during Menem's entire first term. Moreover, major unions in the electricity, telecommunications, oil, natural gas, and railroads sectors cooperated with the privatization of those sectors (Murillo 2000, 2001), and the CGT negotiated its support for the privatization of the pension system and reforms to flexibilize labor markets (Etchemendy and Palermo 1998).

There are several reasons why labor acquiesced to the Menem reforms.[11] These include sheer pragmatism in the face of hyperinflation, memories of the 1973–6 period (when labor mobilization contributed to the collapse of a Peronist government), substantial rank-and-file support for the reforms (Ranis 1995: 215–16), and the fact that unions extracted important organizational benefits in exchange for their support (Murillo 1997, 2000).[12] However, the most decisive factor may have been the unions' longstanding social, political, and organizational ties to Peronism (Levitsky and Way 1998). As Chapter 5 showed, most unions continued to participate actively in PJ politics during the Menem period. Of thirty-nine national unions surveyed by the author, twenty-four reported placing one of its members in the PJ leadership or the government in the 1990s. Several top unionists held posts in the PJ's national leadership when Menem took office, and dozens of others represented the party in Congress. Several others, including Luis Barrionuevo, Roberto Digón, and Jorge Triaca, gained positions in the Menem government. These overlapping leaderships gave much of the union leadership a stake in the government's success and an incentive to limit public opposition to Menem. Unions were also constrained by the persistence of strong Peronist identities among both local union leaders and rank-and-file

---

[10] Ex-President Alfonsín observed in 1990 that if he had adopted similar measures, he "would have been hanged from a lamppost in the Plaza de Mayo" (*La Prensa*, February 21, 1990, p. 5).

[11] See McGuire (1997: 226–38), Levitsky and Way (1998), and Murillo (1997, 2000, 2001).

[12] For example, unions such as the oil workers, light and power workers, telephone workers, and railway workers gained shares of newly privatized companies in exchange for their support for privatization. Similarly, in exchange for supporting the privatization of the pension system, major unions gained the right to participate in the newly privatized pension fund market.

workers. Finally, many unionists had close personal ties to PJ leaders. These ties, which were often forged during periods of shared adversity and struggle against military rule, enhanced union leaders' trust in the government and facilitated communication between union leaders and government officials. In so doing, they lengthened the unionists' time horizons and facilitated the negotiation of variety of deals – including both programmatic accords and individual side payments – that were critical to keeping many unions in the progovernment camp (Levitsky and Way 1998: 176–8).

Strong party–union ties limited the capacity of militant labor factions to mobilize opposition to the neoliberal reforms. During the initial reform period between 1989 and 1991, dissident unions led by former CGT General Secretary Saúl Ubaldini carried out a series of protests against privatization and other economic reforms. However, the bulk of the country's largest and most powerful unions refused to join them, and as a result, the protests failed to mobilize a large number of workers. Although two militant labor organizations, the Argentine Workers Congress (CTA) and Argentine Workers Movement (MTA), broke away from the official CGT and led repeated protests against the Menem government during the mid- and late-1990s, they, too, failed to build broad support within the labor movement.

A second way in which the PJ contributed to the implementation of neoliberal reforms in a democratic context was in its capacity to "contain" its traditional electorate, which meant that relatively few working- and lower-class voters were available for antireform appeals. In the early 1990s, several nationalist and left-of-center political forces explicitly targeted traditional Peronist voters with antireform appeals. These included dissident Peronists such as the Group of Eight and CGT leader Ubaldini, as well as ultranationalist coup leader Aldo Rico's Movement for Dignity and Independence (MODIN). Each of these appeals failed. In the critical 1991 midterm election, which constituted the first electoral test of the Menem reforms, Ubaldini's antireform gubernatorial candidacy in Buenos Aires received just 2 percent of the vote, and the Group of Eight failed to elect a single member to Congress. Although MODIN made modest inroads into the traditional Peronist electorate between 1991 and 1994 (López 1994: 25–35; Adrogué 1995: 49),[13] these gains were short-lived and were largely confined to the province of Buenos Aires[14]. The failure of antireform appeals forced opposition parties to rethink their strategies vis-á-vis the new economic model, and by the mid-1990s, both the UCR and the emerging FREPASO had accepted the fundamentals of the neoliberal model. This political–economic consensus, which was virtually unprecedented in modern Argentina, helped to ensure the consolidation of the Menem reforms.

---

[13] MODIN peaked at 9.2 percent of the vote the 1994 Constituent Assembly elections.
[14] In 1995, after Rico struck an alliance with the PJ, MODIN's share of the vote declined to less than 2 percent.

Party System Stability, Governability, and the Failure of Antisystem Appeals

The PJ's adaptation and subsequent electoral success also contributed to regime stability by helping to reequilibrate what had become an increasingly volatile party system. Although the Argentine party system never approached the level of fluidity observed in Peru and Venezuela, it entered the 1990s in a relatively fragile state. Traditional party identities had begun to erode, and Argentina's predominantly two-party system appeared to be in danger of collapse. Whereas the PJ and the UCR had accounted for 86.6 percent of the vote in the 1983 legislative elections and 80.2 percent of the vote in the 1987 legislative elections, by 1991, this figure had fallen to just 69.5 percent, and in the 1994 Constituent Assembly elections, it dropped to 59.3 percent (Fraga 1995: 34). Much of this decline was caused by the crisis of the UCR, which saw its share of the electorate fall from 52 percent in 1983 to just 17 percent in 1995. Yet surveys found that confidence in, and attachment to, political parties was declining across the board, and in the early and mid-1990s, Argentina was widely viewed as suffering a "crisis of representation" (Novaro 1994; Adrogúe 1995; Landi 1995). Indeed, in the early 1990s, the political space created by the decline of traditional party identities began to be filled by a variety of "outsiders," many of which espoused antiparty and even "anti-politics" views (Novaro 1994). Some of these outsiders were popular cultural figures, such as auto racer Carlos Reutemann and pop singer Palito Ortega. Others, such as former General Antonio Bussi and Aldo Rico, were former military officers with distinctly authoritarian profiles.

Yet Argentina did not follow the Peruvian or Venezuelan path toward party system decomposition during the 1990s. The PJ's continued dominance among the working- and lower-class electorate limited the space available for new parties. Indeed, the only new political force to establish itself during the 1990s, FREPASO, drew the bulk of its votes from the predominantly non-Peronist middle sectors (Gervasoni 1998b). After the UCR and FREPASO formed the Alliance for Jobs, Justice, and Education in 1997, the party system took on a two-party dynamic not altogether different from that of the early and mid-1980s: the predominantly working- and lower-class-based PJ versus the predominantly middle- and upper-middle-class-based Alliance. The PJ and the Alliance accounted for 81.9 percent of the vote in the 1997 midterm elections and 86.8 percent of the vote in the 1999 presidential election.[15]

The reequilibration of the party system contributed to democratic governance in at least two ways. First, it helped Argentina avoid a neopopulist authoritarian outcome of the kind that took place in Peru and Venezuela.

---

[15] The bulk of the remaining vote in the 1999 presidential election went to Domingo Cavallo of the center-right Action for the Republic.

In both Peru and Venezuela, authoritarian neopopulist leaders successfully appealed to lower-class voters who had abandoned established populist and left-wing parties (Roberts 1995; Weyland 1999). In Argentina, the PJ's continued electoral strength among working- and lower-class voters limited the space for such antisystem appeals, at least during the 1990s.[16] Outsider and antisystem candidates repeatedly failed to establish a national presence in the 1990s. The most successful antipolitical establishment outsider, Aldo Rico, peaked at just 9.2 percent of the vote in the 1994 Constituent Assembly election, faded quickly from the national political scene and eventually joined the PJ. Other potential neopopulists, including union leader Ubaldini, former military Governor Antonio Domingo Bussi, and former police commissioner Luis Patti, were even less successful, particularly at the national level.[17] In 1999, both of the leading presidential candidates – winner Fernando De la Rua and runner-up Eduardo Duhalde – were established party politicians, and career politicians captured virtually every one of the country's twenty-three governorships.

Second, the reequilibration of the party system helped Argentina avoid the kinds of governability crises that are frequently associated with weak parties and party system fragmentation (Mainwaring and Scully 1995). Most importantly, the PJ's continued electoral success provided the Menem government with the legislative support it needed to push through its reform agenda without bypassing (or closing down) the legislature. The PJ's majority in the Senate and near majority in the Chamber of Deputies ensured – with the help of small conservative and provincial parties – the relatively smooth passage of the bulk of the executive's most important legislative initiatives. In this way, the PJ's legislative strength prevented the kind of legislative gridlock that undermined reform efforts in countries such as Brazil, Ecuador, and Peru between 1990 and 1992. It also helped to limit executive–legislative conflict, which reduced the likelihood of an institutional crisis caused by a presidential attempt to bypass or shut down Congress, as occurred in Guatemala and Peru.

---

[16] This discussion suggests that characterizations of the Menem presidency as "neopopulist" (Roberts 1995; Weyland 1996, 1999) are somewhat off the mark. Indeed, the differences between the Argentine case and those of Peru under Fujimori, Brazil under Collor, or, more recently, Venezuela under Hugo Chavez are striking. First of all, notwithstanding his plebiscitarian rhetoric, Menem belonged to, worked with, and was generally supported by a powerful political party. As Chapter 7 showed, Menem's relationship to the Peronist rank and file was always mediated by strong, semi-autonomous local organizations, and these organizations provided the government with a range of political benefits. Second, as noted previously, the "delegative" nature of Argentine democracy – particularly in the second half of the 1990s – has often been overstated. Menem's capacity to circumvent or impose his will upon other branches of government never approached that of neopopulist presidents such as Chavez and Fujimori.

[17] Bussi was elected governor of Tucuman province in 1995 but faded soon thereafter.

THE COSTS OF PARTY ADAPTATION

Notwithstanding a variety of democratic deficiencies, Argentina preserved its core democratic institutions and avoided serious governability crises during the 1990s. Given the depth of the economic crisis and the radical nature of the Menem reforms, this was no small achievement. This chapter has argued that the PJ's capacity to undertake radical neoliberal reforms without rupturing its linkages to its traditional working- and lower-class constituencies were critical to these democratic successes. Peronism's ties to organized labor and working- and lower-class activists helped to limit popular sector mobilization against neoliberal reforms and prevent the growth of political forces that opposed the reforms. This enabled the Menem government to carry out rapid and far-reaching reforms without resorting to labor repression, an *autogolpe*, or other antidemocratic measures. Moreover, the PJ's survival as a major political force helped to stabilize the party system, which both limited the space available for antisystem appeals and helped to prevent the kind of executive–legislative deadlock that hindered reform efforts in countries with highly fragmented party systems. Indeed, one of the paradoxes of the Menem presidency is that, notwithstanding the government's clear lack of interest in strengthening democratic institutions, when Menem left office in 1999, Argentine democracy had perhaps never been more stable.

Yet the PJ's transformation also had several important costs for the quality, if not the stability, of Argentine democracy. First, the PJ's radical programmatic about-face undermined the quality of democratic representation. A severe disjuncture between platforms, voting, and public policy may be expected to erode citizens' trust in the responsiveness of political parties and the electoral system (Stokes 2001). Second, the PJ's increasing reliance on patronage and clientelism, together with ample evidence of corruption in the Menem government, further eroded the legitimacy of Argentina's democratic institutions. Public support for political parties, Congress, and the judiciary all declined over the course of the 1990s. Finally, the Menem reforms produced a degree of socioeconomic dislocation that was unprecedented in modern Argentina. Although radical neoliberalism did not harm the PJ's electoral performance during the 1990s, its long-term impact on working- and lower-class representation – and on democracy – remained questionable.

In a context of a growing economy and a Peronist government, as in the 1990s, the political costs of radical labor-based party adaptation were manageable. However, in a context of severe economic downturn, such as that faced by Menem's successor, Fernando De la Rua, these costs became more salient. Under De la Rua's Alliance government (1999–2001), Argentina fell into yet another round of political – economic crisis. After three consecutive years of recession, the economy collapsed in late 2001, resulting in a $140 billion debt default, a meltdown of the financial system, and an eventual descent into depression. The economic collapse was accompanied by a profound political crisis. Public anger at the established parties was made manifest in the October 2001 midterm elections, when the number of blank and spoiled ballots surpassed that of the governing Alliance.[18] Two months later, a massive wave of rioting, looting, and protest forced Fernando De la Rua to resign the presidency. The protests quickly transformed into a full-scale rebellion against the entire political elite. The public mood was crystalized in an extraordinary slogan: *que se vayan todos* ("throw everyone out"). When another round of mass protests led to the resignation of interim President Adolfo Rodriguez Saa barely a week after his election by Congress,[19] the country was thrown into a state of near anarchy. On January 1, 2002, Rodriguez Saa was replaced by PJ Senator Eduardo Duhalde, who became Argentina's third president in less than two weeks.

Duhalde presided over the worst economic collapse in Argentine history. The January 2002 repeal of the Convertibility Law resulted in a massive depreciation of the peso and triggered fears of a return to hyperinflation. With the government in default and the banking system paralyzed, and with United States and IMF unwilling to lend further assistance, the economy entered into a free fall. By mid-2002, a quarter of the workforce was unemployed, and the poverty rate had risen from 22 percent (in 1994) to nearly 50 percent.[20] As the economy descended into depression, Argentina's democratic institutions grew increasingly vulnerable. Public disaffection reached heights that threatened both the established party system and the democratic regime. Surveys revealed a strikingly high level of public hostility toward all of the existing political parties – and toward all politicians in general. A plethora of outsiders emerged as opponents to the political establishment and ascended in the polls, raising the specter of a full-scale party system collapse. Moreover, rumors of a military coup and reports of meetings between military officials and business leaders suggested that, for the first time in more than a decade, democracy itself might be at risk.[21] Although the regime remained intact as of mid-2002, Argentina's democratic future once again appeared uncertain.

The 2001–2 crisis was neither a direct nor an inevitable product of Menemism. The roots of the crisis were primarily economic. A series of external shocks, particularly the Asian and Russian financial crises of 1997–8

---

[18] In the Federal Capital and Santa Fe, the number of blank and spoiled ballots surpassed that of all parties.
[19] Rodriguez Saa was elected by Congress because the vice presidency had been vacant since October 2000, when FREPASO leader Carlos "Chacho" Álvarez resigned the vice presidency in protest over the government's failure to investigate vigorously allegations of bribery in the Senate.
[20] *Clarín*, May 10, 2002.
[21] See *Página 12*, February 25–8, 2002.

and the Brazilian devaluation of 1999, together with the monetary and exchange rate constraints imposed by the Convertibility system, threw Argentina into a recessionary trap from which the De la Rua government was unable to escape. The sustained collapse of the banking system and the absence of any kind of international rescue package allowed the economy to sink to a level of depression that had historically destroyed all but the world's strongest democracies. Had Argentina experienced even slow to moderate growth between 1998 and 2001, it is doubtful that the political system would have fallen into crisis.

Yet the 2001–2 crisis cannot be understood entirely apart from the Peronist transformation. The December 2001 political rebellion revealed both the continued weakness of Argentina's political institutions and a profound crisis of representation. Although Menemism did not cause either of these problems, the PJ's programmatic reversal, its extensive use of patronage and clientelism, and the severe socioeconomic dislocation caused by the Menem reforms eroded public trust in representative institutions and widened the gap between citizens and party elites, which almost certainly accentuated them.

The Peronist transformation was thus double-edged in terms of its consequences for democracy. During the 1990s, the PJ's adaptation and survival were critical to party system stability and democratic governance. Yet radical programmatic and coalitional change did not come cost free. A major legacy of Menemism was a growing disjuncture between Argentine citizens and the political elite. In a context of a severe economic downturn, this disjuncture gave rise to a political crisis whose ultimate regime consequences are – at the time of this writing – still unfolding.

CHAPTER 9

Crisis, Party Adaptation, and Democracy: Argentina in Comparative Perspective

The 1980s and 1990s constituted a new critical juncture in Latin American politics. Changes in the international economy, the exhaustion of statist economic models, and evolving class structures limited the viability of economic policies and political coalitions that had once predominated in the region, and new policy agendas and coalitions moved from the margins to the center of the political stage. As the ISI model entered into a terminal crisis, the labor-mobilizing parties that for decades had been the "fulcrum" of party systems in Argentina, Chile, Mexico, Peru, and Venezuela (Collier and Collier 1991: 40) were confronted with a fundamental challenge. The increased political and economic difficulties associated with traditional statist policies and the diminishing benefits associated with union support created a strong incentive for these parties to change course. For governing labor-based parties, the costs of nonadaptation were potentially very high: Failed strategies could lead to profound economic crisis and party collapse. The parties did not bear these costs alone. Where Latin American labor-based parties failed in the 1980s and 1990s, party systems often fragmented and decomposed, and some democratic regimes weakened and even broke down. Thus, labor-based party adaptation was critical not only to the political success of the parties themselves, but also to the performance and stability of democratic regimes.

This book has examined the capacity of labor-based parties to adapt to the opportunities and constraints posed by changing electoral and economic environments. It has suggested that a dimension of party organization that is generally viewed as detrimental to party success – low institutionalization – may, in a context of crisis, be beneficial to parties. Although the weak routinization of party rules and procedures often results in inefficiency and disorder, it also increases organizational flexibility, which can be critical to party survival. The book argued that mass populist parties may hold a distinct advantage over social democratic, communist, and other labor-based parties in terms of their capacity to adapt to the contemporary challenges of economic liberalization and working-class decline. On the one hand, strong roots in society provide mass populist parties with an important degree of electoral stability. On the other hand, key legacies of populism – such as fluid internal structures, autonomous leaderships, and nonbureaucratic hierarchies – provide them with a degree of strategic flexibility not found in many other mass parties.

The book explored the relationship between party structure and adaptive capacity in the case of the Argentine PJ, a mass populist party that combined a powerful base-level organization with a fluid internal structure. After showing that traditional Peronism was poorly equipped to survive in an environment characterized by working-class decline and the crisis of ISI, the study traced the coalitional and programmatic changes undertaken by the party in the 1980s and 1990s. In the coalitional realm, the weakly routinized nature of the party–union linkage facilitated the dismantling of traditional mechanisms of labor participation, which permitted the PJ's rapid transformation from a de facto labor party into a predominantly patronage-based party. In the programmatic realm, the PJ's fluid hierarchy permitted the entry and rise of reformers, facilitated the removal of old-guard leaders, and encouraged the defection of non-Menemists to the pro-Menem camp. Moreover, the weakness of the PJ's formal leadership bodies enhanced President Menem's autonomy as he devised and carried out a set of radical policy changes. Although many PJ leaders and activists would have preferred a more limited or gradual reform, they lacked effective mechanisms through which to challenge Menem. The Menem government's success in stabilizing the economy, combined with Peronism's stable base among the working and lower classes, helped the PJ win four straight national elections between 1989 and 1995. This political success contributed in an important way to regime stability, for it enhanced democratic governance, helped to stabilize the party system, and limited the availability of working- and lower-class voters for antisystem appeals.

COMPARATIVE EVIDENCE FROM LATIN AMERICA

The central arguments of this book may be further illustrated with reference to the experiences of other historically labor-based parties in Latin America. Six of the major labor-mobilizing parties that emerged during the populist period in Mexico and South America (Collier and Collier 1991; Roberts 1997b) survived into the 1980s. In addition to the PJ, these include Democratic Action (AD) in Venezuela, the Chilean Socialist (PSCh) and Communist (PCCh) parties, the American Popular Revolutionary Alliance (APRA) in Peru, and the Institutional Revolutionary Party (PRI) in Mexico.[1]

---

[1] Although the Bolivian Revolutionary Nationalist Movement (MNR) might also be considered a historically labor-based party, it is not included here because its links to the labor movement

The following section examines these parties' responses to the challenges of economic crisis and working-class decline, the electoral consequences of those responses, and the impact of successful or failed labor-based party adaptation on party system and regime stability in Venezuela, Peru, Chile, and Mexico.

Party organization is, of course, not the only factor that shaped labor-based party responses to the neoliberal challenge. Factors such as the depth of economic crises, the timing of the initial reform attempts, whether or not the labor-based party was in power at the time, the structure of party competition, and the choices of individual leaders all played an important role in determining both parties' strategies and their success or failure in carrying them out (Corrales 2000; Burgess and Levitsky 2003). Nevertheless, comparative evidence from Latin America appears to support the hypothesis that loosely structured labor-based parties – such as those of populist origins – are better equipped to adapt to external shocks than are highly routinized parties. Whereas the most highly routinized parties in the sample, AD and the PCCh, largely failed to adapt and suffered steep electoral decline in the 1990s, the less bureaucratic PSCh and PRI underwent substantial adaptation and experienced at least moderate electoral success. Although APRA also possessed substantial adaptive capacity, its centralized leadership pursued an ill-fated populist strategy that had devastating electoral consequences.

Venezuela

Perhaps the clearest contrast to the PJ case is that of AD in Venezuela. Though similar to the PJ in that it was historically a mass party with close ties to labor (Martz 1966; Coppedge 1994: 27–30), AD was – at least through the 1990s – highly routinized. Whereas the PJ hierarchy is fluid and characterized by substantial turnover, the AD hierarchy was bureaucratic and characterized by the entrenchment of an oligarchic leadership (Martz 1992: 102; Corrales 1997: 98–9).[2] As a result, leadership turnover was relatively low.[3] In addition, whereas PJ leadership bodies lack independent authority and are generally unable to constrain office-holding leaders, AD leadership

---

eroded within a few years of its ascent to power in 1952. Although remnants of the Brazilian Labor Party (PTB) existed in the 1980s and 1990s, the post-1964 military regime effectively destroyed the labor-based party that emerged in the 1940s.

[2] Due to the strength and stability of the party bureaucracy, AD does not experience bandwagoning toward office-holding leaders. According to Coppedge (1994), when AD is in power, the party leadership tends to divide into "ins" (allies of the president) and "outs" (internal opponents). Yet unlike the PJ, in which bandwagoning to the president's faction almost invariably depletes the ranks of the "outs," in AD, the "outs" tend to be stronger than the "ins" (Coppedge 1994: 122–8).

[3] The bureaucracy's "iron control over internal promotions and nominations... blocks the entrance of new blood into the party leadership" (Corrales 1997: 98).

bodies such as the National Executive Committee (CEN) were infused with substantial authority, which limited the strategic autonomy of office-holding leaders. The CEN met weekly, possessed an elaborate (and stable) set of internal rules and operating procedures, and was widely accepted as the primary locus of decision making among party leaders (Martz 1992: 112; Coppedge 1994: 11, 20–1). Although the CEN traditionally granted sitting AD presidents substantial policy-making autonomy (Coppedge 1994: 78), several mechanisms existed to hold presidents accountable to the party. For example, office-holding leaders were forced to resign from the party hierarchy, which meant that they lost direct control over the party bureaucracy (Coppedge 1994: 123). Moreover, sitting presidents met weekly with the CEN, and the CEN, not the president, controlled the party's legislative agenda (Coppedge 1994: 66–7). The AD party structure thus discouraged personalistic leadership. As Coppedge writes, AD leaders must "seek consensus among their colleagues in the national leadership, and if they don't, their initiatives often fail" (1988: 166). The CEN and other party organs also exerted tight discipline over lower-level leaders and cadres. Unlike the PJ, AD routinely expelled cadres who broke ranks with the leadership (Coppedge 1994: 66).

Finally, whereas the PJ–union linkage is informal and fluid, the AD-labor linkage was highly routinized. Beginning in the 1940s, unions gained an "institutionalized presence within the party" through Labor Bureaus within local, state, and national party leaderships (Burgess 1998: 259–60; also Martz 1966: 157–67). Through the 1990s, the national Labor Bureau had a fixed membership, clear rules for functioning, and regularized meetings (Martz 1966: 157; Coppedge 1988: 169–70). It automatically placed representatives on party leadership bodies at the local, state, and national levels, and it was guaranteed large quotas of delegates to the party congress and electoral college (Ellner 1993: 79; Burgess 1998: 259). These arrangements allowed the Labor Bureau to play a "pivotal role in the internal affairs of AD" (Ellner 1989: 103). Thus, union leaders enjoyed "meaningful input into party policies" (Burgess 1998: 261), regularized access to legislative candidacies,[4] and a "virtual veto power over presidential nominations" (Ellner 1993: 92).

AD confronted an environmental challenge in the 1980s that was in many ways similar to that which the PJ faced.[5] In the programmatic realm, long-term stagnation and fiscal crisis, in the context of the debt crisis and declining oil prices, brought the country to "the brink of hyperinflation and economic collapse" in the late 1980s (Naím 1993: 44; also Corrales 1996b: 118–28). In the coalitional realm, both AD and its allies in the Venezuelan Workers

---

[4] According to Burgess, an "unwritten pact" granted unionists between fifteen to twenty seats in each Congress (1998: 260).
[5] On the similarities between the AD and PJ cases, see Corrales (2000, 2002).

Confederation (CTV) had grown increasingly detached from the growing urban informal sector and emerging urban social movements (Ellner 1993: 89; 1996: 97; 1999: 82).

Yet, unlike the PJ, AD responded slowly and ineffectively to these challenges. Whereas the PJ experienced a substantial leadership renovation in the 1980s, the AD hierarchy "gradually ossified," as "ranking officials closed the doors to entry by younger figures" (Martz 1992: 120) and an oligarchy of old-guard leaders – known as the *cogollo* – entrenched itself in power (Coppedge 1994: 49; Corrales 1997: 99). The old-guard leadership responded slowly to the economic crisis of the 1980s. Between 1984 and 1988, the AD government of Jaime Lusinchi adopted a mild heterodox strategy that entailed no major liberalizing reforms (McCoy 1986; Coppedge 1994: 81–3). Although Lusinchi's successor, Carlos Andres Pérez, launched a far-reaching reform program in 1989, the reforms were strongly resisted, both by the AD leadership and by much of Venezuelan society. Unlike the PJ case, in which bandwagoning allowed Menem to gain control of the party after he took office, the CEN remained firmly in the hands of the old-guard *cogollo*. The CEN refused to grant Pérez the freedom from party discipline traditionally granted to AD presidents (Corrales 1997: 97), and the CEN-controlled legislative bloc stalled much of the Pérez reform program in the legislature (Corrales 1996b: 237). In 1991, the anti-Pérez Orthodox faction gained control the party, awarding nine of the ten most powerful CEN posts to Pérez opponents (Corrales 1997: 97). From that point onward, AD "began to behave like the principal opposition party," openly attacking government policies and ultimately forcing Pérez to abandon the bulk of his program (Corrales 1996b: 204, 251–8). Thus, according to Corrales, AD opposition was "the principal reason why Pérez was unable to complete his reform program" (1997: 94).

AD also adapted slowly in the coalitional realm. Not only did the Labor Bureau remain intact throughout the 1980s, but union influence in the party actually *increased* over the course of the decade (Coppedge 1988: 170; Ellner 1989: 98–104; 1993: 79),[6] raising fears in some party quarters that AD was becoming a "labor party" (Ellner 1993: 79). Labor continued to exert substantial influence over party strategy in the 1990s. For example, after Pérez's neoliberal turn, the Labor Bureau used its influence in the party to block key labor market reforms in the legislature (Burgess 1998: 290–2). The stickiness of the party–labor alliance limited AD's capacity to appeal to the growing urban informal sector in the 1980s and 1990s. AD's detachment from the urban poor was made manifest by the February 1989 *Caracazo* riots, which took the AD-dominated CTV "completely... by surprise" (Ellner 1993: 89). Although AD reformed its nomination process in 1991 to strengthen territorial structures at the expense of labor (Ellner 1996: 97), the party never

---

[6] There was a "steady increase" in the number of unionists elected to Congress in the 1970s and 1980s (Ellner 1989: 108–9).

fully abandoned its corporatist structure or appealed successfully to urban marginals.

AD paid a steep electoral price for its failure to adapt. After winning 53 percent of the presidential vote in 1988, AD fell to just 23 percent in 1993, and in 1998, the party trailed so badly in the polls that it withdrew its presidential candidate.[7] AD's electoral decline was accompanied by the decomposition of the Venezuelan party system and the deconsolidation of the democratic regime. The erosion of mass support for the established parties, particularly among lower-sector voters, created an opening for antisystemic political appeals. In 1992, the democratic regime was shaken by two coup attempts, the first of which was led by charismatic junior military officer Hugo Chavez. Six years later, Chavez was elected president with massive popular sector support. In 1999, President Chavez dissolved the 1961 constitution and the legislature via referendum. "Mega elections" held the following year gave Chavez control over virtually all of Venezuela's national-level political institutions. Chavez's concentration of power polarized Venezuelan politics, and in April 2002, a military coup nearly removed Chavez from power. As of mid-2002, the future of Venezuelan democracy was very much in doubt.

Peru

Peru's APRA is another case of failed party adaptation and regime instability. Although APRA possessed substantial adaptive capacity, its centralized leadership pursued what proved to be a highly ineffective strategy in the 1980s. APRA's organizational structure differed somewhat from that of the PJ. Created in opposition, APRA developed a structured and disciplined organization (Graham 1990: 80). Nevertheless, the party maintained clear populist features, particularly a centralized and personalistic leadership. Founder and long-time leader Victor Raúl Haya de la Torre enjoyed charismatic authority over the party (North 1973: 178–86; Graham 1990: 80–1). Largely unconstrained by internal norms of accountability to party organs, Haya was able to impose a series of radical strategic changes on APRA in the 1950s and 1960s, including the abandonment of its Marxist and anti-oligarchic program in favor of alliances with conservatives such as Manuel Prado and ex-dictator Manuel Odría. Hence, although APRA was better routinized and more bureaucratic than the PJ, the centralized authority patterns that emerged around Haya's populist leadership arguably gave the party greater adaptive capacity than AD.

APRA confronted serious coalitional and programmatic challenges in the 1980s, although these challenges differed in some respects from those faced

---

[7] AD won 22 percent of the vote in the 1998 legislative elections.

by the other parties under consideration here. In the coalitional realm, due to APRA's conservative shift in the 1950s and 1960s, as well as the efforts of the 1968–75 military regime to weaken it, APRA's working-class base was substantially eroded in the 1960s and 1970s. The military regime's active support for the communist-led Peruvian General Workers Confederation (CGTP) and creation of alternative channels for popular participation left APRA with only a minimal presence in the labor movement (Sanborn 1989: 94–7; Graham 1992: 40–57). By the late 1970s, the pro-APRA Peruvian Workers Confederation (CTP) had been reduced to a handful of unions, and rapidly growing leftist movements had made substantial inroads into the urban working- and lower-class electorate (Sanborn 1989: 94–9; Roberts 1998a: 203–17). APRA's mass base was further eroded by the expansion of the urban informal sector, which constituted approximately 50 percent of the economically active population by the late 1980s (Roberts 1998a: 240).

In the programmatic realm, although APRA came to power in 1985 in the context of the deepening debt crisis, two factors weakened the incentive for the party to pursue market-oriented reforms. The first factor was timing. When APRA won the presidency in 1985, no regional consensus had yet emerged around orthodox responses to the debt crisis. In fact, few democratic governments in Latin America had successfully undertaken neoliberal reforms, and governments in Argentina, Brazil, and Venezuela were in the midst of heterodox experiments. In addition, Peru's poor economic performance in the early 1980s was widely associated with the IMF-style austerity program implemented by the government of Fernando Belaúnde (Cameron 1994: 42), rather than with populist or heterodox policies. Second, APRA's strategic choices were powerfully shaped by party competition. In contrast to the Argentine and Venezuelan cases, APRA's willingness to undertake a market-oriented shift in the 1980s was conditioned by the existence of a strong electoral challenge from the left (Sanborn 1989; Cotler 1995: 343). The Marxist United Left (IU) easily defeated APRA in the poorest districts of Lima in both 1980 and 1983 (Graham 1992: 175), and in 1983, IU leader Alfonso Barrantes was elected mayor of Lima, which made him a serious contender for the presidency in 1985. For APRA, then, a neoliberal turn could be expected to have severe electoral costs.

APRA responded in a vigorous, but ultimately inappropriate, manner to these challenges. Following Haya's death in 1979 and the party's poor performance in the 1980 presidential election, APRA underwent a substantial leadership renovation. Alan García, a young and charismatic leader, consolidated centralized control over the party after being elected general secretary in 1982. Like Haya, García "had supreme authority and few channels of accountability back to the bases" (Sanborn 1991: 345). This authority allowed him to impose two important strategic changes on the party. First, in the coalitional realm, García ceded the labor movement to the IU and instead targeted the urban informal poor (Sanborn 1989: 111–12; Graham 1992: 169–90; Cameron 1994: 42–6). Second, in the programmatic realm, García shifted APRA to the left. In an effort to compete with the IU, García adopted a staunchly antineoliberal profile, railing against the IMF and calling for limits on debt payments (Sanborn 1989: 110–13; Graham 1992: 90). These strategies were initially successful. APRA won massive support among the urban poor in the 1985 presidential election, propelling García to an easy victory (Cameron 1994: 43).

In power, García continued his strategy of building support among the urban poor. Like Carlos Menem, President García enjoyed substantial programmatic autonomy, often making major policy decisions without consulting the APRA leadership (Sanborn 1989: 118; Graham 1990: 88, 92). Yet unlike Menem, García continued his left-leaning strategy after taking office. In his inaugural address, García announced that the government would limit its debt payments to 10 percent of its export earnings. He also embarked upon a Keynesian reactivation program that included salary increases, job-creation projects, and a variety of social welfare programs (Tanteleán 1989: 203–4; Graham 1992: 101–4). In 1987, without consulting the party leadership, García nationalized the banking system (Sanborn 1989: 118; Graham 1992: 113). The left-leaning strategy proved disastrous. The bank nationalization destroyed the government's relationship with the private sector, which, together with the Peru's increasing alienation from the international financial community and the depletion of foreign reserves produced by the government's reactivation policies, threw the country into a deep fiscal crisis. In his final two years in office, García ignored pleas from party leaders to undertake an orthodox adjustment, and Peru descended into a hyperinflationary crisis (Pastor and Wise 1992; Cotler 1995: 346; Burgess 2000: 16).

Having presided over one of the deepest economic crises in Peruvian history, APRA's electoral fortunes plummeted. From a high of 53 percent of the presidential vote in 1985, APRA fell to 23 percent in 1990 and just 4 percent in 1995.[8] As in Venezuela, APRA's collapse was accompanied by the decomposition of the party system, which paved the way for Alberto Fujimori's successful outsider candidacy in 1990. Fujimori's strongest support was drawn from among the urban poor, much of which had backed APRA and the left in the 1980s (Cameron 1994; Roberts 1995: 95). In April 1992, Fujimori carried out a successful *autogolpe*, which paved the way for nearly a decade of authoritarian rule (Cameron 1997; Levitsky and Cameron 2003).

---

[8] APRA received less than 2 percent of the vote in the 2000 presidential election. The party experienced a modest revival with García's return in 2001, winning 26 percent of the presidential vote and 20 percent of the legislative vote.

Chile

Chile offers a more successful case of labor-based party adaptation. The Chilean Socialist (PSCh) and Communist (PCCh) parties, which had constituted one of the strongest and most radicalized leftist movements in Latin America in the 1960s and 1970s, faced a fundamental set of challenges in the aftermath of the sixteen-year military dictatorship led by Augusto Pinochet.[9] The military regime had dramatically reshaped the economic and electoral environment in Chile. For one, the Pinochet government's neoliberal reforms and restrictive labor laws severely weakened organized labor, and as a result, the level of unionization fell from 32 percent in the early 1970s to less than 10 percent in the mid-1980s (Roberts 1998a: 115; Barrett 2001: 569). At the same time, the success of the neoliberal economic model reduced public support for statist policies. Moreover, the strength of the outgoing regime enabled it to dictate many of the terms of the democratic transition, which resulted in the persistence of "reserved domains" of military and right-wing power that would limit the policy-making autonomy of future left-of-center governments (Valenzuela 1992). These conditions, together with a new electoral system in which only two legislative candidates were elected per district, created an incentive to adopt a more moderate and catch-all appeal. Not only were traditional leftist policies unlikely to garner substantial electoral support, but given the continued power of the military and the right, the pursuit of such policies also risked undermining the fragile democratic transition.

The Chilean left's response to these changes provides further evidence of an inverse relationship between party routinization and adaptive capacity. The PCCh and PSCh responded to the neoliberal challenge in strikingly different ways, and research by Kenneth Roberts (1998a) suggests that these diverging strategies can be attributed, in part, to differences in party structure. The PCCh is a "highly structured and institutionalized" party with "a well-developed bureaucracy" (Roberts 1998a: 47). It maintains "an extensive party apparatus and a highly developed cellular structure," and the party hierarchy is "capable of imposing a range of sanctions...on militants who violate disciplinary norms" (Roberts 1994: 20). According to Roberts, this structure limited the PCCh's capacity to innovate in the face of environmental change (1994: 19–27; 1998a: 47–50). The party's rigid structure "screened out innovative or 'heretical' ideas that emanated from external sources while suppressing the emergence of such ideas from within the party itself" (1994: 27). As a result, the PCCh maintained a Marxist program into the 1990s, staunchly opposing the neoliberal model (Roberts 1994: 16–18; McCarthy 1997: 23–4). It also opted to "bunker down with its core constituencies"

---

[9] For a detailed analysis of the challenges facing the Chilean left in the 1980s, see Roberts (1998a).

(Roberts 1998a: 159), maintaining close ties to organized labor and making little effort to appeal to a broader constituency (McCarthy 1997). The result was political marginalization and electoral decline (Roberts 1998a: 134–5, 159). After peaking at 16.2 percent of the vote in 1973, the PCCh vote fell to just 3.2 percent in 1999.

By contrast, the less routinized PSCh and its sister party, the Party for Democracy (PPD), adapted more successfully to the neoliberal challenge. The PSCh, whose origins in the 1930s were populist (Drake 1978), was a "loosely structured party organization" with relatively "lax disciplinary norms" (Roberts 1998a: 48). As a result, it tends to be a "very open, dynamic, and flexible party, with a high predisposition to change and adapt" (Roberts 1994: 22). Unlike the PCCh, the PSCh underwent a far-reaching leadership and ideological renovation in the 1980s. It absorbed a range of new political and economic ideas that enabled it to shed its Marxist profile in favor of a more social democratic orientation (Roberts 1994). The party also loosened its ties to organized labor in favor of a more middle-class-oriented, catch-all strategy (McCarthy 1997; Roberts 1998b: 10).[10]

The adaptive process was even more pronounced in the PPD, which was created by the PSCh in 1988 to campaign against Pinochet in the plebiscite that brought an end to authoritarian rule. The PPD is "essentially a party of notables" with "few roots in the labor movement" and "little base-level organization to speak of" (Roberts 1998b: 10). The party's lack of a real bureaucracy or trade union ties permits rapid leadership turnover and substantial leadership autonomy (Plumb 1998: 101; Roberts 1998b: 10). The PPD adapted even more extensively than the PSCh in the 1990s. Adopting a media-based, issue-oriented strategy (Plumb 1998: 95–9), the party "quickly carved out an independent niche as a progressive but non-ideological catch-all party that appealed to a broad range of unaffiliated moderate leftists and secular centrists" (Roberts 1998a: 138). Lacking any "institutional legacies, traditions, rituals or other anchors with the past limiting its freedom of movement" (Plumb 1998: 101), the PPD erased its socialist heritage in favor of a more "post-materialist" appeal (Plumb 1998: 96–8).

Both the PSCh and PPD were relatively successful in the electoral arena in the 1990s. In addition to forming part of the governing Democratic Concertation, the parties earned a combined 24 percent of the vote in both the 1993 and the 1997 elections, which is more than double the average Socialist vote during the 1957–73 period (Roberts 1998b: 16). In 2000, PPD leader Ricardo Lagos was elected president. The PSCh/PPD's successful adaptation contributed both to the stability of the party system and to its shift from polarized pluralism to a more moderate and consensus-based multiparty

---

[10] According to Roberts, PSCh "made a transition from a class-mass party to a...catch all professional-electoral party" that has "largely ceased to encapsulate popular sectors within its ranks" (1998b: 10).

system (Scully 1995). Both of these outcomes have been associated with Chile's regime stability in the 1990s (Scully 1996: 102–5; Roberts 1997a).

Mexico

Finally, the Mexican PRI is a case of moderately successful adaptation. Although it is less personalistic than other Latin American mass populist parties, the PRI shares important populist features, including a strong element of working-class and peasant mobilization from above (Collier and Collier 1991). Notwithstanding its name and image, the PRI was never highly routinized. The PRI's formative period was relatively unstable. The party originated in 1929 as the Revolutionary National Party (PNR), which largely served as a personal vehicle for Plutarco Calles (Collier and Collier 1991: 225–6). In 1938, President Lázaro Cárdenas dissolved the PNR and replaced it with the Party of the Mexican Revolution (PRM). Cárdenas replaced the PNR's territorial structure with a corporatist structure based on labor, peasant, and popular "sectors" (Garrido 1984: 239–51). Eight years later, the PRM was transformed into the PRI. Although the sector system remained intact, the party hierarchy was restructured, leadership was centralized, and union influence was reduced (Pacheco 1991: 78).

Between the 1940s and the 1970s, the PRI's internal structure became more routinized. Although the organization was largely informal, and although the ambiguities in the party statutes provide the National Executive Committee (usually dominated by the sitting president) with substantial discretionary power (Langston 1996: 7–9), a relatively stable set of internal rules, procedures, and norms emerged (Langston 1996: 2–10). The sector system became entrenched, and labor enjoyed stable representation in the party leadership and a steady quota of legislative candidacies through the 1980s (Middlebrook 1995: 101–4). Efforts to dismantle the sector system, such as party president Carlos Madrazo's proposal to replace it with direct primaries in the mid-1960s, were fiercely and successfully resisted by labor (Hernández 1991: 225; Zamitíz 1991: 123). Nevertheless, as elections became competitive in the 1980s, the informal rules of the game that had structured intraparty life since the 1940s began to unravel (Pacheco 1991: 81–3; Langston 1996, 2001). Thus, the PRI may be said to have *deinstitutionalized* in the 1980s.

Two features of the PRI organization contributed to its strategic flexibility in the 1980s and 1990s. First, its leadership was highly centralized (Burgess 2000: 20). Thus, the CEN, which was always dominated by the sitting president, had a substantial degree of discretion in setting (and modifying) intraparty rules, selecting (and removing) party leaders, and imposing candidates (Langston 1996: 7–9). Indeed, according to Langston, "discretion of the president" was traditionally the "rule of the day" (1996: 17). Second, the party hierarchy was nonbureaucratic. Due to the combination of a powerful presidency, the absence of tenure security or stable career paths, and the impossibility of presidential reelection, presidential successions tended to generate significant leadership turnover in the party hierarchy. Incoming presidents regularly "housecleaned" the party hierarchy and stacked it with allies from their own *camarilla*, or patronage network. At times, the new leaders brought in as part of these housecleanings lacked long careers in the party hierarchy, as was the case with Luis Donaldo Colosio, whom President Carlos Salinas imposed as party president in 1989. Hence, the PRI was not characterized by entrenched oligarchies in the party hierarchy, but rather was open to far-reaching leadership renovation. Consequently, despite its "bureaucratic" image, there was reason to expect the PRI to be relatively flexible and open to change.

The PRI differs from the other cases under consideration here in that, in addition to confronting serious programmatic and coalitional challenges, it was also compelled to adapt to a context of political liberalization and increasingly competitive elections (Collier 1992, 1999). The simultaneous nature of these challenges generated important internal contradictions and trade-offs for the party (Collier 1992, 1999). For example, the Salinas government's emphasis on economic liberalization was accompanied by a degree of retrenchment in the area of political liberalization, which may ultimately have had electoral costs for the party.

The PRI was relatively successful in adapting to these multiple challenges (Burgess 2000: 6–10). This was particularly the case in the programmatic realm, as the PRI abandoned its commitment to ISI and oversaw a substantial liberalization of the Mexican economy. This process began under President Miguel De la Madrid (1982–8) and was accelerated and deepened under the presidency of Salinas (1988–94). The Salinas reforms – which included trade liberalization, an opening up to foreign investment, the deregulation and privatization of several major industries, the reprivatization of commercial banks, and a constitutional reform permitting the sale of communal lands – culminated in Mexico's entry into the North American Free Trade Agreement (NAFTA) in 1994. Despite resistance by organized labor and many old-guard PRI leaders, Salinas was able to bring a substantial number of technocrats into the government and party leadership and – taking advantage of the PRI's centralized leadership – impose the reforms on the party. The economic reforms were quite successful. Inflation was substantially reduced, and both foreign investment and economic growth picked up considerably.

The PRI was less successful in the coalitional realm. By the 1980s, it was clear that long-term social structural changes had eroded the vote-mobilizing capacity of the PRI's corporatist sector-based system (Hernández 1991: 224–5; Collier 1992: 136). The decline in support for the PRI among the emerging middle and urban informal sectors was made manifest in 1988, when it suffered a striking electoral decline in urban centers such as the

Federal District (Collier 1992: 75, 118; Langston 1996: 10–13). The 1988 debacle triggered a major intraparty reform initiative led by Salinas and Colosio. Convinced that the sector system had been the primary cause of the PRI's poor performance, the reformers sought to "restructure the PRI around a territorial base" (Langston 1996: 12–14). The PRI's "territorialization" was, together with the National Solidarity Program, aimed at establishing a stronger presence among the urban poor (Hernández 1991: 229–31). The move away from a corporatist structure was also aimed at creating a party that was "more centrally based in the growing urban middle classes" (Collier 1992: 120; also Hernández 1991: 225). These efforts came to fruition in the PRI's fourteenth National Assembly in 1990. The Assembly passed several reforms that weakened labor's influence, including the establishment of individual membership (rather than collective membership through the sectors), the elimination of sectoral representation in the party leadership, and the strengthening of territorial representation (Hernández 1991: 242; Langston 1996: 14–15). These initiatives met fierce resistance from labor, however. Union leaders blocked the proposed dismantling of the sector system and obtained a quota of 15 percent of the delegates to the party congress (Hernández 1991: 237; Zamítiz 1991: 124; Middlebrook 1995: 305). Three years later, the party congress reestablished sectoral representation in the leadership (Burgess 1998: 151), and by 1994, "the basic contours of the organizational and political bargains between [labor] and the PRI had been restored" (1998: 153). Although the percentage of legislative candidacies awarded to unions declined from 25 percent in 1982 to 16 percent in 1991 (Alarcón-Olguín 1994: 18), labor's legislative representation remained roughly on par with what it had been in the 1960s (Middlebrook 1995: 103). The PRI never fully recovered its urban electoral base. Hence, whereas Salinas could take credit for far-reaching economic reforms when he left office, the party "had hardly been successful in consolidating a middle class or an informal-sector constituency" (Collier 1999: 234).

The economic recovery associated with the Salinas reforms enabled the PRI to make important gains in the 1991 legislative elections. However, these gains proved short-lived. The PRI vote declined steadily over the course of the 1990s, and the PRI suffered an unprecedented defeat in the 2000 presidential elections. Although this decline was to some extent a product of the 1994–5 economic crisis and the parties' failure to appeal to new urban voters, the PRI's electoral performance in the 1990s must be understood in the context of political liberalization. Not only were elections much fairer in the 1990s than they had been in previous decades, but much of the anti-PRI vote reflected opposition to authoritarian rule, rather than opposition to the government's economic program (Dominguez and McCann 1995). Given the dual political-economic crisis faced by the Mexican regime beginning in the early 1980s, the fact that the PRI continued to win elections through 1997, and that it remained a leading political force in 2000, suggests at least

TABLE 9.1. *Electoral Performance of Six Latin American Labor-Based Parties in the 1980s and 1990s (Lower House Legislative Elections)*

Labor-based/populist party	1980s[a]	1990s	Absolute change	Relative change
Justicialista Party (PJ)	40.7	39.2	−1.5	−3.7
Chilean Socialist Party (PSCh)	13.0	12.2	−0.8	−6.2
Institutional Revolutionary Party (PRI)	61.1	49.5	−11.6	−19.0
Democratic Action (AD)	46.7	22.7	−24.0	−51.4
Chilean Communist Party (PCCh)	14.0	6.0	−8.0	−57.1
American Popular Revolutionary Alliance (APRA)	38.3	14.6	−23.7	−61.9

Note:
[a] Because Chile was not a democracy in the 1980s, electoral data for the PSCh and PCCh are taken from legislative elections from during the 1960–73 period.

some adaptive success. Had the PRI failed to adapt programmatically, its decline would almost certainly have been more precipitous.

As a result of the PRI's relative electoral success, the Mexican party system was gradually transformed from a hegemonic system into a relatively stable three-party system in the 1990s. Although the gradual nature of the PRI's decline clearly prolonged the democratic transition, it helped to ensure that when the transition finally occurred, it was a relatively smooth one. Arguably, had the PRI not adapted as successfully, the chances of a violent transition would have been greater and the prospects for the emerging regime less certain.

Table 9.1 compares the six parties' electoral performance during the crisis period of the 1980s to that of the postresponse period of the 1990s. The PJ and PSCh, both of which underwent far-reaching adaptation, maintained stable electoral bases in the 1990s. The PRI, which underwent a partial adaptation, suffered a moderate electoral decline.[11] AD, the PCCh, and APRA, which adapted slowly or, in the case of APRA, inappropriately, suffered steep electoral decline.

Comparative evidence from Latin America thus provides some initial support for the hypothesis that loosely structured labor-based parties are better equipped to adapt to environmental shocks than are routinized or bureaucratic working-class parties. Although changes in the macroeconomic environment provided a powerful incentive for labor-based parties to adapt, the variation in responses to these changes suggests that an environment-centered approach is insufficient to explain party adaptation. And although

---

[11] The figures for the PRI are somewhat misleading, because the elections in the 1990s were much fairer and more competitive than the elections in the 1980s.

the choices and strategies of party leaders such as García, Menem, Pérez, and Salinas were undoubtedly critical to their parties' success or failure, the cases also make clear that the parties varied considerably in the degree to which they permitted leadership renovation and autonomous decision making. Whereas the loosely structured hierarchies of the PRI and PJ facilitated leadership renovation and imposed few constraints on office-holding leaders, in the more bureaucratic AD and the PCCh, entrenched old-guard leaders limited the capacity of reformers to carry out adaptive strategies. As the case of APRA makes clear, however, strategic flexibility is no guarantee that leaders will choose appropriate strategies. Indeed, autonomous leaders may choose strategies that are highly destructive for their parties.

The comparison also provides some support for the argument that labor-based party adaptation was positively related to regime stability in Latin America in the 1980s and 1990s. Latin American countries confronted profound social and economic crises beginning in the early 1980s. These crises were particularly deep in countries with labor-mobilizing party systems (Roberts 2002). Where established labor-based parties adapted and led the process of change, as in Argentina and Mexico, labor-mobilizing party systems tended to remain more stable, which contributed to both governability and regime stability. Where established labor-based parties failed to adapt, as in Peru and Venezuela, party systems weakened and even decomposed. As a result, working- and lower-class voters became available for neopopulist antisystem appeals. Although labor-based party failure was certainly not the only cause of the regime crises in Peru and Venezuela, these failures contributed in an important way to the crises of representation out of which both Fujimori and Chavez emerged.

Implications for Future Research

The results of this study suggest several implications for future research. For one, they call into question some widely held assumptions about party institutionalization. Much of the literature on parties and party systems associates higher levels of institutionalization with (positively evaluated) political outcomes such as greater stability and more effective representation (Huntington 1968; Dix 1992; O'Donnell 1994; Mainwaring and Scully 1995; McGuire 1997; Mainwaring 1999). By stabilizing expectations and lengthening time horizons, institutionalization brings a critical degree of stability to politics. In a context of crisis or rapid environmental change, however, such stability may prove costly, at least to individual parties.[12] High levels of institutionalization may limit the choices available to actors and slow down or even prevent efforts to find creative responses to crises. By contrast, lower levels of institutionalization, though generally inefficient

---

[12] Schedler (1995) makes a similar argument with respect to party systems.

and often chaotic, may provide greater opportunity for innovative responses to crises. Like buildings that are built to give during earthquakes so as to prevent their collapse, organizations may require a degree of internal flexibility to help ensure their adaptation and survival in times of crisis.

A second implication is that there is a clear need for more systematic research on informal and weakly institutionalized party organizations. As has been argued with respect to political regimes (O'Donnell 1996) and party systems (Mainwaring 1999: 21), the dominant literature on political parties tends to take formal institutionalization for granted. Virtually all of the leading concepts and theories in the parties literature are based on studies of parties in the advanced industrialized countries, particularly Western Europe. Because most of these parties are relatively well institutionalized, such studies incorporate little variation along these dimensions. Yet variation along these dimensions may have important implications for party behavior. As this study has shown, the degree of routinization may affect the speed with which parties adapt to environmental change. Expanding the range of cases used in comparative studies to include informally structured and weakly institutionalized parties (which could be accomplished by incorporating more parties from middle- and lower-income cases) would likely produce fruitful refinements of existing conceptual and theoretical frameworks.

Third, the results of this study suggest the need for more research on Latin American party organizations. Whereas a substantial body of literature exists on most of the major parties in the advanced industrialized countries, no comparable pool of research exists for Latin American parties. Filling this research gap is important for at least three reasons. First, given that political parties remain central political actors in virtually all Latin American countries, a lack of knowledge about how they function limits our understanding of politics in those countries. Second, the paucity of empirical studies of Latin American party organizations limits our capacity to undertake the kinds of comparative analyses that have so enriched the European parties literature.[13] Without good secondary material to draw from, comparative studies of complex organizations such as parties are difficult to carry out. Finally, as mentioned previously, theoretically informed studies of Latin American and other non-European parties would expand the range of cases that scholars can draw on as they generate and refine their concepts and theories.

BEYOND MENEMISM: THE TRANSFORMATION OF PERONISM AND
THE FUTURE OF WORKING-CLASS REPRESENTATION IN ARGENTINA

When Fernando De la Rua of the Alliance defeated PJ candidate Eduardo Duhalde to capture the presidency in October 1999, the Menemist era came

---

[13] Examples include Panebianco (1988), Kitschelt (1994a), and Katz and Mair (1994, 1995).

to a close. The PJ's defeat was rooted in the breakdown of the Menemist electoral coalition, which had combined the traditional Peronist base with independent and conservative voters who supported the Menem government's economic program. Although Duhalde retained the bulk of the traditional Peronist vote, this latter group, no longer perceiving Peronism as indispensable for economic stability and increasingly concerned about issues of corruption and institutional integrity, abandoned the PJ for the centrist Alliance and center-right candidate Domingo Cavallo.[14] The PJ's performance in 1999 was hardly a complete failure, however. It remained Argentina's largest party, and it retained control of the Senate and captured fourteen of twenty-three governorships, including those of the three largest provinces (Buenos Aires, Córdoba, and Santa Fe).

Out of power, the PJ quickly fell into a state of fragmentation and disorder. Although Menem retained the formal title of PJ president, his power within the party diminished considerably. The Menemist-dominated National Council lost relevance, and power fell into the hands of the Peronist governors, particularly Carlos Ruckauf (Buenos Aires), José Manuel De la Sota (Córdoba), and Carlos Reutemann (Santa Fe). The governors each played their own political game, and as a result, Peronism rarely spoke with a single voice. Some PJ leaders, such as Menem, positioned themselves to the right of the De la Rua government, advocating additional market-oriented reforms such as the dollarization of the economy. Others, such as Duhalde and Santa Cruz Governor Nestor Kirchner, positioned themselves to the left of De la Rua, calling for substantial changes in the neoliberal model. Still others, including De la Sota and Reutemann, focused on creating an image of efficiency and good government.

The PJ's fragmentation proved costly when De la Rua's resignation unexpectedly thrust the party back into power in December 2001. Because the vice presidency had been vacant since Vice President Carlos Álvarez's resignation in October 2000, it fell to the Peronist-controlled Congress to choose an interim president. Dominated by governors who had their eyes fixed on the presidency, and lacking a central bureaucracy capable of facilitating collective action or imposing internal discipline, Peronism failed to respond to the crisis in a coherent or far-sighted manner. Party bosses initially chose San Luis Governor Adolfo Rodriguez Saa as interim president – only to withdraw their support for him when it became clear that he, too, had longer-term presidential ambitions. They also repeatedly undercut the authority of Rodriguez Saa's successor, Duhalde, preventing

---

[14] To an extent, then, the unraveling of the Menemist coalition was a product of the Menem government's economic success. Only when economic reforms had been consolidated and economic stability could be taken for granted did issues of clean government and accountability gain salience, and *only then* did independent and center-right voters abandon the PJ.

him from establishing a position of leadership in the party. The 2001–2 crisis thus exposed the dark side of the PJ's flexible, nonbureaucratic structure. In the absence of a centralized bureaucracy or a unifying authority figure, Peronism responded to the crisis in an anarchic – and ultimately destructive – way.

Yet, as in the past, the PJ's descent into anarchy may also contribute to its survival and future renovation. Peronism's fragmentation virtually ensures that the party as a whole will not go "down with the ship" in the wake of the Duhalde government's failures. It also produced (albeit unintentionally) a "let a thousand flowers bloom" strategy in which competing Peronists experimented with a variety of new profiles and strategies. Such decentralized experimentation could result in yet another round of innovation and adaptation.

Menemism's longer-term implications for Peronism are uncertain. On the one hand, the PJ's adaptation during the 1990s permitted its survival as an organization and a collective identity. Political organization, as Roberto Michels observed nearly a century ago, is "the weapon of the weak in their struggle with the strong" (1911/1962: 21). Thus, unlike in Peru, where the collapse of organized labor and left-of-center political parties during the 1990s left the working- and lower-classes without any organized bases for collective action (Roberts 1998a), the primary political organization and identity of the Argentine working- and lower-classes remained largely intact. On the other hand, the PJ's adaptation and survival came at a severe cost in terms of its working-class linkages. By the end of the decade, organized labor was more marginal, and Peronism's traditional redistributive goals more removed from the policy agenda, than at any time since 1943. Indeed, the sharp increase in non-Peronist working- and lower-class protest (such as provincial riots and highway blockades by unemployed workers) in the late 1990s suggests that the PJ's hold over the popular sectors may have begun to erode.

The PJ's capacity to defend or advance working- and lower-class interests in the future thus remains unclear. In the programmatic realm, Peronism's future is relatively open. The Menem presidency did not permanently transform the PJ ino a market-oriented party. Indeed, Duhalde and other Peronist leaders sought to steer the party in a more nationalist and left-of-center direction after 1999. Although the *Duhaldistas* stopped short of a return to the traditional Peronist program, the post-1999 debate made it clear that the PJ's programmatic orientation remained up for grabs.

Peronism's coalitional changes appear to be more permanent. Although the post-Menemist PJ continued to draw the bulk of its support from the working and lower classes, its linkages to these sectors had been thoroughly transformed. In urban areas, union-based linkages had been substantially eroded and were replaced, in large part, by clientelistic linkages.

The transition from labor politics to machine politics may limit the PJ's capacity to take up and sustain a redistributive agenda in the future. Given the long-term decline of industrial unionism, these changes are unlikely to be reversed. Hence, although the PJ remained Argentina's "party of the poor" at century's end, its days as a labor-based party were almost certainly over.

References

Abós, Alvaro. 1984. "De lo Plebeyo a lo Social." *Unidos* 2, no. 4 (December): 55–67.
Abós, Alvaro. 1986. *El Posperonismo*. Buenos Aires: Editorial Legasa.
Aboy Carlés, Gerardo. 1996. "De Malvinas al Menemismo. Renovación y Contrarenovación en el Peronismo." *Sociedad* (November): 5–31.
Acuña, Carlos. 1995. "Algunas Notas Sobre los Juegos, las Gallinas y la Lógica Política de los Pactos Constitucionales (Reflexiones a Partir del Pacto Constitucional en la Argentina)." In Carlos H. Acuña, ed. *La Nueva Matriz Política Argentina*. Buenos Aires: Nueva Visión.
Adrogué, Gerardo. 1995. "El Nuevo Sistema Partidario Argentino." In Carlos H. Acuña, ed. *La Nueva Matriz Politica Argentina*. Buenos Aires: Ediciones Nueva Visión.
Alarcón-Olguín, Victor. 1994. "The PRI under Salinas de Gortari's Presidency." Paper prepared for the Eighteenth International Congress of the Latin American Studies Association, Atlanta, GA, March 10–12, 1994.
Aldrich, John H. 1995. *Why Parties? The Origin and Transformation of Political Parties in America*. Chicago, IL: University of Chicago Press.
Alvarez, Carlos. 1987. "La Historia Llama a la Puerta." *Unidos* 5, no. 14 (April): 9–25.
Alvarez, Sonia E., Evelina Dagnino, and Arturo Escobar, eds. 1998. *Cultures of Politics/Politics of Cultures: Re-visioning Latin American Social Movements*. Boulder, CO: Westview Press.
Ansell, Christopher K. and Arthur L. Burris. 1997. "Bosses of the City Unite! Labor Politics and Political Machine Consolidation, 1870–1910." *Studies in American Political Development* 11 (Spring): 1–43.
Ansell, Christopher K. and M. Steven Fish. 1999. "The Art of Being Indispensible: Noncharismatic Personalism in Contemporary Political Parties." *Comparative Political Studies* 32, no. 3 (May): 283–312.
Appleton, Andrew M. and Daniel S. Ward. 1997. "Party Response to Environmental Change: A Model of Organizational Innovation." *Party Politics* 3, no 3: 341–62.
Arias, Maria Fernanda. 1998. "From Rebellion to Rupture: Peronist Party Politics in Neuquén, 1961–1973." In James P. Brennan, ed. *Peronism and Argentina*. Wilmington, DE: Scholarly Resources, Inc.

Arias, Maria Fernanda and Raúl García Heras. 1993. "Carisma Disperso y Rebellion: Los Partidos Neo-Peronistas." In Samuel Amaral and Mariano Ben Plotkin, eds. *Perón: del Exilio al Poder*. Buenos Aires: Cántaro Editores.

Armada, Arturo and Mario Wainfeld. 1990. "Perspectivas del Peronismo de los Noventa." Unpublished manuscript. Buenos Aires.

Auyero, Javier. 1997. "The Politics of Survival: Problem-Solving Networks and Political Culture among the Urban Poor in Contemporary Buenos Aires." Ph.D. dissertation. Department of Political and Social Science, New School for Social Research.

Auyero, Javier. 1998. "(Re)Membering Peronism. An Ethnographic Account of the Relational Character of Political Memory." Paper delivered at the Twenty-First International Congress of the Latin American Studies Association, Chicago, IL, December 24–26, 1998.

Auyero, Javier. 2000. *Poor People's Politics: Peronist Survival Networks and the Legacy of Evita*. Durham, NC: Duke University Press.

Banfield, Edward C. and James Q. Wilson. 1963. *City Politics*. Cambridge, MA: Harvard University Press.

Bárbaro, Julio. 1985. "Peronismo y Sindicalismo." *Unidos* 3, no. 6 (August): 149–52.

Barrett, Patrick S. 2001. "Labour Policy, Labour–Business Relations and the Transition to Democracy in Chile." *Journal of Latin American Studies* 33, no. 3 (August): 561–97.

Bartolini, Stefano and Peter Mair. 1990. *Identity, Competition, and Electoral Availability*. Cambridge, UK: Cambridge University Press.

Beliz, Gustavo. 1988. *CGT, El Otro Poder*. Buenos Aires: Editorial Planeta.

Beveraggi Allende, Walter. 1954. *El Partido Laborista, El Fracaso de Perón y el Problema Argentino*. Montevideo: Editorial Accíon.

Bianchi, Susana and Norma Sanchís. 1988. *El Partido Peronista Feminina*. Buenos Aires: Centro Editor de America Latina.

Bonasso, Miguel. 1997. *El Presidente Que No Fue: Los Archivos Ocultos del Peronismo*. Buenos Aires: Planeta.

Borón, Atilio. 1992. "Becoming Democrats? Some Skeptical Considerations on the Right in Latin America." In Douglas A. Chalmers, Maria do Carmo Campello de Souza, and Atilio Boron, eds. *The Right and Democracy in Latin America*. New York: Praeger Publishers.

Buchrucker, Cristián. 1987. *Nacionalismo y peronismo*. Buenos Aires: Sudamericana.

Buchrucker, Cristián. 1988. "Unidad y Diversidad en las Corrientes Internas del Justicialismo." In Jose Enrique Miguens and Frederick Turner, eds. *Racionalidad del Peronismo: Perspectivas Internas y Externas Que Replantean un Debate Inconcluso*. Buenos Aires: Planeta.

Buchrucker, Cristián. 1998. "Interpretations of Peronism: Old Frameworks and New Perspectives." In James P. Brennan, ed. *Peronism and Argentina*. Wilmington, DE: Scholarly Resources.

Burdman, Julio. 1997. "Las Elecciones Legislativas de 1997: Analisis Socio-Político y Político-Electoral." Centro de Estudios Unión para la Nueva Mayoria Cuaderno No. 263. Buenos Aires: Centro de Estudios Unión Para la Nueva Mayoria.

Burgess, Katrina. 1998. "Alliances under Stress: Economic Reform and Party–Union Relations in Mexico, Spain, and Venezuela." Ph.D dissertation. Department of Political Science, Princeton University.

Burgess, Katrina. 1999. "Loyalty Dilemmas and Market Reform: Party–Union Alliances under Stress in Mexico, Spain, and Venezuela." *World Politics* 52, no. 1 (October): 105–34.
Burgess, Katrina. 2000. "Reinventing Classic Populist Parties: Party Crisis and Change in Mexico, Bolivia, Venezuela, and Peru." Paper delivered at the Twenty-Second Meeting of the Latin American Studies Association, Miami, FL, March 16–18, 2000.
Burgess, Katrina and Steven Levitsky. 2003. "Explaining Populist Party Adaptation: Environmental and Organizational Determinants of Party Change in Argentina, Mexico, Peru, and Venezuela." *Comparative Political Studies* (forthcoming).
Cameron, Maxwell A. 1994. *Democracy and Authoritarianism in Peru: Political Coalitions and Social Change*. New York: St. Martin's Press.
Cameron, Maxwell A. 1997. "Political and Economic Origins of Regime Change in Peru: The Eighteenth Brumaire of Alberto Fujimori." In Maxwell Cameron and Philip Mauceri, eds. *The Peruvian Labyrinth*. University Park, PA: Pennsylvania State University Press.
Canitrot, Adolfo. 1980. "Discipline as the Central Objective of Economic Policy: An Essay on the Economic Programme of the Argentine Government since 1976." *World Development* 8: 913–28.
Cantón, Dario. 1986. *El Pueblo Legislador: Las Elecciones de 1983*. Buenos Aires. Centro Editor de América Latina.
Cárdenas, Emilio Jorge. 1998. "Refurbishing the Argentine Judiciary: A Still-Neglected Theme." In Joseph S. Tulchin with Allison W. Garland, eds. *Argentina: The Challenges of Modernization*. Wilmington, DE: Scholarly Resources.
Carnota, Fernando and Esteban Talpone. 1995. *El Palacio de la Corrupción: Droga, Negociados y Enriquecimiento en el Consejo Deliberante*. Buenos Aires: Editorial Sudamericana.
Castells, Manuel and Alejandro Portes. 1989. "World Underneath: The Origins, Dynamics, and Effects of the Informal Economy." In Alejandro Portes, Manuel Castells, and Lauren A. Benton, eds. *The Informal Economy: Studies in Advanced and Less Developed Countries*. Baltimore, MD: Johns Hopkiins University Press.
Catterberg, Edgardo. 1985. "Las Eleccion del 30 de Octubre de 1983: El Surgimiento de una Nueva Convergencia Electoral." *Desarrollo Económico* 25, no. 98 (July–September): 259–70.
Catterberg, Edgardo. 1991. *Argentina Confronts Politics: Political Culture and Public Opinion in the Argentine Transition to Democracy*. Boulder, CO: Lynne Rienner.
Catterberg, Edgardo and Maria Braun. 1989. "Las Elecciones Presidenciales Argentinas del 14 de Mayo de 1989: La Ruta a la Normalidad." *Desarrollo Económico* 115 (October–December): 361–74.
Cavarozzi, Marcelo. 1984. *Sindicatos y política en Argentina*. Buenos Aires: CEDES.
Cavarozzi, Marcelo. 1986. "Political Cycles in Argentina since 1955." In Guillermo O'Donnell, Philippe C. Schmitter, and Laurence Whitehead, eds. *Transitions from Authoritarian Rule: Latin America*. Baltimore, MD: Johns Hopkins University Press.
Cavarozzi, Marcelo. 1988. *Peronismo y Radicalismo: Transiciones y Perspectivas*. Buenos Aires: Centro Editor de America Latina.
Cerruti, Gabriela. 1993. *El Jefe: Vida y Obra de Carlos Saul Menem*. Buenos Aires: Planeta.

Chalmers, Douglas A., Carlos M. Vilas, Katherine Hite, Scott B. Martin, Kerianne Piester, and Monique Segarra, eds. 1997. *The New Politics of Inequality in Latin America: Rethinking Representation and Participation*. Oxford, UK: Oxford University Press.
Chumbita, Hugo. 1987. "En busca del movimiento perdido." *Unidos* 5, no. 16 (October): 63–71.
Chumbita, Hugo. 1989. *El Enigma Peronista*. Buenos Aires: Puntosur.
Ciria, Alberto. 1972. "Peronism and Political Structures, 1945–55." In Alberto Ciria, ed. *New Perspectives on Modern Argentina*. Bloomington, IN: Indiana University Latin American Studies Program.
Ciria, Alberto. 1983. *Politica y cultura popular: La Argentina peronista, 1946–55*. Buenos Aires: Ediciones de la Flor.
Collier, David and Steven Levitsky. 1997. "Democracy with Adjectives: Conceptual Innovation in Comparative Research." *World Politics* 49, no. 3 (April): 430–51.
Collier, Ruth Berins. 1992. *The Contradictory Alliance: State–Labor Relations and Regime Change in Mexico*. Berkeley, CA: International and Area Studies.
Collier, Ruth Berins. 1999. "The Transformation of Labor-Based One-Partyism at the End of the Twentieth Century: The Case of Mexico." In Hermann Giliomee and Charles Simkins, eds. *The Awkward Embrace: One-Party Domination and Democracy*. Capetown: Tafelberg.
Collier, Ruth Berins and David Collier. 1991. *Shaping the Political Arena*. Princeton, NJ: Princeton University Press.
Compston. Hugh. 1995. "Union Participation in Economic Policy Making in Scandinavia, 1970–1993." *West European Politics* 18, no. 1 (January): 98–115.
Conniff, Michael L., ed. 1982. *Latin American Populism in Comparative Perspective* Albuquerque, NM: University of New Mexico Press.
Conniff, Michael L., ed. 1999. *Populism in Latin America*. Tuscaloosa, AL: University of Alabama Press, 1999.
Coppedge, Michael. 1988. "La Politica Interna de Acción Democrática Durante la Crisis Economica." *Cuadernos del CENDES* 7: 159–79.
Coppedge, Michael. 1994. *Strong Parties and Lame Ducks: Presidential Partyarchy and Factionalism in Venezuela*. Stanford, CA: Stanford University Press.
Cordeu, Mora, Silvia Mercado, and Nancy Sosa. 1985. *Peronismo: La Mayoría Perdida*. Buenos Aires: Sudamericana-Planeta.
Cordoba, José. 1994. "Mexico." In Williamson, John, ed. *The Political Economy of Policy Reform*. Washington, DC: Institute for International Economics.
Corrales, Javier. 1996a. "State-Ruling Party Relations in Argentina and Venezuela, 1989–1993: Neoliberalism through Party Building." Paper presented at the conference "Economic Reform and Civil Society in Latin America," Weatherhead Center for International Affairs, Harvard University, April 12, 1996.
Corrales, Javier. 1996b. "From Market Correctors to Market-Creators: Executive-Ruling Party Relations in the Economic Reforms of Argentina and Venezuela, 1989–1993." Ph.D dissertation. Department of Government, Harvard University.
Corrales, Javier. 1997. "El Presidente y su Gente: Cooperación y Conflicto entre los Ámbitos Técnicos y Políticos en Venezuela, 1989–1993." *Nueva Sociedad* (November–December): 93–107.

Corrales, Javier. 2000. "Presidents, Ruling Parties, and Party Rules: A Theory on the Politics of Economic Reform in Latin America." *Comparative Politics* 32, no. 2 (January): 127–50.
Corrales, Javier. 2002. *Presidents without Parties. Economic Reforms in Argentina and Venezuela in the 1990s*. University Park, PA: Pennsylvania State University Press.
Cotler, Julio. 1995. "Political Parties and the Problem of Democratic Consolidation in Peru." In Scott Mainwaring and Timothy R. Scully, eds. *Building Democratic Institutions: Party Systems in Latin America*. Stanford, CA: Stanford University Press.
Cukierman, Alex and Mariano Tomassi. 1998. "Credibility of Policymakers and of Economic Reforms." In Federico Sturzenegger and Mariano Tomassi, eds.*The Political Economy of Reform*. Cambridge, MA: MIT Press.
Dalton, Russell J., Scott C. Flanagan, and Paul Allen Beck. 1984. "Electoral Change in Advanced Industrial Democracies." In Russell J. Dalton, Scott C. Flanagan, and Paul Allen Beck, eds. *Electoral Change in Advanced Industrial Democracies: Realignment or Dealignment?* Princeton, NJ: Princeton University Press.
De Ipola, Emilio. 1987. "La Difícil Apuesta del Peronismo Democrático." In Jose Nún and Juan Carlos Portantiero, eds. *Ensayos Sobre la Transición Democrática en la Argentina*. Buenos Aires: Puntosur.
De Ipola, Emilio. 1989. "Ruptura y Continuidad: Claves Parciales para un Balance de las Interpretaciones del Peronismo." *Desarrollo Económico* 29, no. 115 (October–December): 331–57.
Delich, Francisco. 1982. "Despues del Diluvio, la Clase Obrera." In Alain Rouquié, ed. *Argentina, Hoy*. Mexico City: Siglo Veintiuno Editores.
De Riz, Liliana. 1981. *Retorno y Derrumbe. El Ultimo Gobierno Peronista*. Buenos Aires: Hyspamerica.
De Riz, Liliana. 1996. "Argentina: Democracy in Turmoil." In Jorge I. Dominguez and Abraham F. Lowenthal, eds. *Constructing Democratic Governance: South America in the 1990s*. Baltimore, MD: Johns Hopkins University Press.
Deschouwer, Kris. 1994. "The Decline of Consociationalism and the Reluctant Modernization of Belgian Mass Parties." In Richard S. Katz and Peter Mair, eds. *How Parties Organize: Change and Adaptation in Party Organizations in Western Democracies*. London: Sage Publications.
Diamond, Larry. 1999. *Developing Democracy: Toward Consolidation*. Baltimore, MD: Johns Hopkins University Press.
Dimaggio, Paul J. and Walter W. Powell. 1991. "Introduction." In Paul J. DiMaggio and Walter W. Powell, eds. *The New Institutionalism in Organizational Analysis*. Chicago, IL: University of Chicago Press.
Di Tella, Guido. 1983. *Perón-Perón 1973–1976*. Buenos Aires: Hyspamerica.
Di Tella, Torcuato. 1965a. *El Sistema Político Argentino y la Clase Obrera*. Buenos Aires: Eudeba.
Di Tella, Torcuato. 1965b. "Populism and Reform in Latin America," In Claudio Véliz, ed. *Obstacles to Change in Latin America*. London: Oxford University Press.
Di Tella, Torcuato. 1968. "Stalemate or Coexistence in Argentina." In James Petras and Maurice Zeitlin, eds. *Latin America: Reform or Revolution*. Greenwich, CT: Fawcett Publishers.
Di Tella, Torcuato. 1998. "The Transformations of Peronism." In James P. Brennan, ed. *Peronism and Argentina*. Wilmington, DE: Scholarly Resources, Inc.

Dix, Robert H. 1992. "Democratization and the Institutionalization of Latin American Political Parties." *Comparative Political Studies* 24, no. 4 (January): 488–511.

Domínguez, Jorge I. and James A. McCann. 1995. "Shaping Mexico's Electoral Arena: The Construction of Partisan Cleavages in the 1988 and 1991 National Elections." *American Political Science Review* 89, no. 1 (March): 34–48.

Downs, Anthony. 1957. *An Economic Theory of Democracy*. New York: Harper and Row.

Downs, Anthony. 1967. *Inside Bureaucracy*. Boston, MA: Little, Brown and Company.

Drake, Paul. 1978. *Socialism and Populism in Chile, 1932–52*. Urbana, IL: University of Illinois Press.

Duverger, Maurice. 1954/1963. *Political Parties: Their Organization and Activity in the Modern State*. New York: John Wiley & Sons.

Eldersveld, Samuel J. 1964. *Political Parties: A Behavioral Analysis*. Chicago, IL: Rand McNally.

Ellner, Steve. 1989. "Organized Labor's Political Influence and Party Ties in Venezuela: Acción Democrática and Its Labor Leadership."*Journal of Interamerican Studies and World Affairs* 31, no. 4 (Winter): 91–129.

Ellner, Steve. 1993. *Organized Labor in Venezuela, 1958–1991: Behavior and Concerns in a Democratic Setting*. Wilmington, DE: Scholarly Resources, Inc.

Ellner, Steve. 1996. "Political Party Factionalism and Democracy in Venezuela." *Latin American Perspectives* 23, no. 3 (Summer): 87–109.

Ellner, Steve. 1999. "Obstacles to the Consolidation of the Venezuelan Neighborhood Movement: National and Local Cleavages." *Journal of Latin American Studies* 31: 75–97.

Escobar, Arturo and Sonia E. Alvarez, eds. 1992. *The Making of Social Movements in Latin America: Identity, Strategy, and Democracy*. Boulder, CO: Westview Press, 1992.

Escolar, Marcelo. 2001. La Posibilidad del *Gerrymandering* Político: Estabilidad y Concentración Geográfica del Voto Partidario." In Ernesto Calvo and Juan Manuel Abal Medina (h), eds. *El Federalismo Electoral Argentino: Sobrerepresentación, Reforma Política y Gobierno Dividido en la Argentina*. Buenos Aires: Editorial Universitaria de Buenos Aires.

Etchemendy, Sebastián. 1995. "Límites al Decisionismo? El Poder Ejecutivo y la Formulación de la Legislación Laboral: 1983–1994." In Ricardo Sidicaro and Jorge Mayer, eds. *Política y Sociedad en los Años del Menemismo*. Buenos Aires: Universidad de Buenos Aires.

Etchemendy, Sebastián. 2001. "Constructing Reform Coalitions: The Politics of Compensations in Argentina's Economic Liberalization." *Latin American Politics and Society* 43, no. 3 (Fall): 1–35.

Etchemendy, Sebastián and Vicente Palermo. 1998. "Conflicto y Concertación: Gobierno, Congreso y Organizaciones de Interés en la Reforma Laboral del Primer Gobierno de Menem." *Desarollo Económico* v. 37, no. 148 (January–March): 559–90.

Fara, Luis. 1989. "Luchas Reivindicativas Urbanos en un Contexto Autoritario. Los Asentamientos de San Francisco Solano." In Elizabeth Jelin, ed. *Los Nuevos Movimientos Sociales*. Buenos Aires: Centro Editor de America Latina.

Fernández, Arturo. 1993. *Las Nuevas Relaciones Entre Sindicatos y Partidos Politicos*. Buenos Aires: Centro Editor de America Latina.

Ferreira Rubio, Delia and Matteo Goretti. 1998. "When the President Governs Alone: The Decretazo in Argentina, 1989–93." In John M. Carey and Mathew Soberg Shugart, eds. *Executive Decree Authority*. New York: Cambridge University Press.

Ferreira Rubio, Delia and Matteo Goretti. 2000. "Executive–Legislative Relationship in Argentina: From Menem's *Decretazo* to a New Style?" Paper presented at the conference "Argentina 2000: Politics, Economy, Society and International Relations," Oxford University, May 15–17, 2000.

Fraga, Rosendo. 1995. *Argentina en las Urnas, 1916–1994*. Buenos Aires: Editorial Centro de Estudios Unión para la Nueva Mayoria.

Franklin, Mark N., Thomas T. Mackie, and Henry Valen, eds. 1992. *Electoral Change: Responses to Evolving Social and Attitudinal Structures in Western Countries*. Cambridge, UK: Cambridge University Press.

Fraser, Nicholas and Marysa Navarro. 1985. *Eva Perón*. New York: W.W. Norton.

Furci, Carmelo. 1984. *The Chilean Communist Party and the Road to Socialism*. London: Zed Books, Ltd.

García, Raúl Alberto and Néstor Montenegro, eds. 1986. *Hablan Los Renovadores*. Buenos Aires: Ediciones de la Galera.

Garrett, Geoffrey. 1998. *Partisan Politics in the Global Economy*. New York: Cambridge University Press.

Garrett, Geoffrey and Peter Lange. 1991. "Political Responses to Interdependence: What's 'Left' for the Left?" *International Organization* 45: 539–64.

Garrido, Luis Javier. 1984. *El Partido de la Revolución Institucionalizola: la Formación del Nuevo Estado en Mexico (1928–1945)*. Mexico City: Siglo Veintiuno.

Gerchunoff, Pablo and Juan Carlos Torre. 1996. "La politica de Liberaliazcion Economica en la Administracion de Menem." *Desarrollo Económico* 36, no. 143 (October–December): 733–68.

Gerlach, Luther P. and Virginia H. Hine. 1970. *People, Power, Change: Movements of Social Transformation*. New York: Bobbs-Merrill Company.

Germani, Gino. 1965. *Política y Sociedad en Una Época de Transición: De la Sociedad Tradicional a la Sociedad de Masas*. Buenos Aires: Editorial Paidós.

Germani, Gino. 1973. "El Surgimiento del Peronismo: El Rol de los Obreros y de los Migrantes Internos." *Desarrollo Económico* 13, no. 51 (October–December): 435–88.

Germani, Gino. 1980. "Categoria de Ocupación y Voto Político en la Capital Federal." In Manuel Mora y Araujo and Ignacio Llorente, eds. *El Voto Peronista: Ensayos de Sociologia Electoral Argentina*. Buenos Aires: Editorial Sudamericana.

Gervasoni, Carlos. 1997. "La Sustentabilidad Electoral de los Programas de Estabilización y Reforma Estructural: Los Casos de Argentina y Perú." Paper prepared for delivery at the Twentieth International Congress of the Latin American Studies Association, Guadalajara, Mexico, April 17–19, 1997.

Gervasoni, Carlos. 1998a. "Del Distributionalismo al Neoliberalismo: Los Cambios en la Coalición Electoral Peronista Durante el Gobierno de Menem." Paper prepared for the Twenty-First International Congress of the Latin American Studies Association, September 24–6, 1998.

Gervasoni, Carlos. 1998b. "Estructura y Evolucion de las Coaliciones Electorales en la Argentina: 1989 y 1995." Unpublished manuscript. Facultad de Derecho y Ciencias Sociales, Universidad Católica Argentina.

Gibson. Edward. 1996. *Class and Conservative Parties: Argentina in Comparative Perspective*. Baltimore, MD: Johns Hopkins University Press.

Gibson, Edward. 1997. "The Populist Road to Market Reform: Policy and Electoral Coalitions in Mexico and Argentina." *World Politics* 49, no. 2 (April): 339–70.

Gibson, Edward and Ernesto Calvo. 2000. "Federalism and Low-Maintenance Constituencies: Territorial Dimensions of Economic Reform in Argentina." *Studies in Comparative International Development* 35, no. 3 (Fall): 32–55.

Gillespie, Richard. 1987. *Soldados de Perón: Los Montoneros*. Buenos Aires: Grijalbo.

Godio, Julio. 1991a. *El Movimiento Obrero Argentino (1943–1955)*. Buenos Aires: Editorial Legasa.

Godio, Julio. 1991b. *El Movimiento Obrero Argentino (1955–1990)*. Buenos Aires: Editorial Legasa.

Godio, Julio and Hector Palomino. 1987. *El Movimiento Sindical Hoy: Historia, Organizacion y Nuevos Desafios Programaticos*. Buenos Aires: Fundacion Friedrich Ebert.

Godio, Julio, Héctor Palomino, and Achim Wachendorfer. 1988. *El Movimiento Sindical Argentino (1880–1987)*. Buenos Aires: Puntosur.

Gonzáles Esteves, Luis and Ignacio Llorente. 1985. "Elecciones y Preferencias Politicas en Capital Federal y Gran Buenos Aires el 30 de Octubre de 1983." In Marcos Victorica, ed. *La Argentina Electoral*. Buenos Aires: Editorial Sudamericana.

Graham, Carol. 1990. "Peru's APRA Party in Power: Impossible Revolution, Relinquished Reform." *Journal of Interamerican Studies and World Affairs* 32, no. 3 (Fall): 75–115.

Graham, Carol. 1992. *Peru's APRA: Parties, Politics, and the Elusive Quest for Democracy*. Boulder, CO: Lynne Rienner.

Gutierrez, Ricardo. 1998. "Renovación, Desindicalización y Neoliberalización del Peronismo." Documento del trabajo. Facultad de Ciencias Sociales, Universidad de Buenos Aires.

Gwartney, James, Robert Lawson, and Walter Block. 1996. *Economic Freedom of the World, 1975–1995*. Vancouver, BC: Fraser Institute.

Hagopian, Frances. 1998. "Democracy and Political Representation in Latin America in the 1990s: Pause, Reorganization, or Decline?" In Felipe Aguero and Jeffrey Stark, eds. *Fault Lines of Democracy in Post-Transition Latin America*. Miami, FL: North–South Center Press.

Harmel, Robert and Kenneth Janda. 1982. *Parties and Their Environments: Limits to Reform?* New York: Longman.

Harmel, Robert and Kenneth Janda. 1994. "An Integrated Theory of Party Goals and Party Change." *Journal of Theoretical Politics* 6, no. 3: 259–87.

Harmel, Robert and Lars Svasand. 1993. "Party Leadership and Party Institutionalization: Three Phases of Development." *West European Politics* 16, no. 2 (April): 67–88.

Harmel, Robert and Lars Svasand. 1997. "The Influence of New Parties on Old Parties' Platforms." *Party Politics* 3, no. 3: 315–40.

Helmke, Gretchen. 2000a. "Checks and Balances by Other Means: Strategic Defection and the 'Re-Reelection' Controversy in Argentina." Paper delivered at the

Annual Meeting of the American Political Science Association, Washington, DC, August 31–September 3, 2000.
Helmke, Gretchen. 2000b. "Ruling against the Rulers: Insecure Tenure and Judicial Independence in Argentina, 1976–1995," Ph.D. dissertation, Department of Political Science, University of Chicago.
Hernández Rodríguez, Rogelio. 1991. "La Reforma Interna y los Conflictos en el PRI." *Foro Internacional* (October–December): 222–49.
Howell, Chris and Anthony Daley. 1992. "The Transformation of Political Exchange." *International Journal of Political Economy* 22, no. 4: 3–16.
Huntington, Samuel P. 1968. *Political Order in Changing Societies*. New Haven, CT: Yale University Press.
Ignazi, Piero. 1996. "The Crisis of Parties and the Rise of New Political Parties." *Party Politics* 2, no. 4 (October): 549–66.
Inglehart, Ronald. 1977. *The Silent Revolution*. Princeton, NJ: Princeton University Press.
Inter-American Development Bank. 1997. *Latin America after a Decade of Reforms: Economic and Social Progress*. Washington, DC: IDB.
Jackisch, Carlota. 1990. *Los Partidos Políticos en América Latina: Desarrollo, Estructura y Fundamentos Programáticos. El Caso Argentino*. Buenos Aires: CIEDLA.
James, Daniel. 1988. *Resistance and Integration: Peronism and the Argentine Working Class, 1946–1976*. New York: Cambridge University Press.
Janda, Kenneth. 1980. *Political Parties: A Cross-National Survey*. New York: Free Press.
Jepperson, Ronald. 1991. "Institutions, Institutional Effects, and Institutionalism." In Walter W. Powell and Paul J. DiMaggio, eds. *The New Institutionalism in Organizational Analysis*. Chicago, IL: University of Chicago Press.
Jones, Mark. 1997. "Evaluating Argentina's Presidential Democracy: 1983–1995." In Scott Mainwaring and Mathew Soberg Shugart, eds. *Presidentialism and Democracy in Latin America*. New York: Cambridge University Press.
Jorrat, Jorge Raul. 1986. "Las Elecciones de 1983: 'Desviacion' o Realineamiento?" *Desarrollo Económico* 101 (April–June): 89–119.
Katz, Richard S. 1990. "Party as Linkage: A Vestigial Function?" *European Journal of Political Research* 18: 141–61.
Katz, Richard S. and Peter Mair, eds. 1992. *Party Organizations: A Handbook on Party Organizations in Western Democracies, 1960–1990*. London: Sage Publications.
Katz, Richard S. and Peter Mair, eds. 1994. *How Parties Organize: Change and Adaptation in Party Organizations in Western Democracies*. London: Sage Publications.
Katz, Richard S. and Peter Mair. 1995. "Changing Models of Party Democracy: The Emergence of the Cartel Party." *Party Politics* 1, no. 1: 5–28.
Keck, Margaret E. and Kathryn Sikkink. 1998. *Activists beyond Borders: Advocacy Networks in International Politics*. Ithaca, NY: Cornell University Press.
Kenworthy, Eldon. 1975. "Interpretaciones Ortodoxas y Revisionistas del Apoyo Inicial del Peronismo." *Desarrollo Económico* 56, no. 14 (January–March): 749–63.
Kesselman, Mark. 1970. "Overinstitutionalization and Political Constraint: The Case of France." *Comparative Politics* 3, no. 1: 21–44.
Key, V. O., Jr. 1949/1984. *Southern Politics in State and Nation*. Knoxville, TN: University of Tennessee Press.

Kirchheimer, Otto. 1966. "The Transformation of Western European Party Systems." In Joseph LaPalombara and Myron Weiner, eds. *Political Parties and Political Development*. Princeton, NJ: Princeton University Press.

Kirkpatrick, Jeane J. 1971. *Leader and Vanguard in Mass Society: A Study of Peronist Argentina*. Cambridge, MA: MIT Press.

Kitschelt, Herbert. 1989a. *The Logics of Party Formation: Ecological Parties in Belgium and West Germany*. Ithaca, NY: Cornell University Press.

Kitschelt, Herbert. 1989b. "The Internal Politics of Parties: The Law of Curvilinear Disparity Revisited." *Political Studies* 37, no. 3: 400–21.

Kitschelt, Herbert. 1994a. *The Transformation of European Social Democracy*. Cambridge, UK: Cambridge University Press.

Kitschelt, Herbert. 1994b. "Austrian and Swedish Social Democrats in Crisis: Party Strategy and Organization in Corporatist Regimes." *Comparative Political Studies* 24, no. 1: 3–35.

Knight, Jack. 1992. *Institutions and Social Conflict*. New York: Cambridge University Press.

Knoke, David. 1990. *Political Networks: The Structural Perspective*. New York: Cambridge University Press.

Koelble, Thomas. 1991. *The Left Unraveled: Social Democracy and the New Left Challenge*. Durham, NC: Duke University Press.

Koelble, Thomas. 1992. "Recasting Social Democracy in Europe: A Nested Games Explanation of Strategic Adjustment in Political Parties." *Politics and Society* 20, no. 2 (March): 51–70.

Koelble, Thomas. 1996. "Economic Theories of Organization and the Politics of Institutional Design in Political Parties." *Party Politics* 2, no. 2 (April): 251–63.

Krasner, Stephen D. 1988. "Sovereignty: An Institutional Perspective." *Comparative Political Studies* 21, no. 1 (April): 66–94.

Lagos, Marta. 2001. "Between Stability and Crisis in Latin America." *Journal of Democracy* 12, no. 1 (January): 137–45.

Landi, Oscar. 1995. "Outsiders, Nuevos Caudillos y Medias Politicas." In Carina Perelli, Sonia Picado, and Daniel Zoviatto, eds. *Partidos y Clase Politica en America Latina en los 90*. San Jose: Instituto Interamericano de Derechos Humanos.

Langston, Joy. 1996. "Why Rules Matter: The Formal Rules of Candidate Selection and Leadership Selection in the PRI, 1978–1996." CIDE Documento de Trabajo no. 58. Mexico City: Centro de Investigación y Docencia Económica.

Langston, Joy. 2001. "Why Rules Matter: Changes in Candidate Selection in Mexico's PRI, 1988–2000." *Journal of Latin American Studies* 33, no. 3 (August): 485–512.

Larkins, Christopher. 1998. "The Judiciary and Delegative Democracy in Argentina." *Comparative Politics* 30, no. 4: 423–42.

Lawton, Judy. 1994. "Clientelist Politics and Peronism in the Squatter Settlements of Greater Buenos Aires: Squatters' Views on Politics and Society." Paper delivered for the Eighteenth Congress of the Latin American Studies Association, Atlanta, GA, March 10–12, 1994.

Levitsky, Steven. 1998a. "Peronism and Institutionalization: The Case, the Concept, and the Case for Unpacking the Concept." *Party Politics* 4, no. 1: 77–92.

Levitsky, Steven. 1998b. "Crisis, Party Adaptation, and Regime Stability in Argentina" *Party Politics* 4, no. 4 (January): 445–71.

Levitsky, Steven. 2001a. "A 'Disorganized Organization': Informal Organization and the Persistence of Local Party Structures in Argentine Peronism." *Journal of Latin American Studies* 33, no. 1 (February): 29–66.

Levitsky, Steven. 2001b. "Inside the Black Box: Recent Studies of Latin American Party Organizations." *Studies in Comparative International Development* 36, no. 2 (summer): 92–110.

Levitsky, Steven and Maxwell Cameron. 2003. "Democracy without Parties? Political Parties and Regime Change in Fujimori's Peru." *Latin American Politics and Society* (forthcoming).

Levitsky, Steven and Lucan A. Way. 1998. "Between a Shock and a Hard Place: The Dynamics of Labor-Backed Adjustment in Argentina and Poland." *Comparative Politics* 30, no. 2 (January): 171–92.

Lewis, Paul. 1990. *The Crisis of Argentine Capitalism*. Chapel Hill, NC: University of North Carolina Press.

Little, Walter. 1973. "Party and State in Peronist Argentina, 1945–55." *Hispanic American Historical Review* 53, no. 4 (November): 644–62.

Little, Walter. 1988. "La Organizacion Obrera y el Estado Peronista." In Juan Carlos Torre, ed. *La Formacion del Sindicalismo Peronista*. Buenos Aires: Editorial Legasa.

Llanos, Mariana. 2001. "Understanding Presidential Power in Argentina: A Study of the Policy of Privatization in the 1990s." *Journal of Latin American Studies* 33, no. 1 (February): 67–99.

Llorente, Ignacio. 1980. "La Composición Social del Movimiento Peronista hacia 1954." In Manuel Mora y Araujo and Ignacio Llorente, eds. *El Voto Peronista: Ensayos de Sociologia Electoral Argentina*. Buenos Aires: Editorial Sudamericana.

Lopez, Artemio. 1994. "El Nuevo Mapa Electoral Argentina IV." Instituto de Estudios Sobre el Estado y Participación (IDEP), Working Paper no, 30. Buenos Aires: IDEP.

López Echague, Hernan. 1996. *El Otro: Una Biografía de Eduardo Duhalde*. Buenos Aires: Planeta.

Luna, Félix. 1984. *Perón y su Tiempo*. Buenos Aires: Sudamericana.

MacKinnon, María Moira. 1995. "Sobre los Orígenes del Partido Peronista. Notas Introductorias." In W. Ansaldi, A. Pucciarelli, and J. Villarreal, eds. *Representaciones Inconclusas: Las Clases, los Actores, y los Discursos de la Memoria, 1912–1946*. Buenos Aires: Editorial Biblos.

Mackinnon, María Moira. 1998. "Unity and Fragmentation: Trade Unionists and Politicians in the Early Years of the Peronist Party (1946–50)." Paper delivered at the Twenty-First International Congress of the Latin American Studies Association, Chicago, IL, September 24–6, 1998.

Madsen, Douglas and Peter G. Snow. 1991. *The Charismatic Bond: Political Behavior in Time of Crisis*. Cambridge, MA: Harvard University Press.

Mainwaring, Scott. 1999. *Rethinking Party Systems in the Third Wave Democratization: The Case of Brazil*. Stanford, CA: Stanford University Press.

Mainwaring, Scott and Timothy R. Scully. 1995. "Introduction: Party Systems in Latin America." In Scott Mainwaring and Timothy R. Scully, eds. *Building Democratic Institutions: Party Systems in Latin America*. Stanford, CA: Stanford University Press.

Manzetti, Luigi. 1993. *Institutions, Parties, and Coalitions in Argentine Politics.* Pittsburgh, PA: University of Pittsburgh Press.

Maor, Moshe. 1995. "Intra-Party Determinants of Coalitional Bargaining." *Journal of Theoretical Politics* 7, no. 1: 65–91.

Maor, Moshe. 1998. *Parties, Conflicts, and Coalitions in Western Europe: Organizational Determinants of Coalition Bargaining.* London: Routledge.

March, James G. and Johan Olsen. 1984. "The New Institutionalism: Organizational Factors in Political Life." *American Political Science Review* 78: 734–49.

March, James G. and Johan P. Olsen. 1989. *Rediscovering Institutions: The Organizational Basis of Politics.* New York: Free Press.

Martucelli, Danilo and Maristella Svampa. 1997. *La Plaza Vacía: Las Transformaciones del Peronismo.* Buenos Aires: Losada.

Martz, John D. 1966. *Acción Democrática: Evolution of a Modern Political Party in Venezuela.* Princeton, NJ: Princeton University Press.

Martz, John D. 1992. "Party Elites and Leadership in Colombia and Venezuela." *Journal of Latin American Studies* 24, no. 1 (February): 87–121.

May, John D. 1973. "Opinion Structure of Political Parties. The Special Law of Curvilinear Disparity." *Political Studies* 21, no. 2: 131–51.

Mayhew, David. 1986. *Placing Parties in American Politics.* Princeton, NJ: Princeton University Press.

McAllister, Ian. 1991. "Party Adaptation and Factionalism within the Australian Party System." *American Journal of Political Science* 35, no. 1 (February): 206–27.

McCarthy, Mary Alice. 1997. "Center-Left Parties in Chile: Party–Labor Relations under a Minimalist State." Paper presented at the annual meeting of the Midwest Political Science Association, Chicago, IL, April 10–12, 1997.

McCoy, Jenifer L. 1986. "The Politics of Adjustment: Labor and the Venezuelan Debt Crisis." *Journal of Interamerican Studies and World Affairs* 28, no. 4 (winter): 103–37.

McGuire, James W. 1992. "Union Political Tactics and Democratic Consolidation in Alfonsin's Argentina, 1983–1989." *Latin American Research Review* 27, no. 1: 37–74.

McGuire, James W. 1993. "Peron y los Sindicatos: La Lucha por el Liderazgo Peronista." In Samuel Amaral and Mariano Ben Plotkin, eds. *Perón: del Exilio al Poder.* Buenos Aires: Cántaro Editores.

McGuire, James W. 1995. "Political Parties and Democracy in Argentina." In Scott Mainwaring and Timothy R. Scully, eds. *Building Democratic Institutions: Party Systems in Latin America.* Stanford, CA: Stanford University Press.

McGuire, James. 1997. *Peronism without Peron: Unions, Parties, and Democracy in Argentina.* Stanford, CA: Stanford University Press.

Menem, Carlos. 1991. "Los Desafios del Justicialismo: Para Cambiar la Historia." Speech delivered at the Movilizacion Peronista para la Actualizacion Politica y Doctrinaria, conference of the Movimiento Nacional Justicialista, Buenos Aires, March 16, 1991.

Merkel, Wolfgang. 1995. *Final de la Socialdemocracia? Recursos de Poder y Politica de Gobierno de los Partidos Socialdemocratas en Europa Occidental.* Valencia: Generakitat Valenciana.

Michels, Roberto. 1911/1962. *Political Parties.* New York: Free Press.

Middlebrook, Kevin. 1995. *The Paradox of Revolution*. Baltimore, MD: Johns Hopkins University Press.

Miguens, José Enrique. 1988. "Las Intepretaciones Intelectuales del Voto Peronista: Los Prejuicios Academicos y las Realidades." In José Enrique Miguens and Frederick Turner, eds. *Racionalidad del Peronismo: Perspectivas Internas y Externas que Replantean un Debate Inconcluso*. Buenos Aires: Planeta.

Mora y Araujo, Manuel. 1980. "Las Bases Estructurales del Peronismo." In Manuel Mora y Araujo and Ignacio Llorente, eds. *El Voto Peronista: Ensayos de Sociologia Electoral Argentina*. Buenos Aires: Editorial Sudamericana.

Mora de Araujo, Manuel. 1988. "La Estructura Social del Peronismo." In Jose Enrique Miguens and Frederick Turner, eds. *Racionalidad del Peronismo: Perspectivas Internas y Externas que Replantean un Debate Inconcluso*. Buenos Aires: Planeta.

Mora y Araujo, Manuel. 1995. "De Perón a Menem: Una Historia del Peronismo." In Roy Hora and Javier Trímboli, eds. *Peronismo y Menemismo*. Buenos Aires: Ediciones El Cielo por Asalto.

Mora y Araujo, Manuel and Ignacio Llorente, eds. 1980. *El Voto Peronista: Ensayos de Sociologia Electoral Argentina*. Buenos Aires: Editorial Sudamericana.

Mora y Araujo, Manuel and Peter Smith. 1980. "Peronismo y Desarrollo: Las Elecciones de 1973." In Manuel Mora y Araujo and Ignacio Llorente, eds. *El Voto Peronista: Ensayos de Sociologia Electoral Argentina*. Buenos Aires: Editorial Sudamericana.

Morlino, Leonardo. 1996. "Crisis of Parties and Change of Party System in Italy." *Party Politics* 2, no. 1 (January): 5–30.

Movimiento Sindical Peronista Renovador. 1986. "Primer Plenario Nacional Sindical del Movimiento Renovador Peronista." Carlos Paz, Cordoba: Movimiento Sindical Peronista Renovador.

Munck, Gerardo. 1998. *Authoritarianism and Democratization: Soldiers and Workers in Argentina, 1976–1983*. University Park, PA: Pennsylvania State University Press.

Murillo, María Victoria. 1997. "Union Politics, Market-Oriented Reforms, and the Reshaping of Argentine Corporatism." In Douglas A. Chalmers, Carlos M. Vivas, Katherine Hite, Scott B. Martin, Kerianne Piester, and Monique Segarra, eds. *The New Politics of Inequality in Latin America: Rethinking Representation and Participation*. Oxford, UK: Oxford University Press.

Murillo, María Victoria. 2000. "From Populism to Neoliberalism: Labor Unions and Market Reforms in Latin America." *World Politics* 52, no. 2 (January): 135–74.

Murillo, María Victoria. 2001. *Partisan Coalitions and Labor Competition in Latin America: Trade Unions and Market Reforms*. New York: Cambridge University Press.

Murmis, Miguel and Juan Carlos Portantiero. 1970. *Estudios Sobre los Orígenes del Peronismo*. Buenos Aires: Siglo XXI.

Mustapic, Ana María. 1996. "El Partido Justicialista. Perspectiva Histórica Sobre el Desarrollo del Partido. La Estrutura del Partido." Buenos Aires: Universidad Torcuato Di Tella. Unpublished manuscript.

Naím, Moisés. 1993. *Paper Tigers and Minotaurs. The Politics of Venezuela's Economic Reforms*. Washington: Carnegie Endowment for International Peace.

Navarro, Marysa. 1981. *Evita*. Buenos Aires: Gedisa.

Nelson, Richard R. and Sidney G. Winter. 1982. *An Evolutionary Theory of Economic Change*. Cambridge, MA: Harvard University Press.

Niño, Carlos S. 1996. "Hyper-Presidentialism and Constitutional Reform in Argentina." In Arend Lijphart and Carlos H. Waisman, eds. *Institutional Design in New Democracies*. Boulder, CO: Westview Press, 1996.

North, Douglass C. 1990a. *Institutions, Institutional Change, and Economic Performance*. New York: Cambridge University Press.

North, Douglass C. 1990b. "A Transaction Cost Theory of Politics." *Journal of Theoretical Politics* 2, no. 4: 355–67.

North, Liisa. 1973. "The Origins and Development of the Peruvian Aprista Party." Unpublished doctoral dissertation. Department of Political Science, University of California at Berkeley.

Novaro, Marcos. 1994. *Pilotos de Tormentas: Crisis de Representacion y Personalizacion de la Política en Argentina (1989–1993)*. Buenos Aires: Ediciones Letra Buena.

Novaro, Marcos. 1995. "Menemismo y Peronismo: Viejo y Nuevo Populismo." In Ricardo Sidicaro and Jorge Mayer, eds. *Política y Sociedad en los Años del Menemismo*. Buenos Aires: Universidad de Buenos Aires.

Novaro, Marcos. 1998. "Shifting Alliances: Party Politics in Argentina."*NACLA Report on the Americas* XXXI, no. 6 (May/June): 11–15.

Nun, José. 1995. "Populismo, Representación, y Menemismo." In Roy Hora and Javier Trímboli, eds. *Peronismo y Menemismo: Avatares del Populismo en la Argentina*. Buenos Aires: El Cielo por Asalto.

O'Donnell, Guillermo. 1973. *Modernization and Bureaucratic-Authoritarianism*. Berkeley, CA: Institute of International Studies.

O'Donnell, Guillermo. 1988. *Bureaucratic Authoritarianism: Argentina, 1966–1973, in Comparative Perspective*. Berkeley, CA: University of California Press.

O'Donnell, Guillermo. 1994. "Delegative Democracy." *Journal of Democracy* 5, no. 1 (January): 55–69.

O'Donnell, Guillermo. 1996. "Illusions about Consolidation." *Journal of Democracy* 7, no. 2: 34–51.

O'Donnell, Guillermo and Philippe C. Schmitter. 1986. *Transitions from Authoritarian Rule: Tentative Conclusions about Uncertain Democracies*. Baltimore, MD: Johns Hopkins University Press.

Offe, Claus. 1984. *Contradictions of the Welfare State*. Cambridge, MA: MIT Press.

Olsen, Johan P. 1983. *Organized Democracy*. Bergen, Norway: Universitetsforlaget.

Orsatti, Álvaro. 1991. "Informalidad y Estructura Productiva en Argentina." In Jacabo Schatan, Dieter Paas, and Álvaro Orsatti, eds. 1991. *El Sector Informal en América Latina*. Mexico City: Centro de Investigación y Docencia Económicas.

Ostiguy, Pierre. 1998. "Peronism and Anti-Peronism: Class-Cultural Cleavages and Political Identity in Argentina." Ph.D dissertation. Department of Political Science, University of California at Berkeley.

Ostrogorski, Moisei. 1902. *Democracy and the Organization of Political Parties*. New York: MacMillan.

Ostrom. Elinor. 1986. "An Agenda for the Study of Institutions." *Public Choice* 48: 3–25.

Otero, Daniel. 1997. *El Entorno: La Trama Íntima del Aparato Duhaldista y sus Punteros*. Buenos Aires: Nuevohacer.

Oxhorn, Phillip. 1995. *Organizing Civil Society: The Popular Sectors and the Struggle for Democracy in Chile*. University Park, PA: Pennsylvania State University Press.

Pacheco, Guadalupe. 1991. "La XIV Asamblea Nacional del PRI." *Estudios Políticos* (October–December): 71–88.
Padgett, John F. and Christopher K. Ansell. 1993. "Robust Action and the Rise of the Medici, 1400–1434." *American Journal of Sociology* 98, no. 6 (May): 1259–1319.
Page, Joseph. 1983. *Perón: A Biography*. New York: Random House.
Palermo, Vicente. 1986a. *Democracia Interna en los Partidos*. Buenos Aires: Ediciones del IDES.
Palermo, Vicente. 1986b. "Transformación Social: Partido y Sindicatos." *Unidos* 4, no. 11–12 (October): 75–87.
Palermo, Vicente. 1994. "El Menemismo, Perdura?" In Aníbal Iturrieta, ed. *El Pensamiento Político Argentino Contemporáneo*. Buenos Aires: Editor Latinoamericano.
Palermo, Vicente and Marcos Novaro. 1996. *Política y Poder en el Gobierno de Menem*. Buenos Aires: Grupo Editorial Norma Ensayo.
Palermo, Vicente and Juan Carlos Torre. 1992. "A la Sombra de la Hiperinflación: La Política de Reformas Estructurales en Argentina." Unpublished paper. Santiago, Chile: CEPAL.
Palomino, Hector. 1987. *Cambios Ocupacionales y Sociales en Argentina, 1947–1985*. Buenos Aires: CISEA.
Panebianco, Angelo. 1988. *Political Parties: Organization and Power*. Cambridge, UK: Cambridge University Press.
Partido Justicialista. 1975. *Carta Organica Nacional*. Buenos Aires: Consejo Nacional del Partido Justicialista.
Partido Justicialista. 1983. *Plataforma de Gobierno*. Buenos Aires: El Cid.
Partido Justicialista. 1991. *Carta Organica Nacional*. Buenos Aires: Ediciones del P.J.
Partido Justicialista de la Provincia de Buenos Aires. 1988. *Carta Organica del Partido Justicialista de la Provincia de Buenos Aires*. Photocopy.
Partido Justicialista Metropolitana. 1986. *Carta Organica*. Buenos Aires: Partido Justicialista Metropolitana.
Partido Peronista. 1948. *Manual del Peronista*. Buenos Aires: Partido Peronista.
Pastor, Manuel and Carol Wise. 1992. "Peruvian Economic Policy in the 1980s: From Orthodoxy to Heterodoxy and Back." *Latin American Research Review* 27, no. 2: 83–117.
Pelinka, Anton. 1983. *Social Democratic Parties in Europe*. New York: Praeger.
Perelli, Carina. 1995. "La Personalizacion de la Politica. Nuevos Caudillos, Outsiders, Politica Mediatica y Politica Informal." In Carina Perelli, Sonia Picado, and Daniel Zoviatto, eds. *Partidos y Clase Politica en America Latina en los 90*. San Jose: Instituto Interamericano de Derechos Humanos.
Perdía, Robero Cirilo. 1997. *La Otra Historia: Testimonia de un Jefe Montonero*. Buenos Aires: Grupo Agora.
Perelli, Carina, Sonia Picado, and Daniel Zoviatto, eds. 1995. *Partidos y Clase Politica en America Latina en los 90*. San Jose: Instituto Interamericano de Derechos Humanos.
Perón, Juan D. 1951/1971. *Conduccion Politica*. Buenos Aires: Editorial Freeland.
Peruzzotti, Enrique. 2001. "The Nature of the New Argentine Democracy: The Delegative Democracy Argument Revisited." *Journal of Latin American Studies* 33, no. 1 (February): 133–55.
Pierson, Paul. 2000. "Increasing Returns, Path Dependence, and the Study of Politics." *American Political Science Review* 94, no. 2: 251–67.

Pinto, Julio. 1995. "Menemismo and Neoconservadorismo." In Ricardo Sidicaro and Jorge Mayer, eds. *Política y Sociedad en los Años del Menemismo*. Buenos Aires: University of Buenos Aires.

Piore, Michael J. and Charles F. Sabel. 1984. *The Second Industrial Divide*. New York: Basic Books.

Pizzorno, Alessandro. 1978. "Political Exchange and Collective Identity in Industrial Conflict." In Colin Crouch and Alessandro, eds. *The Resurgence of Class Conflict in Western Europe since 1968*, vol. 2. New York: Holmes and Meier.

Plotkin, Mariano. 1993. *Manana es San Perón: Propaganda, Rituales Políticos y Educación en el Régimen Peronista, 1946–1955*. Buenos Aires: Ariel.

Plumb, David. 1998. "El Partido Por la Democracia: The Birth of Chile's Postmaterialist Catch-All Left." *Party Politics* 4, no. 1 (January): 93–106.

Pont, Susana Elena. 1984. *Partido Laborista: Estado y Sindicatos*. Buenos Aires: CEAL.

Powell, Walter W. and Paul J. DiMaggio, eds. 1991. *The New Institutionalism in Organizational Analysis*. Chicago, IL: University of Chicago Press.

Powers, Nancy. 1995. "The Politics of Poverty in Argentina in the 1990s." *Journal of Interamerican Studies and World Affairs* 37: 4: 89–137.

Przeworski, Adam and Fernando Limongi. 1997. "Modernization: Theories and Facts." *World Politics* 49 (January): 155–83.

Przeworski, Adam and John Sprague. 1986. *Paper Stones: A History of Electoral Socialism*. Chicago, IL: University of Chicago Press.

Quevedo, Hugo Orlando. 1991. *El Partido Peronista en la Rioja (Tomo II, 1960–1971)*. Córdoba: Marcos Lerner.

Quintar, Aida. 1990. "Flexibilizacion Laboral: Requerimiento de las Nuevas Tecnologias o Fragmentacion del Movimiento Obrero?" *Desarrollo Económico* 30, no. 118 (July–September): 221–35.

Ranis, Peter. 1995. *Class, Democracy, and Labor in Contemporary Argentina*. New Brunswick, NJ: Transaction Publishers.

Roberts, Kenneth. 1994. "Renovation in the Revolution? Dictatorship, Democracy, and Political Change in the Chilean Left." Kellogg Institute Working Paper 203. Notre Dame, IN: Helen Kellogg Institute for International Studies.

Roberts, Kenneth. 1995. "Neoliberalism and the Transformation of Populism in Latin America." *World Politics* 48, no. 1: 82–116.

Roberts, Kenneth. 1997a. "Rethinking Economic Alternatives: Left Parties and the Articulation of Popular Demands in Chile and Peru." In Douglas A. Chambers, Carlos M. Vilas, Katherine Hite, Scott B. Martin, Kerianne Piester, and Monique Segarra, eds. *The New Politics of Inequality in Latin America: Rethinking Participation and Representation*. New York: Oxford University Press.

Roberts, Kenneth. 1997b. "Structural Adjustment and the Adaptation or Breakdown of Party Systems: A Comparison of Chile, Argentina, Peru, and Venezuela." Paper prepared for delivery at the Twentieth International Congress of the Latin American Studies Association, Guadalajara, Mexico, April 17–19, 1997.

Roberts, Kenneth. 1998a. *Deepening Democracy? The Modern Left and Social Movements in Chile and Peru*. Stanford, CA: Stanford University Press.

Roberts, Kenneth. 1998b. "The Chilean Party System and Social Cleavages in the Neoliberal Era." Paper prepared for delivery at the Twenty-First International

Congress of the Latin American Studies Association, Chicago, IL, September 24–6, 1998.

Roberts, Kenneth M. 2002. "Social Inequalities without Class Cleavages in Latin America's Neoliberal Era." *Studies in Comparative International Development* 36, no. 4 (winter): 3–33.

Rodrik, Dani. 1994. "Comment." In John Williamson, ed. *The Political Economy of Policy Reform*. Washington, DC: Institute for International Economics.

Rose, Richard and Thomas T. Mackie. 1988. "Do Parties Persist or Fail? The Big Trade-Off Facing Organizations." In Kay Lawson and Peter H. Merkl, eds. *When Parties Fail: Emerging Alternative Organizations*. Princeton, NJ: Princeton University Press.

Sanborn, Cynthia. 1989. "El Apra en un Contexto de Cambio, 1968–88." In Heraclio Bonilla and Paul W. Drake, eds. *El APRA de la Ideología a la Praxis*. Lima: Centro Latinoamericano de Historia Económico y Social.

Sanborn, Cynthia. 1991. "The Democratic Left and the Persistence of Populism in Peru." Ph.D. dissertation. Department of Government, Harvard University.

Sani, Giacomo and Giovanni Sartori. 1983. "Polarization, Fragmentation and Competition in Western Democracies." In Hans Daalder and Peter Mair, eds. *Western European Party Systems*. Beverly Hills, CA: Sage.

Santoro, Daniel. 1994. *El Hacedor: Una Biografía Política de Domingo Cavallo*. Buenos Aires: Planeta.

Sartori, Giovanni. 1968. "European Political Parties: The Case of Polarized Pluralism." In Robert Dahl and D. E. Neubauer, eds. *Readings in Modern Political Analysis*. New York: Prentice Hall.

Scarrow, Susan. 1996. *Parties and Their Members: Organizing for Victory in Germany and Britain*. New York: Oxford University Press.

Schedler, Andreas. 1995. "Under- and Overinstitutionalization: Some Ideal Typical Propositions Concerning New and Old Party Systems." Kellogg Institute Working Paper 213. Notre Dame, IN: Helen Kellogg Institute for International Studies.

Schlesinger, Joseph A. 1984. "On the Theory of Party Organization." *Journal of Politics* 46, no. 2: 369–400.

Schmitter, Philippe C. 1995. "Transitology: The Science or the Art of Democratization?" In Joseph S. Tulchin (with Bernice Romero), ed. *The Consolidation of Democracy in Latin America*. Boulder, CO: Lynne Reinner.

Schonfeld, William R. 1981. "Oligarchy and Leadership Stability: The French Communist, Socialist, and Gaullist Parties." *American Journal of Political Science* 25, no. 2 (May): 215–40.

Schoultz, Lars. 1983. *The Populist Challenge: Argentine Electoral Behavior in the Postwar Era*. Chapel Hill, NC: University of North Carolina Press.

Scott, James C. 1969. "Corruption, Machine Politics, and Political Change." *American Political Science Review* 63: 1142–58.

Scully, Timothy R. 1995. "Reconstituting Party Politics in Chile." In Scott Mainwaring and Timothy R. Scully, eds. *Building Democratic Institutions: Party Systems in Latin America*. Stanford, CA: Stanford University Press.

Scully, Timothy R. 1996. "Chile: The Political Underpinnings of Economic Liberalization." In Jorge I. Domínguez and Abraham F. Lowenthal, eds. *Constructing Democratic Governance: South America in the 1990s*. Baltimore, MD: Johns Hopkins University Press.

Selznick, Philip. 1957. *Leadership in Administration: A Sociological Interpretation.* New York: Harper and Row.
Seyd, Patrick and Paul Whiteley. 1992. *Labour's Grass Roots: The Politics of Party Membership.* London: Clarendon Press.
Shefter, Martin. 1986. "Trade Unions and Political Machines: The Organization and Disorganization of the American Working Class in the Late Nineteenth Century." In Ira Katznelson and Aristede R. Zolberg, eds. *Working-Class Formation: Nineteenth-Century Patterns in Western Europe and the United States.* Princeton, NJ: Princeton University Press.
Shefter, Martin. 1994. *Political Parties and the State: The American Historical Experience.* Princeton, NJ: Princeton University Press.
Sigelman, Lee. 1979. "Understanding Political Instability: An Evaluation of the Mobilization-Institutionalization Approach." *Comparative Political Studies* 12: 205–28.
Sjoblom, Gunnar. 1983. "Political Change and Political Accountability: A Propositional Inventory of Causes and Effects." In Hans Daalder and Peter Mair, eds. *Western European Party Systems.* Beverly Hills, CA: Sage.
Smith, Peter H. 1972. "The Social Bases of Peronism." *Hispanic American Historical Review* 52 (February): 55–73.
Smith, William. 1989. *Authoritarianism and the Crisis of the Argentine Political Economy.* Stanford, CA: Stanford University Press.
Smith, William. 1990. "Democracy, Distributional Conflicts and Macroeconomic Policymaking in Argentina, 1983–1989." *Journal of Inter-American Studies and World Affairs* (Summer): 1–36.
Smith, William. 1992. "Hyperinflation, Macroeconomic Instability, and Neoliberal Restructuring in Democratic Argentina." In Edward C. Epstein, ed. *The New Argentine Democracy: The Search for a Successful Formula.* Westport, CT: Praeger.
Stokes, Susan C. 2001. *Mandates, Markets, and Democracy: Neoliberalism By Surprise in Latin America.* New York: Cambridge University Press.
Strom, Kaare. 1990a. *Minority Government and Majority Rule* (New York: Cambridge University Press.
Strom, Kaare. 1990b. "A Behavioral Theory of Competitive Political Parties." *American Journal of Political Science* 34, no. 2 (May 1990): 565–98.
Tantaleán, Javier. 1989. "Política Económica del Aprismo." In Heraclio Bonilla and Paul W. Drake, eds. *El APRA de la Ideología a la Praxis.* Lima: Centro Latinoamericano de Historia Económico y Social.
Tarrow, Sidney. 1994. *Power in Movement. Social Movements, Collective Action, and Politics.* New York: Cambridge University Press.
Taylor, Andrew. 1993. "Trade Unions and the Politics of Social Democratic Renewal." In Richard Gillespie and William E. Paterson, eds. *Rethinking Social Democracy in Western Europe.* London: Frank Cass.
Tcach, César. 1990. *Una Interpretación del Peronismo Periférico: El Partido Peronista de Córdoba (1945–1955).* Documento CEDES, no. 54. Buenos Aires: Centro de Estudios del Estado y Sociedad.
Tcach, César. 1991. *Sabattinismo y Peronismo: Partidos Políticos en Córdoba 1943–1955.* Buenos Aires: Editorial Sudamericana.
Thompson, James D. 1967. *Organizations in Action: Social Science Bases of Administrative Theory.* New York: McGraw-Hill Book Company.

Tilly, Charles. 1973. "Does Modernization Breed Revolution?" *Comparative Politics* 5: 425–47.
Tokman, Victor E. 1992. "The Informal Sector in Latin America: From Underground to Legality." In Victor E. Tokman, ed. *Beyond Regulation: The Informal Economy in Latin America*. Boulder, CO: Lynne Rienner.
Tokman, Victor E. 1996. "La Especificidad y Generalidad del Problema del Empleo en el Contexto de América Latina." In Luís Beccaria and Néstor Lopez, eds. *Sin Empleo: Las Características del Desempleo y sus Efectos en la Sociedad Argentina*. Buenos Aires: Losada.
Torrado, Susana. 1992. *Estructura Social de la Argentina: 1945–1983*. Buenos Aires: Ediciones de la Flor.
Torre, Juan Carlos. 1983. *Los Sindicalistas en el Gobierno, 1973–1976*. Buenos Aires: Centro Editor de America Latina.
Torre, Juan Carlos. 1988a. "La CGT y el 17 de Octubre de 1945." In Juan Carlos Torre, ed. *La Formacion del Sindicalismo Peronista*. Buenos Aires: Editorial Legasa.
Torre, Juan Carlos, ed. 1988b. *La Formacion del Sindicalismo Peronista*. Buenos Aires: Editorial Legasa.
Torre, Juan Carlos. 1990. *La Vieja Guardia Sindical y Peron: Sobre los Orígenes del Peronismo*. Buenos Aires: Editorial Sudamericana.
Torre, Juan Carlos. 1998. "The Ambivalent Giant: The Peronist Labor Movement, 1945–1995." In James P. Brennan, ed. *Peronism and Argentina*. Wilmington, DE: Scholarly Resources, Inc.
Trinkunas, Harold. 2000. "Crafting Civilian Control in Emerging Democracies: Argentina and Venezuela." *Journal of Interamerican Studies and World Affairs* 42, no. 3 (Fall): 77–110.
Tsebelis, George. 1990. *Nested Games: Rational Choice in Comparative Politics*. Berkeley, CA: University of California Press.
Valenzuela, J. Samuel. 1992. "Democratic Consolidation in Post-Transitional Settings: Notion, Process, and Facilitating Conditions." In Scott Mainwaring, Guillermo O'Donnell, and J. Samuel Valenzuela, eds. *Issues in Democratic Consolidation: The New South American Democracies in Comparative Perspective*. Notre Dame, IN: University of Notre Dame Press.
Villarreal, Juan. 1987. "Changes in Argentine Society: The Heritage of the Dictatorship." In Monica Peralta-Ramos and Carlos Waisman, eds. *From Military Rule to Liberal Democracy in Argentina*. Boulder, CO: Westview Press.
Wainfeld, Mario. 1983. "El Gobierno Peronista 1973–1976: El Rodrigazo." *Unidos* 1, no. 1 (May): 21–30.
Wainfeld, Mario. 1988. "Patoruzu la Ganó a Isidoro?" *Unidos* 5, no. 19 (October): 17–33.
Wainfeld, Mario. 1990. "No Verguenza de Haber Sido Ni Dolor de ya No Ser." *Unidos* 6, no. 21 (May): 13–17.
Waisbord, Silvio. 1995. *El Gran Desfile. Campañas Electorales y Medios de Comunicación en Argentina*. Buenos Aires: Sudamericana.
Waisman, Carlos. 1987. *Reversal of Development: Postwar Counterrevolutionary Policies and Their Structural Consequences*. Princeton, NJ: Princeton University Press.
Waisman, Carlos. 1999. "Argentina: Capitalism and Democracy." In Larry Diamond, Jonathan Hartlyn, Juan J. Linz, and Seymour Martin Lipset, eds. *Democracy in Developing Countries: Latin America*. Boulder, CO: Lynne Rienner.

Ware, Alan. 1992. "Activist–Leader Relations and the Structure of Political Parties: 'Exchange' Models and Vote-Seeking Behavior in Parties." *British Journal of Political Science* 22 (January): 71–92.
Warner, Carolyn M. 1997. "Political Parties and the Opportunity Costs of Patronage." *Party Politics* 3, no. 4: 533–548.
Welfling, Mary B. 1973. *Political Institutionalization: Comparative Analyses of African Party Systems*. Beverly Hills, CA: Sage Publications.
Wellhofer, E. Spencer. 1972. "Dimensions of Party Development: A Study in Organizational Dynamics." *Journal of Politics* 34: 152–82.
Wellhofer, E. Spencer. 1979a. "The Effectiveness of Party Organization: A Cross-National, Time Series Analysis." *European Journal of Political Research* 19: 205–24.
Wellhofer, E. Spencer. 1979b. "Strategies for Party Organization and Voter Mobilization: Britain, Norway, and Argentina." *Comparative Political Studies* 12, no. 3: 169–204.
Weyland, Kurt. 1996. "Neopopulism and Neoliberalism in Latin America." *Studies in Comparative International Development* 31, no. 1: 3–31.
Weyland, Kurt. 1999. "Neoliberal Populism in Latin America and Eastern Europe." *Comparative Politics* 31, no. 4: 379–401.
Weyland, Kurt. 2001. "Clarifying a Contested Concept: Populism in the Study of Latin American Politics." *Comparative Politics* 34, no. 1 (October): 1–22.
Wilson, Frank. 1994. "The Sources of Party Change: The Social Democratic Parties of Britain, France, Germany, and Spain." In Kay Lawson, ed. *How Political Parties Work: Perspectives from Within*. Westport, CT: Praeger.
Wilson, James Q. 1973/1995. *Political Organizations*. Princeton, NJ: Princeton University Press.
Wolfinger, Raymond. 1972. "Why Political Machines Have Not Withered Away and Other Revisionist Thoughts." *Journal of Politics* 34 (February): 365–98.
Wolinetz, Steven B. 1990. "The Transformation of Western European Party Systems." In Peter Mair, ed. *The West European Party System*. Oxford, UK: Oxford University Press.
Yannuzzi, María de los Angeles. 1995. *La Modernizacion Conservadora: El Peronismo de los 90*. Buenos Aires: Editorial Fundacion Ross.
Zamítiz, Héctor. 1991. "La Reforma del PRI en el Contexto de la Reforma del Estado (Actores y Dinámica Política de la XIV Asamblea Nacional)." *Estudios Políticos* (July–September): 109–39.
Zorrilla, Ruben H. 1983a. *El Liderazgo Sindical Argentino: Desde sus Origenes Hasta 1975*. Buenos Aires: Ediciones Siglo Veinte.
Zorrilla, Ruben H. 1983b. "Líder, Elite, y Masa en el Peronismo." *Todo Es Historia* (December): 28–37.
Zucker, Lynne G. 1977. "The Role of Institutionalization in Cultural Persistence." *American Sociological Review* 42 (October): 726–43.
Zucker, Lynne G. 1983. "Organizations and Institutions." In Samuel B. Bacharach, ed. *Research in the Sociology of Organizations*, vol. 2. Greenwich, CT: JAI Press.

Index

Abal Medina, Juan Manuel, 47, 79
Abasto, Angel, 132
Abós, Alvaro, 103
Action for the Republic, 182t, 226n15
activists. *See* party activists
AD. *See* Democratic Action (AD)
adaptation. *See* party adaptation
agrupaciones, 67, 69–73, 69t, 75, 89,
    109–10, 124, 198–202. *See also*
    local party organization
  autonomy of, 70–2, 89, 177–8,
    197–202, 201t
  base units (UBs) and, 69–72
  collectivist, 213–16
  as *de facto* party organization, 70–1,
    109–10
  exchange-based, 204–9
  financing of, 69, 71–2, 109–10, 126,
    130–2, 195
  union sponsorship of, 130–2
Alchouran, Guillermo, 179
Alfonsín, Raúl, 100–1, 103–5, 119, 183,
    218–19, 224
Alliance for Jobs, Justice, and
    Education, 182t, 183, 226,
    227n17, 228–9
Alvarez, Carlos "Chacho," 172,
    191n10, 247
Alvarez, Juan José, 60n3, 214
American Popular Revolutionary
    Alliance (APRA) (Peru), 2, 6–9,
    11n14, 22, 26, 81, 232–3

economic failure of, 6, 9, 26, 238
electoral performance of, 7–9,
    185n202, 238, 244t
failed adaptation of, 236–8, 244–5
linkage to organized labor of, 237
party structure of, 236
Andreoni, Guerino, 160, 170
Ansell, Christopher, 88, 169
antisystem appeals, 6, 226–7
anti-verticalists, 48, 51
Argentine Workers Congress (CTA), 31,
    137, 225
Argentine Workers Movement (MTA),
    31, 137, 225
Arias, Arnulfo, 22
Arias, Cesar, 86, 170
armed forces. *See* military
Atanasoff, Alfredo, 136
Australian Labor Party, 7, 89
Austrian Socialist Party, 7, 61t
autonomy
  local PJ, 88–9, 197–202, 201t
  local PJ and limits of Menemism,
    177–82
  movement organization and, 43–4,
    51
  mutual, 87–90
  party activists and local, 197–202,
    201t
  party leadership, 13
  party weakness and presidential,
    157–77

271

autonomy (*cont.*)
   strategic, 25–6, 144–5, 158–62, 169
   strategic constraint v. strategic, 18–19, 20–1
Auyero, Javier, 141–2
Azcurra, José, 136, 149

bandwagoning, 31, 33, 87, 144, 233n2, 235
   collapse of Renovation faction and, 158–61, 235
Barrantes, Alfonso, 237
Barrionuevo, Luis, 123, 131, 164n92, 170, 224
base units (UB), 40, 59, 61–4, 64t, 66–8, 69t, 71–2, 86, 126, 128, 130, 187–90, 188t, 193, 195t, 197–8, 198n20, 203
   activities of, 67, 109–10, 215, 126–8, 187–191, 202, 203–5
   agrupaciones and, 69–72
   alternatives to, 212, 215
   autonomy of, 66–7, 215
   bottom-up v. top-down, 210–11
   collectivist, 213–15
   diverse forms of, 67–9, 69t
   finance of, 66–7, 69, 71, 130–2, 178, 195–8, 195t, 203
   low routinization of, 66, 86
   machine, 198, 203–9, 206t, 209t, 210
   modern-amateur, 198, 203–6, 206t, 209
   party activists and, 67, 187–90, 192–3, 193t, 195–9, 195t, 202–16
   social linkages of, 62–65, 64t
   traditional v. modern-amateur v. machine, 203–4, 206–7, 206t, 209, 209t
   unions and, 62–4t, 130–1, 140
   yuppification of, 210
Bauza, Eduardo, 86, 148, 165–8, 166n102, 180
Belaúnde, Fernando, 237
Beliz, Gustavo, 70, 85n103, 86, 157
Bittel, Deolindo, 45, 52, 92, 92n6, 94

blue-collar workers 38, 95–7
   informal sector v., 6, 95–7, 140
   white-collar workers v., 6, 95–8
Bolivia, 10, 22, 221, 223, 232n1
Borda, Osvaldo, 128, 131, 136, 160, 160n53
Bordón, José Octavio, 130, 148, 172–4, 173n51, 183, 191
Born, Jorge, 223
Bouer, Saúl, 126
Brazil, 12, 76, 89, 156, 218, 220–1, 227, 227n16, 230
Brazilian Workers Party (PT), 79, 81
Bretton Woods, 5
British Labour Party, 8, 8n9, 38, 61t, 82, 115
Brito Lima, Alberto, 50
Britos, Oraldo, 148, 171n141, 173n51
Brunelli, Naldo, 130, 136
Buenos Aires (province of), 32, 46, 48n24, 51, 74, 84n97, 84n100, 93, 105, 110, 112, 120, 124–5, 128–9, 131, 134, 134t, 175–6, 179–80, 182, 184, 247
Buenos Aires Peronism, 128–30
Bunge y Born, 145, 163
bureaucracy
   central, 20–1, 76, 88, 198, 215, 239–40
   fluidity of PJ, 79–82, 86–7, 232
   PJ lacking central, 3, 26, 30, 37, 40–1, 65–73, 75–6, 79–82, 88–9, 144, 158–61, 170, 178–82, 215, 247
"business Peronism" (La Matanza), 127–8
Bussi, Antonio, 226–7
Busti, Jorge, 175, 176n176

C de O. *See Comando de Organización*
cadre organizations, 27, 43, 47–51, 70n37, 198–9
Cafiero, Antonio, 31, 54, 56, 73n54, 76n61, 81, 92, 92n5, 94, 109, 111, 113, 116n36, 121, 121n60, 128, 148, 155, 158–60, 162–5, 173–5, 176n176

Index

Calabró, Victorio, 48
Cámpora, Hector, 47–8, 48n25, 199n25
Caracazo, 235
Cardozo, Ruben, 116n36
career paths, 20, 36, 79–82, 86–7, 144, 158–9, 233
Carpinetti, Julio, 111
Cassia, Antonio, 116n36
Castillo, José Luis, 116n36, 131, 136, 160
Castillo, Ramón, 38
Catamarca, 45, 73, 73n55, 81, 114, 171, 175, 177n177, 179, 181
Catholic Church, 98, 119n51
Catterberg, Edgardo, 105
caudillos, 51, 74, 200, 207. *See also* leader(ship)
Cavallo, Domingo, 81n86, 146, 155, 169, 181, 226n15, 247
Celestes, 161, 164–5, 167, 170
Center Democratic Union (UCeDe), 70n40, 99, 100n26, 106, 120, 120t, 145, 153t, 154, 179, 182t, 183, 193
Center of Resistance Operations, 42
CGT (General Labor Confederation), 1, 31, 40–1, 50, 82, 104–5, 105n35, 113, 119, 125, 136–7, 136n117, 147, 224–5
  loss of control over union deputies by, 135–6
  general strike against Menem by, 167, 224
CGT. *See also* organized labor
CGT-Azopardo, 111
Chaco, 45, 73, 75, 181n198
Chamber of Deputies, 135–6, 172, 175, 182t, 183, 219–20, 227, 229, 247
  union representation in, 133–5, 134t, 135t
charismatic organizations, 36–41, 46, 48
Chávez, Hugo, 9, 227n16, 236, 245
Chica Rodriguez, Juan José, 132, 136
Chile, 2, 7–9, 104, 220–1, 223, 231, 233, 239–41

Chilean Communist Party (PCCh), 7–8, 12, 34, 42, 61t, 76, 81, 88, 198, 232–3
  electoral performance of, 240, 244t
  failed adaptation of, 239–40, 244–5
  party structure of, 233, 239
Chilean Socialist Party (PSCh), 22n30, 81–2, 232–3
  electoral performance of, 240, 244t
  party structure of, 239–41
  successful adaptation of, 239–40, 244
Christian Democratic Party (Argentina), 80
Chumbita, Hugo, 116
civic associations, 68, 69t, 214–15
class structure. *See also* middle class; upper class; working class
  changes in, 1, 6, 94–9
  middle, 6, 95–100, 102–6, 118–20, 140, 154t, 210–12
  upper, 154t, 222–3
  working/lower, 24, 27–8, 38, 41, 62–5, 94–100, 105–7, 141, 143, 183–5, 191, 210, 213–16, 222, 227–8, 247–9
clientelism, 107, 141–3, 202–11, 213, 228, 230, 248
clubs, 63–4, 64t
cogollo, 235
collectivist organizations, 213–16
Colombia, 22
Colosio, Luis Donaldo, 242–3
Comando de Organización (C de O), 27, 43, 47, 49–50, 70n37, 198–9
communist parties, 7–8, 12, 22, 25, 27–8, 42, 82, 88, 198, 232–3, 237, 239–40. *See also* Chilean Communist Party; French Communist Party
competition
  identification v., 85, 89, 98–9
  oligopolistic, 98
conservers, 20–1, 26, 87
Convertibility Law, 146, 149, 155–6, 166, 173, 182, 184, 229–30
Convocation of Peronist Workers, 124

Cooperative, 130
Coppedge, Michael, 12, 234
Corach, Carlos, 159, 170
Córdoba, 32, 75, 81, 84n103, 93, 105, 115, 118, 120, 122, 130, 134t, 159, 173, 177n177, 180–1, 247
corporatist structure, 82–4, 130, 242–3
Corrales, Javier, 156–7, 160, 235
Corrientes, 73, 74n55, 81, 84, 84n97–100, 114, 180–1
corruption, 180–1, 210, 228
Costa Rica, 156, 221
Cozzi, Hector, 127, 132–3
critical juncture, 4–7, 231
Cuba, 105, 199

Dal Lago, Adalberto "Tito," 205–6, 208
Dante Gullo, Juan Carlos, 199
de facto laborism, 91–2, 94, 107
De Gennaro, Victor, 160
De la Madrid, Miguel, 242
De la Rua, Fernando, 127, 137, 227–9, 246–7
De la Sota, José Manuel, 109, 109n6, 115n34, 119n50, 121n60, 122, 137, 148–9, 159–60, 160n54, 160n58, 162, 166n102, 173–6, 176n176, 181, 247
De la Vega, Carlos, 179
debt crisis, 5, 104
  Alliance government and, 228–30
  government autonomy reduced by, 5–6
  neoliberalism, ISI exhaustion and, 91, 100–1
  Peru and, 105, 237–8
debt payments, opposition to, 50n32, 104–5, 119
Decrees of Necessity and Urgency (NUD), 219–20
D'Elia, Luis, 210
deindustrialization, 6, 26, 91, 94–8, 102, 140
democracy, 9, 108–9, 116, 119
  alternatives to, 221
  costs of party adaptation and, 227–30

delegative, 26, 219, 227n16
horizontal accountability and, 219–21
Menemism and 219–30
military coup and, 48, 218, 221
party adaptation and, 8–9, 33–4, 217–18, 225–7, 231–2, 245
party system decomposition and, 8–9, 218–19
Peronism and, 221–30
stability of Argentine in 1990s, 217, 219–27
Democratic Action (AD) (Venezuela), 2, 7–8, 11n14, 12, 34, 42, 44, 61t, 76, 79, 81–2, 88, 150, 157, 198, 232
economic failure of, 26, 234–5
electoral performance of, 8–9, 236, 244t
failed adaptation of, 233–5, 244–5
linkage to organized labor, 82, 234–5
party structure of, 12, 233–4
routinized nature of, 41, 79, 81–2, 88, 233–4
Digón, Roberto, 112, 122, 130, 200, 224
Di Tella, Guido, 115, 147n15
Doctrinal Peronism, 199
dollarization, 247
Domato, José, 180
Domínguez, Jorge, 127
Downs, Anthony, 12, 20, 87, 98
Drewes, Hector, 208
Duhalde, Eduardo, 70, 80, 81nn86–7, 92n5, 111, 124–5, 133, 148–9, 149n29, 162, 167, 172–4, 227
Buenos Aires party machine of, 128–9
opposition to Menem by, 173–6, 176n176, 179
as president, 229, 247
as presidential nominee, 175, 246–8
virtual veto power of, 175
Durand, Ricardo, 45
Duverger, Maurice, 11–12, 42

Index

economic boom, 156
economic elite
  PJ and, 27, 145–6, 222–3
  unions and, 222–3
Economic Emergency Law, 145
economic environment
  changes in, 5–6, 10, 100–1
Ecuador, 12, 22, 220
Eldersveld, Samuel, 76, 88–9
election(s)
  boycott of, 45
  campaign strategy for, 14, 103, 108–9, 167–8, 118–19, 204–9, 206t, 211–12
  constitutional reform for (re-), 166, 168, 173, 176, 176n176, 219, 219n2, 221
  entrepreneurial strategies for, 206t, 207–9
  identification v. competition in, 85, 89, 98
  material exchange-based strategies for, 204–9, 206t, 209t
  media-based strategies and, 212
  of Menem(ist), 76n61, 81, 101, 120, 144, 162, 168, 172, 174, 182–5
  PJ losing of, 53, 91, 105–6, 108, 246–7
  PJ winning of, 2, 55, 81, 119–20, 120t, 155, 162, 168, 172, 227
  Renovation success in, 112–13, 118–20, 120t
  results of, 105–6, 119–20, 120t, 182–5, 182t, 244t
  of unionists to Chamber of Deputies, 94–5, 133–5, 134t, 135t, 224
electoral cushion, 13–14, 64, 85–6
electoral volatility, 6, 8, 226
electorate
  of belonging, 13, 65, 85
  failure to adapt to, 8, 105
  independent, 98, 102, 104, 107, 118–20, 183, 185, 247
  new center of, 98, 102, 105–6, 119–20
  party strategy and, 10, 12
  traditional Peronist, 41, 85, 105–6, 183–5, 225
El Salvador, 217
employment
  industrial, 95
  retail and service, 95
  unemployment rates and, 175, 195–6, 229
environment (external)
  changes in, 5–7, 10–12, 94–101
  routinization and adaptation to, 19
Escobar, Jorge, 64, 177
exchange-based organizations, 202–9. *See also* machine UBs
  agrupaciones/municipal, 204–8
  punteros/neighborhood, 204, 206–7

Falklands/Malvinas Islands, 100, 199, 221
Farmache, Horacio, 47
Federal Capital, 31–2, 63–4, 67–8, 70–1, 75, 80, 93, 100, 110, 112–13, 118, 122, 124–7, 130–1, 134t, 159, 176, 183, 188–90, 199–200, 201t, 205, 208–13, 213t
Federal Council, 53–4
Federal Current, 174–5
Federal League, 128–9, 133, 175–6, 196
Federal Parliamentary Group, 172
Federal Union, 175–6
Figueroa, Julio Mera, 170
Fish, M. Steven, 88, 169
flash parties, 218
flexibility
  leadership fluidity and, 3, 19–20, 24, 31, 59, 81–2, 86–7, 245
  low routinization and, 18–22, 84–6
  rootedness and, 13–14, 21–4, 58
  stability and, 13–15, 22–4, 86
food distribution, 187–8, 188t, 205–6, 208
Force, the, 49n26
Formosa, 48, 80, 114, 130, 175, 180–1, 184
France, 2, 6, 87
Franco, Mario, 51

French Communist Party, 7, 42, 76, 87–8, 198
French Socialist Party, 2, 6, 156
FREPASO (Front for a Country in Solidarity), 135, 135n106, 174, 182t, 183, 191, 197, 197n19, 211, 225–6, 227n19, 229n19
Frondizi, Arturo, 44n15, 45, 218
Front for a Country in Solidarity. *See* FREPASO
Front for Peronist Victory (VP), 70, 110, 126
Fujimori, Alberto, 9, 227n16, 238, 245
FUMPE, 199

Gabrielli, Rodolfo, 130, 174–5
García, Alan, 9, 105, 105n105, 185n202, 237–8
García, Roberto, 75, 80, 113n17, 115, 116n36, 117n40, 118n47, 131n96, 148, 159–60, 170
  as acting president of PJ, 165–8
Gay, Luis, 38
Gazia, Rodolfo, 168
G'Dansky, Carlos, 128
General Labor Confederation. *See* CGT
Gerlach, Luther P., 30, 42
German Social Democratic Party, 8, 42, 61t, 115
Gervasoni, Carlos, 183–4
Gibson, Edward, 28
Gonzalez, Erman, 80, 177, 212
government
  career advancement, as source of, 72, 75, 158–9, 161–2
  patronage and resources of, 69–70, 73, 109–111, 123–30, 195–7, 195t
  takeover of PJ leadership, 158–9, 161–2, 165–9
governors, 74, 128–30, 136–7, 156, 167, 171–6, 178–82, 247
Great North, 175–6
Greater Buenos Aires, 31–2, 63, 70, 95, 100, 131, 192, 201–2, 212
Green List, 85n103, 111n8, 113–14
Grosso, Carlos, 54, 109–10, 112, 113n17, 115n34, 122, 124–7, 148, 159–60, 167, 173, 211n67

Group of "25," 50, 83, 108, 108n4–5, 129, 131, 170, 200
  collapse of, 160
  failure to establish new linkage to PJ, 116–17
  as junior partner within PJ, 121, 123
  Renovation and, 108, 110–118
  "62" Organizations supplanted by, 111–13, 115, 122
Group of Eight, 171–2, 174, 191, 191n10, 225
Group of the East, 122
growth rates, lower, 5
Guatemala, 227
Guerreño, Hugo, 196, 214–15, 214n73
guerrilla movement. *See* Montoneros.
Gurlioli, Mario, 55

Haime, Hugo, 150, 153–5, 184n201
Haya de la Torre, Victor Raúl, 236–7
health insurance, 136–7, 156
Hine, Virginia, 30, 42
horizontal accountability, 219–21
human rights, 104–5, 119, 217–18, 220, 222
Huntington, Samuel, 16–17, 17n24
hyperinflation, 6, 8, 101, 146, 149n33, 150, 155, 155n37, 156, 217, 219, 221–3, 229, 234, 238

Ibañez, Diego, 52, 93n7, 94, 103, 172
identification, competition v., 85, 89
identity
  erosion of Peronist, 102, 211
  ritual of, 103
Iglesias, Herminio, 51, 93, 103, 111–12
Illia, Arturo, 218
IMF (International Monetary Fund), 5, 105, 105n35, 119, 153t, 154, 229, 237–8
importing-substituting industrialization (ISI), 1, 5, 33, 100–1, 231, 242
incentives
  material, 195–7, 203–16
  nonmaterial, 197–202
Independent Centers, 38
inflation. *See* hyperinflation

Index

informal mass party, 58–84
  informal organization and, 65–84
  mass organization and, 60–5
informal party organization, 3, 14–15, 24, 29–31, 51, 58–60, 65–76, 82–4, 109–11
  municipal-level (*agrupaciones*), 69–72
  national-level, 75–6
  neighborhood-level, 66–8, 69t
  party-union linkage, 82–4
  research needed on, 246
  roots of Peronism's, 41–9
informal sector, 1, 6–7, 95–7, 140, 235, 237–8, 242
Institutional Revolutionary Party (PRI), 2, 7, 11n14, 22, 79, 82, 232
  adaptation of, 242–5
  electoral performance of, 243–4, 244t
  linkage to organized labor of, 82, 241–3
  party structure of, 241–2
institutionalization, 15–24
  and adaptation, 3, 14–15, 17–22, 25–6, 245–6
  aggregation/disaggregation of, 17–18
  causal analysis of, 17–18
  concept/definition of, 15–18
  informal, 3, 14–15
  routinization and, 16–18
  value infusion and, 16, 16n23, 17
Intransigence and Mobilization (IM), 50
Intransigent Party (PI), 99, 100n26, 106, 120, 120t
Intransigent Radical Civic Union, 45
Iron Guard, 43, 47, 49–50
ISI. *See* importing-substituting industrialization

Joga, Vicente, 148, 168, 175
Juan D. Perón Institute, 75
Juarez, Carlos, 51, 53, 74nn55–6, 110, 181
Justicialist (Peronist) Party (PJ), 1–4. *See also* Peronism; Peronist Party (PP)
  activists, 186–216

activists' views of neoliberalism, 191–2, 192t
assessing coalitional shift of, 139–43
central bureaucracy weak in, 3, 30, 37, 40–1, 43, 51, 57, 65–7, 70–3, 75–6, 88–9, 144, 247
class structure change and, 94–8, 102
collapse of union linkage to, 107–39
Commission of Ten of, 79, 162
commitment to during adversity, 17
corruption and, 180, 210
decline of union influence in, 25–6, 107–43, 134t, 135t, 222, 232
democracy and, 26–7, 219–30
democratization of, 108–9, 116–17, 119
deunionization of, 25, 33, 107–43
electoral base of, 28, 41, 65, 94–8, 105–6, 108, 120, 140, 183–5
electoral performance of, 105–6, 119–20, 120t, 182–5, 182t, 226, 244t
elections lost by, 52–3, 91, 105–6, 108–9, 183, 246–7
elections won by, 2, 55, 119–20, 120t, 155, 162, 168, 172, 182–5, 227
failure to reach institutional settlement in, 44–8, 51–5
Federal Council of, 53–4
financing of, 69–73, 109–111, 106n6, 195–7, 203–11
flexibility of, 3, 31, 47, 85–6
formal structure, 59–60
fragmentation of, 42–4, 49–51, 53–5, 75–6, 180, 247–8
government takeover of party leadership of, 162, 165–9
hierarchy of, 59–60, 79–82
horizontal and vertical links absent in, 75–6, 87–9, 144–5, 158, 169–70, 177–82
ideology/platform of, 27–9, 102, 104–5, 118–19, 140–3, 145–9, 173, 181, 198–202, 248–9
incentives for capturing the center by, 98–100, 105–6
inefficiency of, 25, 84–5, 247–8

Justicialist Party (*cont.*)
    as informal mass party, 58–84
    informal structure of, 29–31, 65–76
    internal elections in, 59–60, 80–1, 108, 114, 117–18, 118n47, 121, 123
    as internally fluid organization, 3, 24–6, 47, 51–9, 76–84, 86–7, 232
    leaders' views of neoliberalism, 148, 150–3, 151t, 152t
    leadership selection in, 79–82, 86–7, 93, 116–18, 122–5
    legalization of, 47
    legislative strength of, 227
    limits of Menemism in, 177–82
    linkages to working and lower classes in, 62, 65, 140, 210, 215–16, 222–5, 227, 231
    local fiefdoms of, 51
    machine politics consolidation in, 123–39
    machine politics, material exchange and, 203–16
    mass organization of, 60–5, 64t
    material exchange in 1990s and, 203–11, 215, 232
    members' views of neoliberalism, 153–5, 153t, 154t
    Menemism and, 56, 57n66, 121–2, 144–82
    Menem's circumvention of, 162–5
    Menem's party-conforming strategy for, 156–7
    middle-class voters and, 103–6, 118–20, 140, 210–12
    military coup against, 48
    municipal-level informal organization of, 67, 69–72, 69t, 89, 109–10, 124, 126–7, 151t, 177–9, 181–2, 195, 197–202, 201t, 204–9
    mutual autonomy of higher- and lower-levels of, 87–90, 177–82
    National Council of, 26, 30, 47, 52–6, 59, 75–80, 86–7, 112, 114, 117–18, 133, 134t, 136, 141–3, 142t, 149, 151, 151t, 158, 161–9, 173, 247
    national organization of, 75–6, 87–8, 144–5, 156, 158, 169–70
    neighborhood-level organization of base units, 59, 61–4, 64t, 66–70, 69t, 71–2, 75, 109–10, 125–7, 187–91, 188t, 192–3, 193t, 195, 195t, 197–8, 203–9, 206t, 209t, 211–12
    neoliberal economic policies of, 2, 17, 145–9
    neoliberalism and adaptation by, 9, 26, 33
    neoliberalism, machine politics, and, 140–3, 142t
    neo-Menemists and, 159–61, 165, 167, 170
    nonadaptation and crisis 1983–5 of, 103–6
    Orthodox faction of, 54–5, 70n38, 76n60, 78, 109–10, 112, 114–15, 119n51, 121, 125, 127, 170–2
    patronage-based territorial organizations of, 1–2, 109–11, 123–30, 130–2, 232
    patronage-based territorial organizations replacing unions in 26, 109–11
    professional staff lacking in, 30, 75
    provincial-level organization of, 72–6, 109–11, 177–82
    punteros and, 62, 66–7, 69, 71–2, 109–10, 125–7, 140, 152, 192–3, 193t, 198n20, 204, 211
    reform of, 2, 108–18, 145–9, 177–82, 232
    Renovation faction of, 54–7, 59, 78, 80–1, 84, 108–23
    reorganization by Perón of, 46
    reorganization from bottom up, 46
    Reorganizing Junta, Board of Analysis and, 46
    response to neoliberal policies of, 147–55, 163–4
    rules and procedures of, 76–84
    semi-anarchic nature of, 42–9, 51–6, 75, 84–5, 247–8
    as a social democratic party, 115, 119, 123, 148, 148nn22–3

Index

social linkages of, 62–5, 64t, 68, 69t
social work of, 141, 143, 187–91, 201–2, 205–6, 206t, 213–16
strategic autonomy of, 25–6
strategic choices facing leaders of, 101–3
Superior and Coordinating Council, 43
Superior Council/Superior Command, 47, 52–4, 79
Tactical Command of, 43, 47
tercio (quota) system, 25, 51, 82–4, 86, 108, 111
  elimination of, 113–18, 118n47, 124–5
  two parallel authority structures for, 53–5
ultraverticalist faction of, 51–2
union influence in, 1–2, 28, 48–9, 52, 92–4
union linkage to, 28, 38–40, 62, 82–4, 92–4, 106, 108–123, 130–9, 134t, 135t, 138t, 139t, 222–5, 228
union representation in legislative bloc of, 93–4, 112–18, 134–6, 135t
union representation in National Council of, 112–18, 133, 134t,
urban, 91–3, 95–7, 102, 107, 140
weakly routinized nature of, 24, 31–3, 37, 39–40, 44–9, 51–9, 76–90
weakly v. highly institutionalized, 17
weakness of formal statutes of, 52, 59–60, 76–7
weakness of leadership bodies, 77–9, 161–9
weakness *vis-á-vis* government, 75–6, 157–69
women's branch of, 40, 47, 51, 115, 121, 200, 204
working/lower-class support for, 26–8, 41, 65, 65n20, 96–8, 105–6, 140, 183–5, 210, 213–15, 225, 227, 246–9
youth branch of, 47, 121, 200, 204–5

Keynesianism, 1, 5, 28, 101, 148n24, 171
kickbacks, 69–70, 69n36
Kirchner, Nestor, 168, 174–5, 247
Kitschelt, Herbert, 12–13, 99n23
Koelble, Thomas, 12–13
Kohan, Alberto, 86

La Matanza, 31–2, 61–3, 65n20, 66–7, 70, 70n37, 71, 124–7, 131–8, 138t, 141, 142t, 143, 152, 152t, 188, 189n7, 190, 196–7, 200–1, 203–5, 207–8
La Matanza Peronism, 127–8
La Pampa, 73, 80, 110, 130, 179–81
La Rioja, 51, 73, 80, 110, 114, 177n177, 181, 184
labor. *See* CGT; organized labor; union
labor-based part(ies), 1–3
  adaptation, adaptive capacity of 1–3, 7–8, 13–15, 19–24, 231–45
  coalitional challenges to, 1, 5–7, 10, 94–100, 231–2
  definition of, 4
  democracy and, 7–9, 217, 245
  mass populist parties, rootedness and flexibility and, 21–4, 58
  organizational approach and, 9–12
  Peronism as, 24, 27–9, 36–41, 57, 91–4
  Peronism as no longer a, 249
  programmatic challenges to, 1, 5–6, 10, 100–1, 231–2
  unions and, 1, 4–5, 5n7, 6, 7, 37, 82–4
labor-based parties, European. *See* social democratic parties
  adaptation of, 7–8
  Latin American v., 5–7, 22–3, 36, 38–9, 58, 79, 82, 115
labor-based parties, Latin American
  collapse of, 8–9, 218–19
  comparative analysis of, 231–45
  decline in Latin America, 2, 2n2
  dual challenge facing, 4–7
  European v., 22–3, 36, 38–9, 58, 79, 82, 115
  new critical juncture facing, 4–7, 231

labor market flexibility, 146–7, 156, 224
Labor Party (PL), 38–9, 82
labor roundtables, 121–2, 124, 132–3
Lafalla, Arturo, 130, 176n176, 180
Lagos, Ricardo, 240
Lamberto, Oscar, 160n53
Langston, Joy, 241
Latin America, comparison within. *See also* American Popular Revolutionary Alliance (APRA); Chilean Communist Party; Democratic Action (AD); Institutional Revolutionary Party (PRI)
   Chile, 7–9, 232–3, 239–41, 244–5, 244t
   Mexico, 7, 232–3, 241–5, 244t
   party adaptation, party system stability, and democracy, 7–9, 217–18, 231–45, 244t
   Peru, 2, 7–9, 232–3, 236–8, 244–5, 244t
   Venezuela, 7–9, 232–6, 244–5, 244t
leader(ship). *See* charismatic organizations; populism
leader(ship) (party)
   autonomy from, 88–90, 197–200
   autonomy of, 13, 19–21, 23, 87–8, 157–82
   career paths and relationship to, 79–82, 144, 158–9
   change of, 11
   charismatic, 23, 36, 39, 46, 236
   circumvention of, 53, 144, 162–5
   economic crisis and, 155–7
   entrenchment v. fluidity of, 19–20, 24, 31, 59, 79–82, 86–7, 245
   government takeover of PJ, 158–9, 161–2, 165–9
   housecleaning of, 86–7, 159, 242
   hub-and-spokes relationship with, 88, 145, 169–77
   local, 71–2, 141–3, 142t, 145, 152–3, 152t, 177–9, 181–2
   national, 75–6, 77–82, 87–8, 148, 151–2, 151t, 247
   limits of national, 177–82
   non-charismatic personalism of, 88
   office-holding, 26, 74–6, 88, 158–9, 161–2, 165, 168
   oligarchic, 14, 20, 23, 26, 233
   and party adaptation, 11–12
   party hierarchy and selection of, 20, 39, 46–8, 52–6, 79–82, 86–7, 93, 117, 122–5
   personalistic, 23–4, 30–1, 39, 48, 57n66, 73–4, 74n55, 233, 236–8
   populist, 22–4, 34, 37, 39, 92, 232–3, 237, 241
   power-seeking nature of, 31, 87n107, 158
   provincial, 45, 48, 51, 53, 72–5, 74nn55–56, 109–10, 112–13, 115, 122, 125–30, 175, 196, 177–82, 247
   renovation, 13, 19–20, 79–82, 86–7
   strategic choices facing, 101–3
   strategic constraint v. strategic autonomy of, 18–21
   tenure security in, 20, 80, 87, 158–60
   Venezuelan AD, 235
   weakness of bodies of, 77–9, 87, 144, 155–69
left-of-center governments, 6–7, 237–40
left-of-center groups, 43, 50, 199–200, 208–9, 214–15
left-of-center groups. *See* "March 11"; Montoneros; Peronist Youth (JP)
Leninist parties, 21
Lescano, Oscar, 135–6, 167
liberalization, political, 242
Liberators of America, 50
lineas internas, 72
LIPEBO (Buenos Aires Peronist League), 72–3, 128–9, 132
local party organization, 59, 61–4
   activities of during 1990s, 186–91
   agrupaciones, 69–72
   alternative forms of, 216
   autonomy of, 88–9
   base units, 66–9, 69t
   changes in, 109, 111, 123–9, 202–11
Lonardi, Eduardo, 41
López Arias, Marcelo, 148

Index

López Rega, José, 48, 92
lower class, 7, 26–8, 37–38, 41, 62, 65, 65n20, 95–7, 102, 105, 107, 140, 196, 210, 213–15, 235, 237–8, 243
Luder, Italo, 48, 52, 93–4, 103, 103n30, 104
Lusinchi, Jaime, 235

machine (party) consolidation, of PJ
  alternatives to, 211–16, 213t
  assessing PJ shift to, 139–43
  Buenos Aires province, Duhaldist, 128–9
  collectivist organizations v., 213–16
  costs of, 209–11
  decline in union influence due to, 123–5, 133–9, 134t, 135t, 138t, 139t
  erosion of working-class linkages due to, 202–11
  Federal Capital, rise and fall of system with, 126–7
  La Matanza (business) Peronism and, 127–8
  material exchange in 1990s with, 203–9, 206t, 209t
  other provincial cases, 130
  reformist challenges to, 210
  three cases of, 125–9
  union response to, 130–3
machine UBs, 203–9, 206t, 209t. See also exchange-based organizations
  campaign innovations and, 204–5, 207–8
  centralized coordination of, 205–6, 206t
  traditional, modern-amateur v., 206–7, 206t
Mackie, Thomas, 11
Mainwaring, Scott, 12, 76
Manzano, José Luis, 77, 107, 148, 159, 161, 165–7, 166n102, 170, 170n135, 172n46
"March 11," 199, 208–9, 214, 214n70
March for Democracy, 104
Marcos, Novaro, 177, 187

Marín, Ruben, 80, 110, 167–8, 171n141, 175, 176n176
market-oriented policies, 2, 7, 10, 25, 101–2, 119, 140–1, 144, 145–9, 221–5, 235, 239, 242, 247. Also see neoliberalism
Martinez, Carlos, 93
Martinez de Hoz, José, 100
mass organization, informal, 60–5
mass parties, 13–14, 22–4
mass populist parties, 22–4
Massaccesi, Horacio, 183
Matera, Raul, 113
Matzkin, Jorge, 160n53
Maurette, Fernando, 88
Mayo, Marcelo, 213
McAllister, Ian, 89
McGuire, James, 16–17, 36n2, 45n17, 50n31, 83n91, 85, 138
media-based electoral strategies/media-based politics, 8, 102–4, 108, 118, 177–8, 186–7, 211–13, 217, 226, 240
Mendoza, 32, 46, 105, 113–15, 118, 120, 122, 130, 134t, 173, 179–82
Menem, Carlos, 3, 33, 50–4, 80–1, 101, 107, 110
  bandwagoning, collapse of Renovation faction and, 158–61, 235
  Bordonismo challenge to, 173–5
  circumvention of PJ leadership, 144, 16–25
  Decrees of Necessity and Urgency (NUD) used by, 219–20
  democracy and, 217–27
  democratic governance under, 221–3
  Duhalde, Eduardo, challenge to, 173–6, 176n176, 179
  economic boom under, 156
  economic crisis and leadership of, 155–7
  economic elite and, 145–6, 222–3
  election of, 76n61, 81, 101, 120–1, 144, 162, 168, 174, 182–5, 182t
  failure of internal challenges to, 169–77

Menem (cont.)
  Federal Council and, 53
  fiefdom of, 51
  hub-and-spokes relationship of,
    169–77
  as lame duck, 172–3
  leadership of, 156–7, 165–9
  "live and let live" strategy of, 178
  local party leaders views of, 151t,
    152–3
  local politics, mutual autonomy and,
    177–9, 181–2
  loyalists of, 159, 176, 221
  market-oriented policies of, 2, 17,
    25–6, 140–3, 142t, 145–9, 223–5
  Menemist factions (Celestes, Rojo
    Punzó) and, 161, 164–5, 170
  national party leaders views of,
    148–9, 151–2, 151t
  neo-Menemists and, 159–60, 165
  organized labor and, 167, 121–2,
    135–7, 140–3, 142t, 146–7,
    223–5
  outsider candidates and, 177
  party activist views of, 147, 191–2,
    192t, 194, 194t
  party members' views of programs
    of, 153–5, 153t, 154t
  party-conforming strategy of, 156–7
  personalistic leadership of, 31
  Productive Revolution of, 162
  provincial party leaderships and,
    177–82
  public approval and, 171, 175
  reelection, constitutional reform and,
    166, 168, 173–4, 176, 176n176,
    219, 219n2, 221
  Renovation and, 54, 56, 56n65,
    57n66, 109–10, 121, 158–61, 170
  strategic autonomy of, 25–6, 144–5,
    157–77
  takeover of PJ leadership by, 165–9
  Twelve Apostles of, 162
  union leaders' views of, 140–2, 142t
Menem, Eduardo, 79n82, 80, 165–6,
  166n109
Menemism, 57n66, 76n60, 81, 129,
  159–61, 164–5

Celeste and Rojo Punzó factions of,
  161, 164–5, 167, 170
electoral success of, 182–5, 185t
internal challenges to, 169–77
limits of, 177–82
neo-, 159–61, 165
origins of, 169–70
unions and, 121–2
Mercuri, Osvaldo, 72, 128
Mesa de Enlace Sindical, 117, 122
metalworkers union. *See* UOM
Mexico, 2, 7–8, 22, 79, 82, 82n90, 146,
  217, 221, 223, 231–3, 241–5. *See
  also* Institutional Revolutionary
  Party (PRI)
Michels, Roberto, 11–12, 14, 248
micro-Peronism, 202
middle class, 6, 95–100, 102
  alienation of, 103–6, 210, 242–3
  appeals to, 102, 118–20, 140,
    211–12
migrants, 27, 31n48, 38
Miguel, Lorenzo, 48, 52, 52n37, 80, 94,
  94n15, 103, 112, 172–3
military, 45, 103–4, 111n8, 220
  civilian control of, 220
  coup, 41, 46–8, 92, 218–19, 221–2
  repression, 42, 49, 92, 94–5, 98,
    104, 104n32
military rule, 33, 41–3, 49, 92, 92n5,
  95, 98, 100, 104, 111, 111n8
Miranda, Julio, 64, 72, 113, 131, 180
Misiones, 80, 130, 180–1, 184
MODIN (Movement for Dignity
  and Independence), 70, 182t, 191,
  225
Monteverde, Liliana, 68
Monteverde, Roberto, 122
Montoneros, 27, 29, 43–4, 47, 49–51,
  199
Morato, Gustavo, 117, 118n47, 121n60
Morato, Ricardo, 77, 80n84
Mouriño, Javier, 51n33, 212
movement, Peronist, 40, 42–3, 50–1,
  70, 121
  cadre organizations and, 43–4, 47
  clandestine organization of, 41–2, 49
  institutional fluidity of, 43–9

lack of discipline within, 42–6
neo-Peronist parties and, 43, 45
"partyization" of, 45–51
semi-anarchic state of, 41–2, 44, 48, 141, 222
Superior Council/Superior Command of, 47, 52–4, 79
tolerance in, 44
movement organizations, 41–4
municipal-level organization. *See* local party organization
mutual autonomy, 87–90, 177–82

Nacul, Miguel, 180
National Commission on Disappeared People (CONADEP), 103–4
National Council (PJ), 26, 30, 47, 52–5, 59–60, 75–9, 117–18
   Executive Board of, 59–60, 86–7, 133, 158, 167–8
   fluidity of leadership of, 79–80, 86–7
   lack of professional staff, 30, 75
   leadership selection and, 55–6, 59–60, 79–80, 114–18
   and Menem, 159–67
   Menemization of, 165–9
   Menem's circumvention of, 162–6
   provincial party branches and, 48, 59, 73, 76, 88, 115, 177–82
   Renovation and, 53–7, 78–9, 112–15, 117–18
   response to neoliberal reforms, 149, 151, 151t, 155, 162–4
   union representation in, 112–15, 117–18, 133, 134t, 136–7, 139t
   weakness of, 26, 30, 47, 52–5, 75–9, 112–15, 157, 169n128, 247
national government. *See* government
neighborhood-level party organization. *See* base units (UB); *punteros*
neoliberalism, 1–2, 5–7, 144. *See also* market-oriented policies
   activist's views of, 191, 192t, 199–202, 201t
   adaptation of PJ to, 8–9, 24–6, 33, 217, 228

in Chile, 2, 239
debt crisis, ISI exhaustion and, 100–1
and democracy, 221–30
economic crisis, leadership and, 149–50, 155–7
economic elite and, 145–6, 222–3
and electoral success, 182–5
and hyperinflation, 146, 149n33, 150, 155–6, 155n37
machine politics and, 140–3, 142t
Menem reforms and, 145–9, 223–5
in Mexico, 242
party weakness, presidential autonomy and, 157–77
Peronist opposition to, 148, 150–1, 169–77, 199–202, 201t, 248
Peronists' views of, 148, 150–5, 151t, 153t, 154t, 199–202, 201t
union response to, 141–3, 142t, 146–7, 223–5
neo-Menemism, 159–61, 165
neo-Peronist parties, 43, 45–6, 83–4
neopopulism, 218, 226–7, 227n16
nested games, 12
Neuquén, 43, 45, 48, 48n24, 75, 84n98, 130, 181
New Current of Opinion, 83
Non-Aligned Movement, 166
noquis, 69, 69n36
North, Douglass, 16, 18
Norwegian Labour Party, 21, 61t

Obeid, Jorge, 176n176
Ocampo, Mate, 214n69
O'Donnell, Guillermo, 219
Odría, Manuel, 22
oligarchy, 14, 20, 23, 26, 233
Olivos Pact, 174, 183, 219, 219n2
Olsen, Johan, 21
Onganía, Juan Carlos, 100
Operation Ambulance, 170
Orange List, 73, 113n17, 122, 130
organized labor, 1, 4. *See also* CGT, unions
   alliance with Peronism, PJ, 1, 28, 37–9, 137–9, 222–5
   in Chile, 239–40

organized labor (*cont.*)
  as core constituency of PJ, 27–8
  decline in influence in PJ, 2, 25, 33, 107, 115–18, 120–5, 127–9, 133–9, 134t, 135t, 140, 143, 167, 232, 248–9
  deindustrialization and, 91, 94–8
  fragmentation of, 113–15, 117, 123–5, 127–8
  as "friendly lobbyist," 136–7
  informal sector and, 6, 95–6
  linkage to Peronism, PJ, 1, 24–5, 28, 33, 38–41, 45–8, 59, 62, 82–4, 92–4, 102–3, 107–18, 120–5, 136–9, 140, 224–5, 248–9
  linkages to political parties (general), 1, 4–6, 82
  Menem and, 121–2, 135–7, 140–3, 142t, 146–7, 167, 223–5
  in Mexico, 82, 241–3
  origins of Peronism and, 37–9
  Perón and, 38–41, 45–6
  in Peru, 237–8
  Renovation and, 108–9, 111–18, 120–3, 139
  in Venezuela, 82, 234–6
  weakening of, 1, 6, 95–6, 232, 239, 244
  white collarization and, 6, 96–7, 97t
Ortega, Ramon "Palito," 79, 81n86, 175, 177, 179–81, 326
Orthodox Peronism, 50, 53–4, 108–18, 121, 125, 127, 130, 170–1, 200–1
  electoral failure of, 103–6
  Menem and, 121, 170
  Renovation challenge to, 108–18
Ostiguy, Pierre, 65, 85, 99n4

Padgett, John, 169
Padró, Raúl, 64
Panebianco, Angelo, 11–14, 16n23, 23–4, 35–6
paramilitary groups, 27, 42–3, 47, 49–50, 199
party activists, 186–7
  activities during 1990s of Peronist, 187–91, 188t

  alternatives to machine politics for, 211–16, 213t
  collective goods for neighborhoods from, 195–6
  collectivistist organizations and, 213–16
  decline of, 186–7 212–13, 213t
  ideological nature of, 186, 191, 201
  left-of-center, 199–200
  links to neighborhoods, 203–4, 210
  local autonomy and, 197–202, 201t
  machine politics and, 202–16, 206t, 209t
  Menem and, 193–4, 194t, 202
  micro-Peronism and, 202
  neoliberalism and, 191, 192t
  nonmaterial incentives of, 195, 198
  participatory channels lacking for, 193–4
  punteros and, 192–3, 193t, 203
  social work of, 177–81, 200–1
  stability under Menem, 191–4, 202
  state resources and, 186, 195–7, 210
  timing of entry into party of, 193, 193t
party adaptation
  approaches to explaining, 10–12
  costs of, 227–30
  and democracy, 7–9, 26–7, 217–18, 221–7
  environmental change and, 10–11
  failed, 7–10, 103–6, 217, 231, 233–6, 236–40, 244–5
  institutionalization and, 17–22
  integrated approach to, 11–12
  organizational approach to, 9, 11–24
  party leadership and, 11
  populist parties and, 22–3
  routinization and, 18–22
party change. *See* party adaptation
party failure, 7–10, 103–6, 217, 231, 233–40, 244–5
Party for Democracy (PPD), 240–1
party organization
  adaptation and, 3–13, 24, 84–90, 231–3, 244–6
  bureaucratic, 13–15, 20–4, 23t, 82, 86, 233, 239, 245

Index

charismatic, 36, 36n2, 37
importance of, 187–90
informal, 3, 14–15, 24, 29–31, 58–9, 82–4, 246
institutionalization and, 3, 13–18, 245
as intervening variable, 11–12
Latin American, 3, 233–41, 246
loosely structured, 41–4, 49, 51, 58, 65–76, 233, 240, 244, 247
mass, 13–14, 22–4, 40, 60–5, 186–7
path-dependent development of, 35–6
patronage and, 67, 69, 72–5, 109–11, 178, 202–11
research needed on, 4, 15, 246
societal rootedness of, 13–14, 22, 60–5
statization of, 203–10
strategic flexibility of, 13–14, 19–24, 245
types of, 22–4, 23t
weakly routinized, 3, 14, 19–26, 37, 39–40, 44–9, 51–8, 76–90, 248
party strategy, 9–12, 101–6, 108–9, 118–19, 145–9, 248
party system(s)
Argentine 98–100, 222–3
decomposition of, 7–9, 217–18, 231, 245
integrated v. stalemated, 222–3
labor-mobilizing, 9, 217, 231
multi vs. two, 10
realignment of, 8, 217
reequilibration of, 226–7
party–union linkage, 1, 7, 82, 92–4
AD, 82, 233–5
APRA, 237–8
Chilean Communist, 239–40
Chilean Socialist, 240
informal nature of Peronist, 33, 82–4
low routinization of Peronist, 3, 25, 33, 40, 48, 51, 82–4, 108, 111–15
PRI, 82, 241–3
transformation of Peronist, 25, 33, 86, 102, 107–8, 111–18, 120–3, 123–5, 130–9, 134t, 135t, 138t, 139t, 140–3
partyization of Peronism, 49–51
path dependence, 35–6
patronage, 140, 228, 230. *See also* machine UBs.
costs of, 209–11, 228–30
increased role in PJ of, 109–111, 202–9
party activists, base units (UBs), and, 67, 186, 195–7, 195t, 202–11
party organization and, 67, 69, 72–5, 109–11, 178, 202–9
patronage-based party, 1–2, 25, 33, 107, 123–4
substitution of union resources with, 26, 107, 109–11, 123–30
Patti, Luis, 227
Pedraza, José, 116, 118n47, 129, 132, 160
Pepe, Lorenzo, 148
Perdía, Roberto Cirilo, 215
Pérez, Carlos Andres, 9, 150, 157, 235
Perón, Eva (Evita), 29, 39–41, 189–90, 200, 202–3
Perón, Isabel, 46, 48, 52–3, 79, 81, 103, 218
Perón, Juan Domingo, 2, 17, 24, 27–9, 35, 37
Cámpora support by, 47–8
challenges to charismatic authority of, 44–7
creation of Peronist party by, 38–41
death of, 48
and democracy, 222
election of, 38, 48
in exile, 41–7, 92
lack of routinization and, 38–40, 44–7
organized labor and, 38, 40, 45–7, 82–3
overthrow of, 41, 218
rise to power of, 38
Vandor and, 45–7
Peronism. *See also* Justicialist (Peronist) Party (PJ)
adaptation, survival of labor-based populist party and, 24–7

Peronism (*cont.*)
    anti-Peronism v., 98–9
    authoritarian image of, 88n110,
        103–4, 108, 112, 119, 143
    as charismatic organization, 36–41,
        44
    decentralized nature of, 43–4, 51,
        65–76, 87–9, 177–82, 197–202,
        215, 247
    democracy and, 221–30
    deunionization of, 25, 33, 107–43
    as an identity, 65, 141–3, 190–1
    ideology of, 27–9
    informally organized nature of, 14,
        29–31, 41–9, 51, 56–7, 59–60,
        65–76
    internal conflict within, 43–8, 52–6,
        84–5, 108–18, 171–82, 247–8
    as labor-based party, 27–9, 36–8,
        40–1, 45–6, 57, 91–4, 249
    as movement, 40, 42–3, 50–1, 70,
        121
    as movement organization, 41–9
    as an organization, 29–31
    organized labor and, 28, 33, 38–40,
        45–8, 50, 52, 57, 82–4, 86, 92–4,
        102–3, 106–9, 111–18, 120–3,
        123–43, 134t, 135t, 138t, 139t,
        146–7, 167, 172, 222–5, 248–9
    origins of, 37–41
    partyization of, 49–51
    as pragmatic, 29
    proscription of, 41–7, 222
    repression of, 41–2, 49, 92
    research on, 29–31
    semi-anarchic state of, 36–7, 41–9,
        51–7, 84–5, 247
    social bases of, 27–8, 32, 37–8,
        64–5, 94–100, 107–8, 118–20,
        140–3, 183–5, 225–7, 248–9
    subculture of, 65, 190–1, 211, 216
    urban v. provincial, 31–2
    women's branch of, 40, 47, 51, 115,
        121, 200, 204
    working/lower classes and, 26–8,
        37–8, 41, 64–5, 94–8, 140–3,
        189–90, 196, 210, 213–16, 218,
        225, 227, 248–9
    youth branch of, 47, 121, 200,
        204–5
Peronism for Everyone, 199–200
Peronism of Hope, 72, 131
Peronist Convergence, 73, 113
Peronist Current, 175–6, 176n175
Peronist Grouping of Insurrectionary
    Resistance, 42
Peronist Loyalty, 200–1, 207, 215
Peronist Militancy, 171–2
Peronist Militancy and Renovation
    (MyRP), 72n50, 127–8, 205,
    207–8
Peronist movement. *See* movement,
    Peronist
Peronist Neighborhood Front
    (FREPEVE), 213–14, 214n69
Peronist Party (PP), 38–41
    as charismatic party, 36–7
    collapse of, 41–2
    fluid hierarchy of, 39–40
    foundation of, 35, 37–9
    linkage to unions of, 38, 40, 82–3
    mass organization of, 40
    movement structure of, 40
    personalistic nature of, 39
    as populist party, 22, 37, 39–40
    state role in, 39
    top-down nature of, 39
    weakly routinized nature of, 38–41
    Women's, 40
Peronist Unity Front (FUP), 49n26, 126,
    200
Peronist Youth (JP), 43, 49n26, 50–1,
    199
Peru, 2, 6, 8–10, 22, 24, 34, 81, 105,
    105n105, 185, 185n202, 217–18,
    220–1, 223, 226–7, 227n16, 231,
    233, 236–9, 244–5. *See also*
    American Popular Revolutionary
    Alliance (APRA); Fujimori,
    Alberto
Peruvian General Workers
    Confederation (CGTP), 237
PI. *See* Intransigent Party (PI)
Pico, Juan Manuel, 131
Pierri, Alberto, 72, 72n50, 73, 125,
    127–8, 176, 207–8

Pinochet, Augusto, 2, 239
Piris, Juan Carlos, 61
PJ. *See* Justicialist (Peronist) Party (PJ)
Pocovic, Juanita, 200
poor. *See* lower class
Popular Union (UP), 45–6
populism, 22–3, 22nn29–31, 37–41, 232
populist part(ies), 14, 22–4, 236, 241
  adaptive capacity of, 22–4, 232–3
  challenges facing, 5–7, 94–103
  Peronism as, 24, 31–2, 36–41, 232
  types of, 22, 22n30
postindustrialism, 6, 107, 140
power games, 12
PRI. *See* Institutional Revolutionary Party (PRI)
privatization, 145, 153t, 154, 224n12
Productive Revolution, 162
Progressive Current, 175
proscription of Peronism, 41–7, 222
provincial-level party organization, 43, 45, 51, 72–5, 88
provincial-level politics, 48, 109–10, 111–15, 177–82
punteros, 62, 66–7, 69, 71–2, 109–10, 125–7, 140, 152, 152t, 192–3, 193t, 195t, 198n20, 203–8, 210–12, 214. *See also* base units (UB)
PURN (Single Party of the National Revolution), 38–9

Quilmes, 31–2, 61–3, 65n20, 66–8, 71n42, 72, 110, 137–8, 138t, 141, 142t, 152, 152t, 188, 190, 196, 199, 206, 208–9, 213–15

Rachini, Juan, 104n32
Radical Civic Union. *See* UCR
reelection (constitutional reform), 166, 168, 173, 176, 176n176, 219, 219n2, 221
Renovation, 56–7, 59, 70, 73, 75–6, 78–81, 174, 181
  Celestes and, 161, 164, 170–1
  collapse of, 121, 149, 158–61, 170

  as *de facto* social democracy, 123
  defeat by Menem, 121
  defeat of Orthodox faction, 109–18
  democratization of PJ by, 56, 108–9, 111–8, 118n47, 222
  dismantling of party–union linkage, 111–18
  electoral success of, 118–20, 120t
  emergence of, 108–9
  finance of, 119–11, 109n6
  "Group of 25" and, 108, 110–18
  leadership of, 54, 109
  legacies of, 120–3
  Menem and, 54, 109–10, 121, 158–61, 170–1
  New, 173
  organized labor and, 108–9, 111–18, 120–3, 139
  public office, patronage, and informal party building as basis of, 109–11
  strategic changes by, 118–19
Renovation Front, 111
Reorganizing Junta, 46
Reutemann, Carlos, 79–80, 86, 137, 177, 179–81, 226, 247
Reviglio, Victor, 56, 116n36, 123n68, 130, 180
Revolutionary Peronism, 50
Reyes, Cipriano, 38
Rico, Aldo, 225–7
Riera, Fernando, 113
Rio Negro, 51, 75, 84n97, 102, 130, 181n198
Rivas, Olijela, 72, 180
Rivela, José, 71n42, 72
Roa, Raúl, 71
Roberts, Kenneth, 12, 217, 239
Robledo, Angel, 48, 51, 113
Rodriguez, Enrique, 136
Rodriguez Saa, Adolfo, 229, 249
Rodriguez Saa, Alberto, 171n141
Roggero, Humberto, 148
Rojas, Isaac, 147
Rojas Pinilla, Gustavo, 22
Rojo Punzó, 161, 164, 170
Romá, Rafael, 128, 175
Romero, Juan Carlos, 176n176

Romero, Julio, 55, 55n63, 74n55, 169n130
Rose, Richard, 11
routinization, 16–18
  failed efforts at, 18, 45–8, 51–7
  formal or informal, 18
  high v. low, 18–22, 246
  organizational flexibility and, 18–19
  party adaptation and, 19–22, 231–3, 244–5
routinization, high, 18–19
  AD and, 233–4
  Chilean Communist Party and, 239–40
  costs of, 19, 231, 246
  of leadership bodies, 20
  of party hierarchy, 20
routinization, low (weak), 19
  Chilean Socialist Party, 240
  costs of, 84–5, 247–8
  flexibility and, 18–22, 85–90
  of leadership bodies, 21, 77–9
  of party hierarchy, 20, 39, 79–82
  of party rules and procedures, 76–7
  of party-union linkage, 40, 82–4, 111–15
  in PJ, 24–6, 38–41, 45–9, 51–8, 76–90
Ruckauf, Carlos, 92, 137, 175, 176n176, 247
Russia, 24, 156, 229
Russo, Federico, 127–8, 200–1, 207–8

Saadi, Ramon, 148, 171–2, 181
Saadi, Vicente, 44n15, 45, 50, 54–5, 55n57, 74n55, 103, 105n38, 112
Salinas, Carlos, 242–3
Salta, 43, 45, 48, 48n24, 80, 84n97, 130, 175, 179, 181
San Juan, 64, 80–1, 84, 177, 177n177, 180–1
San Luis, 73, 80, 110, 130, 180–1, 184, 248
Sani, Giacomo, 85
Santa Cruz, 68, 73, 81, 93, 113, 130, 175, 179, 180–1

Santamaría, José Maria, 131
Santiago del Estero, 48, 48n24, 51, 73, 74n55, 80, 84, 84n99, 110, 114, 177n177, 180–1
Sapag, Elías, 45
Sapag, Elias and Felipe, 45
Sartori, Giovanni, 85
Schiavo, Eduardo, 214n70
schools, 63, 64t
Scioli, Daniel, 80, 177, 212
Selznick, Philip, 16
Shefter, Martin, 140
Simó, Alejo, 93
Single Party of the National Revolution. *See* PURN
"62" Organizations, 25, 45, 47–8, 50–2, 54, 78, 83n92, 86, 92–4, 104, 109–10, 117–18, 131
  collapse of, 111–8, 120–3, 121n60, 124–5
  Menem and, 121
  origins of, 82–3
  Renovation and, 108–18, 121–2
soccer clubs, 63–4
social democratic parties (social democracy), 6, 8, 11–12, 22, 24–5, 27–8, 36, 38, 42, 60–1, 61t, 115, 119, 123, 148
social security (pension system), 145, 149n31
social work, 141, 143, 202, 213–15
socialist parties, 6–7, 199, 239–40, 244–5, 244t
  electoral decline of, 11n13
  shift to center of, 2
sociedad de formento, 63–4, 64t, 65n22
Solidarity (Poland), 2
Soviet bloc, 1
Spain, 2, 156
Spanish Socialist Workers Party (PSOE), 7, 61t, 115, 148n22
state. *See* government
State Reform Law, 145
Storino, Ernesto, 79
Superior and Coordinating Council, 43
Superior Council/Superior Command 47, 52–4, 79

Index

Supreme Court, 164, 219, 220–1
Swedish social democrats, 6, 61t

Tactical Command, 43, 47
tenure security/insecurity, 20, 79–80, 159–61
tercio (quota) system, 25, 51–2, 82–4, 86, 108, 111
  elimination of, 86, 113–17, 118n47, 124–5
  origins, 83–4
  Renovation and, 108, 111, 113–18
  weakly routinized nature of, 82–4, 86, 113–14
Thatcher, Margaret, 2
Toledo, Hugo, 72, 128
Toma, Miguel Angel, 155, 160n53, 161n60
trade unions. *See* unions
Triaca, Jorge, 104n32, 224
True Peronism, 72
Tucuman, 43, 48, 61, 64, 68, 72, 73n56, 79, 81, 84n98, 113, 131, 135, 177, 177n177, 179–81
two-party system, 10, 99

UB. *See* base units (UB)
Ubaldini, Saúl, 50n32, 113, 125, 225
Ubaldinismo, 50, 50nn31–2, 113, 117–18, 122
UCeDe. *See* Center Democratic Union (UCeDe)
UCR (Radical Civic Union), 78–9, 85, 98–9, 101, 103, 105–6, 120, 120t, 164, 173, 182–3, 182t, 219n2, 226
UCR Renovating Juntas, 38
ultra-loyalists, 39
union(s), 192t. *See also* organized labor; Group of "25"; "62" Organizations
  AD and, 82, 234–5
  APRA and, 237–8
  Chilean Communist Party and, 239–40
  Chilean Socialist Party (PFCh) and, 240
  collapse of mechanisms of participation in PJ and, 25, 33, 86, 111–18, 120–5, 143, 232
  decline of influence in PJ, 2, 25, 33, 107, 115–18, 120–5, 127–9, 133–40, 143, 167, 232, 248–9
  domination of PJ, 2, 45, 48, 52, 92–4, 104, 125, 139
  government positions of leaders of, 224
  informal sector and, 6, 95–8, 140
  Labor Roundtables and, 132–3
  as linkage to working and lower classes, 28, 38, 41, 45, 91–3, 96–7, 102–3, 106–7, 141, 143, 203, 248
  machine politics and, 123–33, 139–43
  mechanisms of participation in PJ, Peronism, 25, 40, 47, 59, 82–4, 86, 108–9
  membership, 38, 96, 146, 239
  military and, 103–4, 104n32
  neoliberalism and, 136–7, 140–1, 142t, 143, 146–7, 172, 224–5
  participation in Peronist Party, 38–41
  participation in PJ and, 45–8, 50–2, 59, 62, 64, 64t, 82–4, 92–4, 111–18, 120–37, 133–9, 138t, 139t, 167, 224–5
  PJ electoral defeat and, 102–6
  PRI and, 82, 241–3
  representation in Chamber of Deputies, 93–4, 112–15, 134–6, 134t, 135t, 224
  representation in Peronist leadership, 38, 40, 47, 82–4, 94, 115, 117–18, 133–4, 134t, 136, 224
  responses to machine politics, 130–3
  role during proscription period, 41–6, 49, 92
  sponsorship of *agrupaciones* by, 130–2
  sponsorship of base units, 62, 64, 68, 69t
  strikes by, 48, 167, 224–5

union(s) (*cont.*)
  violence and, 102
  weakly routinized nature of mechanisms of participation in PJ, Peronism, 3, 24–5, 40, 46–8, 82–4, 86, 111–15
  white collar v. blue collar, 95–7, 97t
union factions
  Gestión y Trabajo (GyT), 113
  Group of 25, 83, 108, 110–18, 113n17, 121–4, 160, 170
  Menem for President Labor Roundtable, 121–2
  "62" Organizations, 93–4, 104, 108–18, 113n17, 116n38, 121–2
  Ubaldinismo, 113, 117–18, 122
United Left (IU) (Peru), 237–8
United Officers Group (GOU), 38
United States, 76, 147, 148n 24, 154, 154t, 166, 229
upper class
  democracy and, 221–3
  Menem and, 145–7
UOM (metalworkers union), 45, 48, 50, 79, 93–4, 96, 122n66, 124, 127–8, 130, 136, 140, 146

Vaca, Eduardo, 148, 171n141, 173n51
Vandor, Augusto, 45, 45n18, 46, 82, 116n38
Vanrell, Antonio, 123n68
Velasco Ibarra, José María, 22
Venezuela, 2, 7–10, 26, 34, 42, 44, 61t, 76, 79, 81–2, 88, 150, 156–7, 198, 217–18, 221, 226–7, 227n16, 231–6, 244–5. *See also* Democratic Action (AD)
Venezuelan Workers Confederation (CTV), 234–5

Vernet, José Maria, 79–80, 93, 121n60, 130, 159, 162, 165
Videla, Jorge, 100

West Ocampo, Carlos, 136n117, 167–8
white-collarization, 6, 94–5, 97–8, 97t, 102, 105–6, 108
Wilson, Frank, 11
women, 40, 47, 59, 120, 189–90, 196, 200–1, 204–5, 213
women's branch, 13, 40, 47, 51, 115, 121, 200, 204
Women's Peronist Party (WPP), 40
working class, 7, 237, 241
  blue collar v. white collar, 6, 96–8
  decline of industrial, 1, 6, 11n13, 22, 24, 33, 91, 94–8, 146, 232
  emergence of Peronism, and 37–8
  informal sector and, 6, 95–7, 102, 105, 140
  linkage to Peronism via unions, 28, 38, 41, 45, 91–3, 96–7, 102–3, 106–7, 141, 143, 203, 248
  Peronism's transformation and future representation of, 34, 246–9
  and populism, 22
  as social base of Peronism, 24, 26–8, 33, 37–8, 40–1, 58, 60, 62, 65, 91, 94–9, 105–7, 120, 140, 183–5, 189–91, 196, 213–16, 225–7
  white collarization and, 6, 94–5, 97–8, 97t, 102, 105–6, 108

Yoma, Jorge, 176
youth, 59, 98, 104, 120, 188, 188t, 200, 204
youth branch, 13, 47, 121, 200, 204–5
Yrigoyen, Hipólito, 218

Zanola, José, 116n38, 172